In Adeline R. Tintner's previous ~~~~~ *The Book World of Henry James*, s~~~~~ revealed how James appropriated ~~~~~ classics for his own use. The works of literary giants like Shakespeare, Milton, and Balzac re-emerged from his pen transformed and uniquely Jamesian. But James also relished popular culture, and it, too, bursts forth in his fiction. In *The Pop World of Henry James: From Fairy Tales to Science Fiction*, Tintner leaves behind the oak-panelled library to follow the trail of James's "grasping imagination" through the popular culture of his time.

For James, the germ of an idea might be found anywhere. The fairy tales he read as a child, like "Little Red Riding Hood," "Sleeping Beauty," and "Bluebeard," he reworked again and again throughout his career, along with the myths of Pandora and Alcestis. Both the romantic cult of Orientalism and the great scandals recounted daily in the newspapers had captured the imagination of the public, and both *The Arabian Nights* and the Dreyfus Affair found their way into James's novels and stories. The Victorian sensation novels of Miss Braddon, the potboilers of American popular novelists like F. Marion Crawford, the science-fiction novels of James's friend H. G. Wells, and a wealth of other sources from popular life and literature suggested plots, themes, and motifs to the Master.

Tintner is uniquely qualified to lead the search for the stimulating influences in James's world. As Madeleine B. Stern observes in her foreword, Tintner "has at her disposal an almost universal frame of reference that enables her to take 'iconic voyages' through James's texts, to be 'alert to his fictional strategy,' to find without hunting his sources, to engage in his 'admirable commerce of borrowing and lending...stealing and keeping.' As a result, she is able to describe minutely the means by which James molded the papier-mâché of popular literature into masterpieces."

published by UMI Research Press, and she has co-edited, with Leon Edel, *The Library of Henry James* (1987), also published by UMI Research Press. She is past president of the Henry James Society and serves on the editorial boards of the *Journal of Pre-Raphaelite Studies* and the *Henry James Review*.

# The Pop World of Henry James

## From Fairy Tales to Science Fiction

## Studies in Modern Literature, No. 89

Other Titles in This Series

No. 56
*The Museum World of Henry James*
Adeline R. Tintner

No. 80
*When the Master Relents:*
*The Neglected Short Fictions*
*of Henry James*
George Bishop

No. 82
*The Book World of Henry James:*
*Appropriating the Classics*
Adeline R. Tintner

No. 83
*Henry James: The Indirect*
*Vision, Second Edition,*
*Revised and Enlarged*
Darshan Singh Maini

No. 84
*Leon Edel and Literary Art*
Lyall H. Powers, ed.

No. 90
*The Library of Henry James*
Leon Edel and
Adeline R. Tintner, eds.

# The Pop World of Henry James
## From Fairy Tales to Science Fiction

by
Adeline R. Tintner

U·M·I Research Press

Ann Arbor / London

Produced and distributed by
UMI Research Press
an imprint of
University Microfilms Inc.
Ann Arbor, Michigan 48106


Library of Congress Cataloging in Publication Data

**Tintner, Adeline R., 1912-**
  The pop world of Henry James.
  (Studies in modern literature ; no. 89)
  Bibliography: p.
  Includes index.
  1. James, Henry, 1843-1916—Knowledge—Literature.
2. Popular literature—History and criticism.
3. Popular culture in literature.   I. Title.   II. Series.
PS2127.L5T56   1988      813'.4      88-27725
ISBN 0-8357-1855-7 (alk. paper)

British Library CIP data is available.

*For Leon Edel*
*In Friendship and Homage*

Gustave Doré, *The Enchanted Castle,* 1862

"Do you remember in Doré's illustrations to Perrault's tales, the picture
of the enchanted castle of the Sleeping Beauty? Back in the distance . . .
surrounded by thick baronial woods which blacken all the gloomy horizon,
on the farther side of a great abysmal hollow of tangled forest verdure, rise
the long facade, the moss-grown terraces, the towers, the purple roofs of
a chateau of the time of Henry IV. Its massive foundations plunge far
down into the wild chasm of the woodland, and its cold pinnacles of slate
tower upwards, close to the rolling autumn clouds. . . ."

"Gabrielle de Bergerac"

# Contents

# Figures

# Foreword

Everywhere there are connections, though they are often unlikely. To perceive such connections is to perceive what has not been perceived before. It is also to add facets, to enrich, to enlarge what is connected.

The tracing of connections between the plastic world, the printed world, the world itself, and Henry James is an art that Adeline Tintner has made peculiarly her own. It is an art that involves detection: the ferreting out of covert as well as overt allusions, analogues, and verbalisms; the picking up of stated clues; and the discovery of clues hidden between lines. But the art does not stop with detection, which is merely the initial perception. The detection of original or source is followed—must be followed—by the expert delineation of the transmutation of the source.

Henry James, who was saturated with the literature that preceded and surrounded him, provides Tintner with a seemingly limitless field for the tracing of connections and the reconstruction of sources. Having identified the source, the connection, she proceeds to show how James elevated that source into art and, by his particular alchemy, metamorphosed it into a re-creation. She does indeed "carefully parse his improved versions" which, in the end, yield up the treasure of a new language.

Tintner has done this before. In *The Museum World of Henry James* she applied her special technique to the connections between the visual arts and Jamesian art; in *The Book World of Henry James* she applied it to the connections between the so-called classics, from Shakespeare to Balzac, and Henry James. Now, in *The Pop World of Henry James,* she applies it—most brilliantly—to the fascinating connections between popular subliterature and its Jamesian transmutations.

Tintner's arena here is a vast one. Since James's fiction subsumed the books and legends that made mass entertainment, that arena encompasses fairy tales, classical myths, biblical legends, sensation novels, and science fiction. The tracing of connections between a continent of subliterature and a master of literature, and the reshaping of the former by the latter are presented in a cornucopia of masterly perceptions and reconstructions.

Out of this horn of plenty comes a network of correspondences. Tintner begins her huge mosaic with a study of fairy tales "encoded in the text" of Henry James. She demonstrates, for example, how Perrault's *contes,* "Sleeping Beauty," along with "Bluebeard" and "Cinderella," form a basis for James's metaphors and supply him with images. "Sleeping Beauty" appears and reappears in the stories until in "Flickerbridge" the tale is recast in a "new and inverted version" in which unconsciousness becomes the "foil to the heightened consciousness of society and of women within it." The fairy tales that James had read he assimilated and appropriated, a process that includes, as Tintner skillfully points out, interweaving, incorporating, reconstructing, paralleling, revising, repatterning.

So too with biblical legends whose circumstances James makes contemporary. In a dazzling reconstruction of her own, Tintner depicts the parallel between Milly of *The Wings of the Dove* and Hezekiah, King of Judah, both of whom, reprieved from death, display their riches. To James nothing was alien. His borrowings from eastern sources are traced in their changing forms in *Roderick Hudson, Watch and Ward, The Europeans, What Maisie Knew,* and *The Golden Bowl.* James's Orientalism was derived not only from the *Arabian Nights,* but from F. Marion Crawford's *Mr. Isaacs* and Beckford's *Vathek* and especially from Pierre Loti; and always James reshaped those influences to his own purposes in figures of speech and mise-en-scènes, in attitudes, in "icons," in characterizations and events.

Similarly James availed himself of classical legends, revamping Greek mythology until it became "Jacobean instead of Homeric." Of enormous interest is his manipulation, his modernization of "Pandora" into his "new woman" who is self-created, and his conversion of her "box" into a pun. Euripides is present in *The Ambassadors* and an "Olympian aura" in the allegorical mock-epic "The Velvet Glove," while Virgilian lines and elements are interspersed through *The Ambassadors* and "Crapy Cornelia." To all these interweavings Tintner, cicerone par excellence, holds the telltale thread.

When she approaches English popular literature she finds analogues likely and unlikely, but even when unlikely, carefully explained. Just so the legend of Saint George from *The Golden Legend* is refashioned in "The Lesson of the Master" into "a bit of transformed hagiography." Of extraordinary interest is Tintner's analysis of James's single "pure 'sensation' story" of bigamy, murder, and insanity, "Georgina's Reasons," as an "enhancement" of *Lady Audley's Secret* and *Aurora Floyd* (which James reviewed), bestsellers of the popular and prolific Mary Elizabeth Braddon. The luring path of transmigration is followed, from Braddon's *The Doctor's Wife,* out of *Madame Bovary,* into *The Portrait of a Lady.* Seeds of "The Turn of the Screw" are found in Tom Taylor's "Frank

Leslie" serial *Temptation,* as well as in Charlotte Brontë's *Jane Eyre:* seeds of relationship, theme, even the atmosphere of corruption. Through Tintner's eye, which little if anything escapes, we become witness to Dickensian filterings in "Julia Bride," correspondences with Mrs. Humphry Ward's *Marriage à la Mode,* the re-emergence of Mrs. Margaret Oliphant as Mrs. Harvey in "Broken Wings." In a highly innovative pastiche, "the brew of Bantling" in *The Portrait of a Lady* is presented as a blend of "literature, life, and art." Indeed Henry James is shown to have turned much of Victorian subliterature to his lofty purposes.

Nor did he abstain from such use of his readings in American publications for mass entertainment. We glimpse traces of that Sunday-school-library favorite, Maria Cummins's *The Lamplighter,* for example, in James's early fiction. And in "The Private Life" we unearth borrowings from Edward Everett Hale's "My Double; and How He Undid Me." In James's re-creation, however, Hale's invention of a double becomes the far more intricate "story of a *double* double." In James's fictive family relationships Tintner discovers hints from America's best-loved author of juveniles, Louisa May Alcott. In the plot of "The Beldonald Holbein" she finds resemblances to a story by Clara Sherwood Rollins, "A Burne-Jones Head." Traces of F. Marion Crawford are pursued in James; and "cameos of his friends," Annie Fields, widow of the American publisher James T. Fields, and the writer Sarah Orne Jewett, are recognized when they are reproduced in his novels.

The discoveries are made; step by step the alchemical transmutation of sources is pursued. In an insightful section Tintner examines the methods by which James uses the tales of Rudyard Kipling and makes them his own. She proceeds to expose the connections between James's interest in events that made journalistic headlines and his work: between the Baccarat scandal and his story "The Real Thing"; between his presence as a juror in a divorce hearing and his narrative "The Given Case"; between the Affaire Dreyfus and *The Ambassadors* where that infamous scandal eddies as an undercurrent. And finally, the critic alive to influences exposes the methods by which James in his *Sense of the Past* reversed the science fiction visions of H.G. Wells; how, in short, a writer centered in futurity "fed the imagination" of a writer centered in the past.

James's plea that the reader cooperate with the writer can never be more substantively fulfilled. Tintner's saturation in her subject is both productive and creative. James's life, letters, and notebooks, the books in his library, his public and publisher relations, his conscious and even his unconscious are Tintner's familiars. But in addition to this specialized core of knowledge she has at her disposal an almost universal frame of reference that enables her to take "iconic voyages" through his texts, to be "alert to his fictional strategy," to find without hunting his sources, to engage in his "'admirable commerce of borrowing and lending . . . stealing and keeping.'" As a result, she is able to describe minutely the means by which James molded the papier-mâché of popular literature into masterpieces. Her findings are no mere exercises in discovery, but re-viewings of Henry James. This arena and this technique *she* has appropriated. The Tintner Connection has penetrated the secrets of Henry James.

*Madeleine B. Stern*

# Preface

In the previous volume in this series, *The Book World of Henry James,* I attempted to show in concrete detail how certain literary classics served James's purposes and the extent to which he "appropriated" them (his term) and re-worked them. Of himself James wrote, "If a work of imagination, of fiction, interests me at all . . . I always want to write it over in my own way," adding, "I take liberties with the greatest." One generous critic of my earlier volume has assumed that James paid attention only to the greatest works of literature. "One would imagine him as paying the compliment of a critical and corrective rewriting only to works worth the effort of redemption."

I have called this volume *The Pop World of Henry James* because I want to emphasize that James remodeled the low as well as the high. Popular culture in its varied forms—Victorian sensation novels, the contemporary craze for Orientalism, American magazine stories, scandals both private and public—served his purpose. He did not hesitate to publish in the sensational press. Writing in his preface to a volume of the New York Edition, which contained some of his ghostly tales, he spoke about "the felt challenge of some experiment or two in one of the finer shades, the finest (*that* was the point) of the grue-some," recalling the appearance of one of his stories "with a large picture, in a weekly newspaper."

James makes the point very clearly. "The gruesome gross and obvious might be charmless enough, but why shouldn't one, with ingenuity, almost infinitely refine upon it?—*as one was prone at any time to refine almost on anything*" (emphasis mine). And it was in no boasting fashion that he said of a piece of work he had just completed, "It is of an *ingenuity!*"

By calling this book *The Pop World of Henry James* I do not associate him invidiously with Andy Warhol and a whole school of art that seems worlds away from Henry James's fiction. Actually, the impulse that made James go to the popular literature of the time in which he wrote is very much like that with which Warhol approached the popular art of today. James had done somewhat the same thing to Louisa May Alcott, to the popular writings of Dickens and

Kipling, to the fairy tales of his youth as Warhol did to popular visual material in producing an elite art. A Warhol can of tomato soup is not the soup can we see at the grocer's. Its transposition from a shelf in a supermarket onto a base in an art gallery removes it from the class of utility into the class of aesthetic contemplation. James, however, would have changed the can of tomato soup to a tureen of some special concoction worthy of Brillat-Savarin's approval. Though James said of himself, "I should so much have loved to be popular!," and near the end of his life resorted to writing his own blurbs, my study assumes that it was not really the desire for fame that drove James to popular literature of all kinds, but his deep psychological needs as well as an artistic itch to handle these forms of fantasies going as far back as the classic fairy tales and ancient myths, as well as going forward to the science fiction fables of H.G. Wells.

What has popular literature, which is manufactured for and consumed by the masses, to do with the writer of the elite, Henry James? The large amount of popular culture absorbed in his fiction (even jury duty, which, although not a form of literature, has its records and its special written disciplines) is a remarkable revelation that James lived in the world. He wrote for and in a busy, populated metropolis, or not far from it, all his life. His ability to be constantly excited by what took place in the world lifted him out of the libraries and into the arena, even if the arena was often occupied only by newspaper accounts and literary records of the worldly life as he found it—in Daudet's version of Little Red Riding Hood, Zola's journalism and the Dreyfus affair, or in Kipling's literature for children.

Even in the works of writers for whom he had no respect, like F. Marion Crawford and Edgar Fawcett, James found material to serve his purpose. He would surely not do such writers' themes the way they had done them; he would improve on them and yet preserve the merits of their plots and the basic themes worth saving. But he took them for himself and made them into art. As he wrote to Wells, "My sole and single way of perusing the fiction of Another is to *write it over* . . . as I go. Write it over, I mean, re-compose it, in the light of my own high sense of propriety and with immense refinements and embellishments."

He had written "I take liberties with the greatest." The popular works he adapted are evidence that the lowest served him as well as the greatest. He saved "bad" books from oblivion by lifting them into his realm. But then even bad books had something good in them, at least those that had some interest for him. At a time when young art historians and museum directors are planning "blockbuster" exhibitions on the "High and Low: Modern Art and Popular Culture," it is most appropriate to concern ourselves with how James, now enshrined as a modernist forerunner, handled the icons of popular art. We should be able to recognize the catholicity of his interests.

His kinds of reading seem to have ranged from Clara Rollins, an unknown American writer of twenty, to Miss  Braddon, the prolific sensation novelist.

He reacted to the European infatuation with the Near East and the Orient. His diaries from 1909 on, recording his intense around-the-clock social life in London, show that his appetite for life was enormous. It is not a question of his coming out of the library; he was never totally there, although as a boy he devoured books, and when he bought Lamb House he stayed there long enough not only to write the last three novels of the major phase but to read omnivorously in his spare time. Yet James never separated himself either from his continental social life or his English country-house life, and even though he managed to fill his library as well, his heavy social schedule continued until the last few months of his life.

Fairy tales had the deepest hold on James's sensibility, as far back as his earliest memories went. We are not surprised at their "tug," since we are all aware of the role fairy tales and fables play in the evolution of a child's psyche. James's fiction—early, middle, and late—is inundated with fairy-tale recollections and references, but the fact that in eight different stories he employs seven of the eight classical Perrault *contes* that act as the core of his *données* is astonishing evidence for his dependency on them. An older narrator of one of James's early stories, reflecting on the tastes of his boyhood, asks, "Do the instructors of youth nowadays condescend to the fairy-tale pure and simple?" We know that in our own time it is no longer a question of condescension, nor was it with James himself, because of the general interest in the significant relationship between "lullaby-literature," as James called it, and the development of the adult psyche. The Greek legends appear early, middle and late, but not in such great profusion, because he was less sensitive to classical mythology than he was to fairy tales. This may have been because, in many ways, he anticipated Freud in making the connection between unconscious behavior and the fairy tale plots handed down through the centuries, especially in the case of Perrault's tales that were meant first for the adults of the court of Louis XIV. James also may have worked through some of his own personal dilemmas through these tales, for Bettelheim tells us that that is why children will always love fairy tales—fairy tales help them to handle their problems. James kept his childlike needs throughout his life, and at the end they took over his last short stories and his autobiographies.

Just the way James resorted chiefly to Perrault's *Contes* for his versions of fairy tales without our thinking of Perrault as a classic of literature, so he had to read Homer and Hesiod, Sophocles, Euripides, and Virgil to get at the corpus of ancient myths and legends. These writers differ from the authors included in *The Book World of Henry James* in that they are trapped within the immutable story line of a myth, unlike Shakespeare and Milton when they resorted to popular or biblical legends. In this book it has seemed more appropriate to treat the ancient writers merely as reservoirs of the popular art of their times, rather than as creators of classics. It is the ancient legend that enchanted James, rather than the individual author's treatment, with the possible exception of Euripides' *Bacchae*.

At many places the reader may wonder why certain authors like Kipling and Wells are treated as part of mass culture rather than as classics. The reader may think that such persons should have been included in my earlier book about the classics in James's book world. But these are authors who, although known mostly to academics now, were extremely popular in their own day.

Sir Joshua Reynolds said of Raphael that he was "always imitating and always original." Similarly, James could not read even a sensation story without making an original version of it. He always needed "to measure his mind with something" as he has a character say in a early story. The canonical literary status of a pop work of literature had little to do with the amount of stimulation it would give him, "if I find any interest in it at all." What this interest comprised we find as we carefully parse his improved versions.

The pop world of James includes not only popular literature—the best-sellers of his day and the day before—but also other popular forms of culture, the movies that he saw and relished, the scandals in the press, and the scandals of society, including divorce hearings and the Dreyfus affair. *The Reverberator,* James's short novel of 1888 based on a private scandal, that of May McClellan's reportage in an American newspaper about the private life of the Venetian society that had welcomed her has been fully discussed by Leon Edel in *Henry James: The Middle Years* (pp 228–30). The scandals I investigate are the public ones that involved everyone. Popular culture in its plastic form I considered in my first volume, *The Museum World of Henry James,* for James was fascinated by the world around him in all its forms of art, as well as by its literature and theatre. Those forms find their way into his fiction. They animate and stimulate his keen interest and intelligence as the classics had done. But what he remodels them into is never popular. He endows the sensation novels of Mrs. Braddon with a depth and extension all his own and draws her themes and situations into his own complex realm of consciousness.

Marcia Jacobson, in her fine *Henry James and the Mass Market,* argues that James resorted to popular forms to make himself into a popular author. Discussing James in a general contextual fashion, she stops short of demonstrating how he could remake a bestseller, other than by incorporating its surface features, while still referring back to the original work. Doing this, he created a completely new work of art that was not popular.

From my analysis, a given work of contemporary popular art on which he does focus acts only as a stimulus, since it was part of modern life, for the creation of a work that could not be popular under any terms. James must have felt at heart that his recreation of popular culture could never be accepted by the mass of readers, for the example of Ray Limbert in James's story "The Next Time" shows that he understood how certain people, try as they might, could never write for readers with tastes different from their own. James's intention was to use the material of popular art to make it into a permanent work of art, something that would make one think about life in its most serious form; the appeal was to consciousness rather than to sensation.

James was drawn to popular literature of all kinds, from the beginning of his career to the end; fairy tales, myths, and ghost stories intrigued him. Popular novels and popular authors stirred his creative powers. The exercise of his ingenuity seemed to be James's chief incentive, though he would have been happy if the mass of readers had applauded him for his feats.

Wells and Kipling were popular, and he envied them this, but his redoing of some of their works was not so much to appeal to and win over their audiences as to stimulate his own powers of invention and recreation. James was not catering to Wells's audience but pepping up his own thinking by looking into Wells's "Future" and using it as point of departure for his own "Past." Naturally, he would have liked to have been widely recognized for what he *did* do, but his drive toward clarification always succeeded in making a subject, fairly simple in its original presentation, infinitely complex in its final development, a result that was anathema to the mass of readers.

Then, by a most ironic turn, James, who hated any form of personal notoriety, whose first interview with the daily press was his last, became himself a pop hero and figure for the turn of the century. And now in the 1980s the figure of James himself has been brought in and named in two novels—one a mass market paperback and the other a historical pop novel by Gore Vidal. But this is beyond the limits of the present volume.

The chronology I follow is that of the appearance in time of the given type of popular literature. Within each category and within each specific tale, I try to follow the chronology of James's fiction. Thus I begin with fairy tales, move to tales from the Bible, then go to Oriental tales. From there I range through the later periods of English and American popular literature; the press, with its social and political scandals; and certain major nineteenth-century writers in England whose fiction stimulated James. The final chapter is devoted to the effect of the popular form of science fiction invented by H. G. Wells. This, with its rush to futurity, compelled James to make the same leap backward into the past.

The interested reader of this book will, in a sense, still have some work to do. These analyses are only the tip of the iceberg. There are probably many sources in popular literature that I have not probed, which should encourage others to look around for themselves.

# Acknowledgments

I wish to thank Daniel Mark Fogel for his careful reading of this manuscript and his interest in my entire project. I am grateful to Juliet McMaster, professor of English at the University of Alberta in Edmonton, Alberta, Canada, for calling my attention to Thackeray's and Dickens's use of fairy tales. I wish to thank Justin Schiller for having obtained for me an edition of *The Child's Own Book,* which, though as late as 1869, repeats the material and figures of the editions of the 1840s and 1850s which James read as a child. I also wish to thank Mark Piel, the head librarian of the New York Society Library in New York City, and his assistants for easy access to popular nineteenth-century fiction.

I wish to thank Elizabeth Armour who has, as usual, produced a legible manuscript. I wish to thank the editors of the following journals for permission to use material that first appeared in a somewhat modified form in their journals: *A.B. Bookman's Weekly, Colby Library Quarterly, The Henry James Review, Journal of Narrative Technique, Manuscripts, Markham Review, Modern Fiction Studies, Modern Language Studies, Notes and Queries, Notes on Modern American Literature, Studies in Short Fiction* and *Topic.* Unless otherwise specified, illustrations are of materials in my own collection, photographed by Kenneth Chen.

# 1

# Fairy Tales

*I scarce know what odd consciousness I had of roaming at close of day in the grounds of some castle of enchantment. I had positively nothing to compare with this since the days of fairy-tales and of the childish imagination. Then I used to circle round enchanted castles, for then I moved in a world in which the strange "came true." It was the coming true that was the proof of the enchantment, which, moreover, was naturally never so great as when such coming was, to such a degree and by the most romantic stroke of all, the fruit of one's own wizardry.*

Henry James, *The Sacred Fount*

## Perrault: "The Fairies of the *Grand Siècle*"

Strange though it may seem to those who consider James a realist and recorder of the consciousness of supersubtle fry, fairy tales intrigued him all his life. He wrote in one of his New York Edition prefaces, "the whole fairy-tale side of life has used, for its tug at my sensibility, a cord all its own."[1] Since James was concerned above all with human consciousness, to relieve it and yet call attention to it he created analogies within his tales of *other* forms of consciousness in art and literature. His invocation of fairy tales in his stories represents the transmitted literary relics of the human race that reach back to the unconscious.

In 1907 James wrote to Miss Elizabeth Jordan, editor of *Harper's Bazaar*, in answer to her "note asking me to consult, on the question of my favourite fairy tale the dreadfully dim & confused & obscure memories of my antediluvian childhood. I'm not very sure I *had* a favourite fairy-tale—so beguiling and absorbing to me were *all* such flowers of nursery legend." His principal source in infancy had been "a fat little Boy's—or perhaps Child's—Own Book which contained all the 'regular' fairytales dear to that generation" (fig. 1), but he

THE

# CHILD'S OWN BOOK,

AND

## Treasury of Fairy Stories.

*ILLUSTRATED BY TWO HUNDRED AND FIFTY ENGRAVINGS,*

BY EMINENT ARTISTS,

"In mirth and play no harm you'll know
When duty's task is done."

PUBLISHED BY ALLEN BROTHERS,
NEW YORK:
1869.

Figure 1. Title Page of *The Child's Own Book and Treasury of Fairy Stories*
(New York: Allen, 1869)

adds that he read also "Perrault & Mme. D'Aulnay, . . . the Brothers Grimm & H. C. Andersen."[2]

Although in his work James goes back to his childhood consciousness as a metaphor for his adult consciousness, he does this by referring to his memory of fairy tales. He often pits a fairy tale against its adult application. He wrote several fairy tales for grown-ups who have not lost their memories of childhood feelings, wishes, and sorrows. (He said he was more interested in the tragedies of life than in the happinesses). Especially in his later fiction, after 1900, these submerged frames of reference come to the surface in metaphors of children's games and fairy tales. Maggie's feelings are so expressed in *The Golden Bowl*[3] and in "Crapy Cornelia."[4] In *The Whole Family* chapter, Charles Edward uses the pebbles of Hop o' My Thumb as a figure in his effort to find Goward.

In James's letters to Goody Allen, a fairy tale is the unifying, mock-serious theme. The last seventeen years of James's life were marked by a lively correspondence with Jessie Allen, a descendant of the Earl of Jersey, and in 1902 he begins addressing her as "Goody" Allen, from the eighteenth-century fairy tale, "Little Goody Two Shoes," credited to Oliver Goldsmith (fig. 2). Goldsmith is fresh in James's mind because in 1900 James had written a preface to *The Vicar of Wakefield*. When James revises "The Siege of London" for the New York Edition in 1908, he puts in a reference to "The Diverting History of John Gilpin" by Cowper, which may have occurred to him when he was remembering *The Child's Own Book* in response to Elizabeth Jordan's request for a favorite fairy tale, for in that little book there is reprinted the poem by Cowper illustrated by diverting illustrations (fig. 3).

In *The Sense of the Past* notes, James writes of "the sort of Cinderella quality . . . of the younger one," the Milman sister to whom Ralph Pendrel is attracted. In a letter of 1901 to Sir Edmund Gosse, James remembers the legend of Stevenson as "a story": "So he's placed—the *Puss in Boots* or *Hop o' my thumb,* or whatever, of Biographic Literature." James's friendship with Edith Wharton had for him the quality of a fairy tale, as he remembered The Mount, her Lenox home, as well as her traveling conditions. In describing his trip to France in the Whartons' motorcar, he tells how the servants go on ahead by train "to have our rooms ready and our 'things out,'" adding "which makes the whole thing an expensive fairy tale."

What I have been sketching so far are the random interjections with their fairy-tale allusions in letters, criticism, and fiction, especially in James's late period, but even in his first novel, *Watch and Ward,* James furnishes his heroine's Oriental fantasies by way of the children's edition of fairy tales he had read as a youngster. Nora, as a child, holds *The Child's Own Book,* a collection of fairy tales reprinting many from *The Arabian Nights,* with her finger at the history of *The Discreet Princess.* She thinks Hubert "looks like the *Prince Avenant.*"[5] Nora "had grown up in the interval, from the little girl who slept

and the young eagles shall eat it." Now this bird she taught to speak, to spell, and to read; and as he was particularly fond

of playing with the large letters, the children used to call this Ralph's Alphabet:
A B C D E F G H I J K L M N O P Q R S T U V W X Y Z.

Some days after she had met with the raven, as she was walking in the fields, she saw some naughty boys, who had taken a pigeon, and tied a string to its legs, in order to let it fly, and draw it back again when they pleased; and by this means they tortured the poor animal with the hopes of liberty and repeated disappointment.

This pigeon she also bought, and taught him how to spell and read, though not to talk; and he performed all those extraordinary things which are recorded of the famous bird that was some time since advertised in the Haymarket, London, and visited by most of the great people of the kingdom. This

H

Figure 2.   "Goody Two-Shoes"
From *The Child's Own Book and Treasury of Fairy Stories*, p. 97.

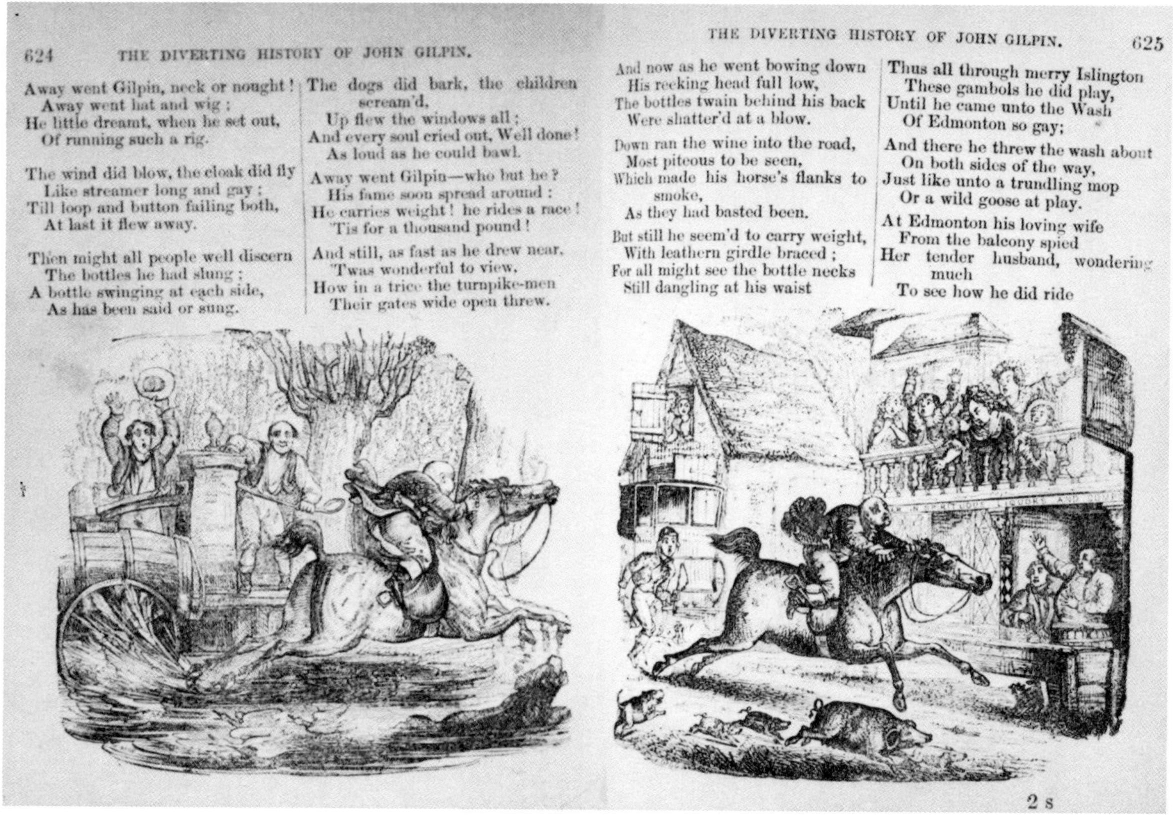

624 THE DIVERTING HISTORY OF JOHN GILPIN.

Away went Gilpin, neck or nought!
Away went hat and wig;
He little dreamt, when he set out,
Of running such a rig.

The wind did blow, the cloak did fly
Like streamer long and gay;
Till loop and button failing both,
At last it flew away.

Then might all people well discern
The bottles he had slung;
A bottle swinging at each side,
As has been said or sung.

The dogs did bark, the children scream'd,
Up flew the windows all;
And every soul cried out, Well done!
As loud as he could bawl.

Away went Gilpin—who but he?
His fame soon spread around:
He carries weight! he rides a race!
'Tis for a thousand pound!

And still, as fast as he drew near,
'Twas wonderful to view,
How in a trice the turnpike-men
Their gates wide open threw.

THE DIVERTING HISTORY OF JOHN GILPIN. 625

And now as he went bowing down
His reeking head full low,
The bottles twain behind his back
Were shatter'd at a blow.

Down ran the wine into the road,
Most piteous to be seen,
Which made his horse's flanks to smoke,
As they had basted been.

But still he seem'd to carry weight,
With leathern girdle braced;
For all might see the bottle necks
Still dangling at his waist

Thus all through merry Islington
These gambols he did play,
Until he came unto the Wash
Of Edmonton so gay;

And there he threw the wash about
On both sides of the way,
Just like unto a trundling mop
Or a wild goose at play.

At Edmonton his loving wife
From the balcony spied
Her tender husband, wondering much
To see how he did ride

2 s

Figure 3. "The Diverting History of John Gilpin"
From *The Child's Own Book and Treasury of Fairy Stories*, p. 625.

with *The Child's Own Book* under her pillow and dreamed of the *Prince Ave-nant,* into a lofty maiden who reperused *The Heir of Redclyffe*" (WW, 102–3).

But this particular source retreats from the text of the fiction; the basic model for James will be one he had used earlier—in 1865 in "The Story of a Year," in 1869 in "Gabrielle de Bergerac," and in 1871 in "Master Eustace"— the *Contes* of Perrault. They will continue to be the source for a series of stories in which seven of the eight classic tales by Perrault are encoded in the text. In his earliest tale, "The Story of a Year," James had not completely worked out his narrative strategy of naming the fairy tale itself somewhere in his own story and then later repeating echoes of his importation to alert the reader to see a parallel between it and his own story of contemporary life. To clarify the influence that each tale had on James in each stage of his writing life (and the fairy tales run through all of it), I trace the presence and meaning of each one of the seven Perrault *Contes* as it appears. When a Perrault tale features importantly more than once, I attempt to show how the treatments differ and why.

### "The Fairies" in "The Story of a Year" and "The Bench of Desolation"

At the age of twenty-two, in his earliest publicly acknowledged story, "The Story of a Year" (1865), the young Henry James drew his first extended metaphor from a Perrault fairy tale. His source was "The Fairies," with its figure of a young woman given the ability to pour forth jewels from her mouth as a reward for her kindness to an old woman who turned out to be a powerful fairy. When James's hero, Lieutenant John Ford, or "Jack," disappoints Elizabeth Crowe, or "Liz," his secretly engaged fiancée, the allusion is made overt.

> "I was going to say this, Lizzie: I think for the present our engagement had better be kept quiet". Lizzie's heart sank with a sudden disappointment. Imagine the feelings of the damsel in the fairy-tale, whom the disguised enchantress had just empowered to utter diamonds and pearls should the old beldame have straightway added that for the present mademoiselle had better hold her tongue. Yet the disappointment was brief. I think this enviable young lady would have tripped home, talking very hard to herself, and have been not ill-pleased to find her little mouth turning into a tightly clasped jewel-casket. Nay, would she not on this occasion have been thankful for a large mouth,—a mouth huge and unnatural—stretching from ear to ear? Who wish to cast their pearls before swine? The young lady of the pearls was, after all, but a barnyard miss."[6] (fig. 4)

The fairy tale does not explain or elucidate the story; it simply provides a metaphor. This, the first mention and use of a Perrault fairy tale, is interesting for us and would have been, in a sense, the most appealing to Americans. The miracle of the loaves and the fishes has been translated into money. The figure could be an apt illustration of what the rich American girl meant to Europeans. In "A London Life," a story written over twenty years after this one, another

Figure 4.    Gustave Doré, *The Good Sister*, 1862
            Illustration for "The Fairies" in Charles Perrault's *Contes*.

Perrault tale does more than supply an image for the wealth contained within a woman: Selina Wing could be seen as having pearls and diamonds pop out of her mouth for her English husband, Lionel Berrington.

Like his first tale, James's last, "The Bench of Desolation" (1909), in his final collection of short stories, *The Finer Grain,* also depends heavily on "The Fairies" with its vivid figure of pearls and diamonds coming out of a lucky girl's mouth. The younger James in 1865, determined to make his own living in writing, was the first of his family actually to do so. He found pearls coming out of his mouth, his words turning into money. In 1909 the older James, beaten by life but taken over by the rich Edith Wharton as a companion on her motor trips, returned to "The Fairies." He referred to the trips themselves as part of a fairy tale in which he was whisked around and "facilitated" by a woman who undoubtedly also got on his nerves, so that "The Bench of Desolation" is both his "fairy-tale and a nightmare" all in one.

In his first story James uses the picture of unlimited wealth as a symbol of a desired engagement in all its emphatic contour; in the last story it means only money itself, after Kate Cookham had given snakes and venom. On the first page of the story Kate Cookham is a witch but on the last page she is a fairy godmother, first the bad sister and then the good. The fairy-tale atmosphere of "The Bench of Desolation" is suggested in the very first paragraph, although transmuted, for "the ugly, the awful words" uttered by Kate Cookham (who accuses poor Herbert Dodd of breach of promise), "were like the fingers of a hand that she might have thrust into her pocket for extraction of the monstrous object that would serve best for . . . a gage of battle."

Just as "The Fairies" had contrasted the behavior of the "bad sister" with the behavior of the "good sister," who was rewarded by the gift of mouthing jewels, so the first section of James's six-part story is devoted to a picture of this bad sister and the second section to the good sister, Nan Drury, whom Dodd marries. Kate had been, in Perrault's words, "disagreeable and arrogant" whereas Nan had "gentleness and sweetness of disposition" and was "also one of the prettiest girls imaginable," with "pretty teeth," "pretty eyes," and a "regular God-given distinction of type" (XII, 379). A threatened breach of promise suit does not take place, for Herbert Dodd pays Kate her four hundred pounds, or part of the four-hundred-pound settlement she requires; then he lives his "nightmare," with his wife and children finally dying from the poverty Kate has imposed on him.

In the fourth section of the tale, Kate, having disappeared from the scene, reappears totally changed. A sedate and tasteful exterior has replaced her blatant "vulgarity"; she is now a "mature, qualified, important person." She suddenly arrives at Herbert's "bench of desolation" on the shore and watches him, a "limp, undistinguished . . . shabby man on the bench" (XII, 390). The "sharp terms of her transformed state" that can take place only in legends and folklore are such that Kate has now become the woman who, in deed and in fact, offers Herbert diamonds and pearls, or their modern equivalent (XII, 391).

His fate, Herbert realized, was "at once a fairy-tale and a nightmare." He is amazed by "the fantastic fable, the tale of money in handfuls, that he seemed to have only to stand there and swallow and digest and feel himself full-fed by." By this reversed figure, James has the hero eat the money rather than have it drop out of his mouth. Herbert realizes "the whole of the rest was a nightmare, and most of all his having thus to thank one through whom Nan and his little girls had known torture" (XII, 412). Since Dodd is weak and since Kate had invested profitably all the money she got from him, he is overwhelmed by "so *much* money—so extraordinarily much" (XII, 421). Kate appears to him like the girl in the tale, who "scattered diamonds right and left."[7]

We recall the figure from Perrault's "The Fairies" in "The Story of a Year," and the effect is the same here, only digested and reformed into James's own version of the fairy tale. He had perhaps suggested the fairy-tale tie-in to himself a few months before he wrote "The Bench of Desolation" when he used a picturesque and unique version of the figure from the fairy tale in a letter to Gosse. From his club June 4, 1909 James wrote to his friend in a letter now in the Library of Congress that he was experiencing "a horror of black cold and wet—fires and overcoats and rivers of mud," whereas Gosse was one of the "Happy fugitives" from all this: "You breathe of course a golden air and perspire in pearls and diamonds." Kate Cookham changes from the bad sister to the good sister, for this is a story of transformation, as in the more traditional older tales recorded by the Brothers Grimm. It occurs in "The Frog King," "The Ugly Duckling," and others in their collection. James has blended a series of fairy-tale actions, built on the basic frame of "The Fairies." However, this is the least popular *conte* by Perrault. One of the earliest to stimulate James in his own fantasies was "Sleeping Beauty."

## "Sleeping Beauty" in "Gabrielle de Bergerac," "A Passionate Pilgrim," and "Flickerbridge"

The fairy tale that haunted James most, so that he built three stories completely around it (two early, when he was in his twenties, and one later, when he was almost sixty), was "Sleeping Beauty." Each of James's three stories not only contains explicit references to that fairy tale but also admits to being a retelling of the legend based in part on the illustrations of the tale by two such different artists as Gustave Doré and Edward Burne-Jones. The legend of the Sleeping Beauty, with all its pictorial, metaphorical, and psychoanalytical implications appears first in "Gabrielle de Bergerac." In James's only piece of historical fiction (located in prerevolutionary France and written in 1869 while James waited to go abroad to Europe alone), there is a striking passage that accurately describes one of the illustrations by Doré for the Perrault fairy tale, "La Belle au Bois Dormant," first published in 1862. The legend partially spills over into James's next story, "A Passionate Pilgrim" (1871), written just after he returned from that first solo trip to Europe. It reappears later in 1902 in "Flickerbridge," where it totally envelops the story. This time it is Burne-Jones, whose "The Briar Wood" series at Buscot Park, Faringdon, England, a painted retelling of the Sleeping Beauty tale in four large panels, feeds James's imagination.

How this most popular of Perrault's tales operates in James's stories is a matter for investigation, a process which can illuminate both James's artistic strategies and his deep personal problems. The first tale in which it appears, "Gabrielle de Bergerac," is seen through the eyes of a little boy, the appropriate witness of a fairy tale. Here the Sleeping Beauty of noble birth, Gabrielle, is awakened to love by Coquelin, the child's tutor, a man of plebeian birth. She rejects a noble suitor, flees to Paris with her lover, and leads a life of penury, culminating in the death of both of them on the scaffold as Girondists.

The story proceeds from part 1, presented as a state of the listless inactivity of all participants, to part 2, their awakening under emotional stress as the hero triumphs over a ruined castle's dangers. The third part shows how the couple breaks with the aristocratic family. In spite of this separation from the nobility, they are sacrificed to the revolution. In its way, this division in the story corresponds to Perrault's tale, where first there is the casting of the spell of sleep by which the good fairy transmutes the death sentence of the young princess; second, the prince's penetration of the wood and his awakening of the Sleeping Beauty to life, love, and sex; and third, the threatened devouring by the prince's mother, the ogress, of the couple's children. Although all ends happily, Perrault has demonstrated that life is not a bed of roses after the young couple's marriage.

James uses the spell of sleep to characterize the condition of prerevolutionary France, the "volcano" on which "we slept." The world represented by the prerevolutionary Bergerac was a "somnolent sort of life" (II, 99). "We slept a great deal." The young chevalier's father belonged to a type "completely obsolete" (II, 100), while the child himself "was listless and languid." Although "a desultory elegance" reigned at the chateau, his father was "taciturn and apathetic" (II, 107), while the aristocratic suitor whom Gabrielle will reject had "a tired, jaded, exhausted look" (II, 108). The child's ailing mother is always in bed, and much of the private conversations take place either there or are overheard in bed by the child, who has an illness conveniently produced by James to create a situation solved by eavesdropping in bed, that recurrent piece of furniture in a Perrault tale.

Gabrielle herself "led a life of unbroken monotony" surrounded by "unclipt garden walks" (II, 113), an approximation of "the interlacing brambles and thorns" surrounding Perrault's Sleeping Beauty. It is only Coquelin "with the plebeian stamp" who "opened a way for the girl's fancy into a vague, unknown world" (II, 114). Even the "light" that the stars of their sky "flung down" was "languid" (II, 118). This part of the story, in which all seem to be asleep, also stresses that the characters are children. Coquelin's drawings "are meant for . . . children," and Gabrielle says, "we too are children" (II, 126), although we know she is twenty-two years old.

Section 2 brings in the fairy tale itself in the specific version that James wants the reader to recognize as an analogue of his *nouvelle.* Coquelin used to "tell me fairy-tales till the eyes of both of us closed together." James then summons up the forest scene by Doré in which the Prince is seen asking wood-cutters what the castle in the back section of the picture is, a castle with an ancient and mouldering wing, set in the mysterious dark forests Doré is known for. By way of teaching his young charge, the tutor in the story told stories that "belonged to the old, old world." James likens their effect to a precise verbal rendering of Doré's picture.

> Do you remember Doré's illustrations to Perrault's tales, the picture of the enchanted castle of the Sleeping Beauty? Back in the distance, in the bosom of an ancient park and surrounded by thick baronial woods which blacken all the gloomy horizon, on the farther side of a great abysmal hollow of tangled forest verdure, rise the long facade, the moss-grown terraces, the towers, the purple roofs, of a chateau of the time of Henry IV.

Then follows a detailed description of that plate by Doré (frontispiece). "I never look at the picture without thinking of those summer afternoons in the woods and of Coquelin's long stories. His fairies were the fairies of the *Grand Siècle,* and his princes and shepherds the godsons of Perrault and Madame d'Aulnay. They lived in such palaces and they hunted in such woods" (II, 131–32).

The old chevalier telling the story, whose childhood antedated the French revolution, could not have seen the illustrations by Doré first published in France except when he was already an old man. James himself could not have seen them as a child, for in 1862 he was already nineteen years old, so apparently the narrator and James himself were grown-ups interested in fairy tales, or at least in Doré's version of them. After this testimonial to Doré's effect on James, the story continues to show that the picture itself is the hub around which the tale revolves. The distinctive feature of the castle in James's tale is the ruined wing, which had its own platforms, a place separate from the rest of the castle where Gabrielle and the young chevalier sit while Coquelin goes climbing. A fissure in the castle makes descent almost impossible for Coquelin, and his life is in danger. His finally successful penetration of the ruin awakens Gabrielle to the recognition of their love.

James never reprinted the story and felt it was a failure because he didn't have enough facts to write historical fiction. One wonders whether the real reason was that he could not accept as a parallel for his story a Sleeping Beauty who is awakened, lives in sexual harmony, and engages in a reciprocal relationship with a man.

The metaphor of the Sleeping Beauty is repeated in "A Passionate Pilgrim" (1871). When James again wishes to show the awakening of love, he alludes to Perrault's version by using the French title to the story. Miss Searle, like the Sleeping Beauty, is awakened by Clement Searle's kiss of her hand (fig. 5). "Meeting her eyes the next moment, I saw that they were filled with tears. The Belle au Bois Dormant was awake" (II, 264). But the hero dies before they can consummate their love. "A Passionate Pilgrim" was one of the three tales written after the year abroad that marked James's own awakening, and the only one of the three that he put into his New York Edition. What James called the "inexpert intensity of art" of such an early tale describes the forceful use once more of Sleeping Beauty as part of the art of *his* fable (II, 10). He is still enchanted by the notion of a period of latency that characterizes the meaning of the fairy tale, for it is announced on the first page of a *nouvelle* even longer than "Gabrielle de Bergerac." In speaking of the "latent preparedness of the American mind for even the most delectable features of English life" (II, 227), James joins the fairy-tale atmosphere of the story to his own awakening to the world of Europe and to England specifically.

His meeting with the hero introduces us to someone still in a dream, with a "spiritless droop of his head" (II, 229). This is the American Clement Searle, the claimant to an English estate, in love with England and with his dream of being the prince who awakens the Sleeping Beauty. His view of taking over the estate is an analogue of the prince's forcing his way into the brambles of the enchanted castle, only he is the very opposite of the successful prince of Perrault's tale. We are prepared for this when, in the opening scene at the Red-Lion Inn, someone jokes with the exhausted Searle by telling him that instead of dying he might marry the estate-owner's sister, Miss Searle. The atmosphere of lassitude continues with the next scene at Hampton Court, during a day that "yielded that dim, subaqueous light which sleeps so fondly upon the English landscape." The "rooms of the great palace . . . follow each other . . . with a sort of regal monotony." All seems asleep, as one passes through "anterooms, drawing-rooms, council-rooms, through king's suite, queen's suite, and prince's suite." There are "vast cold tarnished beds and canopies. . . . The whole tone of this long-drawn interior is immensely sombre, prosaic, and sad. . . . I seemed to be the only visitor" (II, 237–38).

It is in Hampton Court palace that the narrator meets Searle; "the dark red palace, with its formal copings and its vacant windows, seemed to tell of a proud and splendid past" (II, 240). James is now a realist in his own time, but the experience in the lifeless sleeping palace is similar to the prince's excursion into the silent castle of the Perrault fairy tale. "The silence of the place was dreadful,

Figure 5.   Gustave Doré, *The Prince about to Waken Sleeping Beauty*, 1862
Illustration for "The Sleeping Beauty" in Charles Perrault's *Contes*.

and death seemed all about him" (P, 13). Joined by the narrator, the poor Searle, born "an aristocrat" and "with a soul for the picturesque," penetrates the hills of Warwickshire to find Lockley Hall the estate to which he feels he has a right.[8]

The narrator and Searle investigate the English fields with the same sense of discovering a world of wonder as the prince in the fairy tale. They finally enter Lockley Hall's precincts through "an untrimmed woodland," like "the wood" where "the tall trees, the brambles and thorns separated of themselves" (P, 10), and here we recognize the brambles of the fairy tale. The men travel through the house, which, like the sleeping castle, is filled with "old pictures, old tapestry, old carvings, old armor" (II, 254). The majolica "has stood for a hundred years, keeping its clear, firm hues in this aristocratic twilight" (II, 255). The time, a hundred years, is exactly the fairy-tale time.

The sleeping princess is finally introduced, but in a typically Jamesian, converted form: "she was neither young nor beautiful" (II, 257). Like the Sleeping Beauty whose clothes, Perrault had the prince note, "were like those to which his grandmother had been accustomed" (P, 15), this one's "dress was out of taste and out of season" (II, 258). Then follows the key sentence: "Miss Searle was to the Belle au Bois Dormant what a fact is to a fairy-tale, an interpretation to a myth" (II, 259). James here tells the reader "the uses of enchantment" for him as a writer. He applies the fairy tale to his own reality. Miss Searle describes her life. " 'It's extremely quiet' " (II, 259), but she is on the threshold of her awakening. When her brother returns, a "signal change had been wrought in her since the morning." She is now dressed like a princess, and her identification with Perrault's heroine is complete.

Both mature lovers find their fairy-tale roles hard to play; Searle is sick and Miss Searle says, " 'It's a hard part for poor me to play.' " The narrator, however, encourages her in the role. " 'You have begun to care for something outside the narrow circle of habit and duty. . . . It's a great moment. I wish you joy!' " (II, 276). The American claimant is a reversed Sleeping Beauty himself. When the present owner kicks him out of the house, he responds, " 'What a dream! . . . What an awakening!' " (II, 285). This marks the point when his health once more fails and he " 'confound[s] his identity with that of the earlier Clement Searle' " (II, 291), slipping into a state of fatally damaged health. Coincidentally, "the Belle au Bois Dormant was awake" (II, 264), and the dying Searle sends for her. But although she is free now that her brother has been accidentally killed, her prince is also dead. Once again "Sleeping Beauty" has been converted into a tragedy, no longer allowed its traditional happy ending.

James's third redoing of the Perrault tale, in "Flickerbridge" (1902), takes place after many years of realistic writing and the occasional reworking of the fairy tales, all sunk within tales of contemporary social life in England. It appears now as a totalizing metaphor, realized by the main character, an impressionist painter who chooses the world of a sleeping beauty, not this time a beautiful young princess but, paradoxically and parodically, an elderly spinster who lives in a sleepy, old-fashioned town in England removed from modern life. The young painter is an American who not only repudiates his ambitious young American fiancée but also leaves his elderly spinster because she will be ruined by publicity and destroyed as his version of Sleeping Beauty.

The fairy tale of "Sleeping Beauty" has always had more appeal than its seven companions in Perrault's *Contes* but, from the 1860s to the 1890s in England, the sleeping woman became an almost obsessive subject for certain painters whose chief poetic source was Tennyson's poem "The Day Dream" (1842), a completion of the 1830 first section of the poeticized fairy tale[9] (fig. 6). Henry James seems to have shared this predilection for the tale as well as certain characteristics of the men who painted sleeping women in poses of unconsciousness, new to Western art. Of these painters, Burne-Jones, the most committed to the actual fairy tale, was someone whose studio James visited from 1884 until the painter's death in 1898. Burne-Jones attached this sleeping girl to the fairy tale, painting her more than once. Like his fellow artists, he wished to keep the princess from being awakened, thus modifying Doré's version of Perrault.

These painters did not see the sleeping woman in a stage that inevitably would and should end in awakening. They put their women to sleep forever, as it were, and to understand this we must see them trying to stop a world that was moving and changing too rapidly, bringing a change in women's self-awareness. The creation of their particular subject matter fulfilled a need to reduce the speed with which the confrontation between men and women and a redisposition of their rights and responsibilities to each other was taking place toward the end of the century. James had, earlier in 1888, predicted that the "essential, latent antagonism of the sexes" that was "founded on irreconcilable interests" would get worse because women were changing.[10]

One way of explaining James's need for the fairy tale early in his career is that, first, it helped him accept the waiting period necessary for adulthood to take place, which for him meant waiting to go to Europe on his own. Further, in creating a hero who gets to Europe too late and with impossible illusions about it, he represented his own fears. Did he think as early as 1869 that his discovery of Europe was too late for his tale to profit by? Was it a sign of his nervousness that the "Sleeping Beauty" has to end in disaster? The lovers in "Gabrielle de Bergerac" at least discover each other, even though they die with the old Régime. In the later tales no one wins.

In "Gabrielle de Bergerac" and "A Passionate Pilgrim," Sleeping Beauty is at least awakened by love. In "Flickerbridge," the hero urges Sleeping Beauty to stay asleep and, since it will be impossible to keep her that way, leaves her, as well as her namesake and his fiancée, the so-different, young Addie Wenham. The reasons for this change may be twofold. First, the model for the story

THE SLEEPING PALACE.

I.

THE varying year with blade and sheaf
  Clothes and reclothes the happy plains;
Here rests the sap within the leaf,
  Here stays the blood along the veins.
Faint shadows, vapours lightly curl'd,
  Faint murmurs from the meadows come,

Figure 6.   John E. Millais, *The Sleeping Palace*, 1857
            Illustration for "The Day Dream" in Moxon's *Tennyson*.

is no longer Doré's version of Perrault's *Contes* but the four panels illustrating the tale that Burne-Jones had painted for the dining room of Lord Faringdon at Buscot Park, which were shown publicly at the Whitechapel Gallery in 1890 and 1891 before their final installation. James could have seen them not only there but also at the painter's studio or at Agnew and Sons. Second, in the 1870s, James had written the first praise for Burne-Jones's big show at the Grosvenor Gallery, and his friendship with the painter grew close shortly after that.

In Burne-Jones's world of Sleeping Beauty, all the figures remain sleeping forever. The only wide-awake figure is the prince unlike Doré's figures caught in interrupted activities that one knows will be resumed. Doré was faithful to Perrault, but Burne-Jones invents his own tale, borrowing from Tennyson's poem up to the kiss, which he eliminates. Even though William Morris's quatrains printed in the catalogue and meant to be read in front of the paintings mention the kiss, it is never pictured.[11] Burne-Jones completely ignores Morris's last quatrain, with its encouragement to wake the princess, "Come fated hand the gift to take, / and smite this sleeping world awake." When he was asked why he had not awakened the princess, Burne-Jones replied, "I wanted to stop with the princess asleep and to tell them no more."[12] Henry James follows Burne-Jones's Sleeping Beauty panels closely in "Flickerbridge." The painter's response to the pressures of Victorian industrial society was to put the world to sleep in the habiliments of the Middle Ages, a form of passive aggression as opposed to the active aggression of the Arts and Crafts movement embodied in Morris's workshops; "the more materialistic science becomes, the more angels shall I paint," Burne-Jones is reported to have said.[13]

This interest in unconsciousness as a foil to the heightened consciousness of society and of women within it is directly mirrored in "Flickerbridge," for even a James hero, interested in consciousness above all, retreats to its opposite when he wants or needs a rest. Burne-Jones spent twenty years in painting and repainting the inertness of his sleeping councilors and scullery maids as a reaction to Victorian England's catastrophic rush into modernism; James wrote one story that acts with the same type of resistance against the same kind of dangers. The hero, Frank Granger, repudiates the busy world of Parisian impressionist painters and, to recuperate from his postflu asthenia, visits an elderly spinster relation of the energetic young writer and fellow countrywoman, Addie Wenham, an example of the "new" woman from whom he will in the end be alienated.

Arriving at the small town, the young man—whose surname, Granger, suggests the name of Burne-Jones's studio, The Grange, in North Fulham—"let himself go as a convalescent. . . . It helped him to gain time, to preserve the spell even while he talked of breaking it."[14] Granger has stumbled into this fairy land like Burne-Jones's prince, who, like most Burne-Jones young men, is as pale as a convalescent. Like the prince, too, Granger fears to wake the princess. And he declares to Miss Wenham, "'I've found . . . just the thing one has ever heard of that you must resemble. You're the Sleeping Beauty in the wood'" (XI, 340).

Frank Granger feels that the entire place contains the past, "hushed to sleep round him," and although "one might love it . . . how one might spoil it! To look at it too hard . . . was positively to wake it up. Its only safety, of a truth, was to be left still to sleep" (XI, 337). That the town of Flickerbridge has also been asleep for a hundred years is indicated in that Miss Wenham "would know about the past generations, would have warrant for . . . the long, muddy century of family coaches" (XI, 338).

The Sleeping Beauty matter enters even before the first dialogue takes place between Frank Granger and the spinster from sequestered time: "He had been treated of a sudden . . . to one of the sweetest, fairest, coolest impressions of his life. . . . He had held his breath for fear of breaking the spell; had almost from the quick impulse . . . to prolong, lowered his voice and *moved on tiptoe*" (XI, 334; my italics). This is a precise description of the Burne-Jones prince as he hesitates to break the spell, because James had noticed a small but significant detail in *The Briar Wood* panel: the prince is standing "tiptoe" on his left foot, while cautiously lifting his right, picking his way noiselessly among the brambles, careful not to take "instant freedom" with "supreme beauty" (fig. 7).

Granger tries to prevent Addie, his fiancée, from coming up and "ruining" the place. The repetition of the words "kill," "ruin," "fatal," and "fatally" echoes the lines by Morris placed under the Briar Rose panels, which involve the brutal and violent destruction of a sleeping, dreaming world. "The sword that smites" the beautiful old remnant of another century, Flickerbridge and its lady, is newspaper publicity, "a publicity as ferocious as the appetite of a cannibal" (XI, 348), wielded by the young woman whom Granger ultimately rejects.

The fairy tale of Sleeping Beauty in the Perrault version had focused not only on passivity but also on rebirth, on unconsciousness as a *temporary* retreat from activity to be necessarily followed by a rebirth. James had kept to the double lesson of the fairy tale in his 1869 and 1871 reworkings. But in his 1902 version, which is more saturated with the legend since Flickerbridge, where time has stopped, encapsulates the whole sleeping world of the fairy tale, James contributes some independent twists to the tale, twists that cannot but make the post-Freudian reader try to guess at the reasons for the writer's preoccupations. Bruno Bettelheim, the chief Freudian explicator of fairy tales today, sees this fairy tale as having as its central topic a "period of passivity," an inactive period that can free the budding adolescent from worry, but also as a period during which the adolescent learns that things continue to evolve. The happy ending

Figure 7. Sir Edward Burne-Jones, *The Prince on Tiptoe among the Brambles*, The Briar Rose Series: The Briar Wood, 1871–1890 *(Courtesy of the Faringdon Trust, Buscot Park, Faringdon, England)*

assures him that he will not remain forever in a state of doing nothing even if it seems as if this period of unconsciousness will last for a hundred years:

> After the period of inactivity which typically occurs during early puberty, adolescents become active and make up for the period of passivity; in real life and in fairy tales they try to prove their young manhood or womanhood, often through dangerous adventures. This is how the symbolic language of the fairy tales states that after having gathered strength in solitude they now have to become themselves. Actually, this development *is* fraught with dangers: an adolescent must leave the security of childhood, which is represented by getting lost in the dangerous forest; learn to face up to his violent tendencies and anxieties, symbolized by encounters with wild animals or dragons.[15]

This is *not* what happens to James's hero of 1902. He repudiates the life of activity with young Addie and would stay forever with the old Addie if the young one were not due to destroy "the deep doze of the spell," the silence of Flickerbridge. When he decides to leave he knows he "could never return" (XI, 347). He regrets that she shall be brought to "self consciousness" by machinery "all organized to a single end. That end is publicity. . . . 'You'll be only just a public character'" (XI, 348). What the old Sleeping Beauty has taught Granger is " 'that you've made me see her [his fiancée] as I've never done before'" (XI, 349).

This idiosyncratic version of the fairy tale was the most acceptable one to James in 1902, for he did not see that the latent period of sleep is a preparation for life, a period of passivity to be replaced by one of activity. He viewed the state of unconsciousness as an end in itself and the awakening as a destruction of the ideality of the passive state. Burne-Jones accepted the sleeping girl, but James rejected even her. The sleeping girl unawakened into sexual life was a theme of a large number of other English paintings such as Albert Moore's group of drowsy young women in settings without men and Lord Leighton's swooning and slumbering maidens in such popular pictures as *The Garden of the Hesperides* and *Summer Moon*.

In addition to being part of the social circle of these painters, James shared certain temperamental affinities and homoerotic tendencies with them. In James's story, as well as in Burne-Jones's Briar Rose series, both writer and painter stop short of the kiss with which the Prince is to awaken the sleeping princess, because of their own anxieties and timidities before the fully aroused woman (fig. 8). This was how such temperaments neutralized the effects of Rossetti's fatal woman (Mrs. Jane Morris in her various incarnations, Moreau's and Beardsley's Salomé and other fin de siècle versions of *la belle dame sans merci*). James seemed to want to keep his women friends sleeping so far as their sexuality in relation to him was concerned, just as the facts of Burne-Jones's life make it clear that in his later years he preferred young women to whom he related imaginatively rather than physically.

Figure 8.  Sir Edward Burne-Jones, *Sleeping Beauty*, The Briar Rose Series: The Briar Wood, 1871–1890

*(Courtesy of the Faringdon Trust, Buscot Park, Faringdon, England)*

But James goes further than even the painters do in Frank Granger's rejection of heterosexuality. His falling in love nonsexually with the spinster—"'You're the Sleeping Beauty in the wood'" (XI, 340)—doesn't keep him from worrying about *her* possibly normal sexual feelings for *him:* "She gazed at him with her queerest, kindest look, which he was getting used to, in spite of a faint fear, at the back of his head, of the strange things that sometimes occurred when lonely ladies, however mature, began to look at interesting young men from over the seas as if the young men desired to flirt" (XI, 341). James's prince is not only *not* going to wake the Sleeping Beauty, whom he wants to remain asleep, but he recognizes simply by crossing the place's threshold that "quick intimacies and quick oblivions were a stranger to its air" (XI, 346). He (and after him, the young Addie) would so ruin his sleeping princess and her virgin world that he could "never return." He tells Miss Wenham, "'You can never be again what you *have* been. I shall have seen the last of you'" (XI, 348). The last line of the story repudiates the young Addie. "'We're not engaged. Goodbye'" (XI, 350).

Given this Freudian interpretation of the Sleeping Beauty, "Flickerbridge" has to be read today as a manifesto of Frank Granger's repudiation of heterosexuality if not Henry James's. It is the state of forswearing women as sex objects and of running away from the very notion of the penetration of the female. It is the desire for sterility, for death in life, for the elimination of sexual characteristics in a woman, and for fleeing from healthy sexual relations. And yet the story is told with such consummate art that James has contributed a new and inverted version of Perrault's tale. He goes further than the painters, none of whom seem to have been overt homosexuals, but whose desirable women are anesthetized, made unconscious and thereby manageable. "Flickerbridge" was written in the winter of 1899–1900, during a period of frequent letter writing to the young Norwegian-born sculptor, Hendrick Andersen, with whom James seems to have fallen in love. "Flickerbridge" can thus be seen as James's use of the Sleeping Beauty fairy tale as a symbol of his final repudiation of women presented as his hero's choice. He has not chosen men—yet; he simply has rejected women.

After 1902 James never again wrote a story in which a man has a continuing strong passion for a woman, with one exception. John Marcher fails May Bartram in "The Beast in the Jungle." Abel Taker in "Fordham Castle" is an old man useless to his wife; John Berridge rejects the Princess in "The Velvet Glove"; Sidney Traffle is simply an impotent old voyeur in "Mora Montravers"; White-Mason rejects the lively and vulgar Mrs. Worthingham in "Crapy Cornelia"; and Herbert Dodd, a limp wreck in all respects, is simply shoveled up by his bad fairy in "The Bench of Desolation." Mark Monteith in "A Round of Visits" is merely a devitalized man in a New York hell. Only in "The Papers" (1903) does a young couple stay together, but he is called Jacques and she

Rosalind, and we know Shakespeare's Jacques was finished with women. Howard, however, seems satisfied with Maud, his *"mannish* Rosalind" (my italics). Although Amerigo shows at first, on pressure from her, some passion for Charlotte, he soon forgets it. Strether retreats from love, and the two heroes of the unfinished novels are the targets of passion, not the agents. By this time James could make only women the carriers of passion, with Merton Densher the one exception for a short period of time. He rejects Kate in the end.

James clung to the fairy tale of the Sleeping Beauty during two periods in his life when he had to make a choice. In the years from 1869 until 1875, he had to choose between America and Europe. He needed the fairy tale that stood for sleeping, nature's way of waiting until a mature decision can be made, because with its insistence on a passage of time in which nothing takes place, it allowed itself to be used symbolically. It satisfied James's need for time out in which to rest in order to make the right choice between difficult alternatives. We even find it surfacing in a few sentences in *Roderick Hudson* (1875), just when James was still postponing his choice of permanent residence. He places it when Christina's duty, like his own, is to make a choice, for her that of the proper husband. The reader is told by the Cavaliere: "She must choose a name and a fortune—and she will!"[16] a sentence followed shortly after by Christina's wish to go to sleep on the grass. "But that would have been unheard of," she says. "'Oh, not quite,' Prince Casamassima answers, 'There was already a Sleeping Beauty in the Wood!'"[17] She marries her prince and lives unhappily ever after. The next year James resolved his own problem by choosing England for his permanent address, and Sleeping Beauty retreats temporarily as a usable icon.

It appears only once more, twenty-five years later, when again James is faced with making a choice. This time it was even more disturbing, for now it involved his choosing between women and men as objects of his deepest emotional attachment. First his hero is drawn to the grotesque Sleeping Beauty as a relief from her active double, but even she will be ruined by being discovered. The Sleeping Beauty has to be awakened, but neither Burne-Jones nor Henry James at the fin de siècle wants to witness it. For them heterosexual sex was out. For Burne-Jones it was burnt out; for James, the younger man of the two, it was repudiated. This rejection of both women is a fact of the story. We can only speculate that it represents James's own repudiation of women done through his character's. Since it was written when his strong emotional response to Hendrik Andersen was at its peak, we can further speculate that he had made his choice and that, like Frank Granger's last word in the story, he had said "Good-bye" to women. Edel's account of James's life from this point on makes this conjecture credible. In James's last version of Sleeping Beauty he took away from it its essential ingredient, the *postponement* of heterosexual fulfillment, and converted it to the *elimination* of heterosexual intercourse. At this stage the story seems to be unconscious witness to James's choice in favor of homoeroticism. We shall probably never know whether or not he moved from that stage to active homosexuality.

### "Bluebeard" in "A Passionate Pilgrim" and *The Sense of the Past:* Curiosity and Violence

When we look at the next Perrault *conte* we must take into consideration other accounts of Bluebeard that were available to James as early as 1866, the date of "A Day of Days" in which the legend first makes its appearance in a tale by James. To Thackeray and Daudet, two authors James admired, he might have owed a debt that amplified the story in Perrault. Their interest in Bluebeard material made clear to James that the story was alive and stimulating to two older writers of international repute at the time. Thackeray's connection with the James family and Henry James Senior made all his works fascinating to the young Henry, and we find traces of his influence in James's tales of the 1870s.

The Bluebeard legend was particularly interesting to Thackeray, as Juliet McMaster has shown us.[18] As we can see from his little picture-book of 1833, *The Awful History of Bluebeard,* the idea of the curious woman, which travels all through folk literature into Wagner's *Lohengrin* and even modified in Puccini's *Turandot,* seems to have fascinated Thackeray (as it had Dickens as well in his tale of Captain Murderer in "Nurse's Stories"), for he makes at least three versions of Bluebeard's tale, with numerous other unnamed parallels in his fiction, not including his unpublished play. It is to either the wife-killing Bluebeard or the overcurious Fatima that Thackeray pays attention. "Bluebeard's Ghost," reprinted in book form in Thackeray's *Early and Late Papers, Otherwise Uncollected* (Boston: Ticknor and Fields, 1867), must have been in the James household. It shows Mrs. Fatima Bluebeard, after having escaped Bluebeard, considering marrying either Captain Blackbeard or Sly, the lawyer. Sly's subterfuge of pretending to be Bluebeard's ghost is unmasked by Blackbeard, who wins Fatima's heart. A few years later, "Barbazure," a burlesque of G. P. R. James's style, alludes to the two horsemen, Fatima's brothers, who save her in the fairy tale. This does a turn on the two horsemen by which inclusion G. P. R. James usually began his romantic novels.

Our James begins by stressing the curious female in his first two Bluebeard tales where the legend does not control the entire story but contributes metaphorically to the curiosity of the narrator. Adela Moore in "A Day of Days" gets bored and wishes that her brother, Herbert, were a Bluebeard so that she could do something forbidden. "She felt a delectable longing to do something illicit, to play with fire, to discover some Bluebeard's closet. But poor Herbert was no Bluebeard; if she were to burn down his house he would exact no amends" (I, 141). Adela does, however, try to pry into the secret of Thomas

Ludlow, a friend of Herbert's, who arrives at their house unannounced. Later, Adela's sense of mischief is stimulated by the fact that the young man, Ludlow, is on his way to Europe; she sees whether she can keep him from going. "The reader has been put into the key of our friend's conversation; it is only needful to say that in this key it was prolonged for half an hour more" (I, 161). The "key" might be the key to Bluebeard's room, the room of the young man's consciousness and will which Adela wishes to control or, again, it might be the musical key. Needless to say, it reenforces the Bluebeard connotation.

In 1871 James wrote "Master Eustace," which is dominated by Shakespeare imagery and ideas about *Hamlet*, but the reference to Bluebeard appears here in a more pervasive role. The teller of the tale, an unmarried retainer of a certain Mrs. Garnyer, became for her employer "housekeeper, companion, seamstress, guest" and "gave her . . . my best judgment on all things." She regarded Mrs. Garnyer as a "younger and weaker sister," suggesting that she herself is a Sister Anne. "Her own confidence stopped always short of a certain point; a little curtain of reticence was always suspended between us. But it was a magical web. . . . Of course, I had fits of immense curiosity. . . . I never pried, I never pressed her, I lingered near the door of her Bluebeard's chamber, but I never peeped through the keyhole. She was a poor lady with a secret; I took her into my heart, secret and all" (II, 348). The secret in the closed room is that Eustace (the story's Hamlet) is the son of Mr. Cope (the story's Claudius), and a bastard; it is something from which Eustace never recovers, and it kills his mother. In this sense one can say that the secret is closer to Bluebeard and was worked out further than the reference to "The Fairies" in "The Story of a Year," but not completely.

After these two early uses of the tale of Bluebeard and his wives, James's late, last, and most extended reference to it may have been stimulated by reading his friend Daudet's "The Eight Mrs. Bluebeards" in *Scenes and Fancies* which, with "The Romance of Red Riding Hood," constitutes Daudet's excursion into fairy tales, although his novel, *Le Petit Chose,* suggests "Le Petit Poucet." Daudet kept quite close to the original figures, except he put them into little satirical playlets. Bluebeard, in Daudet's version, is shown in the first scene praying to God that he be released from his curse of killing all his wives. Please, he begs God, let him not kill Evelina, his eighth wife. Sister Anne appears as she always does, and Bluebeard likes her and her role, saying how like Balzac's Cousine Bette she is. All the other seven wives have been confined—that is, their corpses have been—in the old turret, and Evelina, of course, disobeys the instruction not to use the key for that building. The reanimated wives have a scene in which they talk to each other and reveal that they have been killed because of the seven vices of sloth, hatred, wantonness, and so forth. The new wife is going to be killed because of curiosity, the eighth vice. While her husband is gone, Evelina commits all the sins which Anne takes note of in addition to curiosity, so when her husband comes home he has to kill her and keep the fairy tale continuing.

Bluebeard is unhappy because, by his being chained to the age-old fairy tale, he is forced to murder many wives. He prays to be relieved of it, but custom and the categorical imperative, so to speak, make him do again what he has always done, and he kills his eighth, fifteen-year-old wife. He tells Sister Anne (each one of the wives has a sister Anne, who in this version always betrays the new wife) not to go out on the turret, "for nothing is coming. This is a serious drama in which we are acting, and there is nothing of tradition about it. . . . That's eight! (Turning to my feminine readers) Warning to ladies."[19] Daudet changes the Perrault ending and makes it a total tragedy. Nobody survives except Bluebeard, who must continue to act his thankless wife-murdering role.

In its last appearance in James, the Bluebeard material serves as the armature of an extended, three-page metaphor in *The Sense of the Past* when the people of 1820, whom Ralph Pendrel has summoned up from the past, begin to be uneasy about him and to sense that he may not be the person he pretends to be. The metaphor appears in the conversation between Molly Milman, the girl from the past, and Ralph in which she teases him about all the fiancées in America he may have concealed. Although the famous illustration by Doré seems to be behind the figure of Bluebeard offering the key to the room to his wife (fig. 9), at this late date the figure is probably more closely related to the illustration in *The Child's Own Book,* James's childhood compendium of fairy tales (fig. 10). Its appearance early in that part of the novel, which had been completed by James and did not form part of his notes, indicates that it was written around 1900. In the next few years his interest in fairy tales was to center around his memories of that jam-packed little volume to which he referred when asked by Elizabeth Jordan what his favorite fairy tale had been.

Molly Milman accuses Ralph in his 1820 guise of having left behind him in the States a number of sweethearts.

> "I don't *hold* a man single who drags about twenty hearts: he's no better than Bluebeard himself—unless found out in time."
>
> "Fortunately I'm found out in time then," Ralph again laughed—"that is in time to give you the key of the dreadful room and yet trust in spite of it to your courage—not to say to your regard."
>
> "'Regard' is a fine word when you mean my foolish curiosity! . . . If I stare you out of countenance . . . it's because I'm not ashamed of my curiosity, or of any other good reason for looking at you! I thank you for the key, as you call it, . . . and I'm sure I already see the poor things strung up in their dreadful row."[20]

Figure 9.　Gustave Doré, *Bluebeard Gives the Key to His Wife*, 1862
Illustration for "Bluebeard" in Charles Perrault's *Contes*.

country.  He desired her to be sure to indulge herself in
every kind of pleasure; to invite as many of her friends as
she liked; and to treat them with all sorts of dainties, that her
time might pass pleasantly till he came back again.  ' Here,'
said he, ' are the keys of the two large wardrobes.  This is
the key of the great box that contains the best plate, which
we use for company; this belongs to my strong box, where
I keep my money; and this belongs to the casket, in which
are all my jewels.  Here also is a master-key to all the rooms
in the house; but this small key belongs to the closet at the
end of the long gallery on the ground floor.  I give you
leave,' said he, ' to open, or to do what you like with all the
rest except this closet; this, my dear, you must not enter,

nor even put the key into the lock, for all the world.  If you
do not obey me in this one thing, you must expect the most
dreadful of punishments.'  She promised to obey his orders
in the most faithful manner; and Blue Beard, after kissing
her tenderly, stepped into his coach, and drove away.

5                          F

Figure 10.    Bluebeard Gives the Key to the Locked Room to Fatima
From *The Child's Own Book and Treasury of Fairy Stories*, p. 65.

Her mother answers, "'I should think very ill of you if you had broken no heart—I had clean broken a dozen before I patched up my husband's; and if Molly will expect you to do as much now yourself, it's no more than you'll expect of her. . . . It isn't to me . . . that I ask you to confess. . . . Well, I confess to *one!*'" (SP, 209).

In this case, James has kept the emphasis on the curiosity of the woman and the giving up of the key to her. Curiosity is apparently not only Miss Milman's vice but also the hidden vice of Ralph himself, who through that curiosity (which makes a good historian) has willed himself into the lives of these people who have lived and died almost a hundred years ago. That his faculty for resurrecting the past will end presumably with the death of one of the members of this group, very much the way Bluebeard was responsible for the death of more than one, is what we can foresee from the notes James left.

The violence of the traditional Bluebeard has been softened to a kind of psychological violence, a violence by time—time that has been engineered by this hypersensitive hero-historian. It is unlike Thackeray's sense of violence which also, however, does not exhibit itself in action in the unpublished play tentatively named by Juliet McMaster "Bluebeard at Breakfast" (Princeton University Library). What that Bluebeard does in his conversation with his butler, Butts, is, in a Socratic manner, to play on Butts's distaste for his wife of long standing. He never gets to the actual murder; all he is interested in is in presenting the male who is "driven to murder, eventually by a provocative wife" (BB, 215). This inactive Bluebeard resembles Daudet's Bluebeard which, contrived ten years later, is another extenuation of the criminal, fairy-tale villain. It is the ultimate male defense of the ultimate uxorphobic act, a defense that seems to have been widely shared at the time, even though James never saw Thackeray's unpublished play.

Bettelheim seems to agree with our three writers that the chief stress in the original Bluebeard tale is the curiosity of the woman: "the female must not inquire into the secrets of the male. . . . [W]hen the male gives the female a key to a room, while at the same time instructing her not to enter, it is a test to her faithfulness to his orders, or, in a broader sense, to him." At a certain time "only one form of deception on the female's part was punishable . . . by death: sexual infidelity" (B, 300), and execution was the punishment. On one level, Bettelheim argues, "Bluebeard" is a tale "about sexual temptation," yet on another level it "is a tale about the destructive aspects of sex" (B, 301). It is related to jealousy, and in this respect Miss Milman's quizzing Ralph Pendrel about his other sweethearts and the guise of Bluebeard shows her anxiety about *his* faithfulness. And as Perrault added, in his second moral to the tale, times now have changed. "Now, it's quite a different thing; / Be his beard what hue it may— / Madam has a word to say!" (P, 43). By his inclusion of the Bluebeard tale in "Master Eustace," James has put his finger on its relevance to the extreme jealousy and fixation Eustace has on his mother and to his sexual jealousy of her second husband, actually the boy's real father. James's *Hamlet* is reenforced by this reference, which expands the Shakespearian material to include the recorder of the unconscious, the fairy tale. In the Bluebeard tale's last introduction, in *The Sense of the Past,* what is added is the curiosity on the part of the girl of the 1820s—which can never be satisfied—and the suggestion of the death that will result from Ralph's curiosity under the aegis of scholarly interest in the past: the death of Nan, the younger Milman girl, with whom he is having an unscheduled, and as far as the unalterable facts of the past are concerned, doomed love affair.

## "Cinderella" in "Mrs. Temperly": "Analogies Drawn from Legend and Literature"

The early period of James's use of fairy tales culminates in 1875 in his own fairy tale—which is also not a fairy tale. "Benvolio," which begins "Once upon a time (as if he had lived in a fairy-tale)," immediately qualifies itself as "not a fairy-tale," even though the hero was "as pretty a fellow as any fairy prince."[21] Benvolio is cursed by having to make a choice between two ways of life, the scholarly, inherent in the young woman Scholastica, or the worldly, personified by the Countess (a parable for America or Europe as the choice for Henry James himself at the time). And the resolution of the tale, which is the lack of resolution, makes quite clear that James is giving up fairy tales for the time being. The story ends, "I rather regret now that I said at the beginning of my story that it was not to be a fairy-tale; otherwise I should be at liberty to relate" that Benvolio missed both women but that he finally "brought Scholastica home" and began to produce again only dull poetry. "But excuse me" he finishes the tale with, "I am writing as if it *were* a fairy-tale!" (III, 401). He is telling us that, although the trappings are those of a fairy tale, all does not end happily as in fairy tales because life is not like that and reality takes over. We recall his writing to Miss Jordan many years later that he "got through" Perrault, Mme. D'Aulnay, Grimm, and Andersen "very early indeed, & began to prefer 'stories of Real Life.'"[22]

After a twelve-year hiatus, James wrote "Mrs. Temperly" (1887), his version of the Cinderella story. It is only after the tale has progressed two-thirds of the way that James's young narrator, Raymond Bestwick, who is courting the elder daughter of a strong-minded, older cousin, Maria Temperly, realizes that his beloved is the Cinderella of the household. "Mrs. Temperly" is told in the manner of such stories of the 1880s as "The Lesson of the Master" and, before it, "Lady Barberina," in which some literary myth or legend implanted within the story emerges in the language, in the figures of speech and in figures from art, a system of semiotics possibly inherited from Charles Peirce. "Mrs. Temperly" concerns Raymond Bestwick's love for Dora Temperly, a daughter of the lady who gives the title to the story, but he is rejected temporarily because the ambitious mother has other daughters to marry off first to princes or their equivalents in society. Our unsuccessful artist, the aspirant fiancé, is made to wait indefinitely, but he watches with exasperation and a sense of doom the way in which Dora is exploited by her mother to further her social ambitions.

At this point in "Mrs. Temperly," "the idea came to him [Raymond] at once . . . that she was the Cinderella of the house, the domestic drudge, the one for whom there was no career. . . . He was ashamed of this fancy, I say, and yet it came back to him; he was even surprised that it had not occurred to him before. Her sisters were neither ugly nor proud . . . but her mother, like the mother in the fairy-tale, was a *femme forte*."[23] From that point on, the Cinderella legend appears reconstituted in this international tale of an ambitious mother who takes her three daughters to Paris to get them married to titled husbands.

From now on, the reader, who has been clued in on the fairy tale, can follow the analogy in the ball Mrs. Temperly gives. There the two younger girls, Tishy and Effie, are greeted more as daughters than Dora, the plain older girl, "who struck many people as silent, shy and angular" (VI, 202). The music and details are chosen by Dora herself; she "is not in it, she is not of it, and yet she too works for the common end" (VI, 223). The "taste" had been Dora's, Raymond muses, just as in *The Child's Own Book* of James's childhood, the ugly sisters "called up Cinderella to consult with her about their dress, for they knew she had a great deal of taste."[24] Cousin Maria's pleasure in her ball elicits from her a statement that reminds the reader of the fatal hour of twelve at which the enchantment ends in the fairy tale. "If it will only keep on to the end!" (VI, 224). Raymond notices that Dora's mother

> had arranged things beautifully to keep her [Dora] occupied with other people; . . . that she had half a dozen flustered young girls on her mind, whom she was providing with programmes, seats, ices, occasional murmured remarks and general support and protection. When the concert was over she supplied them with further entertainment in the form of several young men . . . whom she inarticulately introduced to them. . . . It was strange to Raymond to see her transformed by her mother into a precocious duenna. (VI, 224–25)

James appears to have remembered the details of his fairy-tale compendium because Dora, at the ball, follows in the footsteps of Cinderella who, while there, paid her sisters "a thousand attentions" (COB, 75) and, after she marries the Prince, "as amiable as she was handsome," gave her sisters "magnificent apartments in the palace" and, after a time, "married them to two great lords of the court" (COB, 80).

James's "Cinderella" is "not a fairy-tale," as James had said of his own "Benvolio," since in real life there are no fairy tales. The fairy tales always turn out well, but here Raymond, the unsuccessful artist, cannot marry Dora, the plain sister, with more marriageable younger sisters, until they have been found suitable husbands. "Cousin Maria's conscientious exactions promised him a terrible probation. And in those intolerable years what further interference, what meddlesome, effective pressure, might not make itself felt?" (VI, 232). "Cinderella" ends happily for the heroine, but "Mrs. Temperly" does not.

The effect of the narrative strategy of introducing the notion of Cinderella as the role model for the heroine in the young lover's consciousness is to make the reader go back and pick up the clues earlier in the story that prepare for this revelation. For Cousin Maria, Mrs. Temperly, is at first presented as a devoted though ambitious mother. On the second reading we are able to see her hypocrisy and the machinations hidden within her amiable exterior. The "tone of graceful, reasonable concession" with which, at the outset of the tale, she greets what she considers the ridiculous and premature demand by Raymond for the hand of Dora is a red herring to conceal her artful programs for the girls. Yet the reference on the very first page to the lamplighter "with the long wand who touched into flame the tall gas-lamp" prepares the reader for the ambience of the fairy godmother's magical wand even though the reader does not yet know that this fairy tale will be invoked. And Cousin Maria is anything but a horrible stepmother, though Raymond's love for her plain daughter seems to interest her not at all. Before she and her family leave for Paris, he says to her, "if things go as you like over there Dora will marry some foreign prince," the mention of "prince" furthering the Cinderella suggestions, though Raymond "knew that her mother deemed her peculiar" (VI, 200).

"In his artistic imagination Raymond had analogies for her, drawn from legend and literature" (VI, 202), but as yet we are not given the exact analogy, until the case for it builds up in his mind. "She was original and generous and uncalculating, besides being full of perception and taste in regard to things he cared about" (VI, 202). He doubted whether she would be married to a prince because "the foolish race of princes would be sure not to appreciate her" and because "her gentleness would not go so far as that" (VI, 203). In the fairy tale, Cinderella has also an exceptionally "sweet and gentle nature" (P, 67). Tishy and Effie, Dora's two younger sisters, are presented as being as worldly as Cinderella's two ugly sisters. Like the fairy-tale stepmother, Cousin Maria has "Napoleonic plans" for the girls. For Raymond, Dora "was like a figure on the *predella* of an early Italian painting or a mediaeval maiden wandering about a lonely castle, with her lover gone to the Crusades" (VI, 202). James's vision of his own interpretation of the fairy-tale heroine reappears once more in his defining of Nan Midmore's quality in *The Sense of the Past* as being "the sort of Cinderella quality" (SP, 319) that goes with a "longish, narrowish, almost colourless face (with the forehead, markedly high and clear, such as to recall a like feature of some mothering Virgin by Van Eyck or Memling . . . )" (SP, 281).

The first two sections of the tale follow Raymond's unsuccessful courtship of the plain sister. Just so did the stepmother in the fairy tale keep Cinderella near the fire and focus her attention only on her two daughters at Cinderella's expense. In section three of James's tale, five years have passed, and we find Raymond has returned to Paris after his family misfortunes have increased and his own career has not improved. He arrives at a prosperous and chic household decorated with masterpieces by Cabanel and with evidence of Cousin Maria's "headway . . . in a society tired of its own pessimism" (VI, 215). It is in the middle of section four, the last of the tale, while dining with the successful family and the fashionable marquise who has made that success possible, that Raymond realizes that Dora was "the Cinderella of the house," and from then till the end, this modernized fairy tale, but without a happy ending, rises to the surface of James's story.

We are tempted to speculate that the second of the two morals with which Perrault's tale ends points out the chief reason for Dora and Raymond's failure to live happily ever after. James would have read the moral not in *The Child's Own Book* but in the Doré-illustrated Perrault volume that we know he did read. "Godmothers are useful things / Even when without the wings. / Wisdom may be yours and wit, / Courage, industry, and grit / What's the use of these at all, if you lack a friend at call?" (P, 78). What defeats happiness in this tale is the lack of a godmother, a dea ex machina, someone interested in the lovers' plight. No one is, for in this society Dora and Raymond do not count.

Fourteen years after *The Sense of the Past,* Cinderella reappears in a metaphor in *The Sacred Fount* set in an Edwardian Country house, "the castle of enchantment."[25] "We're like the messengers and heralds in the tale of Cinderella, and I protest, I assure you, against any sacrifice of our *dénouement*. We've still the glass shoe to fit" (fig. 11). This is a conversation the narrator is having with Mrs. Briss. He goes on in the next paragraph, "I took pleasure at the moment in my metaphor; but this was not the case, I soon enough perceived, with my companion. 'How can I tell, please,' she demanded, 'what you consider you're talking about?'" (SF, 258). He has misjudged the application of Cinderella to the present concerns, and the reference simply reinforces the narrator's lack of the sense of reality.

The main thrust of Cinderella is sibling rivalry between Cinderella and her stepsisters. But James's treatment diminishes that aspect of the story and emphasizes now the maltreatment of one child by her biological mother. The being degraded by the mother herself is a new twist and might, as Freud said about fairy tales, be a screen for the memory of James's own childhood. Perhaps the mother might be a reversal for the father in James's own case, because he may

Figure 11.   Gustave Doré, *Cinderella Tries on the Glass Slipper*, 1862
Illustration for "Cinderella" in Charles Perrault's *Contes*.

have figured himself as not being considered important enough in the family romance. The significance of James's version of the tale is first that there is no fairy godmother to ease the situation, that if you are a Cinderella in real life you may easily never get your prince—not even if he is a loving commoner. But your mother might easily be the bad stepmother, and that is just your bad luck, as well as that of your appreciative suitor. Stephen Sondheim, in his *Into the Woods,* a musical redoing of fairy tales, created a Cinderella who, though she wins her prince, does not live happily ever after, nor do the other fairy-tale heroines and heroes of his play live through their lives as Perrault and Grimm retold them. James's point of view has finally, in 1988, permeated popular American culture.

The second importance of James's version is that the Cinderella fantasy exists in the mind of Dora's lover, not in her own mind. He views the vise he is in as just another version of the folk tale but without its wish fulfillment, the happy conclusion. As I have suggested, this tale might be a screen for James's own disappointment in the way his parents, dead for years at the time he wrote the story, had treated him. Here it might be the mother herself. Mrs. Temperly is described as being "a man as well as a woman—the masculine element was included in her nature," and the music played at her ball seemed to be "a glorification of Cousin Maria's practical genius" (VI, 224). Mrs. Temperly's name, Maria, makes the identification with James's mother, Mary James, even more tempting, since we know she was the practical and strong-willed parent.

The story may also present a remodeled and concealing picture of James's relations with his own brothers and sister, a speculation made feasible because the tale of Cinderella has been designated by modern psychoanalysis as the tale of sibling rivalry (B, 236). When we look at James's life at the time of his writing of "Mrs. Temperly" (first called "Cousin Maria" in its periodical appearance in August 1887), we see that he had been spending the time from December 1886 through the summer of 1887 in Florence more or less in the constant company of Constance Fenimore Woolson. If (as Bettelheim reviews the feelings stirred up in the child by his oedipal guilt which the tale of Cinderella allays) we see the transposition of the repressed feelings of desire for the mother transferred to another woman about whom the child feels the same guilt for not being able to sustain a sexual relation with her, then we have the relation between James and Miss Woolson as it has been suggested by Leon Edel.

The tale can be viewed as a set-up for making James think of Cinderella as a screen for his own feelings. (It is conceivable that living near Miss Woolson made him remember his feelings for his mother.) His feelings of "guilt and anxiety" (B, 243) are stirred up by his relation to a woman, Miss Woolson, the only close personal relation with a woman we know anything at all about. Bettelheim points out that many variants of the Cinderella story show that sibling rivalry has as its "real source . . . the child's feelings about his parents"

(B, 238) and that Cinderella's degradation is because of an oedipal entanglement between her and her father. In terms of James's personal history, it would seem that the *agon* of this tale requires very little of the self-sacrificing Dora-Cinderella and that it is really a story of the struggle between the will of Cousin Maria and that of the young painter-suitor of her daughter. It is clear Cousin Maria wins, and, since she is the main character, the tale is named after her. The reason why the struggle between James's mother and himself rises to the surface at this time may be that a woman was courting him and trying to put him into the vise of obedience and subordinateness that he had felt, and that all the children in the James household seem to have felt, with their mother.

### "Riquet with the Tuft" in "A London Life"

"Riquet with the Tuft" ("Riquet à la Houppe") is one of the least known and read of Perrault's fairy tales for a good reason: it seems unnecessarily complicated. It involves three young people who have been endowed by a witch with different properties. Riquet, an ugly but very clever young prince, falls in love with one of two sisters. She is the one born beautiful but stupid, whereas her younger sister is ugly but extremely clever. To compensate for these unfortunate combinations, the ugly boy has been given the power to make the beautiful sister, with whom he falls in love, clever. She, in turn, has been given the power to make the ugly boy handsome. Since she has accepted a deal with the young prince that if he makes her clever she must marry him within a year, she is forced to marry him. Since she makes him handsome, it no longer is a disaster for her. It is love, we are told, that can transform these young people and give them the good qualities they lack. The younger sister is ignored in the fairy tale but the moral ("what we love is always fair, /clever, deft, and debonair") allows the possibility of her happiness.

James brings into one of his longest tales, "A London Life" (1888), the tale of "Riquet with the Tuft," which the two little boys of Selina and Lionel Berrington choose to have read to them. James can only have chosen this tale, which is so difficult for children to keep straight, because it creates a parallel to his story. Unlike the fairy tale, however, James's story does not turn out all right. Lionel Berrington is the ugly boy; he has the tuft of hair like Riquet and has chosen the beautiful sister. But instead of Selina's becoming clever when he marries her, she becomes uncontrollably idiotic. She ruins their marriage and her own position in society by eloping with an army officer. The situation is made close to the fairy tale because her sister, who is not beautiful as she is but who is clever like the ugly sister in Perrault's tale, is the one Lionel thinks he should have married. Laura Wing, the sister, is disturbed because she has found herself in a horror story rather than in a fairy tale that comes out all right. Because of her fears of how Selina is ruining her own life, as well as those of her immediate family, Laura hysterically tries to force a proposal of marriage from Mr. Wendover, a young man who has just met her and who, as yet, entertains no inclinations toward marrying her. Lady Davenant stands for the fairy godmother who, upon the two sisters' births, had given beauty along with stupidity to one and brains but not beauty to the other. Lady Davenant helps to straighten out Laura's difficulties.

The fairy tale itself, as written in Perrault, is built on the balanced form that James repeated four years later in "The Wheel of Time"(1892). In the latter, it seems to many a reader that the pattern is too mechanical. The fable of an ugly girl, Fanny Knocker, jilted by a fastidious and beautiful young man, is repeated when the ugly daughter of the once-beautiful-now-grown-old young man is similarly jilted by a second beautiful young man, the son of the once-ugly-but-now-beautiful woman. But it is the very balancing that gives away the fairy-tale model and the source for a contemporary London version.

"Riquet with the Tuft," as first treated by James in "A London Life," carries out completely the basic formula of the Perrault tale. Because of this complete rendering it and "Mrs. Temperly" are the first two James tales to be completely dominated by a fairy tale that is actually named in the story. In Perrault's version Riquet assures the beautiful but reluctant princess that, since she likes everything about him except his looks, she has the power to make him handsome. When she asks how, he answers, "It will happen of itself, if you love me well enough to wish that it be so," since the fairy gave her that power at birth. Perrault adds: "Some people assert that this was not the work of fairy enchantment, but that love alone brought about the transformation. They say that the princess, as she mused upon her lover's constancy, upon his good sense, and his many admirable qualities of heart and head, grew blind to the deformity of his body and his face" (P, 89). The moral that is added in rhyme is as follows: "Here's a fairy tale for you, / Which is just as good as true. / What we love is always fair, / Clever, deft, and debonair" (P, 89).

The ingredients of the fairy tale have been somewhat changed to fit James's modern parallel. In the once-upon-a-time version, the son born to the queen is "ugly and misshapen," with a hump on his back but with "plenty of brains" and with the gift of imparting to the person "whom he should love best the same degree of intelligence which he possessed himself." James stressed this aspect in "A London Life" in the relation between Lionel Berrington and his sister-in-law, Laura Wing. He makes it explicit in a scene in which Laura reads the story of "Riquet with the Tuft" to her two little nephews. It is in this scene that Lionel tells her he wishes he had married *her,* and not her sister, Selina, who is now betraying him. Lionel himself is identified with Riquet with the Tuft not merely because of the way his hair grows.

In the fairy tale, the figure of Riquet is balanced by the neighboring princesses—the one who is beautiful and the other who has good sense; "the beauty of the elder and the wit of the younger" (P, 82). It is in the distinction between the two girls that James sees the interest. The two Wing girls, Laura and Selina, are created from this model of the beautiful elder sister and the clever younger sister. In Perrault's tale the ugly daughter is made with "so much good sense that her lack of beauty will scarcely be noticed" (P, 82).

James sets the atmosphere of the fairy-tale world on the first page of the story, with a schoolroom, the society of the two little nephews Scratch and Parson, and Lady Davenant, the modern fairy godmother who "took an interest in Laura partly perhaps to make up for the tepidity with which she regarded Selina."[26] Lady Davenant tells Laura that she "is not so smart as Selina," meaning fashionable, and Laura answers, "the worse she [Selina] is the better she looks," so that it is clear that Selina is the beautiful sister and Laura the witty one. Lady Davenant says that Lionel's mother "wishes it had been you," rather than Selina that Lionel had married (VII, 98). "Lionel is as idiotic as a comic song, but you have the cleverness for two." This reverses the model of "Riquet with the Tuft" with a change from a clever to a silly boy, yet keeps the relation between the two girls.

After this set-up let us follow the fairy-tale format. The elder sister in "Riquet with the Tuft" "would have willingly surrendered all her beauty for her sister's, for half her sister's cleverness" (P, 83). The "ugly little man" she meets in the forest is Riquet, and he consoles her by saying, "Beauty is of such great advantage that everything else can be disregarded, and I do not see that the possessor of it can have anything much to grieve about." Riquet tells her that he is "able to bestow as much good sense as it is possible to possess on the person whom I love the most." When she assures him that she will marry him in a year "a complete change came over her. She found herself able to say all that she wished with the greatest of ease" (P, 85).

"A London Life" establishes the atmosphere of the schoolroom by paying attention to the "primitive wood-cuts illustrative of nursery tales" that Lionel's mother had made when he was young (VII, 104). Laura's two nephews "had placed themselves in position for a story. . . . Scratch wanted an old story and Parson a new" (VII, 105). The "matter was settled for 'Riquet with the Tuft.'" James gives both an old story and a new story, the new one being the one we are reading, based on the old one (VII, 106)—though the fairy tale never seems to get read as the two children begin to argue about family matters.

Suddenly their father comes in. By bringing Lionel back into his old nursery, James puts him into the fairy-tale world and into this particular one. "I like this place," he says of his old nursery. "I was a rough one, my dear; I wasn't a pretty little lamb like that pair," implying he was as ugly as Riquet with the Tuft (VII, 113). He tells Laura that Selina is in Paris with Lady Ringrose (a nursery-tale name), and when Lionel and Laura have dinner together, James emphasizes the fairy-tale details. Lionel says to Laura, "I never know how to talk to you—you are so beastly clever" (VII, 117). He is then described as having "the air . . . of being a good-natured but dissipated boy; with his small stature . . . and his hair growing in curious infantile rings," the equivalent of Riquet's tuft. He "had lost one of his front teeth and always wore a stiff white scarf, with a pin representing some symbol of the turf or chase."

Lionel says of Selina, " 'I don't see why *she* couldn't have been a little more like you. If I could have had a shot at you first!' " (VII, 117). Then, in a significant sentence, he says, "she hates me as she'd hate a hump on her back," a figure which, without doubt, identifies him as Riquet, "so ugly and mis-shapen" (VII, 81), although Riquet's "humpback seemed no more than natural in a man who could make the courtliest of bows" (P, 89). "She'd like to stamp on me and hear me crack, like a black beetle" (VII, 118). On another occasion, after an insult from Selina, Lionel says, "Now we'll see who's a beetle and who's a toad!" (VII, 121), reminding us of the Frog King who undergoes the same kind of transformation (fig. 12).

These elements seem to take care of the "Riquet with the Tuft" model, although the remainder of the story is freighted with nursery rhymes, Mother Goose echoes and school-age children. Lady Ringrose, "a clever little woman with a single eye-glass who had read Lecky" (VII, 137), suggests a fairy god-mother turned into a witch who influences Selina. Two young men appear, one of whom looks "like a rosy child and as if he ought to be sent up to play with Geordie and Ferdy; his social nickname indeed was the Baby." Mrs. Schooling, aptly named, "must have been a goose" (VII, 145). Selina is also childish—she "talks a fury and sulks" (VII, 164). Lionel is a child in his great crisis. "Has he told his mother?" (VII, 189). Indeed, Selina and Lionel are like their two little boys.

When Selina elopes with Captain Crispin, Hogarthian elements take over the story and "Riquet with the Tuft" is finished as a pattern. James does, however, include other aspects of the tale in a later story, "The Wheel of Time" (1892), which also deals with British society in London. The name of the fairy tale does not appear in "The Wheel of Time" as it does in "A London Life." Once apparently was enough. But the mechanics of the fairy tale are there all the same, and in this story they completely dominate the plot. The tale begins, as the fairy tale does, with a daughter who is clever and not beautiful. In the fairy tale the ugly clever girl has no problems; the beautiful sister is stupid and hence miserable. In "The Wheel of Time," Lady Greyswood, like Lady Dave-nant, wants to do something for the clever and unbeautiful girl. Mrs. Knocker, the girl's mother, herself had not been beautiful, whereas her beautiful friend, Lady Greyswood, having led an impoverished life, wants her third son, Maurice Glanvil, to marry the rich but ugly Fanny Knocker, who is having a hard time attracting beaux.

Maurice is very handsome and has a passion for photography; he only

# RIQUET WITH THE TUFT.

THERE was once upon a time a queen who had a little son; he had a hump upon his back, on account of which he was named Riquet with the Tuft; and was, besides, so very ugly, that people hardly knew, for a long time, whether he had the form of a human creature. A fairy, who by chance was present at the prince's birth, told his parents, that for all his ugliness, he would make himself pleasing to every one, by his great wit and talents; and she said, too, this was not all, for she would also bestow on him the power of giving the very same charms to the person he should love best. All this was some comfort to the queen, who was in great grief at the thought of having brought such a frightful little creature into the world. It is true, as soon as he began to talk, he said the most charming things that could be; and all that he did was done in so

Figure 12.   "Riquet with the Tuft"
From *The Child's Own Book and Treasury of Fairy Stories*, p. 236.

wants a bride whose beauty will stimulate him to take photographs of her. He says, "How can a fellow have the air of having been bribed with gold to marry a monster?" (This reference does not make "The Wheel of Time" a "Beauty and the Beast" story in the strict sense because, although the moral is also that beauty appears in the face of someone who loves, the double set of girls attaches itself more closely to "Riquet with the Tuft." Further, "Beauty and the Beast" was not a Perrault story, as all the others are.) When the two young people have met and Fanny falls in love with Maurice, Mrs. Knocker suggests that it would help her daughter if she felt that Maurice was "prepossessed in her favour." It would "perhaps cheer her up, as it were, and encourage her, so that by the very fact of being happier about herself she may make a better impression."[27] What ruins the courtship for Fanny is that, sweating in a torrid spell, she looks too ugly for Maurice to go through with it. He retreats by leaving for Boulogne.

In section three of the story we leap ahead twenty-five years. Maurice Glanvil is now a fifty-year-old widower. The handsome young man he meets happens to be the son of Fanny Knocker. This is a story of transformation. In contrast, Maurice's "short, colourless, insignificant" daughter, Vera, was the disappointing fruit of a beautiful mother and handsome Maurice (VIII, 474). Vera shows her father the picture of the handsome young man's mother, who in the portrait is also handsome. It turns out to be Fanny Knocker, who survived her sorrow at Maurice's abandoning her and became beautiful through her husband's love.

Fanny now "embodied success, whereas he himself . . . was a failure not to be surpassed." From a handsome, confident youth, Maurice has turned into one of James's "poor gentlemen." He thinks of the portrait "in whom there was just enough of Fanny Knocker to put a sort of defiance into the difference" (VIII, 480). She is now, as Mrs. Tregent, "splendid and serene" (VIII, 480). Her reputation is great; "everyone adores her—she's so clever . . . and quite one of the most charming" (VIII, 480). She is clearly modeled on the younger sister of the two princesses in "Riquet with the Tuft." When he meets her, again in section four of the story, "it was above all clear to him that she wasn't Fanny Knocker—was simply another person altogether." In her face "the proportions and relations had changed, and the expression and the spirit: she had . . . found oblivion and activity and appreciation" (VIII, 483).

We are reminded again of the fairy tale of Riquet when Mrs. Tregent says to Maurice, "'You care greatly for that'" (speaking of the beauty of his wife now dead). "He hesitated a moment. 'Don't you?' She smiled at him with her basking candour. 'I used to. That's my husband,' she added, with an odd, though evidently accidental, inconsequence. . . . 'He was very good to me.' " From this statement one remembers that James has the fairy tale behind him and that it is Fanny's husband's appreciation that changed her looks, something Fanny's mother had suggested to Maurice's mother when the young people were first meeting each other years ago. At this moment the transformation now also takes place with Maurice. "In this little hour he felt his situation change—something strange and important take place" (VIII, 484).

In section five of the story Maurice tells her that he " 'can't get over . . . the difference between your youth and your maturity!' " (VIII, 485). He remarks on " 'the transformation' " (VIII, 486), but she answers, " 'I can't flatter myself that I've had two identifies' " (VIII, 486). Maurice now berates their mothers and Fanny herself for his having been such a fool as to reject her. " 'You ought to have warned me, they ought to have warned me, that there would be wizardry in the case, that you were to be the subject, at a given moment, of a transformation absolutely miraculous.' " His companion "had the advantage of being to all intents and purposes a different person from the one he talked of, while he suffered the ignominy of being the same" (VIII, 491). " 'You wore a disfiguring mask, a veil, a disguise. One fine day you dropped them all and showed the world the real creature' " (an echo of "Beauty and the Beast" as well as of "Riquet with the Tuft") (VIII, 492).

Finally, "He seemed to understand now by what miracle Fanny Knocker had been beautified. . . . [I]t had come by living for others" (VIII, 493). When she asks, showing the passion that she had once felt for him, " 'Hadn't I a single redeeming point?' " he answers, " 'It was I who was wanting—it was I who was the idiot!' " (VIII, 492). Glanvil is refused by her now. He is worried that Arthur, her son, will not like his daughter, Vera, because she is so short, and "one must remember that in that respect, at her age, she won't change" (VIII, 498). In section six Arthur leaves for Spain; Vera gets a chill and dies. This fairy tale really turns out badly. "Riquet of the Tuft" has been turned around and given a bad ending. "Unlike Fanny Knocker, Vera was never to have her revenge" (VIII, 502).

It is significant that James did not include "The Wheel of Time," his second attempt at incorporating "Riquet with the Tuft," in the New York Edition of 1908–1909. Could it be that James recognized it as too mechanical, showing that aspect of the Perrault tale—the mechanical situation of the two sisters, their formal division and double transformation—to be not really acceptable for his definitive edition? James's story is too pat, too artificially ironical, although the details are very fine indeed and the paradoxical elements amusing; also, as the main tragedy of the two ugly girls, it is touching. But the notion of transformation, of the change in a woman when she does meet with success in life, is basically Perrault's morality, which James divides into two related cases.

Since, of these tales, "A London Life" did make the New York Edition selection, included in volume X with "The Spoils of Poynton" and "The Chaperon," we may pay attention to a few words in the preface to that volume that betray James's conscious attitude to his ingenious strategy. In making an apology for having represented Selina, the wicked girl, as an American, he adds that Laura Wing was "the candid outsider." He had a feeling as an author that, in this story, "I had my right oppositions" (AN, 135). "They seemed to ensure somehow the perfect march of my tolerably simple action; the straightness, the artful economy of which—save that of a particular point where my ingenuity shows to so small advantage that, to anticipate opprobrium, I can but hold it up to derision—hasn't ceased to be appreciable." He then apologizes for making the interview with Wendover and Lady Davenant not in Laura's consciousness. He feels that it would have been better to have done it through Laura's sense and that "without this flaw the execution might have appeared from beginning to end close and exemplary" (AN, 138).

Surely the fairy-tale theme must have had a meaning in a story so strongly marked by its author for its degree of ingenuity. "The Wheel of Time" James rejected for the New York Edition, probably because it was not a good demonstration of the enclosed fairy tale and because that particular tale had once been carefully and fully investigated in its relationship to a human predicament in contemporary London. James probably considered "A London Life" as the more successful version of "Riquet with the Tuft." The fairy tale is named in the story; the themes of beauty being in the eye of the beholder and the opposition between the good sister and the bad sister, the beautiful and stupid sister versus the clever and the not-so-beautiful sister are ingeniously maintained.

Laura searches for her handsome prince, and Lady Davenant acts as her fairy godmother, and it may possibly turn out to have a happy ending—or we are inclined to think it will be so. Laura thinks her sister has been "metamorphosed," that when she was young "she seemed born for innocence." (This is a reference to what happens to the beautiful but stupid sister in "Riquet with the Tuft.") Lady Davenant was to act as the fairy godmother for Laura; "she assumed the general responsibility of providing her with a husband" (VII, 90). The promised protection and the presence of "talk" was what Laura "had dreamed of before she came to England, but in Selina's set the dream has not come true" (VII, 92). This is only the first dream or fairy-tale notion that gets dissipated for Laura.

Her fairy godmother is the complete realist, hard for Laura to accept because she has been bred on fairy-tale-like dreams. The "transformation" is clear here. "She's so changed—so changed! . . . Nothing could have been happier. . . . And now to be so dependent—so helpless—so poor!" The girl is still under the influence of fairy tales, because when Lady Davenant discusses possible suitors, Laura says, "'He must like me first,'" but Lady Davenant tells her she expects too much (VII, 97). When Selina arrives, fairy-tale motifs of transformation continue. Wendover, Selina feels, talks as if "he had been a nursemaid" (VII, 140). After Selina and Crispin leave the box at the performance of *The Huguenots,* which they all watch, Laura tries to force Wendover to propose to her. Then she tells him to go away, since she knows he does not love her. Lady Davenant, attempting to play the fairy godmother, tries to persuade him to marry Laura and give the story a happy ending. "She's clever, so charming, so good and so unhappy," but Wendover admits he had no intention of proposing to her, though he thought she was all the things Lady Davenant said she was. In James's characteristic way we are not absolutely assured of a happy ending.

According to Bettelheim, there is no known precedent for "Riquet à la Houppe." It is a beast story transmogrified and explores an exchange of favors between a prince and a princess of opposing attributes. "This is the magical transformation which love achieves: mature love and acceptance of sex make what was before repugnant, or seemed stupid, become beautiful and full of spirit" and "beauty . . . lies in the eye of the beholder." Then Bettelheim decides why this story "loses out as a fairy-tale. While love changes all, there is really no development—there is no inner conflict that needs to be resolved, nor any struggle that lifts the protagonists to a higher level of humanity" (B, 304). But "Riquet with the Tuft" has a connection with a more popular tale that Perrault never included in his classic fairy tales, one that the Grimm Brothers made popular. It is "The Frog King" which, according to Bettelheim, presents the repulsive and disgusting side of sex. The repulsive frog who becomes a prince is at that point transformed into someone beautiful, no longer disgustingly ugly, after the princess is willing to have him in her bed. The story "confirms the appropriateness of disgust when one is not ready for sex, and prepares for its desirability when the time is ripe" (B, 290). It and other stories of its type "warn that trying to rush things in sex and love . . . can have disastrous consequences" (B, 291).

What in 1888 could have stirred James's unconscious to work on a story using a variant of this basic tale as a key motif, as a parallel for a tale he had invented from modern life? The subtext of "A London Life" is undoubtedly reflective of some of his own unconscious reactions to the relationship he had sustained for the past few months in living closely with Constance Fenimore Woolson whose emotional stance to him we know, chiefly from what Edel has revealed in letters she wrote to James. That a fairy tale should also exist in the bowels of "The Wheel of Time" suggests again, as in the case of James's Cinderella story, that certain deep-seated attitudes were activated. It is not that he solved whatever problems he had in this department by writing these relevant tales, but at the very least he projected those problems onto the screen provided by the basic fairy tales. It is significant that he always used Perrault's versions, as if he were in his own way taking care of the literature of the unconscious in its most classical and sophisticated form, that version preferred to the members of the French court, to adults who could make comparisons, rather than to mere children.

James's last two attempts at revising the fairy tales of Perrault for contemporary consumption are "Flickerbridge" (1902), which builds completely on "Sleeping Beauty," and the "Married Son" chapter of *The Whole Family* (1907) which has "Hop o' My Thumb" as a central metaphor. They show signs of personal involvement to a greater degree than any of the preceding experiments. "Flickerbridge," as stated above, was James's official signing off of women, demonstrated through his main character, Frank Granger, the impressionist painter. The reader must continue to bear in mind Freud's injunction that fairy tales screen childhood memories. Granger breaks off with his fiancée because she will without doubt awaken and ruin her cousin, the Sleeping Beauty. The Sleeping Beauty must never be awakened, and, since the world will awaken her, Granger must leave. As for "Hop o' My Thumb," this is the fairy tale James told Miss Jordan was his favorite.

## "Hop o' My Thumb" in *The Whole Family*

We have already mentioned the letter James wrote to Elizabeth Jordan in 1907, answering her request for his favorite fairy tale.

> However, I *had* thrilled, by the nursery fire, over a fat little Boy's—or perhaps Child's—Own Book which contained all the "regular" fairy-tales dear to that generation—an enormous number, amid which I recall Hop O' My Thumb, *Le Petit Poucet,* as my small romance of yearning predilection. I seem to remember that story in some other particularly thrilling and haunting form, with a picture of the old woodcutter & his wife sitting at night in the glow of the fire & the depths of the wood & plotting for the mislaying of their brood [figs. 13, 14]: a very dreadful & romantic image of a strange far-off world in which the enchanting heroism of the small boy, smaller than oneself, who had in that crisis gained immortality, gave one's fond fancy the most attaching of possible companions.[28]

Jordan's request did not precede, but followed, James's completion of the chapter that he had written for the composite novel, *The Whole Family* (1907), for which Miss Jordan had arranged. That chapter is animated by a reference to Hop o' My Thumb. When Charles Edward, who is narrating the chapter, goes to New York to find Harry Goward (whose fiancée Peg had been, until his strange fascination for her aunt), he tells Peg to remember that Harry is just a "prize ass."[29] This he considers a "silver clue" to help him find the young man in New York, like one of the pebbles dropped by Hop o' My Thumb.

In chapter 7 of the novel, James presents a picture of the married son, Charles, as a person who has suffered humiliation at the hands of his large family, made up of father and mother, married sister and her husband, unmarried sister, an aunt who is the younger sister of his mother, and grandmother, a total of at least eight members including himself (which would amount to the number of siblings, parents, and aunt of which the James family was composed when James was a young man). Charles lives in close contact with his family had ever done yet, they thought that as they could contrive no other way, they must some how get rid of their children One night when the children were gone to bed, and the fa got-maker and his wife were sitting over a few lighted sticks, to warm themselves, the husband sighed deeply, and said, ' you see, my dear, we cannot maintain our children any longer; and to see them die of hunger before my eyes, is what I could never bear.    I will therefore, to-morrow morn-

ing take them to the forest, and leave them in the thickest part of it, so that they will not be able to find their way back' this will be very easy; for while they amuse themselves with tying up the fagots, we need only slip away when they are looking some other way   'Ah, husband!' cried the poor wife, ' you cannot, no, you never can consent to be the death of your own children.'   The husband in vain told her to think how very poor they were.   The wife replied, this was true to be sure; but if she was poor, she was still their mother; and then she cried as if her heart would break.   At

Figure 13.   Hop o' My Thumb Overhears His Parents Plotting to
            Abandon the Children
            From *The Child's Own Book and Treasury of Fairy Stories*,
            p. 539.

Figure 14.   Gustave Doré, *Hop o' My Thumb Overhears His Parents Plotting to Abandon the Children*, 1862
Illustration for "Hop o' My Thumb" in Charles Perrault's *Contes*.

and with his young wife, Lorraine. Charles and Lorraine both suffer, because they are artists and his family is composed of business people who manufacture ugly water pitchers. He feels he has "never either said or done a bold thing in my life," and his family believes that he has not "the spirit of a fished-out fly" (WF, 146). His mother, he believes, is "worth all the rest of us put together, and is really worth two or three of poor Father" (WF, 144). He and Lorraine are considered by the family "to be ashamed of ourselves not only for our proved business incompetence, but for our lack of first-rate artistic power as well"; in other words, he is a failure. He admits to being as dependent on his mother as when he was a child waking up from "frightening dreams." The married sister, Maria, comes across, in her confidence, in the way William did in the James family. "It is one of the facts of our situation all round, I may thus add, that everyone wants to get someone else away" (WF, 164), which seems to mirror, at this point in our knowledge of the James family, an image of their feelings.

Since Charles's position is not very good in terms of family relations, he decides to "define" it more and goes off to find Peg's recalcitrant fiancé and bring him to justice by going to New York and locating him "on the glorious impulse of a moment." Knowing Goward is "a mere little frisking prize ass" but "with no moment now to spare, yet wishing not to lose my small silver clue, I just put it here for one of the white pebbles, or whatever they were, that Hop o' My Thumb carried off to the forest, dropped, as he went, to know his way back" (WF, 173) (fig. 15). Charles has been "'saving up' . . . for an exercise of strength and a show of character that would make us of a sudden some unmistakable sign" (WF, 174). He does not want to be like his father, who is distinguished by "his failure *ever* to meet a domestic responsibility" (WF, 175), which sounds very much like Henry James Senior.

The second time James uses the same figure is in his autobiography, *A Small Boy and Others,* where he writes as a small Hop o' My Thumb himself. The very title of the book shows how James mythologized himself under the mantle of "the small boy," his very words in his letter to Miss Jordan, of Hop o' My Thumb, the tiny tot who saved his family. Since Henry was the first to earn money and to have any success as a working writer, and very early at that, it was reasonable for him to see himself as a small hero, who brought his family of siblings out of the woods, as it were. Daudet's novel, *Le Petit Chose,* had been another more extended attempt on the part of the French writer to modernize a fairy tale and to bring it up into contemporary life. We know James had read it, possibly seeing it as setting a precedent for his own autobiography done under the guise of "the little thing" or a small boy.

Just as Daudet had been the little one, *Le Petit Chose,* which, as James reminds us in his essay on Daudet, is Daudet's consciously Dickensian recollection of his own life, so *A Small Boy and Others* could be considered a kind of autobiographical novel of the development of a mind and taste. One difference,

Figure 15.    Gustave Doré, *Hop o' My Thumb Leaves a Trail,* 1862
Illustration for "Hop o' My Thumb" in Charles Perrault's
*Contes.*

however, proclaims its originality: the subtext is always the overcoming of obstacles that other members of the family could not quite handle, by a small boy who follows the "clues" to success, very much as Hop o' My Thumb followed his pebbles. Daudet's small boy is a failure. The presence of "clues" penetrates all the volumes of James's autobiography. They begin early in the book where he missed some of them, for there are "clues I have only lost."[30] The clues change to "seeds" when James tries to "grope for our early esthetic seeds." Like Hop o' My Thumb, James's interest is centered around the family; some of the clues have "tenuity: I had begun to count our wavering steps from so far back and with a lively disposition, I confess, not to miss even the vaguest of them" (AU, 125). James, as a little boy, is picking up "the smallest remembered" clues, as clues to the family's history (AU, 135). When he and his brother go to the Louvre as boys, "it would have been stupid and ignoble, an attested and lasting dishonour, not with our chance, to have followed our straggling clues, as many as we could and disengaging as we happily did, I felt, the gold and silver ones, whatever the others might have been—not to have followed them and not to have arrived by them, so far as we were to arrive" (AU, 199).

The clues sometimes are made from "a golden tissue," and change to the character of "impressions" which, in adolescence, "had begun to scratch audibly at the door of liberation" (AU, 253). The "clues" diminish when the Small Boy's report is over, and they change into "echoes" for a time in *Notes of a Son and Brother,* but they are collected as if they are things, like pebbles: "It was at any rate as if I had from the first collected and saved up the echoes" (AU, 325). The echoes change to the figure of "the cabinet of intimate reference, the museum, as it were, of the soul's curiosities" (AU, 423), but James comes back to "clue," for it is by the "lovely art of foreshortening" by which "I still grasp my capricious clue" (AU, 495). He refers to the power that the "loose clue that I had been able to recover unaided" wields in remembering the family past (AU, 505). The "impressions" he received of distinguished men in 1869 affected him "as a positive fairy-tale of privilege," and the final appearance of "clue," even here surrounded by quotation marks for the first time in the *Autobiography,* illuminates for the young man James the secret of England's idiosyncratic wonder and "genius of accommodation" (AU, 556). The entire book has been a following up of clues in order to create a biography of his family, as Hop o' My Thumb followed his pebbles to save, actually physically, his many brothers and sisters, and bring them back to their parents. The final fairy tale treatment by James suggests thus a happy ending, for, from a saga of sibling rivalry, it becomes, through the hidden fable of the Small Boy, a saga of family solidarity. The sad fact is that there is no ending at all because James died before he completed all three volumes of his autobiography. In the Perrault *Contes* endpiece, Mother Goose is reading the tales to her grandchildren. On the wall is a picture of the favorite tale, *Le Petit Poucet* (fig. 16). Even for Perrault the tale was a symbol of family solidarity.

## "Little Red Riding Hood" in "Covering End"

"Covering End" is James's fairy tale with an indisputably happy ending, possibly because it was to appear as a companion piece to "The Turn of the Screw" in *The Two Magics,* its white magic balancing its companion's black magic. Although a compendium of tags from Mother Goose nursery rhymes, La Fontaine's fables, and childhood rhymes, "Covering End" contains James's one attempt to bring Little Red Riding Hood into his work.

At this point it might be relevant to render account of James's interest in La Fontaine's fables which, according to him, he had translated into English when a "small boy," or at least before the age of fifteen, when he had been judged by his tutor to be good for nothing except for "rendering" those fables into English "with a certain corresponding felicity of idiom" (AU, 183). He must have known them well indeed, for we find a reference ten years later to "the bent and blackened woodcutters of old France, of La Fontaine's Fables" in "Gabrielle de Bergerac." We encounter the fables themselves in "Covering End," written forty years after his original rendering.

The plot of this once-upon-a-time story translated into a contemporary setting is a simple one. Captain Yule stands in danger of losing to the mortgage holder, Mr. Prodmore, his heavily mortgaged estate, Covering End, unless he marries Prodmore's daughter, Cora. He is saved by the fairy godmother, Mrs. Gracedew, a rich, attractive, American widow. By buying up the mortgage for an outrageous amount of money, Mrs. Gracedew at one stroke forces Mr. Prodmore to accede to his daughter's marriage to the suitor she desires, a Mr. Hall Pegg (a humorous pun worthy of a nursery rhyme) and saves the estate for Yule, whom she marries. Mr. Prodmore, who dangles a "heap of gold" and his daughter before Captain Yule, is the big bad wolf, but he is also introduced as the father of Cora, presented as Little Red Riding Hood. Since the wolf, Mr. Prodmore, is Red Riding Hood's father (and in this James shows a remarkable perception of the deeper meaning of the fairy tale), "he has a handkerchief of splendid scarlet silk."[31]

Cora's association with little Red Riding Hood is established by her name, Cora (heart, with its color red), by the "great deal of colour in her cheeks and a great deal more . . . in the extremely high pitch of her new, smart clothes" (X, 249), by her walk through the woods ("'there's such a lovely footpath across the park'" [X, 250]), and by the fact that she is staying with her Granny. Her maid was sick because "'at Granny's she eats too much'" (X, 250). Cora is "as unconscious as the rose on its stem!" (X, 267), and in case we do not get it, Yule asks the butler "'what color is the rose?'" "'Kind of old-fashioned red'"

Figure 16.   Gustave Doré, *Mother Goose Reading to the Children*, 1862
Endpiece to Charles Perrault's *Contes*.

(X, 268). Her father, with his aggressive personality, who wishes to feed her to Captain Yule, thinks Mrs. Gracedew, whom Cora met on the train, is also a wolf tempting his daughter (X, 251). Labeled "wild" and "mad," she is apparently staying at the Blue Dragon (X, 252). The name of Cora's fiancé, Mr. Hall Pegg, recalls the wolf's instruction to Red Riding Hood when she enters her Granny's hallway. "'Pull out the peg and the latch will fall'" (P, 28).

Cora is aware that her father is "feeding" her to Yule "'Don't *kill* me, father: give me time!'" (X, 258). Cora's father is the real wolf as we follow *his* fable, that of the wolf masquerading as a shepherd and eating lambs, from La Fontaine, and about to "kill" his daughter by gobbling up her along with Covering End. This is made very clear in the first encounter between Mother Goose (Mrs. Gracedew) and the prince (Captain Yule). He says, "'The mortgages I speak of have all found their way, like gregarious silly sheep, into the hands of one person—a devouring wolf, a very rich, a very sharp man of money'" (X, 296). She asks (X, 299), "'It's he who's the devouring wolf?'" Yule points out that "'like other devouring wolves, he's not personally adored'" (X, 300), and she responds "'You *are* personally adored; . . . and that, you poor lamb, is why he wants you!'" (X, 300).

The "covering" Mother Goose tale is "Goosy Goosy Gander" of the rhyme: "Whither shall you wander, upstairs and downstairs and in my lady's chamber." When Mrs. Gracedew, the dea ex machina or Mother Goose herself, enters Covering End, the country house that is the center of the story, she quotes the lines in section 3: "'I've been upstairs and downstairs and in my lady's chamber. I won't answer for it even perhaps that I've not been in my lord's!'" (X, 277). She also arrives on the scene likening herself to a figure in a children's poem. "'Did you think I had got snapped down in an old box like that poor girl—what's her name? the one who was poking round too—in the celebrated poem?'" (X, 271). This is picked up again when she says she likes to "'poke round'" (X, 277) and again in "her laugh but rattled the box. 'I want this house!'" (X, 331).

The entire drama is located either on or close to the central staircase of the house, and the action takes place there, probably because James first located his tale in his play *Summersoft*. "Upstairs and downstairs" is a repeated direction. When Mrs. Gracedew appears, it is as if she were "an apparition" (X, 271), and, like Mother Goose, she "gossiped" while "taking notes" (X, 272). (The location of the house in "Gossage" is an invention to emphasize the "Goose".) She gives forth assurance "as by the wave of a great wand, the motion by which she is converted from mere passive alien to domesticated dragon," and all are held by "the magic of her manner." At that point she assumes Mother Goose's traditional costume, pretending to be the castle housekeeper: "she had thrown her handkerchief over her head or made an apron of her tucked-up skirt" (X, 283). When the handsome heir, Captain Yule, proposes to her, he speaks of "the light of such a magic as yours" (X, 347). There is a point in the story when Mother Goose calls Yule " 'Oh, you delightful goose!' " (X, 341), thus making him her consort.

The nursery rhyme attached to Captain Yule (in addition to the mélange of the lamb about to be devoured by the wolf and "the goose" about to be married to Mother Goose) is "Rockabye Baby." Mr. Prodmore spells it out when he asks the Captain whether " 'rocked, as it were, by my friendly hand—in the ancient cradle of your race' " he can part with his house (X, 262). Yule answers, " 'The cradle of my race bears, for me, Mr. Prodmore, a striking resemblance to its tomb.' The sigh that dropped from him . . . might . . . have been a long sad creak, portending collapse" (X, 263), an obvious recall of "When the wind blows / The cradle will rock. / When the bough breaks / The cradle will fall. . . ." The fairy-tale tone of a childish romp is maintained within metaphors as children's games are mentioned. When Mrs. Gracedew talks to the sightseers at Covering End she says, " 'Keep well together, please—we're not doing puss-in-the-corner' " (X, 283), and Captain Yule "had the misfortune of bandaged eyes," as if blind man's buff were being played.

It takes only one hour of magical time to solve all the problems of Covering End. "A sacrifice is averted," as Mrs. Gracedew says, two marriages are arranged, a house is saved, and she remains in her chosen, boxlike, old English mansion with its heir. Mrs. Gracedew has worked her white magic; as her name foretold, she would shed grace like the dew from heaven. It may be that this story was a response to the deep disappointment of James's dramatic years, and it took the form of everything coming out all right. James had just consoled himself with the purchase of his "great, good place," Lamb House. "Covering End" is a true fairy tale since "they lived happily ever after." Although James was to write fairy tales again, of a sort, he never made them true fairy tales. First written as a play, *Summersoft* (1895), then as the tale "Covering End" (1898), this was to be comedy and to make people happy. He never reprinted the story, although in 1907 he made it into a three-act play, "The High Bid."

## Contemporary Versions of "Little Red Riding Hood": James's Sources in Other Treatments

Our Mutual Friend

What distinguishes James's use of Perrault's "Little Red Riding Hood" in "Covering End" is that he never once mentions the fairy tale by name. We have seen that, in almost every other case, he cues us in by naming the chief character or the tale itself. In his version of Little Red Riding Hood, James builds his case with a myriad of details about the big bad wolf who eats lambs and who wants to gobble up a little girl, who in this case turns out to be the wolf's daughter.

There is a park leading to Cora Prodmore's granny's house. So the salient details from the fairy tale are planted in "Covering End." In addition to "Little Red Riding Hood," there are a number of Mother Goose rhymes in "Covering End" as we have already seen above. We are not to think of "Covering End" only as a Little Red Riding Hood story but as carrying, in addition to its major thrust of that tale, nursery rhymes, little popular poems, and other elements in the Mother Goose stories that Perrault had also collected.

Little Red Riding Hood has always interested writers, and two versions by James's contemporaries, Dickens and Daudet, may have reinforced his own literary effort. In Dickens's *Our Mutual Friend* (1865) there is a predominance of references to fairy tales and nursery rhymes. Could this aspect of Dickens's novel have been a model for Henry James? We know that as a young man of twenty-two Henry James had reviewed *Our Mutual Friend* when it came out and that he did not like the book. He considered it the worst of all of Dickens's books because there was no natural character in it. However, he excepted from all the other characters the figure of Rogue Riderhood who is more natural and more within the compass of Dickens's comfortable characters.

It is in him that the fairy tale is suggested, for there is a Red Riding Hood motif within *Our Mutual Friend,* and it opens on the third page. Lizzie Hexam, the daughter of Gaffer Hexam, who tours the muddy waters of the Thames in order to find corpses and steal the money on them, is wearing "a cloak with a hood," and she pulls the hood "of a cloak she wore over her head and over her face." Rogue Riderhood enters; he is always accompanied by the description of his "squinting leer," and, when he talks, Lizzie "pulled on her hood again." Rogue Riderhood, whose name of course sounds very close to Red Riding Hood, is associated with Lizzie and her hood, and in this sense she becomes Red Riding Hood. While there never is really anything explicit about the fairy tale in the almost one thousand pages of Dickens's novel, it is only very much later in the book, four hundred pages on, that Riderhood is called "Little Rogue Riding Hood." Parenthetically, Dickens, in his authorial voice, says: "I am tempted into the paraphrase by remembering the charming wolf who would have rendered society a great service if he had devoured Mr. Riderhood's father and mother in their infancy."[32] Rogue Riderhood is the sly and unpleasant fellow who informs on Lizzie's father and who appears frequently within the book in connection with her. Another characteristic that associates him with the wolf is that he wears a fur cap and, as Dickens describes it, the cap suggests a wolf's pelt: the "sodden fur cap . . . that looked like a furry animal, dog or cat, puppy or kitten, drowned and decaying" (MF, 173). In addition *Our Mutual Friend* describes other kinds of nursery tale—"Jack and the Beanstalk" among others, including "Cock Robin"—and often alludes to fairy tales. Mr. and Mrs. Boffin have no child, but, "like the kings and queens in the fairy-tales, I suppose you have wished for one?" (MF, 125).

A second and interacting fairy tale more explicitly referred to in *Our Mutual Friend* is "Cinderella." The reference concerns the relationship of Jenny Wren, the lame little doll's dressmaker, and her boarder, the old Jew, Mr. Riah. She considers him her godmother and calls him that up to the time that she falls for Fledgeby's strategem of making the old Jew seem to be the usurer in the firm owned by Fledgeby himself and not the reverse. She then says to the old Jew after he calls her " 'my Cinderella dear,' " " 'you are not the godmother at all . . . you are the Wolf in the forest, the wicked wolf! and if ever my Lizzie is sold and betrayed I shall know who sold and betrayed her.' " But when she realizes that she has made a mistake she involves the figure of a pumpkin which will carry her to the ball, and Mr. Riah, who is her godmother, plays this game with her. Jenny now sees Fledgeby as "the wolf in a conspiracy."

There are even references to "The Three Little Bears" (MF, 668). The poem of the dance of the water animals, "Will you, Won't you, Will You, Won't You, Come to Dance with Me," is echoed, reminding us of *Alice in Wonderland.* " 'Will you, will you, will you, will you, will you come to the Bower? Oh, won't you, won't you, won't you, won't you come to the Bower?' " (MF, 715). Both *Alice* and *Our Mutual Friend* were written in 1865, and this song must have been a popular one of that year that each literary masterpiece parodies. There are many references to fairies and "the spiteful Fairy at the christening of the Princesses" (MF, 729). Such nonsense rhymes as "Mew says the cat, quack quack says the duck, bow-wow-wow says the dog" are put into the childish Mr. Boffin's mouth.

Every now and then the Little Red Riding Hood motif creeps back into the Riderhood episodes. When they go to find Gaffer's boat, "every post or wall showed the depth of the water, but seemed to hint, like the dreadfully facetious wolf in bed in Grandmother's cottage, 'that's to drown *you* in, my dears!' " (MF, 198). But then again the Cinderella motif enacted between Jenny and Mr. Riah is combined with the Red Riding Hood one. She says to him, " 'You *are* so like the fairy godmother in the bright little books! . . . I can see our features, godmother, behind the beard" (MF, 480). " 'If you'd only borrow my stick and tap this piece of pavement, . . . it would start up a coach and six' " (MF, 481).

Now there are certain indications in "Covering End"—aside from the allusions to Red Riding Hood and the input of so many nursery rhymes and Mother Goose tales and other stories (a mélange that corresponds to the mélange in *Our Mutual Friend*) that suggest that these two works could be interrelated and might give away the fact that James was either rereading or rethinking *Our Mutual Friend* and becoming aware of the presence of such a web of associations of the novel, which he thought was not one of Dickens's best. In the first place, he has the very word "dickens" in its colloquial form enter the story. Mr. Prodmore says to his daughter, " 'Why the dickens are you so late?' " (X, 249). This would be meaningless by itself, but in relation to the other elements that I will mention it might be a further corroborating piece of evidence that James remembered *Our Mutual Friend* in detail. It is also the kind of pun that he often works into his tales, especially around 1898 (see those in "The Figure in the Carpet").

Since *Our Mutual Friend* is about the mud and dust that surround the people who live off the river, we see a passage from "Covering End" that refers to mud: "'Out of the mud, if you prefer. You must pick it up, do you see?'" (X, 255), and in the next sentence, "'When we've brushed it off and rubbed it down a bit, blown away the dust and touched up the rust, my daughter shall gracefully bear it'" (X, 256). We also have the dust that surrounds *Our Mutual Friend* and the material that gives Mr. Boffin the name of The Golden Dustman, golden referring to the money that is made by picking up stuff in the dust. "Covering End" itself is just as much about money as *Our Mutual Friend,* since Mr. Prodmore, the wolf of James's tale, is one who can buy everything. "A heap of gold," which sounds like a quotation from *Our Mutual Friend,* occurs several times in "Covering End." The introduction of Puss in the Corner, Blind's Man Buff, and other children's games in "Covering End" recalls the peppering of such things in *Our Mutual Friend.* The main point about the two is that money is their big theme and that although Dickens and James bring in the magical elements of fairy tales to account for the happy endings, money is what the stories are all about.

In *Our Mutual Friend* the river and the drownings, or foiled drownings, dominate the book, and some verbal echoes of those situations may have carried over into "Covering End." Captain Yule says, "'You mean I floundered like a drowning man—?'" and then Mrs. Gracedew answers, "'Till I plunged in!'" He answers, "'You saved me'" (X, 340). Since Prodmore's money and Mrs. Gracedew's money are rivals for the purchase of the young man, including his house, Mrs. Gracedew wins because, as Captain Yule says, "'You pour out money'" (X, 346).

The case need not be overstressed but James, in his early reading of *Our Mutual Friend* for review, probably had perceived in his glossing of a large book the pattern of many fairy tales—but unfortunately done in no controlled fashion. Since he did not like the book, he waited many years for an appropriate occasion to arise for his creating a story built around similar fairy-tale models and Mother Goose rhymes, but in *his* tale the insertions would dominate the format, which might be possible in a short story. Indeed, most of James's redoings of Perrault's classic fairy tales take place in short stories because there they can help create the form of the story; in a novel the narrative demands are too complex.

*Daudet's Fairy Tale*

James's interest in Daudet extended over a quarter of a century, beginning with his first essay on Daudet in 1875. His long 1883 essay on the French novelist was reprinted in *Partial Portraits* in 1888 after his friendship with Daudet was renewed in Paris in 1884. In 1890 James translated *Port Tarascon,* and in 1897, after Daudet died, James wrote a short piece about him. Alphonse Daudet, too, wrote a series of redoings of the classical Perrault fairy tales. Daudet's story of "The Romance of Red Riding Hood" gives us a heroine who meets first a Mr. Polonius, a professor at the University of N——, who meets this joyful character whose good humor he wonders at, since she is going to be devoured by a wolf. She responds to this by saying, "'For four thousand years the same accident keeps happening to me. . . . When I return to the World (after being devoured by the wolf) I have such a vague . . . remembrance of my previous existences. . . . '"[33]

She next meets a man of letters, two lovers, a lunatic, and a child. She makes them all give in to their impulses. When eight o'clock chimes Red Riding Hood says, "'The time has come; all romances have an end, mine like the rest; it is a little shorter than most, that's all.'" In the eighth scene Polonius comes rushing in, after the noise is heard of the wolf devouring Red Riding Hood. "'Alas! I am always too late. . . . Oh! how wisdom and experience come limping after youth and folly! . . . I never arrive in time to save Red Riding Hood from the jaws of the wolf'" (AD, 172). The lunatic drowns himself: "'I like novels that end badly'" (AD, 173).

Red Riding Hood in Daudet's "The Romance of Red Riding Hood" is not *Little* Red Riding Hood. She is a young woman who seduces but who is bound to meet her fate at the hands of the wolf. Clearly Daudet is not referring to anything but to the tale by Perrault. She will be eaten, and she says to the three or four people whom she has seduces who come to complain to her that soon the wolf will eat her. "'It is my fate, as little Red Riding Hood, to accept that fate without complaining. Do as I do, dear children, never regret a pleasure, no matter how dear you may have to pay for it.'" No child should read this version. In his late novel *La Petite Paroisse* (1895), Daudet cannot resist creating another Red Riding Hood in Elise, the girl commissioned to seduce Richard Fénigan. Like her earlier Daudet incarnation she enjoys cross-roads and detours. We are told that when she knows what she is about, the wolf is the one to be pitied. James received an inscribed copy of *La Petite Paroisse* from Daudet just when he was writing *Summersoft,* the earlier play version of "Covering End."

In Daudet's fairy tales, "Red Riding Hood" and "Bluebeard," the characters are trapped within their roles. Red Riding Hood has to go through the endless ages, seducing and being eaten alive, and in no way can she avoid her fate. Bluebeard prays to be delivered from murdering his wives, but he cannot be. They are caught forever in their neuroses, and, as paradigms, they explain what human neuroses are, if fairy tales are screens for childhood memories. These memories, if they involve unsolved relations with parents, help to appease those neuroses.

James's treatment of some of these fairy tales indicates that he was aware of the neurotic component in his handling of such tales or that the tales indicated neurotic components themselves. For instance, "Sleeping Beauty," as he treats it is his later version, "Flickerbridge," shows that the Sleeping Beauty has to be awakened; her arousal cannot be avoided, so that the hero who is conscious of the old lady's Sleeping Beauty role in this story knows that she is bound to be ruined by his modern fiancée and that he must leave them both. We may view the Red Riding Hood tale as a screening of James's own problems in relating to his father, which he resolves in "Covering End," because Cora flees her father's choice of mate. She flees because, if she does not, she will be gobbled up. She is helped to avoid the situation by the Mother Goose of the story. In James's inverted Cinderella tale, "Mrs. Temperly," not only is the heroine trapped but the young man who wishes to marry her is also trapped. James seems to be adopting Daudet's attitude to fairy tales, that Cinderella will always be Cinderella, only in "Mrs. Temperly" the pattern is inverted; that is, she will continue to be Cinderella and *not* be helped by a fairy godmother. In James's last story, "The Bench of Desolation," there is a rueful solution. The fairy witch becomes a fairy godmother; the two sisters, good and bad, are both in one person, and the victim ruefully accepts her help. Because she has handsful of money, the witch turns into a fairy godmother.

Certain geniuses of literature look so deeply into the human psyche that they foresee what future generations will be obsessed with. Shakespeare was one of these, and so was Henry James. His interest in certain aspects of popular art foretold the taste of the present. His redoings of Perrault's fairy tales anticipated our vital concern with fairy tales today. We have fairy tales being constantly performed in the ballet and today *Into the Woods*, Sondheim's musical comedy, presents a modern interpretation of the basic fairy tales and an interpretation of what the fairy tales really mean. Whereas James showed how real life cannot reproduce a fairy-tale situation, though we would like it to, *Into the Woods* shows that fairy tales themselves can be viewed as capable of revision, since real life changes. Instead of interpreting real life through the fairy tales, the musical theater reinterprets the fairy tales through life and rewrites them.

It seems that James was aware of the incest pattern represented by Little Red Riding Hood, because Cora Prodmore finally avoids it. Subservient to her father, she allows herself to be handed over to Captain Yule to help keep her father's hold on Yule's property, until she meets Mr. Gracedew, who encourages her to stand up for her own happiness and to go off with the young man of *her* choice. James seems to have gone off to Europe early in life to avoid the tentacles of his own family and to avoid his father's hold over his sons' careers and expectations. James probably saw what his father's ambitions did to William, and his instincts for survival made him flee.

The amazing thing is that James saw that the wolf was the father and that he devoured his child, just as little Henry, posing as Red Riding Hood, was devoured by his father, as we may freely speculate. His mother protected him, but his father had the power over his mind, and he knew he had to get away and did. Bettelheim observes that Red Riding Hood's father is never mentioned in the tale and therefore is implicit in the wolf. Mr. Prodmore, the man described as the devouring wolf whose child says, "Don't *kill* me, father," but who wants to sell his daughter to get the house, Covering End, must be the menace for James as well. His father had been dead now for sixteen years, so James could face up to his relation to him.

It is helpful to contrast James's version to the version by Sondheim, *Into the Woods,* which has, as one of its fairy tales, Red Riding Hood. The wolf is actually the prince who, in the second act, is unfaithful to Cinderella. He is an upper-class wolf and in the meaning associated with "wolf" today, a sexually predatory male. The solo the wolf sings in the Sondheim production, after he meets Red Riding Hood walking through the woods, explicitly avows his sexual interest in both the grandmother and in the little girl. However, when we see what goes on in the hut after he has eaten the grandmother and greets the little girl, we realize there is nothing overtly sexual, and the little girl is saved by the hunter. When the prince pursues another woman in act 2, he sounds like the wolf. "The parallel is intended," the actor has been quoted as saying.

Daudet's Red Riding Hood is neither like Sondheim's nor like James's, though it is closer to Sondheim's because it tampers with the fairy tale itself. James maintains the classical version in his equivalent put into modern terms. The wolf is a father, a situation that probes more deeply into the Freudian aspects and the little girl, his daughter, is supposed to be gobbled up by the father in his marrying her to a young man who owns property on which the wolf has his eye. He is, moreover, called a wolf throughout "Covering End." Although James's Red Riding Hood is finally rescued, she is a victim. She is not a victim in the Sondheim musical; she is a pert and all-knowing little girl. In the Daudet version, she is the seductress, a twist original with Daudet. He calls it "The Romance of Red Riding Hood." When Polonius, an old man, recognizes Red Riding Hood in the woods, she claims that for four thousand years she has been devoured by the wolf and " 'four thousand years have I been resuscitated' " (AD, 149). " 'Oh! what an interesting story 't would be to read— and to write—that of little Red-Riding-Hood throughout the ages! M. Perrault has sketched one chapter; happy is he who will write the rest' " (AD, 150). With his close knowledge of his friend Daudet's work, may we not see that James is the "happy . . . he" who wrote "the rest" of Red Riding Hood, joining to it a number of other Mother Goose (*Mère d'Oie*) figures in this one white-magic tale? Daudet shows how Red Riding Hood is trapped in her destiny, as Blue-beard himself is trapped in his. James shows how his Red Riding Hood can get away from her destiny through the help of her good friend, Mrs. Gracedew. He is illustrating the refrain at the end of Cinderella's tale in Perrault: one needs a godmother.

*"Lullaby-Literature" : "Little Girl Devoured by a Wolf"*

Writing about The Wallace Collection's "Strawberry Girl" by Sir Joshua Reynolds, James compared Reynolds's paintings of children to Velasquez's. "Velasquez's children are the children of history; Sir Joshua's, of poetry, or at least of rhymed lullaby-literature: and the two sorts of representations are as far asunder as Wordsworth and Cervantes. An irresistible little ballad-heroine is this Strawberry maiden of Sir Joshua's: her pitifully frightened innocent eyes make her the very model of that figure so familiar to our childish imagination— the Little Girl Devoured by a Wolf"[34] (fig. 17). This was written in 1873 when James was thirty years old.

In 1862, when James was a young adult aged nineteen, Doré published his illustrations of the Perrault *Contes.* Doré's illustrations contain an image of the wolf in bed with Little Red Riding Hood, a version appealing to present-day Freudian points of view (fig. 18). But in *The Child's Own Book,* published earlier, the picture of the wolf in bed with the little girl is even more explicit (fig. 19). Her knees are bent and her body is in a convenient position for sexual intercourse. The sexual implications surely are evident in whatever version James read as a young person, and his description of the Reynolds interpretation, which he connects with Little Red Riding Hood, suggests the violent experience of the loss of virginal innocence.

Perrault's version, which we know was James's favored version of the fairy tales from James's use of French terms and from his quoting within his fiction from "La Belle au Bois Dormant," differs from that of the Brothers Grimm. The first part of the story is the same in both versions: the little girl, dressed in her grandmother's present of a cape or, rather, cap, has been sent by her mother to take some good things to her sick grandmother. She meets the wolf in the forest (fig. 20), but he dare not eat her there because of the woodcutters. Given the address of her grandmother's, however, he precedes the girl there, eats up the grandmother, and lies down in her bed.

In the 1862 edition of the Doré-illustrated Perrault *Contes,* the order of the stories begins with "Le Petit Chaperon Rouge." The story is very short and succinct. At the point where the wolf, after having eaten the grandmother, gets into bed and greets Little Red Riding Hood, he simply says "viens te coucher avec moi." This is immediately followed by "Le petit chaperon rouge se

Figure 17.   Sir Joshua Reynolds, *The Strawberry Girl*, 1773
*(Reproduced by permission of the Trustees of the Wallace
Collection)*

Figure 18.    Gustave Doré, *Red Riding Hood in Bed with the Wolf*, 1862
Illustration for "Little Red Riding Hood" in Charles Perrault's *Contes*.

Figure 19.    Red Riding Hood Being Attacked by the Wolf
              From *The Child's Own Book and Treasury of Fairy Stories*, p. 351.

Figure 20.  Gustave Doré, *Red Riding Hood Meets the Wolf in the Forest*,
1862
Illustration for "Little Red Riding Hood" in Charles Perrault's
*Contes*.

déshabille, et va se mettre dans le lit." Why she gets undressed is unexplained, and from this unexplained undressing we can only assume that she wants the wolf to make love to her. Why else? He had not asked her to take her clothes off, but she had instinctively done so. Since we know that Perrault wrote for adults of the court, we have to assume that he intended the sexual innuendoes. There is no suggestion here that, after the wolf eats the grandmother, he gets into her nightclothes. He simply gets into bed. In the Grimm version he is decently dressed: "Then he put on her clothes, dressed himself in her cap, laid himself in bed and drew the curtains." Perrault does not bother with any of these details. Grimm never puts Red Riding Hood into bed with the wolf. She comments on the largeness of his ears, his eyes, his hands, and his mouth (Perrault mentions teeth), and then "with one bound he was out of bed and swallowed up Red-cap." Grimm has the two devoured ladies saved by a passing woodcutter or hunter.

Perrault's awareness of the sexuality of his tale is made clear by Red Riding Hoods astonishment "de voir comment sa mère-grand était faite en son déshabille." Then she describes how big his arms are, etc., a catalogue of the fact of the wolf's nudity undoubtedly titillating to the court of Louis XIV. [35] After the words " 'the better to eat you with!' . . . the wicked Wolf leaped upon Little Red Riding Hood and gobbled her up." " 'C'est pour te manger!'—Et en disant ces mots, ce mechant loup se jeta sur le petit chaperon rouge, et la mangea." So ends the tale. We can interpret in a symbolic way that the wolf has seduced Little Red Riding Hood; her having been gobbled up literally means she has experienced Donne's little death, death simulated in an orgasm. The late twentieth-century reader cannot avoid such conclusions. It is of note that the wolf "tutoyers" the little girl, which is the language of intimacy as well as the common form of address for children. The scene is totally erotic. In the French version, therefore, Little Red Riding Hood wants to be made love to; she undresses herself when she accepts the invitation of the wolf to "te coucher avec moi." She knows what she is doing, and she does it. Her little death is what she wanted.

It is amusing that the worldly Sir Thomas Lawrence commented on Reynolds's "Strawberry Girl" in a different vein from James. He speaks of "that magnificent display of impudent knowledge that kicks modesty out of doors."[36] But for James at the age of thirty the girl had "pitifully frightened innocent eyes." However, I venture to say that by 1898 in "Covering End," in which Little Red Riding Hood is the understructure, James himself had come to see something deeper in the relation between the wolf and the little girl. For, as Hugh Walpole wrote, James was "aware of all the darkest and most morbid corners of the human heart. . . . [H]e knew *all* the passions . . . and allowed himself to reveal them only by innuendo (and he *did* reveal them thus)."[37] For the wolf is the father of Cora Prodmore, a man who wishes to sell his daughter to a suitor who both owns the desirable property of Covering End and represents the political party useful for Mr. Prodmore's commercial, predatory ends. "'Don't *kill* me, father,'" is Cora's cry. She avoids being eaten up by her father and escapes the Perrault doom. Perhaps James had been given a hint by reacting to Daudet's redoing of Little Red Riding Hood. This particular fairy tale is the only one of the Perrault *Contes* with a bad ending, unless we look on it as a description of satisfied sexuality.

I think that Bettelheim is wrong in thinking that the moral lesson appended at the end of Perrault's version was to be taken seriously. Perrault was writing the tales for the court. Although Bettelheim says that "the threat of being devoured is the central theme," one may question this. Bettelheim admits that there are different levels of meaning. He admits that the adolescent girl has to solve certain problems "if oedipal attachments linger on in the unconscious, which may drive her to expose herself dangerously to the possibility of seduction" (B, 170). Bettelheim discusses the ambivalence of the little girl between the pleasure principle and the reality principle. She is not "yet ready emotionally because she has not mastered her oedipal conflicts." But Bettelheim is discussing this tale from the Grimm version where the grandmother's clothes have been put on by the wolf. "Little Red Cap's danger is her budding sexuality, for which she is not yet emotionally mature enough. . . . [A] premature sexuality is a regressive experience, arousing all that is still primitive within us and that threatens to swallow us up" (B, 173). What about wanting to be swallowed up in an orgasm? "The immature person who is not yet ready for sex but is exposed to an experience which arouses strong sexual feelings falls back on oedipal ways for dealing with it. The only way such a person believes he can win out in sex is by getting rid of the more experienced competitors" (B, 173). She pushes the wolf on to her grandmother. Once the mother figure embodied in the grandmother is out of the way, the daughter can realize "her unconscious wish to be seduced by her father (the wolf)." (B, 175).

The child's "unconscious equation of sexual excitement, violence and anxiety" is what "Djuna Barnes alludes to when she writes: 'Children know something they can't tell; they like Red Riding Hood and the wolf in bed!'" and because "this strange coincidence of opposite emotions characterizing the child's sexual knowledge is given body in 'Little Red Riding Hood,' the story holds a great unconscious attraction to children and to adults who are vaguely reminded by it of their own childish fascination with sex" (B, 176). "It is this 'deathly' fascination with sex . . . experienced as . . . the greatest excitement and the greatest anxiety—that is bound up with the little girl's oedipal longings for her father" (B, 176).

Why should Henry James think of this tale in 1898? Even before then, at the end of August 1895, it was posted to Ellen Terry as a play entitled *Summersoft*. What took place in his life to make him dredge up Red Riding Hood? Leon

Edel has traced the series of small girls who gradually grow up to late adolescence in the end-of-the-century stories and novels by James. Edel attributes this
to a reliving of James's childhood hurts, stimulated by the failure of *Guy
Domville* and its subsequent trauma. I would add that Alice, James's sister, had
died in 1892 and that in January 1894, Constance Fenimore Woolson committed
suicide. Deprived of two female intimates, James began to feel like a little girl
himself, and, like Red Riding hood, he wanted to seduce his father, so he made
himself into a little girl. As Edel puts it, "In resuming the disguise of a female
child, the protective disguise of his early years, James performed imaginative
self-therapy. The record of these stories can be seen as the unconscious revisit-
ing of perceptions and feelings to minister to adult hurts. As his old feelings . . .
had defended his childish self long ago against the brutal world, they now served
as aid against the new brutalities."[38] He possibly could only do this when the
two women to whom he was closest, Alice and Constance, were no longer
witnesses.

It is worth remembering here Freud's mention in discussion of a patient's
dream, that "the question arises whether the hidden content in the fairy-tales of
the wolf that ate up . . . 'Little Red Riding Hood' may not simply be infantile
fear of the father."[39] Extremely relevant is the passage in the essay "The Occur-
rence in Dreams of Material from Fairy-Tales" (1913). In it Freud writes that
"in some people a recollection of their favourite fairy-tales takes the place of
memories of their own childhood: they have made the fairy-tales into screen-
memories."[40] We can apply this, to a certain extent, to the fairy-tale content of
James's tales. In other words, the fairy-tale elements, especially those of the
classical fairy tales, disguise his own childhood anxieties which he embeds in
the fantasy he is inventing.

We have said above that Cora, the timid and intimidated daughter in "Covering End," might be a screen for James's own feelings about his father. The
word "covering" in the title has all kinds of meaning, manifest and latent, which
would conform to the subtext of the fairy tale. For instance, to cover means to
copulate, used about animals (a horse covers a mare), in this case the mare
covering the horse, for Mrs. Gracedew covers, in the sexual sense, Captain
Yule. There is, as well, another more general meaning of cover, for Mrs.
Gracedew also protects him from the wolf, as she protects, as a mother figure
(Mother Goose) Prodmore's daughter, Cora.

If Cora's drama with her father might be the screen for James's memory
of his own relation to his own father, then we would see being played out in an
unconscious way one of the elements of the family drama that has never been
broached, that is, Henry's feelings for his father. Sibling rivalry as well as
fraternal incest has been speculated about. Henry's relation to his mother has
been advanced as a cause for his homoeroticism, but never, for such a cause,
his relation to his father. James's attempt at self-analysis by becoming a fictive

young girl in Edel's terms may not have worked, since a decade later he developed a crippling nervous breakdown. Bettelheim observes,

> All through "Little Red Cap" no father is mentioned. . . . This suggests that the father is present but in hidden form. The girl certainly expects her father to rescue her from all difficulties, and particularly those emotional ones which are the consequence of her wish to seduce him and to be seduced by him. What is meant here by 'seduction' is the girl's desire and efforts to induce her father to love her more than anybody else, and her wish that he should make all efforts to induce her to love him more than anybody else. (B, 178)

The wolf and the hunter contain both these aspects. "'Little Red Cap' speaks of human passions, oral greediness, aggression and pubertal sexual desires. . . . The fairy tale carries within itself the conviction of its message; therefore it has no need to peg the hero to a specific way of life. There is no need to tell what Little Red Riding Hood will do, or what her future will be. Due to her experience, she will be well able to decide this herself" (B, 183).

The French version by Perrault is somewhat pornographic, ending with the "swallowing up" of Little Red Cap. The Grimm version has her saved and learning from her terrible experience. The French version is one of sexual initiation, though a moral is drawn from it. We remember the eighteenth-century attitude from its paintings. Boucher's little girls take the place of amorous adults, and Greuse's moralistic paintings exhibit his typical little beauties who spill milk while they display their breasts. Why at this particular moment did James want to be loved by his father? We never hear that question asked in the various psychoanalytical interpretations of his tales, nor am I equipped to answer it.

That Mrs. Gracedew is the savior or the hunter of the tale is made clear from James's first notes about the tale. "She 'steps in' . . . with a certain beautiful beneficence and passion," and what interests James is "the combination of this function of hers . . . and the intensity . . . of her American character."[41] In February 1895 (right after *Guy Domville*'s failure), there is another note (N, 185). He still has the picture of the saving American woman "with everything else confused and crude" (N, 185). There is no suggestion of Red Riding Hood here yet. In the white-magic story it is Mother Goose herself, and also the hunter in Red Riding Hood, a combination that Mrs. Gracedew seems to embody. They appear in the contemporary tale about the predatory landlords of the stately homes of England and about the rich American who saves it all for the original owners.

James could not identify with Mrs. Gracedew, but at this time he could identify with Cora Prodmore, since he was seeing himself as a small and young girl in many stories, including the girl and governess in "The Turn of the Screw." In the book in which the tale is published, there is the black magic of ghosts seen by a young woman who clearly loves the master as a father figure, but she can get nowhere near him, so, like other people with father fixations, she turns her attention to the son of the master and literally kills him through mind control, by having created a ghost for him. Although "Covering End" is white magic and the saving figure of Mrs. Gracedew rescues the house and its owner as well as poor Cora from being devoured by her father's plans, it still has the scary story of Red Riding Hood and the wolf behind it, a tale which might have acted for James as the fulfillment of the unconscious wish to go to bed with his own father. For his father had never usurped the domination of the symbols of James's fictional fantasies. It is William who stands out in the sibling rivalry pattern, but for what are the siblings rivals if not for the father's love? Henry knew he had his mother's love since he was called "angel" and was known as mother's favorite by the rest of the family. The clear cut sexual message of Little Riding Hood, which we of the twentieth century accept so easily, may account for James's uncharacteristic omission of the name of this fairy tale from what is clearly his own version of it. As Hugh Walpole wrote of James's peculiarities, "There was no crudity of which he was unaware but he did not wish that crudity to be named."[42] Fairy tales give concrete support to Freud's metaphors.

Robert Darnton, in *The Great Cat Massacre,* offers an alternate, non-Freudian interpretation of the fairy-tale and folk-tale world.[43] Darnton's thesis is that the folk-tale world is what the peasant created out of the conditions of his living. Darnton quotes from "Little Red Riding Hood": " 'Undress and get into bed with me.' " As she goes through her whole story of what various big things " 'you have,' " he ends up with " 'it's for eating you better,' " and he eats her. Darnton finds that the conditions of paucity of food and the threat of wolves among the peasants are what determined all this. In this point of view, Darnton opposes Eric Fromm and Bruno Bettelheim. He points out that adolescents are confronted with adult sexualities. The wolf is a ravishing male. Yet Darnton thinks that in the Freudian interpretation these fairy tales have been taken into a mental universe that never existed before psychoanalysis. We, in turn, must ask why, then, these tales have persisted to the present day and why writers like Daudet and James have felt that the tales have had relevance for modern or contemporary consciousness. Bettelheim wrote that the *id* is the wolf as well as the father, who is also the hunter. This mixing of symbols allows Red Riding Hood to get into bed with her father. The nightmare quality of Red Riding Hood existed even during the Age of Reason, Darnton argues, for historical and sociological reasons. But it was not the Age of Reason for the peasants, only for the intellectuals, and we cannot use his argument to explain the striptease prelude to the wolf's devouring of the little girl.

There is a brief but evocative reference to the fairy tale of "The Children in the Wood" at the close of *The Ambassadors*. It emerges as a figure for death as a way to peace. Strether likens Miss Gostrey and himself to "the Babes in the Wood; they could trust the merciful elements to let them continue at peace. . . . [H]e might, for all the world, have been going to die—die resignedly; the scene was filled with so deep a death-bed hush, so melancholy a charm"[44] (fig. 21).

## Biblical Tales in *The Wings of the Dove* and "Mrs. Medwin"

The popular role of the Bible follows alongside the realm of the fairy tale, for we must consider that it was the only literature of the illiterate transmitted through oral tradition and the art of the cathedrals during the Middle Ages and up through the nineteenth century. James's recourse to the Bible itself is minimal. As I have traced previously, whatever strong biblical stories appear in his work, he seems to get through the genius of Milton, for we see Milton strongly in *The Wings of the Dove* and *The Golden Bowl*. However, within the first of those paired novels, there is an echo of the Bible that has not been filtered through another individual writer's imagination; and it occurs at the same time in two short stories as well.

Although it is well known that the title of *The Wings of the Dove* (1902) is derived from the King James version of the Bible, Psalms 55 and 68, it has not been noted that the sentence that describes Milly's giving up hope and accepting death, "She turned her face to the wall," contains an exact quotation from the same translation of the Bible, II Kings, 20:2.

> In those days was Hezekiah sick unto death. And the prophet Isaiah the son of Amoz came to him, and said unto him, Thus saith the Lord, Set thine house in order, for thou shalt die, and not live.
> 2. *Then he turned his face to the wall,* and prayed unto the Lord . . . (emphasis mine.)

It contains also a slightly altered quotation from Isaiah 38:2.

> In those days was Hezekiah sick unto death. And Isaiah the prophet the son of Amoz came unto him, and said unto him, Thus saith the Lord, Set thine house in order: for thou shalt die and not live.
> *Then Hezekiah turned his face toward the wall,* and prayed unto the Lord . . . (emphasis mine.)

James used the biblical sentence four times. In *The Wings of the Dove* it first occurs near the end of James's novel. Mrs. Susan Shepherd Stringham (her middle name is Christological in connotation) is telling Merton Densher that Milly has given up her desire to live. "They came to it almost immediately. He was to wonder afterwards at the fewness of their steps. 'She turned her face to the wall.'"[45] It occurs again when Densher reports to Kate that Milly, after judge, and was found guilty : so that he was condemned to be hanged for the crime. As soon as he found what his death must be, he sent for the keeper of the prison, and owned to him all the crimes he had been guilty of in his whole life.

Thus he made known the story of the two children ; and, at the same time, told what part of the wood he had left them to starve in. The news of this matter soon reached the uncle's ears, who was already broken-hearted for the many ills that had happened to himself, and could not bear the load of public shame that he knew must now fall upon him, so he lay down upon his bed, and died that very day. As soon as the tidings of the death of the two children were made public, proper persons were sent to search the wood for them ; and after a great deal of trouble, the pretty babes were at last found stretched in each other's arms ; with William's arm round the neck of Jane, his face turned close to hers, and his frock pulled over her body. They were quite covered with leaves, which in all that time had never withered; and on a bush near this cold grave there sat a robin redbreast, watching and chirping ; so that many gentle hearts still think it was this kind bird that did bring the leaves and cover the little babes over with them.

Figure 21. "The Children in the Wood"
From *The Child's Own Book and Treasury of Fairy Stories*, p. 69.

having been told that he and Kate were "secretly engaged," is dying. Kate asks, " '*That* was what made her worse?' "

> He watched her take it in—it so added to her sombre beauty. Then he spoke as Mrs. Stringham had spoken. 'She turned her face to the wall.' (NYE, XX, 321)

The image is so vivid and striking that it is invariably cited when critics retell the plot of the story. What makes its choice by James so apposite is that there is a touching parallel between Milly and Hezekiah, King of Judah. They both react the same way when they know about their impending deaths. In addition, both have received a temporary reprieve from their deaths. Hezekiah gets fifteen more years of life from the Lord, who hears his prayer. ("I have heard thy prayer, I have seen thy tears: behold, I will add unto thy days fifteen years" [Isaiah 38:5]).[46] Milly also gets a reprieve from Sir Luke Strett, the great London medical specialist. " 'Hard things have come to you in youth, but you musn't think life will be for you all hard things. You've the right to be happy.' " He continues, " 'Worry about nothing. . . . It's a great rare chance.' " And when Milly asks the doctor, " 'Shall I at any rate suffer?' " he responds, " 'Not a bit.' " " 'And yet then live?' " " 'My dear young lady,' " said her distinguished friend, " 'isn't to 'live' exactly what I'm trying to persuade you to take the trouble to do?' " (NYE, XIX, 246). There is another verbal link to *The Wings of the Dove;* Isaiah 38:14 contains a passage (not found in II Kings) in which Hezekiah says, " 'I did mourn as a dove,' " which might link him again with Milly.

However, we find the most striking parallel between Hezekiah's and Milly's careers when, after having received their reprieves from death, they invite their well-wishers to see the exhibition of their wealth in their palaces. Hezekiah, like Milly, gives a big reception for his potential enemies, one of whom, the son of the King of Babylon, having "heard that he had been sick, and was recovered," sent him "letters and a present." Hezekiah "was glad of them, and showed them the house of his precious things, the silver, and the gold, and the spices, and the precious ointment, and all the house of his armour, and all that was found in his treasures: there was nothing in his house, nor in all his dominion, that Hezekiah showed them not" (Isaiah 39:2). Then the Lord tells Hezekiah through Isaiah, "Behold, the days come, that all that is thine house, and that which thy fathers have laid up in store until this day, shall be carried to Babylon: nothing shall be left, saith the Lord."[47]

Milly also gives her party in her rented Venetian palace with royal luxury. There are "more candles" than her "common allowance—she grew daily more splendid: they were all struck with it and chaffed her about it" (NYE, XX, 203). In this scene Milly is called "a princess" by Mrs. Stringham in an extended metaphor that designates her a member of reigning royalty, as Hezekiah was "a king of Judah." " 'I do see that it's quite court life,' " Densher remarks (NYE,

XX, 210). "The effect of the place, the beauty of the scene . . . the golden grace of the high rooms, chambers of art in themselves" summon up a Veronese version of a biblical scene of wealth (NYE, XX, 213). During the festivities Kate covets Milly's pearls, which become a symbol of her wealth. Kate spells out to Densher that he is to marry Milly so that when her death takes place he shall "in the natural course be free" (NYE, XX, 225). Milly's treasures will eventually belong to her despoilers. Kate ends up with Milly's fortune, as Babylon ends up with the treasures of Hezekiah. It is not too farfetched to assume that, along with the other biblical associations, Hezekiah's "brief life" in Isaiah and II Kings occurs as a parallel to Milly's life—to her initial and final illness, her reprieve, and her hospitality to her friends in her palace with its treasures, her friends who are also her despoilers and who will eventually inherit her wealth. It is appropriate, therefore, that when Hezekiah and Milly accept their doom, they turn their faces to the wall.

That James had been thinking of the biblical quotation just when he was writing *The Wings of the Dove* seems to be corroborated by the fact that it occurs in his fiction in two other stories written at approximately the same time that he was working on the novel. The first of these stories, "The Abasement of the Northmores," published in 1900 in *The Soft Side,* adheres to the action in the King James version of Hezekiah's life. The heroine of the story, Mrs. Hope, "stricken, chilled to the heart, accepted perforce her situation and turned her face to the wall. In this position, as it were, she remained for days, taking heed of nothing and only feeling and nursing her wound. . . . She was beaten. She leaned thus, motionless, muffled, for a time of which, I say, she took no account; then at last she was reached by a great sound that made her turn her head. It was the report of the appearance of Lady Northmore's volumes" (XI, 125). Like Hezekiah, Mrs. Hope rallies and comes back to life.

The other example occurs in "The Beldonald Holbein," which appeared in *Harper's New Monthly Magazine,* October 1901. James had begun to work on *The Wings of the Dove* in July 1901, so it is possible he was doing the short story and the novel exactly at the same time. The phrase assumes the meaning it will take on in the novel, that of death, but in the story it is used in a tragicomical, metaphorical sense when it refers to Mrs. Brash, the victim of the story, who had become, in the eyes of a social set in London, a Holbein portrait. The "poor old picture, banished from its museum and refreshed by the rise of no new movement to hang it, was capable of the miracle of a silent revolution, of itself turning, in its dire dishonour, its face to the wall. So it stood . . . till they happened to pull it round again and find it mere dead paint" (XI, 306). These examples show that James was infusing the biblical cliché with fresh meaning by trying to apply it more originally and imaginatively to situations in contemporary life.

*Scott Homer: A Biblical Satan*

James's relation to the Devil has a long history and appears first in the 1870s when he reviews certain books about John Milton. In 1875 James agreed with David Masson that "Milton's Satan was an exalted poetic conception, in which the idea of evil was constantly modified by the beauty of presentation."[48] His connection with Milton that year manifested itself in the redoing of his "L'Allegro" and "Il Penseroso" in "Benvolio," but the Devil himself as a figure waited until around 1900 when James began thinking about the Temptation and the bitter but necessary consequences of the eating of the fruit of the Tree of Knowledge, especially seen that year in a story of that name concentrating on the expulsion from Paradise, set in modern terms.

In *The Wings of the Dove* the figure of Satan appears in Lionel Croy and in Lord Mark, though Satan had been metaphorically suggested earlier in 1892 in "Collaboration," a tale in which the narrator acts as a "tempter," a "mere mocking Mephistopheles handing over" the Frenchman's "pure spirit to my literally German Faust." But this satanic figure, as well as Lionel Croy and Lord Mark, is attached to both Goethe and to Milton. Although Rowland Mallet in *Roderick Hudson* answers Christina's question, "'Do you believe anything at all?'" with "'I believe in the grand old English Bible,'" figures from the Bible do not occur often in James's fiction.

The Devil is a different story. He is the one figure in the Bible whose two appearances of note, that in Job and that before Christ in the Gospels, seem to have caught James's imagination and are suggested first in "Mrs. Medwin" (1901) and later in *The Wings of the Dove* (1902). But it is in "Mrs. Medwin" that we are given definite clues that point to the biblical Satan, rather than the one from Milton who confronts us in Lord Mark in *The Wings of the Dove*. In "Mrs. Medwin," we are given the traditional figure of the Devil from the Bible, if we gather together the clues; for Scott Homer's role in the tale is indisputably that of the Devil.

In a letter to Mrs. Cotes in 1900, James had written, "we are both . . . conscious that a work of art must make some small effort to *be* one; must sacrifice somehow and somewhere to the exquisite. . . . So we open the door to the Devil himself—who is nothing but the sense of beauty, of mystery, of relations, of appearances, of abysses of the whole—*and* of EXPRESSION! That's *all* he is; and if he is our common parent I'm delighted to welcome you as a sister and be your brother."[49] He might have been thinking out his story, "Mrs. Medwin," about another sister and a brother, for which he had made notes in 1898 but which did not appear until 1901, and which was probably written out closer to the time of the letter than to the time of his *Notebook* recordings.

In his tale, we read on the first page that a Miss Mamie Cutter considered herself "a pair" with her half-brother Scott Homer, both Americans living by their wits, and she especially since she has made it in British society. Scott is, like the Devil, distinguished for his "perfection of indifference." He is distinguished for "impudence," for "shabbiness," "cleverness," and a "history." If the Devil is "relations," "what possible relation with him could be natural enough to meet it?" In other words, he was ready for any relation with his "easy, friendly, universally acquainted eye." He comes to cadge money from his sister, who makes a lot of it by being paid for getting people into society, and Scott is so impressed that he brings early in the story the name of his own basic character: "What the devil are they [people] kind to you *for?* (XI, 259). His "long black legs" suggest the Devil of the traditional figure whose legs might have been a model for Scott Homer's "long lean loose" legs. He wears a "scant, rough Inverness cape" (XI, 258) as so many nineteenth-century configurations of the Devil do.

Since Mamie had said, "I'm just what I am,'" so Scott answers "*I'm* what I am too. Nothing less and nothing more'" (XI, 259). Moreover, only the Devil dares to pretend to be God and to take over for his own use God's definition of himself. These are paraphrases from Exodus 3. When Moses asks God (who had appeared to him in a burning bush to elect him to take the children of Israel out of the land of Egypt) what he should say to the people when they ask the name of God, God answers, "I AM THAT I AM!" and he said, "Thus shalt thou say unto the children of Israel, I AM hath sent me unto you" (Exodus 3:14). Scott adds that he is "clever and amusing and charming," in other words, a tempter. "'We *are* a crew!'" (XI, 260). This is Miltonic and from *Paradise Lost*. The English, he says, "think me . . . diabolically American" (XI, 260).

Within two pages he has identified himself as the Devil, or at least a member of the Devil's family, through an expletive and through an adverbial phrase. He constantly exhibits an "easy play of intelligence." His relation to his sister is the result of "a community of fatigue and failure, and after all, of intelligence. There was a final cynical humour in it" (XI, 261). She wants him not to "ruin me." She tells him to "come back at seven sharp—not a minute before and not a minute after," and if he does this she will give him "two five-pound notes." This Devil, situated in modern London, does not require someone's soul, merely cash. Mamie is also perhaps his sister, Sin, but she expects to do "the impossible," getting the socially undesirable Mrs. Medwin into society, and only God and the Devil can do the impossible. Mamie explains to her client that she has had "a descent from" her brother, "a wretch." The "descent" is of course a biblical word as well as a Miltonic one. He " 'disappears abroad. But he always turns up again, worse than ever.'"

Here we recognize a paraphrase from the Book of Job in chapter 1 when the Lord asks Satan, "Whence comest thou? Then Satan answered the Lord and said, From going to and fro in the earth, and from walking up and down in it." Scott is "awfully clever—awfully traveled, and easy." Like the Devil, he is one who cannot keep his word; he comes at six-thirty instead of at seven, as his sister asked him to do, and pleading "fatigue" goes for "half an hour" on "that old sofa upstairs." When Mamie returns she finds out that Lady Wantridge had gone up, too, and had talked with Scott. He quotes her as being eager "to make too much of anything," and if it is something she "doesn't want to do, she'll make as much as Moses," a biblical reference probably referring to how Moses made a lot out of the treatment of the Jews to get them out of the land of Egypt, also from Exodus 3. Scott tells Mamie that he gets "on with everybody," as the Devil did. He adds, "'you don't know the curiosity we any of us inspire'" (XI, 270).

This again is a reminder of James's letter, where he defines the Devil as "the sense of mystery . . . abysses." Scott tells his sister that people will pay them because "'They're dead, don't you see? And *we're* alive'" (XI, 270). And they are so used up they are even "'not afraid—not even of me!'" (XI, 270), that is, they are so bored they will even play with the Devil. Lady Wantridge had "a sharpened taste for life, and, with all sorts of things behind and beneath her, more abysmal and more immoral, more secure and more impertinent." So she at first declined to put through Mrs. Medwin, Mamie Cutter's client: "she quite doubted that Mamie herself had measured the job."

Could the intrusion of this word "job" used as a pun remind us of the book in the Bible in which Satan makes his appearance and tells God that Job is "perfect and upright"? This is because "thou hast blessed the work of his hands. . . . But put forth thine hand now, and touch all that he hath, and he will curse thee to thy face." So God tells Satan to turn the tide of Job's fortune, which Satan does do. The reference to Moses substantiates our thesis that this tale is involved with biblical quotations, especially from the Old Testament. Mamie "interposed," which is a Miltonic word if not biblical, but Milton is associated with Satan, naturally.

Scott asks Lady Wantridge whether she can forgive him, and she answers for what. That gives Mamie an idea, since Lady Wantridge likes his oddity—"one of your odd Americans" (XI, 277). She insists that her friend cannot meet him because "'he appears to have done something that has made a difference in his life.'" . . . "'Is it then something too terrible?'" Scott (whose name begins with S like Satan) knows she will ask him down. He has seen them charmed by him "'at Cannes, at Pau, at Shanghai'" (XI, 279); "'it has just been my life.'" Mamie tells Mrs. Medwin that Lady Wantridge wants her brother at Catchmore, her country house. "'He shan't go unless she [Mrs. Medwin] comes. She must meet you first—you're my condition'" (XI, 280). She also arranges, after the tea to which Mrs. Medwin was invited, that as far as the weekend at Catchmore went "'He shan't go *now* unless he takes you'" (XI, 281). This involved "a separate fee."

The last paragraph includes "whirlwind," a word from the Book of Job, in which God appears to Job. It occurs in the description of the party given at Catchmore in which Scott and Mr. Medwin make up a small, intimate, and funny party for the Grand Duke, for Mrs. Medwin was included "after a brief whirlwind of wires and counterwires," a party from which Mrs. Medwin sends "the new cheque" and at which Scott *"was* the feature" (XI, 281). The Devil as agent of interrelatedness in this tale of purchased favors is a hero in a society corrupt in its values. James here plays with the idea that lack of relations is a cardinal sin.

Peter Quint and Miss Jessel in "The Turn of the Screw," according to Donal O'Gorman, are demons or agents of the Devil inhabiting Bly, the name of which area might possibly be connected with Defoe's "The Devil lies at Blye Bush."[50] The veracity of O'Gorman's discovery depended on whether or not James owned the set of Defoe in which the *Political History of the Devil* is included. Recent work on James's library shows that he did indeed own that particular set of Defoe, so that the hypothesis appears to be substantiated.

Lionel Croy and Lord Mark of *The Wings of the Dove* also possess demonic characteristics, but it is in the black-comedic figure of Scott Homer in "Mrs. Medwin" that the traditional operatic figure of the Devil, the charming Mephistopheles of *Faust,* as costumed by nineteenth-century producers and envisaged by Delacroix's popular engravings of *Faust,* that the charming, seductive aspect of the Devil, the Devil whom James describes in his letter to Mrs. Cotes, appears for the only time in James. Peter Quint and Miss Jessel are evil spirits with little attraction the reader can feel, since they create intense sensations of repulsion, but Scott Homer is the seducer, the entertainer and the desirable guest at country-house parties of the bored aristocracy in a corrupt society. In the short story of 1901, the period in which the devils of *The Wings of the Dove* were being created in James's mind, the fair side of the Devil appears in Scott Homer. But the society in which he lives is totally evil itself, so he becomes simply the flower of that society. He is named Scott Homer possibly to unite Sir Walter Scott, who wrote the famous *Letters on Demonology and Witchcraft* (1830), with Homer because of the universality of the *Iliad* and the *Odyssey* which underlines also the universality of the Devil, he "who is nothing but the sense of beauty . . . *and* of EXPRESSION!" (IV, 131).

# 2

# James the Orientalist

*The joy of masquerading as an Oriental*
Henry James, Introduction to *Impressions* by Pierre Loti

The traditional view of Henry James as the observer of the civilized people of the Western world and the recorder of their highly refined consciousness has never considered him as one who responded to the romantic cult of Orientalism. Yet this movement, which started with William Beckford's *The History of the Caliph Vathek* (1786) in England at the end of the eighteenth century and through Byron influenced the French Romantic school of 1830, both writers and painters, swept a whole generation off its feet and found a place in James's fiction. Stemming originally from the Napoleonic conquest of Egypt, it provided a palette, a geography, and an exotic manner of living at strong variance with everything that the civilized West seemed to stand for during the nineteenth century. But it provided at the same time a needed outlet for the emotions. As a catharsis it depended on an acceptance of cruelty as a stimulus for creativity and on the subjugation of women during a period when women were first beginning to establish some kind of equality with men.

Most Europeans did not remain in the East, but many who did go, if only for a short visit, especially the French, never forgot it in their work; witness Delacroix's one trip from which he painted all his life. William Holman Hunt's journey to Palestine intensified the minuteness of his vision and produced a biblical symbolic picture so strong it scared Henry James as a child, as he recorded it in his *Autobiography*.[1] But the vividness of Hunt's *The Scapegoat* provided James in his mature years with a powerful icon of sacrifice for the Oriental chapter of *The Golden Bowl* (1904), supported by other references to the Orient, creating in their totality an ambience of mystery, suffering, and wiliness.

English novelists from Disraeli through E. M. Forster had at least one Oriental tale in their oeuvre, and the more prolific of the American novelists, like F. Marion Crawford, could create a bestseller in *Mr. Isaacs* (1882), about a Persian entrepreneur moving in a setting of India. Among the French novelists, Flaubert had his *Salammbô* (1862) and his *Tentation de Saint-Antoine* (1874). James owned not only those two works and read them with interest, though with his highly critical point of view, but also Maxime Du Camp's *Souvenirs Littéraires,* and it was with Du Camp that Flaubert had made the trip to the Orient that produced his own two Eastern novels.[2] In Flaubert's *Tentation de Saint-Antoine* James had expected the figure of Saint Anthony to be used as a symbol for temptation experienced by a modern Parisian, and he places the failure of the book in its too heavily researched pictorialism of the East.[3]

In spite of his skepticism about the worth of Flaubert's Oriental "failures," James was not one to deny the seduction of current styles in art and literature. There is more than a trace of Orientalism in James's work, though, unlike Flaubert, Gautier, Daudet, and Sand, he resisted devoting either an entire novel or an entire tale to the pull of the East, chiefly because he had never been there. He often displays his fascination with *The Arabian Nights,* the one great source of literary Orientalism that the eighteenth century brought to the West and which in the third decade of the nineteenth century was popularized in Lane's English translation.

James was delighted as a young man by James Morier's *The Adventures of Hajji Baba of Ispahan* (1828), another compendium of Oriental tales wrapped around a young scamp and adventurer from Ispahan (fig. 22). Beckford's *Vathek,* which was probably the first European Oriental tale closely imitating Eastern literature, had occasioned Morier's work, and we now know James probably read *Vathek* early in life.[4] Gobineau had praised *Hajji Baba* in his *Nouvelles Asiatiques* (1876), which James reviewed that year for *The Nation* in an unsigned article.[5] These literary works seem to have been the source for the Orientalism that appears in James's fiction up to the 1880s, when other literature and art begin to present another East for his imagination to work on.

In the 1870s James especially felt the impact of the Orientalist painters such as Jean-Léon Gérôme (1824–1904) and Alexandre-Gabriel Decamps (1803–60) as well as Eugène Delacroix (1798–1863) whose early masterpiece, *The Death of Sardanapalus* (1826) (fig. 23), James wrote about enthusiastically when it was exhibited in Paris in 1876, the same year as Moreau's *Salomé.*[6] Indeed, during this year when James was writing a regular letter for the *New York Tribune,* he was almost surfeited with the number of paintings of the Orientalists, who by this time constituted a veritable school. By then James had written into his first two novels, *Watch and Ward* running serially in 1871 in the *Atlantic Monthly,* and *Roderick Hudson* (1875), his first published novel, certain figures of speech that contained what he wished to preserve from the Oriental spasm that had seized Europe. They depend on *The Arabian Nights* and on the Orientalist paintings he had seen.

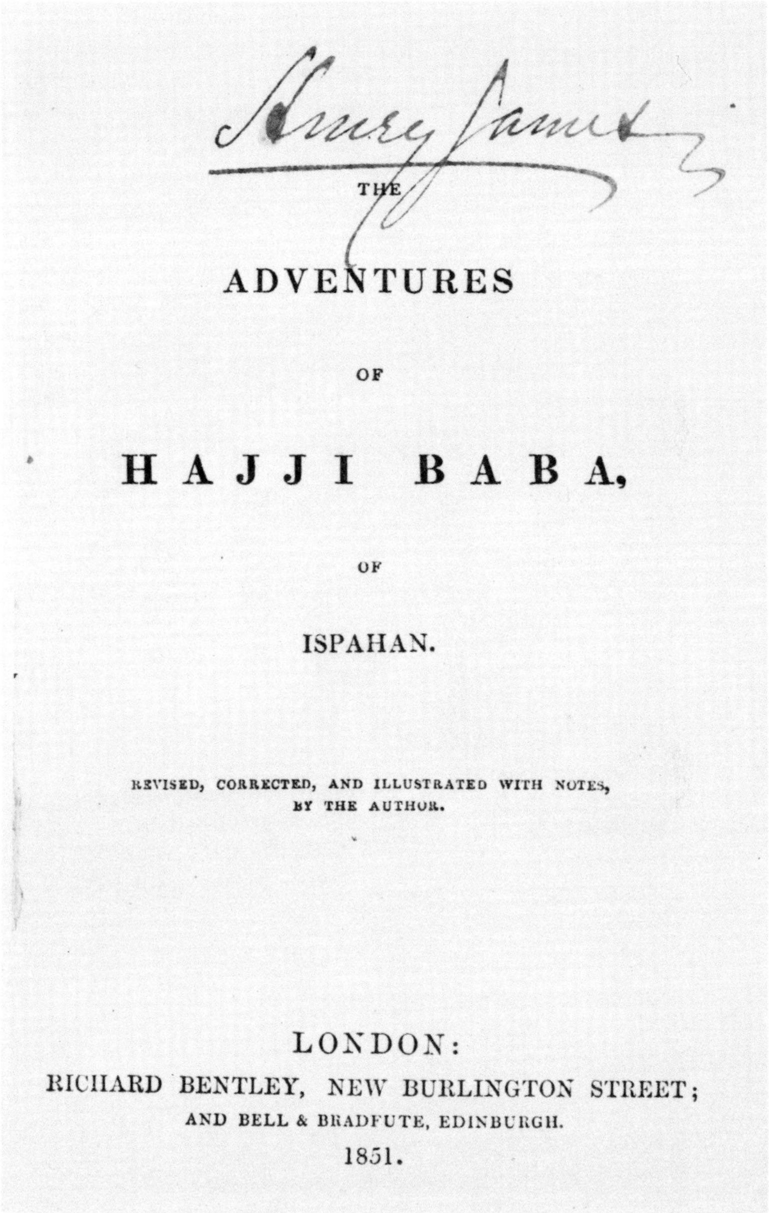

*Henry James*

THE

ADVENTURES

OF

HAJJI BABA,

OF

ISPAHAN.

REVISED, CORRECTED, AND ILLUSTRATED WITH NOTES,
BY THE AUTHOR.

LONDON:
RICHARD BENTLEY, NEW BURLINGTON STREET;
AND BELL & BRADFUTE, EDINBURGH.
1851.

Figure 22.    Title Page from James Morier's *The Adventures of Hajji Baba of Ispahan*, 1851
Henry James's signed copy.

Figure 23.  Eugène Delacroix, *The Death of Sardanapalus*, 1827
(*Musée du Louvre, Paris*)

In his first novel, *Watch and Ward,* James furnishes his heroine's Oriental fantasies by way of the children's edition of fairy tales he had read as a youngster. Nora, as a child, holds *The Child's Own Book,* a collection of fairy tales reprinting many from *The Arabian Nights,* with her finger at the history of *The Discreet Princess.* She thinks Hubert "looks like the *Prince Avenant.*"[7] Nora "had grown up in the interval, from the little girl who slept with *The Child's Own Book* under her pillow and dreamed of the *Prince Avenant,* into a lofty maiden who perused *The Heir of Redclyffe*" (WW 102–3). Hubert says, "'I mean to write a novel about a priest who falls in love with a pretty Mahometan and swears by Allah to win her.'"

> "Oh Hubert!" cried Nora, "would you like a clergyman to love a pretty Mahometan better than the truth?"
> "The truth? A pretty Mahometan may be the truth." (WW,163)

When commenting on his sermons, he says,

> "I can imagine talking to one person and saying five hundred times as much, even though she were a pretty Mahometan or a prepossessing idolatress! I can imagine being five thousand miles away from this blessed Boston—in Turkish trousers, if you please, with a turban on my head and a chibouque in my mouth, with a great blue ball of Eastern sky staring in through the round window, high up. . . ." (WW, 164)

As Roger convalesces, there "came to him, out of his boyish past, a vague, delightful echo of the 'Arabian Nights.' The room was gilded by the autumn sunshine into the semblance of an enameled harem court; he himself seemed a languid Persian, lounging on musky cushions; the fair woman at the window a Scheherezade, a Badoura" (WW, 178).

The feeling for the Orient comes into *Roderick Hudson* (1875) by means of a reference to contemporary paintings of the East. It occurs with startling vividness when Roderick works on his bust of Christina Light for which she is posing, chaperoned by her mother and by Rowland Mallet, who watches with them while Roderick attempts to restyle Christina's hair. When Rowland says, "'But if I were only a painter!'" Christina answers, "'Thank Heaven you are not. . . . I am having quite enough of this minute inspection of my charms.'" Her mother then tells Roderick, "'My dear young man, hands off!'" and she then "gathered up the dusky locks and let them fall through her fingers, glancing at her visitor with a significant smile. Rowland had never been in the East, but if he had attempted to make a sketch of an old slave-merchant, calling attention to the 'points' of a Circassian beauty, he would have depicted such a smile as Mrs. Light's." When Christina remarks that her mother is "'afraid that Mr. Hudson might have injured my hair, and that, *per consequenza,* I should sell for less,'"[8] the slave-market paintings of Jean-Léon Gérôme would be summoned up for the reader, for they were especially popular with American collectors. The exhibition of naked female flesh superbly painted was acceptable when positioned in the slave context of an Oriental genre scene.

Since James the next year was surrounded by Oriental paintings seen in the Paris exhibitions, it is only fitting that he should cater to this taste in *The Europeans* (1878), which shows a signal interest in *The Arabian Nights*. It is the book read by the heroine, who sees Prince Camaralzaman in young Felix; Felix courts her in as romantic a fashion as the Eastern prince. This short novel is the first harbinger of a trio of stories later published in 1883 and 1884 in which Eastern tales now give a real form to James's fiction. The heroine of *The Europeans,* Gertrude Wentworth, "possessed herself of a very obvious volume—one of the series of *The Arabian Nights.* . . . There, for a quarter of an hour, she read the history of the loves of the Prince Camaralzaman and the Princess Badoura."[9]

The tale, in volume 3 of the three-volume Galland edition, is called "The Story of the Amours of Camaralzaman, Prince of the Isles of the Children of Khaledan, and of Badoura, Princess of China." Although James owned the three-volume set of Edward W. Lane's *The Thousand and One Nights* (1839–41), the spelling of the main characters in the story from which he quotes in *The Europeans* is that of the famous French translation by Antoine Galland (1675–1715), the first European translator of *The Arabian Nights*. The tale in Lane's translation of the Arabian Nights is called "The Tale of Kamar-al-Zaman."

We are prepared for *The Arabian Nights* early in the novel by the youthful Felix Young's impression that Boston looks like the East rather than the West. "'Instead of coming to the West we seem to have gone to the East. The way the sky touches the housetops is just like Cairo; and the red and blue signboards patched over the face of everything remind one of Mohametan decorations'" (E, 14). His sister says that, since the young women here do not hide their faces and are bold, they are "'not Mohametan.'" Gertrude acts wickedly like the Princess Badoura. She takes a volume, one of the series of the *Arabian Nights,* where "she read the history of the loves of Prince Camaralzaman and the Princess Badoura. At last looking up, she beheld, as it seemed to her, the Prince Camaralzaman standing before her brilliant, polite, smiling!" (E, 25).

In Gertrude's mind, the story from the *Arabian Nights* begins to be symbolic of her own life. What had happened the day before "seemed to her a kind of dream." The *Arabian Nights* tale concerns a sleeping prince and a sleeping princess who wake each other up, and this theme is carried into the episode in which Gertrude wants to be painted while sleeping because it would amuse her. ("Ah, do paint me while I am asleep") (E, 66). Felix's susceptibility to girls "proves . . . that there are a thousand ways of being good company," an oblique reference to the thousand and one nights. Gertrude adds, "'There must be a thousand ways of being dreary . . . and sometimes I think we make use of them all' " (E, 67). To her Felix's adventures would seem as if she were "reading a romance that came out in daily numbers" (E, 71), just as the tales from *The Arabian Nights* were told. Gertrude, like the sleeping princess, is beginning to awaken. James has thus cleverly used an Eastern fairy tale from *The Arabian Nights* to back up the romance of Felix Young and Gertrude Wentworth, and it seems no accident that the word Paradise, which originally meant a Persian park or pleasure ground, is used twice in *The Europeans*.

The earliest Eastern source for James, then, is *The Arabian Nights,* and the tales from that compendium give a metaphorical structure to some of James's fiction. In *Watch and Ward* the specific tale concerns the handsome prince's marrying the heroine. In *The Europeans* the tale of the sleeping prince and princess serves as an allegory for Gertrude's awakening into life through love.

As late as 1897 the fabulous tale of Ali Baba and the Forty Thieves from *The Arabian Nights* is put into the heated imagination of the little girl in *What Maisie Knew,* when she meets an exotic woman.

> The child had been in thousands of stories . . . but she had never been in such a story as this. By the time he had helped her out of the cab, which drove away, and she heard in the door of the house the prompt little click of his key, the Arabian Nights had quite closed round her.
>
> From this minute the pitch of the wondrous was in everything, particularly in such an instant "Open Sesame" and in the departure of the cab. . . . [10]

Maisie finds herself in a room "with more pictures and mirrors, more palm trees drooping over brocaded and gilded nooks" (M, 128), belonging to Sir Claude's friend, the "brown" lady, who is a very rich American woman presented as an Oriental, probably a Jew as well as a countess. She has a "lemon sofa" (M, 138). (Yellow is a color usually associated with the Orient.) When the countess gives Maisie a shower of sovereigns for her trip, it "was still at any rate the Arabian Nights" (M, 141).

The one place James has invented a complete Eastern character is in "The Impressions of a Cousin" (1883). In the powerful Mr. Caliph there converge a number of sources. Not only *The Arabian Nights* (he is called "Haroun al Raschid" four times) but contemporary novels like Alphonse Daudet's *Le Nabab* (1878) and F. Marion Crawford's *Mr. Isaacs* (1882) seem to be suggested. James had praised the Daudet novel in his article on the French writer, and he wrote "The Impressions of a Cousin" just after publishing his essay on Daudet in the *Century* ( in which magazine he also published the tale at the end of 1883). Since James praises that novel and its hero, it is not a surprise to see that the Nabab himself, M. Jansoulet, described as a "personage out of the

*Thousand and One Nights,"* might be a model for James's Mr. Caliph.[11,12] Daudet's hero is an Oriental entrepreneur who goes broke, as does Mr. Caliph, though Mr. Caliph is not as sympathetic as Jansoulet.

If we turn to *Mr. Isaacs* by Crawford we see that, as in *Le Nabab,* the Eastern element is brought into the West, just as the Oriental figure of Mr. Caliph penetrates the American Hudson River valley and New York itself. There is in *Mr. Isaacs* a concentration, as in the Daudet novel, on the colony of Levantines who have made money in the East and have returned to the European West to enjoy Parisian life. In one of his letters, James remarked how he, like everybody else, has "read . . . 'Mr. Isaacs.'"[13] One feels that since this is Crawford's *Arabian Nights* tale, James probably read it carefully out of curiosity. It is quite readable even today, chiefly for its brilliant depiction of an Indian polo match, a tiger hunt, and, above all, the effect on Westerners of a powerful alien personality.

The Persian hero owns a collection of objects gathered from all over the East, "narghyles . . . from Bagdad or Herat . . . yataghans from Roum and idols from the far East," as well as "two or three superbly illuminated Arabian manuscripts."[14] Mr. Isaacs is like the hero of all the Arabian Nights rolled into one. A perfect shot, this "descendant of Zoroaster" spoke with an Oxford accent, dressed in quiet English dress, and had been romantically carried off by a party of slave-dealers as a youth. Rescued by an Englishman who is going to reappear in the novel, he becomes a millionaire. His attitudes toward women, however, are Eastern; already married to three women, he plans to marry a fourth. He does finally fall in love with a Western girl, but aside from this change, his resemblance to certain aspects of James's Mr. Caliph is interesting. He, too, is connected with *The Arabian Nights.* His room is like the "subterranean chambers whither the wicked Magician sent Aladdin in quest of the lamp," and he shows "Oriental indifference" (Is, 54). The young woman says she has learned all she knows about Mohammedans from "reading the Arabian Nights" (Is, 74). Like Mr. Caliph, Mr. Isaacs is an Oriental relating to Westerners who identify him with *The Arabian Nights:* "'Just think . . . I was entertaining a Sinbad unawares!'" (Is, 157). Like Mr. Caliph, Mr. Isaacs is extremely attractive to women. There the resemblance ends. In addition to these popular novels, there is evidence that James Morier's *Hajji Baba* also had a part in the configuration of the despotic, attractive, but evil Mr. Caliph.

But behind all these sources in contemporary literature there lies the influence of Byron and through him the ultimate source, William Beckford's *Vathek.* In a letter to his friend, the painter Herbert Gilchrist, Henry James late in life commented on a holiday Gilchrist had been taking "among uncanny reminders of the queer Beckford, the superannuated Vathek and those faded glories— though I am doubtless unjust to florid Fonthill itself in calling it faded."[15] This is the only place we know that James indicated he had read *Vathek.* That he had been familiar with it in his younger years seems to be indicated by "superannuated Vathek," showing that the book was a taste of romanticism no longer able to stir his imagination. But this mention is enough to confirm a belief that "The Impressions of a Cousin," James's most Oriental story, is based in part on *Vathek,* for it is there that the first evil caliph appears, he who stimulated Byron to write his own Eastern tales, including "Sardanapalus." Beside the overt reference to *Vathek* in his letter, the link for James to Beckford was through Byron, for Byron was for James the supreme authority of the romantic movement.[16]

In "The Impressions of a Cousin" the very name of the hero-villain is Oriental, embodying a title that offers to the reader at every turn the idea of the absolute power of an Eastern ruler as the distinguishing characteristic of the man. The figure in Delacroix's painting of Sardanapalus himself, reclining on his bed, stout and robed in white as his beautiful slaves and luxurious possessions are going up in smoke, may have been a model for Mr. Caliph, also "clad in white garments from head to foot."[17] Sardanapalus had already appeared in a metaphor in *The American* (1877) just after James reviewed the exhibition of the picture in 1876 in the *New York Tribune.* But to this is added the costume of the many sultans and caliphs that the Orientalists painted. The narrator says, "If I had painted him, it would have been in a high-peaked cap, and an amber-coloured robe with a wide girdle of pink silk wound many times around his waist, stuck full of knives jeweled handles" (V, 127). James had seen Gérôme's *The Guard of the Harem* in his trip to the Wallace Collection in 1873, and the costume in which he dressed Mr. Caliph may have been borrowed from the guard's "amber-coloured robe" and his "wide girdle of pink silk wound many times around his waist" filled with weapons (fig. 24).

Since Haroun al Raschid is mentioned four times, we would feel justified in limiting the test of this Orientalism to *The Arabian Nights,* except that the Caliph Haroun was always considered benevolent. The Moxon Edition of Tennyson's *Poems,* which James's father gave to him as a boy, contains a poem, "Recollections of the Arabian Nights" with fourteen stanzas, each of which ends with the lines, "For it was the golden prime / Of good Haroun Alraschid."[18] The caliph as an essentially bad though personally attractive ruler was Beckford's invention.[19] There comes a point in James's story when the Haroun al Raschid resemblance fades away and the evil, even ruthless, nature of Mr. Caliph is exposed. To point this up, the tale is divided into two halves, the first showing Mr. Caliph as more or less benevolent, the second as the swindler of Eunice's fortune. In talking to him, Catherine Condit, the narrator, has "a prevision of penalties," which excites her (V, 151). But even in the first part the reader of *Vathek* will remember the caliph's one strange "terrible eye," which is more dangerous than the other. Mr. Caliph in James's story also has "his remarkable eye" (V, 126), "his deep bright eye." When "the Grand Turk," as

Figure 24.   J. L. Gérôme, *The Guard of the Harem*, 1859
            *(Reproduced by permission of the Trustees of the Wallace
            Collection)*

he is called, brings in the "most wonderful bouquet of Boston roses that seraglio ever produced," he is merely imitating Oriental potentates bestowing roses on "favorites." The jealousy and competition among Eunice, Mrs. Ermine, and Catherine remind us of a scene in *Vathek* where the caliph dismisses his old favorite for a new one.

In the second part Mr. Caliph tries to make a conquest of Catherine, who finds him almost irresistible. He says "brutal" things to her, a characteristic adjective from *Vathek,* and she is aware that he is trying to "magnetize" her (V, 157). When they reach Eunice's country house, equipped with a "tower" like the Caliph Vathek's, the splendor of a Hudson River villa takes on the splendor of the Orient. Here it is revealed to Catherine that "the captivating Caliph is no better than a common swindler" (V, 165), though she sees Mr. Caliph, with "his diabolical assurance" and his wonderful "air of being anointed and gilded," appear "more than ever like Haroun-al-Raschid" (V, 173). He is counted "a dangerous man to irritate." His eyes "seemed to say, 'Be on your guard; I may be dangerous'" (V, 154). When Mr. Caliph tries to persuade Catherine to get Eunice to marry his stepbrother Adrian (to cover his swindle), he tells her, "'he doesn't want to marry *you,*'" which she thinks is "a little brutal" (V, 156). Throughout the tale, then, there are words suggesting the tortures that Vathek put his people through, for Beckford's novel is filled with the gratuitous murders ordered by the caliph. In a similar way, in James's tale the word "monster" (V, 117) appears along with other words signifying brutality, just as in *Vathek.*

There is also a figure of speech that seems to have been stimulated directly by the final images in *Vathek.* There the burning hearts of the evil ones can be seen through their crystalline breasts.[20] Eunice has been carried away by the "vividness of her passion which is none the less intense because it burns inward and makes her heart glow while her face remains as clear as an angel's" (V, 167), and she stands up for Mr. Caliph as Nourinhar had for the Caliph Vathek. The revelation now that Mr. Caliph is a villain emerges from his attributes of "impudence, cynicism, cruelty," even though, like an Eastern potentate, he is "anointed and gilded" and "more than ever like Haroun-al-Raschid" (V, 173). Why then is he called by the latter's name and not by his grandson's, Vathek's, whom I believe is the real figure behind him? We must remember that James was writing for an American puritanical audience, and the name of Beckford was taboo in polite society. If he was known at all, he was known for his pederasty, a criminal trait attracting Byron, whose reputation was also suspect sexually. Another point favoring *Vathek* as a source is that the end of James's tale reflects *Vathek's* end, for the good young lover in *Vathek,* the blue-eyed Gulchenrouz, lives happily ever after in his childish bliss, just as Adrian also lives happily in his equally childish world. Catherine is very likely to share his happiness and youthfulness, while Eunice and Mr. Caliph seem condemned to each other, for better or worse, like Nourinhar, the young girl who chooses the evil lover, Caliph Vathek, over the youthful prince—she dies for her choice.

The letter from James to Gilchrist proves also that James knew about Beckford's sexual inversion since in it is mentioned a discussion of Otto Weininger's book, *Sex and Character,* which James spent a number of hours reading in his club and which contains a long account of homosexuality. Given such a context, James could not allow *Vathek* to be overtly discoverable in his tale, but the clues to its obvious Orientalism would have to have been suggested by Mr. Caliph's resemblance to the other more acceptable example of Orientalism, Haroun al Raschid. But Mr. Caliph's cruelty, his ability to make Eunice "suffer" (the word occurs frequently), his irresponsibility and whimsicality, his swindler's role, all suggest the first *bad* caliph in literature, Vathek.

What further may have emphasized the Eastern element was the appearance in 1882 of Robert Louis Stevenson's *The New Arabian Nights,* in which the adventures of a Prince Florizel provided six tales with a connecting link. Florimond, the name of the hero of James's story, "A New England Winter" (1884), is close to, yet not a direct copy of Florizel, Stevenson's prince. In the story, Rachel Torrance, an exotic girl from Brooklyn, is provided by Florimond's mother as a distraction for him. She had "a striking, oriental head . . . a manner of dressing which carried out her exotic type. . . . Her coins and amulets . . . were a part of the general joke of one's looking like a Circassian or a Smyrniote—an accident for which nature was responsible."[21] Rachel, with her "oriental head," had a given name like that of a famous Jewish actress; in addition, she reminds Florimond of another "celebrated actress in Paris who was the ideal of tortuous thinness," whom all would recognize as Sarah Bernhardt, another Jew.[22]

James's stories of the 1890s are concerned with the theater and with writers and artists, so the East disappears for a while. When the Orient does make a dramatic return in *The Golden Bowl,* its chief nourishment seems to have come from the works, fictional and autobiographical, of Pierre Loti, which James loved and avidly read. Loti's twenty-three works not only rested on James's Lamb House library shelves but were well read and occasionally annotated.[23] Although an armchair traveler, James succeeds in making *The Golden Bowl* a reservoir of icons from Loti's east. Whereas Eastern fantasies and Orientalist paintings had furnished his fiction up through 1886, now it is chiefly the real East as it passes through the hypersensitive consciousness of a French naval officer and novelist, much of whose life was spent in travel there.

The pagoda image, which has been the focus of so much exegetical energy, appeared even in an invented Eastern tale like *Vathek* and is traditionally acknowledged as part of the Orient's topography. However, it is strikingly present in the many volumes devoted to the East by Pierre Loti in Henry James's library.

The pagoda is part of Loti's oriental furniture, especially when it appears in a mysterious, melancholy garden setting, inscrutable and impenetrable. At this point a glance at James's long-time devoted attention to Pierre Loti will show how James's late East owes its configuration largely to Loti's "East," which James wrote was "of all Easts the most beguiling."[24]

*The Arabian Nights, Hajji Baba, Vathek, Nouvelles Asiatiques,* and the Orientalist painters contributed to the Orientalism of James's early and middle periods. But for the Orientalism of 1904 (*The Golden Bowl*), we need look no further than to the sixteen books by Loti that involve the East, two-thirds of the total number of books James owned by this author, which he read from 1888, when he wrote his first essay on Loti, until at least a year before his death. For James Loti was "a painter," and his scenes had a reality that brought the East vividly to James.

Such a scene provided certain details for the episode dealing with the purchase of the Damascene titles and seems to come from *Au Maroc* (1889). Loti stays at a Jewish household in Fez, where a family of many children set before him "cakes, preserves of watermelon and many little sweets."[25] These and a "good little old red wine" amidst the presence of "the Tables of the Law or inscriptions in Hebrew"[26] may have contributed to the scene at Brighton in *The Golden Bowl,* where the equally many members of the family of the Jewish art dealer serve Adam and Charlotte "heavy cake and port wine" adding "the touch of some mystic rite of old Jewry."[27] Loti's, the outsider's, reaction to this alien scene of an Eastern family is close to that of the other outsider's, Adam Verver's.

The caravan, which Gobineau called "a moveable city" and which Loti called "our little city" that "never changes," is an often recurring icon in Loti's semiautobiographical works, especially in *Au Maroc,* to which James pays a lot of attention in his 1898 preface to Loti's *Impressions. Jerusalem* (1895) as well takes us into "étouffantes montagnes" with wandering, concealing routes. James himself began to use the caravan as a figure of speech in his preface to Loti's book: "we remain in his caravan as disconnected from everything else as it need occur to us to desire," and "it would never be easy to find in any caravan a pilgrim with so absolute an esteem for his emotions,"[28] passages that seem to be a trial run for the figure of speech in *The Golden Bowl.*

As a literary source for the pagoda image, there is almost an embarrassment of riches in Loti. In his *Propos d'exil* (1887), a travelogue about all kinds of pagodas, both mosques and pagodas coexist; "pagodas hindoues à mysterériuses figures . . . mosquées musulmanes . . . églises du Christ" lie "côte à côte," just as Maggie's garden structure appears to her as both a pagoda and a mosque. Loti visits a pagoda in a junglelike garden whose interior he cannot penetrate, for its door resists and "il faut y renoncer."[29]

In *Madame Chrysanthème* (1887) the "gloomy pagodas" give a melancholic atmosphere. But it is in *Les Derniers Jours de Pékin* (1902) that the great imperial pagodas seem to resemble most Maggie's pagoda with its enameled surface and its impenetrable interior.

The "golden pagoda" in which Loti finds himself as one of the visitors in the conquered city remains "one of the last refuges of the unknown . . . incomprehensible for us." The great Rotunda Palace has a "roof of blue enamel," and its surfaces are decorated with enamel plaques and, like Maggie's, they are "dumb, closed palaces."[30] There, Loti, like Maggie, feels "alone in the silence of my lofty garden and my strange palace," which to him is "incomprehensible and terrible."[31] In addition to the concrete details Loti's pagodas and mosques lend to James's images, it is their effect on the consciousness of a sensitive Frenchman that must have attracted James. He wrote that Loti, one of "the rarest of story-tellers," had "his undiscourageable passion for putting on as many as possible of the queerer forms of consciousness encountered in other races and under other skies, of living . . . into conditions exotic and uncomfortable."[32] This adds to the reasons why James chose Loti's East to help him create metaphors for the mysterious, despotic and uncomfortable aspects of his character's problems in *The Golden Bowl*.

But first let us look at the icons of the East that punctuate *The Golden Bowl*, and that are arranged there in an actual as well as metaphorical system that plays a significant role in a novel organized in a particularly complex way. This Oriental note is sounded on the first page of *The Golden Bowl*, where Amerigo looks at the elegant things in London shops "as if, in the insolence of the Empire" they had been the "loot of far-off victories,"[33] possibly Indian. Soon after, we read that Mr. Verver "had pitched a tent suggesting that of Alexander furnished with the spoils of Darius" (G, 40). The prince tells Mrs. Assingham that for his family London is "'quite their Mecca, but this is their first real caravan,'" a prefiguration of the great scene in book 2 where Maggie's caravan dominates a chapter built up on Oriental figures.

The second and much louder Oriental note is soon struck by Mrs. Assingham's Oriental appearance. "Full of discriminations against the obvious, she had yet to accept a flagrant appearance and to make the best of misleading signs" (G, 50), which signs prepare the reader for her later symbolic role, that of a prophetess or sybil from the East who, in the last two chapters of book 1, foresees how Maggie will solve her problems. Here her "richness of hue, her generous nose . . . seemed to present her as a daughter of the South, or still more of the East. . . . She looked as if her most active effort might be to take up, as she lay back, her mandolin or to share a sugared fruit with a pet gazelle" (G, 50).

Back of this figure may lie certain popular pictures: the Bonington watercolors in the Wallace Collection which James praised in 1873 and in which both Scheherezade (fig. 25) and Medora have mandolins; a picture like Edwin Long's

Figure 25.  Richard Parkes Bonington, *Arabian Nights*, 1825
            *(Reproduced by permission of the Trustees of the Wallace*
            *Collection)*

*Love's Labour Lost* (1885), where a pet gazelle accompanies a young Egyptian woman; John Frederick Lewis's Circassian woman lying at rest with a plate of fruit by her side, pictures all available to James. Long was a painter whom James singled out at various art shows in the 1870s and 1880s, not only as a popular purveyor of pictorial anecdotes but as one who made a "clever archeologized representation of oriental subjects."[34,35] But Mrs. Assingham's attitude to her Eastern appearance is something much more sophisticated and probably based on Pierre Loti's example of assuming native dress. Since she looked Oriental, she figured that "if nature had overdressed her . . . her only course was to drown, as it was hopeless to try to chasten, the overdressing." Her game was "that of playing with the disparity between her aspect and her character" (G, 50). Loti liked masquerading as Mrs. Assingham did, being just as solidly French under his Oriental garb as she was American under hers.

The third important cluster of Eastern icons takes place in chapter 12 of book 1 where Adam proposes to Charlotte a marriage in which she will become a virtual slave to the special conditions of his life. She is as bound to the pattern of this billionaire's needs as a favorite is to the harem of a caliph. The proposal takes place at Brighton where the large hotel, probably the Metropole, has always been a center of rich Jewry and exotic peoples; "the big windy hotel swarmed with 'types.' " The wild music they hear, a music that is "violent, exotic and nostalgic," brings in the Orient (G, 169). Adam and Charlotte are there for the purchase of rare Damascene tiles, which are being sold by an Eastern Jew (G, 171) whose family reenact the tribal ceremonial rites on English soil. The scene of this Oriental purchase is created to parallel the purchasing of Charlotte. Although the latter is done in the most polite terms, it is just as much of a purchase. The courtship, without sentiment or pretensions on either side, is a kind of bargain, and it might well be illustrated by a well-known Orientalist picture by Emile-Jean-Horace Vernet, *Judah and Tamar* (1840), which James saw in the Wallace Collection (fig. 26). In it Judah is buying the privilege of enjoying Tamar by giving her his staff, his signet and his bracelet. The giving of the ring makes it look like a commercially arranged Oriental marriage picture.

After the complicity between Amerigo and Charlotte becomes noticeable, Fanny, in her troubled state, acts out her role as prophetess and thus creates the fourth Oriental center. Weighted down with concern over the drama she may have precipitated by arranging the marriage between the Ververs and the prince, she sits on "a great gilded Venetian chair—of which at first, however, she but made, with her brooding face, a sort of a throne of meditation. She would thus have recalled a little, with her so free orientalism of type, the immemorially speechless Sphinx about at last to become articulate." Near her stands the colonel "not unlike, on his side, some old pilgrim of the desert camping at the foot of that monument" (G, 273). The image strongly suggests Elihu Vedder's painting *The Questioner of the Sphinx* (1863) (fig. 27), shown first at the

Figure 26.    Emile-Jean-Horace Vernet, *Judah and Tamar*, 1840
            *(Reproduced by permission of the Trustees of the Wallace
            Collection)*

Figure 27.   Elihu Vedder, *The Questioner of the Sphinx*, 1863
(*Bequest of Mrs. Martin Brimmer; courtesy of the Museum of Fine Arts, Boston*)

National Academy in New York that year and widely known.[36] (In 1895 it was used as an advertisement for Pabst beer.)[37] In this scene Mrs. Assingham prophesies that Maggie will "'see me somehow through!'" and that "'she'll triumph'" (G, 285). Her sense will have to open "'to what's called Evil—with a very big E'" (G, 286).

In book 2 of *The Golden Bowl,* the East is extended to mean more than a symbol of luxury (the things in Bond Street) and more than a symbol of wisdom (Mrs. Assingham). The Orient is now the mysterious, the unknown, and the threatening. If book 1 ends with Mrs. Assingham as an Oriental sybil in modern guise predicting what will happen, book 2 begins with three figures of speech used to describe Maggie's feeling of an unspecified unease. She tries to explain it by picturing it; it is either a "'tall tower of ivory,'" "'an outlandish pagoda . . . plated with hard, bright porcelain,'" with no way of being entered, or "'a Mahometan mosque'" with a "'vision of one's putting off one's shoes to enter.'" In 1876, in one of his letters from Paris for the *New York Tribune,* James had mentioned Gérôme's "hard and brilliant piece of orientalism," the small picture *Santon at the Door of a Mosque,* where a guard watches "a congregation of shoes which the ingoing worshipers have deposited on the threshold of a Mussulman temple. . . . They make a very picturesque, an almost dramatic array."[38]

After Maggie has lunch with Mrs. Assingham and tells her she fears there is something between Amerigo and Charlotte, Mrs. Assingham tells her husband, "We shall have . . . to lie till we're black in the face." Lying means adopting the Oriental code of morality. The little Jewish dealer had been a symbol of the cheating merchant from the East who offered for sale a gilded bowl with a crack in it, but he now shows himself to be a hero. The honesty of the Oriental dealer furnishes the proof of the dishonesty of the prince and Charlotte. This teaches Maggie how evil must be fought by evil's own tactics, and the princess learns to lie.

Chapter 36 of book 2 is invested with all the suggestions of the East we have been given so far and represents the climax in the confrontation between Maggie and Charlotte, when Maggie's victory is initiated through her first lie. Amerigo, Charlotte, Adam, and Mrs. Assingham are playing bridge together while Maggie sits apart. As she looks at them each with knowledge of a relation to her, they seemed to "put it upon her to be disposed of, . . . to charge herself with it as the scapegoat of old, of whom she had once seen a terrible picture, had been charged with the sins of the people and had gone forth in the desert to sink under his burden and die" (G, 457). The "terrible picture" is *The Scapegoat* by William Holman Hunt, and it establishes the desert and its doomed victim as the dominant Oriental icons of the last part of the novel (fig. 28). The weary and dirty goat stands in the desert by the Dead Sea surrounded by animal skeletons that he will soon join.

Figure 28.   William Holman Hunt, *The Scapegoat*, 1854
(*Courtesy of National Museums and Galleries on Merseyside; Lady Lever Art Gallery,
Port Sunlight, England*)

The third Oriental figure picks up the caravan metaphor the prince had used at the beginning of the novel. Maggie sees that the relief of letting her feelings dramatically express themselves is not for her. For her a "range of feelings . . . figured nothing nearer to experience than a wild eastern caravan, looming into view with crude colours in the sun, fierce pipes in the air, high spears against the sky, all a thrill, a natural joy to mingle with, but turning off short before it reached her and plunging into other defiles." To have felt this need to create a noisy scene "would have been to give them [her family] up" (G, 459). Useless as the release for Maggie, the caravan yet represents man's triumph over the desert and prepares the way for Charlotte's ultimate triumph over her imprisonment.

When Maggie has a talk with her father, she gives Adam to understand that he has been her "victim," saying " 'I sacrifice you' " (G, 480). Here the burden of the scapegoat is placed upon him. He "was practically offering himself as a sacrifice." Maggie again says, " 'I sacrifice you . . . to everything and everyone' " (G, 481). The atmosphere of the scapegoat continues in the allusion to the thirst the desert creates as the scapegoat experiences it. The lack of talk with Maggie seems to Amerigo "a privation that had left on his lips perhaps a little of the same thirst with which she fairly felt her own distorted, the torment of the lost pilgrim who listens in desert sands for the possible, the impossible splash of water" (G, 489).

Now the icon of Charlotte being bought and taken into slavery delivered in the Brighton chapter is taken up once more. Her connection with Adam "would not have been figured wrongly if he had been thought of as holding in one of his pocketed hands the end of a long silken halter looped round her beautiful neck. He didn't twitch it, yet it was there; he didn't drag her, but she came" (G, 493). It seems as if he were saying, " 'I lead her to her doom and she doesn't so much as know what is is. . . . She thinks it *may* be, her doom, the awful place over there . . . but she's afraid to ask' " (G, 494). Charlotte now is both the slave *and* the scapegoat, about to be exiled to the great desert of America's center. The focus, therefore, has completely shifted from Maggie's to Adam's and then to Charlotte's identification with the scapegoat. Maggie has maneuvered with the help of the prince, her father, and finally Mrs. Assingham to accomplish this. When Fanny says that Charlotte now knows that Adam has made his choice and that " 'she can't speak, resist, or move a little finger,' " her words recall Hunt's picture. It

made a picture, somehow, for the Princess . . . the picture that the words of others, whatever they might be, always made for her, even when her vision was already charged, better than any words of her own. She saw, round about her . . . the hard glare of nature—saw Charlotte somewhere in it, virtually at bay, and yet denied the last grace of any protecting truth. She saw her off somewhere all unaided, pale in her silence, and taking in her fate. (G, 504)

The prophetess of the book, Mrs. Assingham, continues with her vision. "I see the long miles of ocean and the dreadful great country, State after State—which have never seemed to me so big or so terrible. . . . And it will be—won't it?—for ever and ever! . . . These were large words and large visions" (G, 504–5).

In contrast to James's technique of indicating his Oriental sources in his early fiction by a more or less random location of words and descriptive passages, the operation of such a powerful icon as *The Scapegoat* is much more subtle. In a referred manner, the elements of the picture attach themselves to each character as that character temporarily assumes the role of victim, until the role settles finally on Charlotte. Through her saturation with those elements, metaphorically and realistically (given the nature of her American future), her position as the one and only scapegoat in the cast of characters is clarified.

The desert itself continues to appear in the scene that introduces the last part of the novel, for even the cabman of Portland Place shares the tortures of the desert, and parodies Charlotte's future punishment. The "desert of Portland Place looked blank as it had never looked," a place where "a drowsy cabman, scanning the horizon for a fare, could sink to oblivion of the risks of immobility" (G, 515). As the heat of the desert is transformed to the heat of the August day at the novel's start, so the novel ends on an even hotter day in August a few years later. The East expires on the next page as Maggie remembers the pallor of the Assinghams "as if they had seen Samson pull down the temple." Maggie keeps up the "silken noose" image, recalling Charlotte's "immaterial tether," and notices that "the other end of the long cord" had not "disengaged its smaller loop from the hooked thumb" (G, 522). Toward the very end of the novel the loop as the instrument and machinery of Charlotte's slavery continues. Adam, playing out "his long fine cord," is here seen as an Oriental potentate who treats a woman like an animal.

For the other Oriental icons that create a system within the complex novel, the caravan image, the Damascene tiles, and the pagoda, sources both pictorial and literary were at hand for James. Analyzing first the genesis of the caravan figure, we find at James's disposal many well-known and impressive pictures that evoke with great realism the composition of that phenomenon indigenous to the Orient. James had never been in a caravan, but at the Fine Arts Society he might have seen an 1871 watercolor by Joseph Austin Benwill, *The Head of the Caravan,* (fig. 29), which shows pipes being played on, spears in the air, and, what is pertinent to Maggie, a caravan winding through the many "defiles" made by the mountainous terrain. Léon-Adolphe-Auguste Belly's *Pilgrims Going to Mecca,* a marvelous moving city (as Gobineau and Loti described it), was presented at the Salon of 1861 and exhibited for years in the Luxembourg Museum (fig. 30). The effect of this huge picture, five-and-a-half by nine feet,

Figure 29.   Joseph Austin Benwell, *Head of the Caravan*, 1871
*(Courtesy of the Mathaf Gallery)*

Figure 30. Léon Adolphe Auguste Belly, *Pilgrims Going to Mecca*, 1861 *(Musée du Louvre, Paris)*

was so great that "each visitor seemed to come out of the Salon as if he had himself been a member of the caravan."[39]

No small part was played by Gobineau's *Nouvelles Asiatiques* which James had reviewed almost thirty years before. The story James preferred was the last, "La Vie en Voyage," concerned with the troubled consciousness of a young bride who makes her first caravan trip to live permanently in the Orient with her husband. All aspects of the elements that go to make up a caravan, the relations among its members, and especially the tales that are told to entertain the young woman, present a complex way of life "'all a thrill, a natural joy to mingle with,'" as Maggie phrased it. Some aspects of her sensibility seem to have been inherited from the young woman's in Gobineau's tale. That woman, thrilled by the tales she has heard during her trip, suddenly realizes that they do not represent the reality of the life she is going to lead and, fearful of the unknown Orient, she makes her husband take her back in the next caravan returning to the West. The girl in dread buries her head in her husband's breast, just as Maggie, "for pity and dread," buries hers in Amerigo's in the last line of *The Golden Bowl*.

The Oriental Damascene tiles constitute the only art purchase the reader sees Adam Verver acquire, and they remain the only demonstration of his passion and expertise. The tiles themselves belong to a genre with which James would be familiar from the Oriental courtyard decorated with the Persian tiles that Frederick Lord Leighton had imported into his house on the outskirts of London where James was a frequent guest, as well as in their frequent depiction in the mise-en-scènes of Orientalist paintings and watercolors.

The Orientalism of *The Golden Bowl* is a long way from the Orientalism of the novels and tales written before 1888. James's childhood fascination with the unreal world of *The Arabian Nights* and his almost illicit pleasure in reading about Hajji Baba's thieveries and the inhumane adventures of the Caliph Vathek have given place to the remembered terror of a powerful painting of abandonment and to the continuing love of the melancholic excursions into the real East by a writer whose sensibility was to have almost as great an effect on Henry James as on Marcel Proust.

**3**

# Greek and Roman Legends: "Movements of the Classic Torch round Modern Objects"

## "Dear and Venerable Circe": Homer in the Prose

Although James did not make the same frequent reference to ancient classical myths and legends either in his critical articles or in his fiction as he did to the large body of European literature at his command, he did invoke Homer's *Odyssey* occasionally in his critical work without enlarging on his reactions. It is clear from his early reviews that he was thoroughly grounded in Greek mythology.[1] Bruce Redford has found recently an Odyssean figure in James's *William Wetmore Story and His Friends* (1903).[2] It is contained in the passage where "the gentle ghosts . . . begin to crowd."[3] Later those ghosts "with very little encouragement, would peep out" and "if I were to take an unconsidered step to meet them they would fairly advance upon us in a swarm" (ST, I, 257). Here James may be invoking the scene where Odysseus summons up the spirits of the dead to consult Teiresias, shortly after his year-long stay on Circe's island, though it is unusual for James to seek in Homer a source for metaphor and image at this time. But in 1883 he had written a very short letter of acceptance to an unknown lady for her invitation to a two o'clock social event, presumably tea, for the day before Christmas (fig. 31). He addresses her as Circe, with himself playing the role of Odysseus.

3 Bolton St. Mayfair<br>W

Dear and venerable Circe!

    Yes, I will come on the 24th at 2. for your irresistible sake and that of Xmas eve. You convert into a passive porker grunting a little not ungratefully (or ungracefully) your falsely abjuring, feebly returning, & altogether Odyssean and affectionate

Henry James

Dec. 13th 1883

Figure 31. "Dear and Venerable Circe!" Letter from Henry James to an Unknown Correspondent, December 13, 1883

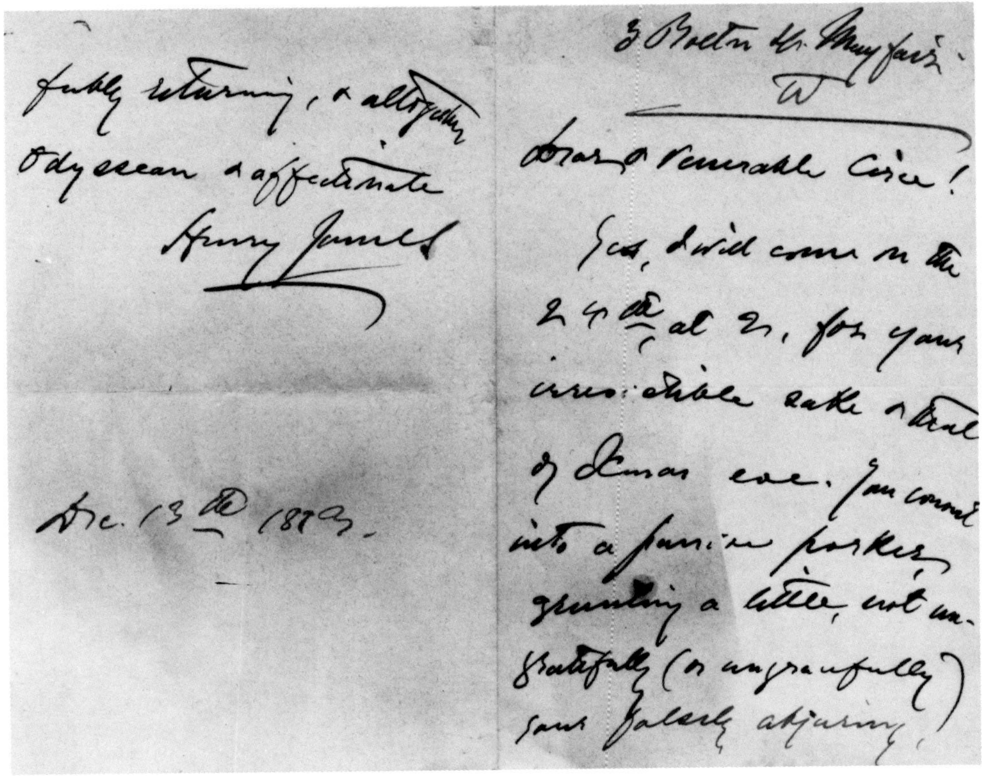

This letter is a microcosm of James's habit of taking over and writing "my way," even in a joke, an episode from a given piece of literature. In the Homeric rendering of the myth of Circe who transformed men into beasts, (*The Odyssey,* X, 236–574) Odysseus hears of how the enchantress, the sun's daughter, lives in a beautiful palace on the Aegean isle. Odysseus sends an investigative advance party led by Eurylochus, who alone refuses Circe's hospitality and who witnesses her transformation of Odysseus's men into swine, thus as a spy bringing the news to Odysseus. With the help of Mercury, who gives Odysseus a plant to protect him from the enchantment, the Greek hero threatens Circe when she attempts to make him also a pig. He extracts from her an oath that she will restore his men into human beings, which she does. She then entertains them all so royally that Odysseus himself forgets his mission and has to be reminded by his men after a year spent with Circe to leave the beautiful witch and her life of luxury and ease. What James has done in his humorous revamping of the legend is to make himself into an Odysseus who has himself been changed into a pig, for which change he calls himself grateful. James undoubtedly knew this story in the *Odyssey* well, for it introduces the episode in which Odysseus must go to the underworld with Circe's help to find the ghosts of Teiresias (*The Odyssey,* XI, 24–26). In doing so he had to keep off the other ghosts that would swarm around after he had filled a trench with blood to summon them up. And it was Circe who told Odysseus how to manage this task successfully.

It is fitting, then, that this letter of 1883 and *William Wetmore Story and His Friends* both refer to the same parts of the *Odyssey.* However, what the "falsely abjuring" refers to I cannot say unless it refers to some exchange between the "venerable Circe" and himself. But the "feebly returning" is an extension of the Homeric tale in order to have an Odysseus who *does* turn into a pig return to Circe's island "feebly," perhaps referring to James's returning home to England from America, after his parents' deaths, referring either to his will or to his physical condition. The legend has become in its nature Jacobean instead of Homeric—and all within two sentences.

Who the "venerable Circe" was we have no idea.[4] Could the word "venerable" be taken at its face value and have referred to one of the truly venerable old ladies James was close to at this period, such as Mrs. Kemble, Mrs. Proctor, or Mrs. Duncan Stewart? I am inclined to think that Mrs. Kemble stands a good chance to be the recipient of the letter because she continued, by her talent and her personality, by her reading and her fine voice, constantly to enchant James. In James's memorial essay after her death, included in *Essays in London and Elsewhere,* he has recourse to the same Homeric reference that was pointed out to us in his life of Story. "Her conversation swarmed with people and with criticism of people, with the ghosts of a dead society," for she "testified even more than she affected to do, which was much, on antique manners and a closed chapter of history."[5] And then he goes on to anticipate the passage from the life of Story. As in that book he had the ghosts assembled as "pictures," here he goes on to relate how the old London of her talk "was in particular a gallery of portraits."

James's portrait of Mrs. Kemble presents an enchantress with her "rules and her riots . . . all her luxuriant theory and all her extravagant practice." James comments on "her rare forms and personal traditions that mocked a little at everything—these were part of the constant freshness which made those who loved her love her so much" (EL, 115). It is to the "grand line and mass of her personality" that the essay is a tribute. It seems an interesting coincidence that at the time of this letter James was writing a story called "A New England Winter" in which a young American painter, Florimund Daintry, living in France, visits his mother in Boston and is caught in the enchantment of a young married woman called, significantly, Mrs. Pauline Mesh. She calls him humorously "'a false and faithless man,'" resembling the "falsely abjuring" Odysseus that James makes himself out to be in his letter. Mrs. Mesh is an enchantress like Circe, although Circe is never directly mentioned.

Mrs. Jack Gardner might very well have been the model for Mrs. Mesh, since she had the reputation for being an enchantress. On January 20, 1881, James wrote to Mrs. Gardner that she must "look out for my next big novel; it will immortalize me. After that, some day, I will immortalize you," and shortly afterward he invented the character of Mrs. Mesh, who lives in a Beacon Street house like Mrs. Gardner's and who entertains young men as the Boston "siren" did.[6] That lady continues in jest to doubt Florimund Daintry's word, "the word of the betrayer." Like Odysseus he is held in her spell for almost a year (his aunt says "Pauline will detain him a year").[7] Finally his mother, who, like Eurylochus, "presented herself at Mrs. Mesh's in the capacity of a spy," takes him away back with her to Europe (VI, 133). Mrs. Mesh receives the news of his departure with a Homer-like figure of speech. "'Oh yes, he's in the midst of the foam, the cruel, crawling foam!'" (VI, 152).

Although the Odysseus-hero is not turned into a pig in this story, it is curious that in a letter to Mrs. Gardner in the spring of 1884 James describes himself as a horse, "poor patient beast," who "shall be waiting in London, and shall get into harness when you arrive. In the meanwhile have pity on the place where the collar is rubbed. I wear a collar always. . . . They are piled up round my poor old head, & when you see me you will scarce distinguish the tip of my nose. I am a ruminant quadruped, too, & I turn it over in my mind that, really, I, at least, am too good a friend of yours to lend a further hand—or hoof—in spoiling you" (May 2, 1884).[8] Why he was thinking in terms of changing into a horse at this particular moment may relate to the fact that, as he was writing this letter, there was appearing the first installment of his tale "Lady Barberina," in which a lady is treated as if she were a highly bred horse up for sale in the international marriage market.[9]

These two stories appeared in *Tales of Three Cities* in October 1884. The first of the three tales was *The Impressions of a Cousin,* which appeared in magazine form just when James wrote his Circe letter. It deals also with a male enchanter, the fat Mr. Caliph with his Eastern arts, but the other two tales, "Lady Barberina" and "A New England Winter" seem to contain allusions to being changed into a beast and to being enchanted by a woman sorceress. So it seems that the figure in the Circe letter fitted the way his imagination was working at this time in his fiction, perhaps the only time when James's inventions involved the metamorphosis of human beings into animals.

James had in his *Notebooks* begun to think not only about "Lady Barberina" but also "The Siege of London" in the spring of 1883, if not earlier for the latter tale. In that story the decadence of the Romans is the theme that is "its little law of composition," and in a letter to Mrs. Gardner of April 1882, we see the Greek material combining with that of the time of Roman decadence, when the early Christians were martyrs. "I am a Greek," James wrote, "as I admire you—& a Christian Martyr as you persecute me" (April 1882). On April 16, 1882, he writes: "You remind me of a Roman lady of the Decadence, at the Circus: I myself being the Christian Martyr!"[10] Then he continues, "I am not at all Roman—I am Greek!" Since "The Siege of London" is also in his mind, he tosses off the two groups of matter that he is handling to produce these rather indirect tributes to classical legends.

## The House of Atreus and Madame de Bellegarde's Crime

In coursing through James's appropriation of the literary heritage of Europe, we have been forced to see that the ancient Greek myths located in the great dramas of Aeschylus, Sophocles, and Euripides were not those temperamentally closest to him. They do figure sparsely in his writing, but they were useful to him only later in life. Then, a play like *The Bacchae* could give him a foundation for the mania of Waymarsh, whose "sacred rage" comes from the Euripidean canon, and for "The Beast in the Jungle," where the Oedipus legend could give him a paradigm for the concept of self-knowledge and self-deception in his own Oedipus, John Marcher.

But the Electra-Orestes struggle was behind his writing of *The American.* It was only in his revision of it for the New York Edition, in 1907, that he made certain changes that emphasized this analogic tie with Greek popular myths in the relation of Claire de Cintré and Valentin to their parents. Royal A. Gettmann pointed out that in the 1907 revision the old marquis's confessional paper included an additional motive for Madame de Bellegarde's murder of her husband and the marrying off of her daughter to M. de Cintré: "It's in order to marry my beloved daughter to M. de Cintré *and then go on herself all the same"* (Gettmann's emphasis).[11] Gettmann himself was uncertain that this added sentence fragment proved the fact of Mme. de Bellegarde's adultery.

Leon Edel has since made available the text of 1890 and a fragment of a new fourth act of 1892 of the dramatization of *The American*. In them, James makes perfectly clear that M. de Cintré had been Mme. de Bellegarde's lover.[12] As a result, the question arises, as Cargill stated: "Did James restore an original feature of the crime or add an implication after dramatization had revealed the weakness of Mme. de Bellegarde's motivation?"[13] A close reading of chapter 8 of the early versions of *The American* (1877 and 1879) seems to answer the question. Newman has encouraged Valentin de Bellegarde to talk to him about his sister, Claire. "'Well,'" says Valentin, "'we are very good friends; we are such a brother and sister as have not been seen since Orestes and Electra.'"[14]

The significant fact about Orestes and Electra in this context is that their mother was Clytemnestra, not only the murderer of their father and her husband, King Agamemnon, but also the lover of Aegisthus, whom she set on her murdered husband's throne. The implication is clear that Mme. de Bellegarde, Claire and Valentin's mother, is an adulteress as well as a murderess. This appears to have been James's intention from the start.

At the end of the same chapter that begins by giving the above information, after Valentin has pointed out to Newman how strange his family is, James added in the revision: "'We're fit for a museum or a Balzac novel.'"[15] This reference to Balzac inserted thirty years later should be viewed as an additional literary reinforcement of the theme of adultery, linked in the earlier editions with the reference to the House of Atreus. In one of the best known short stories in *La Comédie Humaine,* "Les Secrets de la Princesse de Cadignan," Diane de Maufrigneuse was also the victim of an adulterous mother who had married off her daughter to her lover so she could "go on herself all the same." But James's Orestes and Electra do not wreak vengeance on their mother and her lover; they are the victims. Claire de Cintré, the Electra, is immured in a convent after her brother dies in a duel; their mother, Clytemnestra, triumphs; and Newman gives up.

### "Pandora" and the Self-Made Girl: With a Bow to Hesiod and Rossetti

During the period that produced "The Author of 'Beltraffio'" and its intimations of homosexuality, we have, on the other hand, a treatment of a legend from ancient Greek mythology that shows James's great sympathy for women. For James's "Pandora" has behind it all the implications of certain interpretations of Pandora that view the contents of the box the first woman opens as also containing good things. It is difficult on reading this tale to make up our minds whether James is showing fear on the part of men for what Pandora has opened up or is cheering her on for having established in new fields the triumph of the self-made American girl. The great originality of James is that his Pandora has been self-made and not made by the committee of Olympian gods that Hesiod had brought into world literature.

The Panofskys have learnedly and charmingly traced the history of Pandora's iconography.[16] A singular omission in this account, however, is Henry James's "Pandora" (1884), which rings another change on the myth and its meaning. In the Greek versions of the story Pandora is the first woman created in the world and, as her name implies, perfected by the gods through gifts. While married to Epimetheus, Prometheus's brother, she opens one gift out of curiosity, a vessel from which all evils escape, leaving only hope behind. (The early church fathers saw Pandora as Eve, a classical prefiguration of Original Sin.)

Pandora Day, James's heroine, referred to as "the daughter of the Days," is undoubtedly James's clever allusion to Hesiod's *Works and Days,* the *locus classicus* for the Pandora legend. In a real sense, then, Pandora Day is the daughter of the *Works and Days,* the first created woman of "the new type," but created, this time, by herself.[17] According to Mr. Bonnycastle, a Washington host and savant in James's tale, "'she is the latest, freshest fruit of our great American evolution. She is the self-made girl!'" (V, 396). Vogelstein, who is the young secretary of the German legation and who is interested in Pandora, gazes a moment. "'The fruit of the great American Revolution? Yes, Mrs. Steuben told me her great-grandfather—.' But the rest of his sentence was lost in the explosion of Mrs. Bonnycastle's mirth" (V, 396). This laughter echoes the laughter of Jupiter in Hesiod's legend when he thinks of the trick he is going to play on mankind for having stolen fire from the Gods. "But I will give men the prize for fire, an evil thing in which they may all be glad of heart while they embrace their own destruction. So said the father of men and gods, and laughed aloud."

In his book *Hawthorne,* written in 1879, James analyzes Hawthorne's work chronologically, and he comments on the tales of *The Wonder Book:* "I have been careful not to read them over, for I should be very sorry to risk disturbing in any degree a recollection of them that has been at rest since the appreciative period of life to which they are addressed. They seem at that period enchanting. . . . It is in the pages of the Wonder-Book that American children first make the acquaintance of the heroes and heroines of the antique mythology, and something of the nursery fairy-tale quality of interest which Hawthorne imparts to them always remains."[18] Hawthorne's *A Wonder Book,* in the 1884 collected edition, where it appears along with *The Tanglewood Tales* and *Grandfather's Chair,* has as its one illustration Pandora opening a large, decorated chest made of wood, from which the troubles are being released.

Pandora is also the new woman created by Henry James. He has "gifted" her with "strange eyes, a little yellow . . . a nose a little arched," signs by which we recognize the femme fatale. He equips her not with a pottery vase, which stood for Pandora's box in the Middle Ages, or with the little chest or coffer we find accompanying eighteenth-century English Pandoras. It is not the piece of furniture we find in Hawthorne or Longfellow, a wooden decorative chest, not the coffered jewel box Rossetti uses in his Pandora figures, but an ordinary transatlantic trunk, one among many boxes of luggage the American girl (who has invented herself and efficiently manages her puppetlike parents and devilish siblings) brought back from her travels to Greece, the homeland of her namesake.

In this luggage are amassed the elements of culture, gifts with which this self-educated girl has dowered herself and her parents—"The Acropolis," as well as "Pheidias and Pericles." She has even "read . . . Goethe" (V, 373), the author of two plays about Pandora: the first a Prometheus fragment in which Pandora is "a sacred vessel" of gifts, someone who finds out that there is death in the world; the second a play written at the end of Goethe's life in which Pandora stands for renunciation. Pandora Day's mention of Goethe perhaps is there to suggest that German aspect of the legend in the person of Count Vogelstein, whose "curiosity" about Pandora exposes him to the demon of unrequited love. Goethe's *Pandora* expresses the love of an older man for a young girl who leaves him. Count Vogelstein, like Goethe, is an Epimetheus figure. In Goethe's unfinished fragment there would have been a chest that reveals "Science and Art" rather than demons, as in Calderon's version, and Pandora is presented as bringing "Glück und Bequemlichkeit," happiness and comfort (PA, 127). Plutarch's *Moralia* shows how Zeus's gifts to Pandora "signify such external blessings as wealth, successful marriage, and high office" (PA, 129). The last mentioned is what James emphasizes. Pandora, by the time James wrote his legend, was embedded in two traditions, that followed by Hawthorne and Longfellow, where a chest is opened by a curious girl who lets loose evil, and that followed by Calderon and Goethe, where a girl favored by the Gods is presented with a chest whose contents, Science and Art, are also gifts to the world.

The important painter of Pandora during the period was Dante Gabriel Rossetti, who based Pandora on his constant model, Jane Morris. Surely James must have seen Rossetti's studies for Pandora when taken to Rossetti's studio with Charles Eliot Norton in 1869. After Rossetti's death, there was a memorial retrospective show at the Burlington Fine Arts Club in 1883, as well as a Royal Academy showing of that year. In fact, this was the year in which at least six versions of Pandora were on view to the public. The outstanding factor of most of them was the reddish, rosy color that suffused them. Rossetti's large painting (fig. 32), a variation on the first tradition, shows the femme fatale with a jewel box on which is inscribed "Nescitur Ignescitur." "He who is ignorant sets things ablaze"—the unknown ignites; curiosity causes trouble. Curiosity about

Figure 32.   Dante Gabriel Rossetti, *Pandora*, 1871
*(Private collection)*

women's mystery, one might read into the picture, also causes trouble. James has seemed to combine both traditions mentioned above. The first, involving the element of curiosity, has been transferred to the German diplomat. The curious aspects of Pandora that escape his classifying mind stimulate his curiosity. The word "curious," therefore, is used in its two senses in this story. Pandora, with her curious, "strange yellow" eyes and lack of clues as to her background acts as a femme fatale; her "expressions" are "singular," her nose aquiline. "I like novelties," the count tells Mrs. Dangerfield, whose name warns him that he is in a field of danger, should he be affected emotionally by Pandora. The second tradition involves having good things emerge from the opened chest. Pandora gets an ambassadorial post for her fiancé.

One-third of the first chapter of the two-part "Pandora" is devoted to the equivalent of Pandora's box, her trunks which must be opened, chalk-marked and passed through the United States customs. We have been prepared by fifteen mentions of some kind of container that changes from parcel to box to luggage to trunk and by the phrase "human cargo" (V, 357) in the opening sentence, which facetiously refers to people as "parcels" to be delivered. The ship is called "an oblong box" (V, 365). The gifts in Pandora Day's boxes are not the gifts Pandora has been given but those *she* gives. They are the material garnered from the Acropolis and the Parthenon, not from her native Utica. She has filled her trunks, and she unlocks one to be passed by the customs officer. She insists that he open the one with her mother's sea clothes: " 'it has got to be this one' " she says "as she fumbled at the lock of her trunk." Pandora as bearing gifts also gives "high office" to her fiancé as if she herself were a goddess (the fabled, mythological Pandora was half-divine); high office is contained in an envelope as a gift to her from the President of the United States, the modern Zeus.

James calls attention to Pandora's name a number of times, so we know he wants us to think of her legendary predecessor. Pandora is labelled the girl's "pet name" (V, 385). Mrs. Dangerfield is "amused" by the girl's name: " 'you could tell that a girl was from the interior . . . when she had such a name as that.' " In addition to her yellow eyes and aquiline nose, Pandora's kinship with a number of versions of Rossetti's *Pandora* seems to be stressed by James by emphasizing the color of her clothes at the Bonnycastle reception. "She was very prettily dressed, in rose-colour"; again, "she looked brilliant in her rose-coloured dress" (V, 389). She is referred to as the girl in "pink"—then "in rose-colour" (V, 391) and as "a striking pink person" (V, 391). Within three pages the color is mentioned five times.

The second installment of the story takes place two years later (V, 381), in April at a large party. Whereas Mrs. Dangerfield had been the count's guide to Americans on shipboard, now Mrs. Bonnycastle (based on Clover Adams) plays the same role in Washington, once more on a boat, a riverboat. It is in this chapter that the neoclassicism of both the Greek myth of Pandora and of

Washington itself, an Acropolis in parody, joins with the pre-Raphaelite version in Rossetti's *Pandora*. The motto "Nescitur Ignescitur" inscribed on Pandora's box explains, as we have noted, that a fire or flames result from curiosity or from ignorance, or, strictly, "not to know makes one burn with curiosity." The figure is repeated in Count Otto's thought "that the only way to enjoy the United States would be to burn one's standards and warm one's self at the blaze" (V, 382). When Pandora, meeting the German after two years absence, says she supposes he has "found out everything about everything," he answers that there are some things he will never understand, meaning Pandora. She is thus the equivalent of the mysterious Pandora of Rossetti's paintings and drawings. It seems clear that for Count Otto Vogelstein, Pandora is a femme fatale. He falls in love with her unwillingly—she would not be an appropriate wife for a noble German diplomat. This does not keep him from being vulnerable to suffering when it becomes clear that she is not only engaged to another but has been bent on securing an ambassadorship for her fiancé that will put him "in high office" and escalate her socially not only to Vogelstein's own position, but beyond.

In the second section the femme fatale elements, which are part of the "perverse" and the "curious" strain that will become intensified in James's next novel, *The Bostonians,* seem to draw on certain elements suggested by the "perverse," "singular," and "curious" aspects of Rossetti's *Pandora,* all based on Jane Morris's strange beauty and dating from Rossetti's first full-length treatment of her in 1869 and the oil *Pandora* of 1870. It is even possible that when James, in his solo grand tour in 1869, visited the studios of both Morris and Rossetti and saw the portrait of Mrs. Morris in her own home, and other representations of her in Rossetti's studio, he may also have seen the completed or the preparatory studies for versions of Mrs. Morris as Pandora on which Rossetti was working at the time. James was struck by the resemblance to her in the "almost full-length" portrait he saw of her at the Morrises, and the Pandoras are very explicitly frontal, life-size likenesses of Jane Morris.

From the last quarter of the eighteenth century, Pandora was treated as a subject mostly in England; the Royal Academy entry in 1775 by James Barry inspired a long series of Pandoras (PA, 87), which were to include Rossetti's. Now in the City Art Gallery of Manchester (part of the romantic classicism that spread all over), Barry's *The Creation of Pandora,* a huge picture, dominates the room. Included are a "vessel," a "coffer," and a "casket." These variables suggest the fact that James has many variables for *his* contemporary version of Pandora's "box." In naming variables—"cargo," "box," "luggage," "bags," "hampers," "parcels," "trunk," "portmanteau," "coffer"—he just about exhausts all the terms that might be applicable to a covered object acting as Pandora's box in contemporary life. James also repeats "trunk" later, after the early customs scene, to remind the reader to think of these receptacles (V, 390).

The intense curiosity on the part of Epimetheus is seen in Count Otto who, though wanting to know about everything himself, represents "concealment of thought" (V, 357). His curiosity is intense: "he inquired with his eyes . . . with his ears, with his nose, with his palate, with all his senses and organs." He did not believe in emotions—"happiness was an unscientific term"—and his curiosity about Pandora is going to lead to his very unscientific unhappiness. He expects to learn about Pandora from reading "Daisy Miller," but he does not. He pumps information from two properly classified American matrons, Mrs. Dangerfield on shipboard, who warns him against Pandora's provinciality, and Mrs. Bonnycastle, also on the "deck of a vessel," the Washington hostess who instructs him that Pandora is a new type, "the self-made girl" (V, 397), and that "she has lifted herself from a lower social plane, done it all herself, and done it by the simple lever of her personality" (V, 398). Pandora Day is a recognizable type, "her culture" fed by "the journey to Europe," followed by "the effacement of her family" (V, 399). Part of the count's curiosity is satisfied by having Pandora thus "classified," but he wants "to judge really to the end how well a girl could make herself." He meets Pandora and they walk around Washington as if it were Athens, and she is reminded "of the Acropolis in its prime" (V, 401). He experiences being "under a charm which made him feel that he was watching his own life, and that his susceptibilities were beyond his control," (V, 403). He was in the hands of "a young woman in whom he had been unable to persuade himself that he was not interested" (V, 405).

The main conversion James makes of the ancient legend is that Pandora, instead of being fashioned by Hephaestus, creates herself! This is the original contribution of James. Onto this he attaches in eclectic fashion elements from the poets of the tradition he finds assimilable into his modern myth. From Hesiod he takes the laughter of the gods and places it in the throats of the Bonnycastles, whose house in Washington is part of Mount Olympus or the Acropolis. James's Pandora has "singular" expressions (V, 372) because she invented herself. There had been the tradition of the self-made man in America, but Pandora is at that time the rare example of the self-made woman. The type is so new that there are not enough examples to make a classification, which disturbs Count Otto, who can only be happy if he "knows everything."

It is the unknown, the mysterious in Pandora that lets the count's feelings take over his brains. In other words, *he* is the casket, the box that Pandora has opened, and it is *his* desires and emotions, which represent evil to him, that have been let out. That this is so seems to be presented at the beginning of his story. The young diplomat, Count Otto, sees the "human cargo" absorbed in the huge cavity of the ship (V, 357), which is called "an oblong box" (V, 365). He watches with "the consciousness of official greatness." The suggestion as he smugly watches the box of the ship filling up is that he himself is a box. He is "stuffed" like a container "with knowledge" (V, 358). In fact, "His mind contained several millions of facts, packed too closely together for the light breeze of the imagination to draw through the mass." Strictly raised in what he considers scientific thinking, he "had been taught thoroughly to appreciate the nature of evidence" (V, 359). For him everything is "a question of study" (V, 360). The notion of "happiness" to him "was an unscientific term, which he was ashamed to use even in the silence of his thoughts" (V, 358). The casual reader may not pay much attention to this introduction of a young man as a box or container of thousands of tightly confined facts with emotions hidden out of sight, but to someone alert to James's fictional strategy it is readily discernible after the story has been read once. It is a rereading that makes these figures visible.

The count, his German "box" stuffed with facts, is also stuffed with curiosity and a desire to acquire still more facts. In spite of himself, he joins Pandora on deck, "awkwardly, abruptly, irresistibly" (V, 372). The highly significant scene is the disembarcation in the midst of luggage. James is teasing the reader by putting in all these red herrings—all the various coffers, boxes, trunks, parcels, and bags. But what, after all, is the box that Pandora opens? At the end of the story we see that the stuffed box of scientific inquiry that is our German count gradually becomes open through the mysterious, uncalculated, unscientific but mesmeric spell Pandora casts. We also see a pun: even Mrs. Steuben has another form of chest, a bosom sporting "a full-length portrait" of her husband, the commodore.

The irony of the story establishes itself on different levels. First, there is the estimate Mrs. Dangerfield makes of the "'poor girl's'" lack of social position and her warning to Count Otto not to get involved with someone with such a family, and Mrs. Bonnycastle's superior, humorous interpretation of the "self-made" girl's lack of social position. The irony of the outcome is that by means of her charm and her energy, she becomes the social superior of everyone who snubbed her for her undistinguished provenience; at the end she becomes the wife of the minister to Holland, who outranks all the characters of the story, especially Count Otto, who is only the secretary of the German legation.

The triad of older women who pass judgment on Pandora might correspond to the Parcae, but Mrs. Steuben seems to represent, as distinguishable from the two other Northern "fates" (Mrs. Dangerfield and Mrs. Bonnycastle), the spirit of the classical tradition. When the ever-curious Vogelstein asks her, as a third source of information, "'What is the type to which that young lady belongs? Mrs. Bonnycastle tells me it's a new one'" (V, 394), Mrs. Steuben prepares us to see Pandora as just a reincarnation of the Hesiod Pandora, a reincarnation of a permanent figure. "'What we often take to be the new is simply the old under some novel form. Were there not remarkable natures in the past? If you doubt it you should visit the South, where the past still lingers'" (V, 395), to which he impatiently responds, "'All I want to know is *what* type it is! It seems impossible to find out'" (V, 395).

The intense interest in Rossetti the English displayed in 1883 after his death would have presented James with the image of the many versions of Pandora that Rossetti drew and painted from 1869 up to 1879 and which were featured in the two shows given in his memory. The great painting of 1870 and the studies for it and for a later version in 1879 made a total of six different versions of Pandora. Rossetti himself may have seen the Pandora cycle by Henry Howard in Sir John Soane's museum (figs. 33, 34, 35), the only cycle available to the English public that illustrates Hesiod's *Works and Days*. James's familiarity with Sir John Soane's museum is shown in the use he makes of it in "A London Life" (1888).

In the Rossetti poem as well as in the Howard ceiling decoration (and we even find it in the Flaxman series), there are a group of attendants: in Flaxman's *Pandora Attired* (PA, 96), we see three graces and the three hours (morning, noon, and afternoon). In the poem, we find Juno, Venus, and Pallas, the three goddesses (who tempt Paris) and who also appear in triad form in James's story. The three Dresden girls who skate are perhaps the three graces. The jewel box in the Rossetti painting, *Pandora,* is the first representation in Victorian England that features the box in the shape of a miniature trunk, not a jar; the box would fit in with Hawthorne and Longfellow's chest as a piece of furniture. James's interpretation of the box is a pluralistic one.

Swinburne's praise of Rossetti's poem "Pandora," the sonnet invented to be read while one views the painting and inscribed in part on the painting's frame, James noted in an anonymous review in the *Nation* for July 1875. He undoubtedly, therefore, knew of both picture and poem years before he wrote his story "Pandora." Surely the magnetic, mysterious spell that Pandora casts upon her parents, Count Otto, and even the President of the United States seems to derive from the Victorian femme fatale originated and stamped by Rossetti. What is more, Rossetti was mentioned in the one other story James was constructing simultaneously with "Pandora," "The Author of 'Beltraffio.'" Surely, to quote Count Otto, "'the nature of the evidence'" is conducive to believing that Rossetti's *Pandora* went into the creation of James's self-made Pandora.

The originality of James is twofold in importance. One aspect, we have seen, is the idea that the modern Pandora is not the creation of the gods but of herself. She alone gives herself gifts, those of European culture—the best literature, the best art, and travel to the source of that best. The second consists of the manifold changes rung on her accessory, the box or casket, so that its final metaphoric transmutation is found in Count Otto Vogelstein himself, who is conceived of as a "tightly packed," well "stuffed" container of facts and scientific data, with a mysterious attraction to Pandora that results in his falling in love. In other words, his emotions, so well hidden under his official equipment, finally escape from his body, which is no more or less than a human filing

Figure 33.  Henry Howard, *The Gifting of Pandora by the Gods*, 1834
Panel of the Pandora Cycle.
*(By courtesy of the Trustees of Sir John Soane's Museum)*

Figure 34.  Henry Howard, *The Bringing of Pandora to Epimetheus*, 1834
Panels of the Pandora Cycle.
*(By courtesy of the Trustees of Sir John Soane's Museum)*

Figure 35.  Henry Howard, *Pandora's Opening of the Box and Letting Loose Evils in the World*,
1834
Panels of the Pandora Cycle.
*(By courtesy of the Trustees of Sir John Soane's Museum)*

cabinet, and bring trouble into his life. It is the result not of Pandora's curiosity but of his own.

Pandora, gifted of the gods, by disturbing the status quo, by creating her own type and causing society to make new classifications to explain her, causes quite a lot of excitement and disturbs the standard conventional attitudes toward women. But what comes out of the box is not evil. Like Goethe's box before, James's "science" and "art" are disseminated through the world. The name Pandora, "gifted by Zeus," is finally stretched to mean gifted by the President of the United States. His present to her of a ministership puts her now in a position socially superior to the two women who judged her, which adds to the confusion of the disturbed preconceived notions. Count Otto must know that he is delivering a rebuke to Mrs. Bonnycastle when he tells her that Pandora is now a foreign minister's wife and that "there was now grounds for a new induction as to the self-made girl" (V, 412). By "induction" he means in philosophical jargon that there is now a new bit of evidence to reformulate her classification as a human type. Greek mythology has been contoured by James to give a modern shape to one of its most widely known figures, Pandora.

### Oedipus and the Sphinx:
### "The Story of a Year" and "The Beast in the Jungle"

The Oedipus legend has two appearances in James's oeuvre, one early and one late. "A Day of Days" (1866) repeats the confrontation of the sphinx and Oedipus brought up to modern times. Thomas Ludlow, a specialist in "fossil remains" on a visit to a fellow scientist of note, misses him but meets instead his sister; and, as Oedipus is confronted by the hard questions of the sphinx, Ludlow is equally interrogated by Adela Moore in her house, fronted by "three roads" that "went their different ways."[19] Adela, like the sphinx who has killed many a man, had "a past of which importunate swains . . . had been no inconsiderable part; and a great dexterity in . . . outflanking these gentlemen was one of her registered accomplishments," and "for a girl of her age she was unduly old and wise" (I, 148, 140).

Ludlow carries a cane, which with his two legs comprises the answer to the sphinx's famous puzzle: "what is it that walks on four legs in the morning, on two at noon, on three in the evening?" The answer is, of course, man. "'I hope I shall not lose my way,'" he said, "swinging his cane" (I, 150). As he says he does not want to leave her, Adela answers, "'I have seen all the gentlemen can show me' (this was her syllogism)" (I, 151), and he answers, "'I am in your hands'" (I, 151). Since he is about to go to Europe, that is the "great change hanging over" him (I, 155). "'You women,'" he says, "'are strong on asking embarrassing questions,'" and her questions and his answers are the entire story (I, 159). The climax occurs when Adela asks him to answer the question, does he "'really wish to stay?'" (I, 162). "'You ask difficult questions, Miss Moore,'" he answers, but if she orders him, he will stay (I, 163). "He still held Adela's hand, and now they were looking watchfully into each other's eyes" (I, 163). Through various journals of 1864, it is probable that James saw Gustave Moreau's *Oedipus and the Sphinx,* from which he had a precedent for this kind of scene (fig. 36).[20] Realizing Adela wants him to stay, Ludlow leaves for his trip to Europe.

The tale may mean other kinds of things, such as that James, while being pulled by America, still was directed toward Europe, but his method is to imitate and to rewrite the Oedipus legend, which focuses on being questioned. The answer to the riddle that Adela wants is for Thomas to stay, but he escapes her as Oedipus had escaped the sphinx, in this case not by answering questions but by simply leaving. The three roads are the one specific clue to the legend, for it was "where three roads joined" that Oedipus fulfilled the prophecy that he would kill his father. Thomas Ludlow sees that "in front of the house three roads went their different ways." In spite of the differences, the main operation of the story still consists of the give and take of questions and answers of two people who acknowledge the difficulty of choice.

In "The Beast in the Jungle," written almost forty years later, the word "sphinx" is actually brought into a tale that is also a dialogue between the woman questioner, the "impenetrable sphinx" May Bartram, and the Oedipus of the tale, John Marcher. The subject is self-knowledge. A man, haunted by his own fate, in this case does not know the answer though it lies right in front of him in the love for him of the sphinxlike woman. Egypt, the home of the sphinx, is brought into the tale, as are various icons of the classical world. As if trying to find the answer to the questions of his own fate, Marcher travels to "the depths of Asia" after May's death, and visits "the temples of gods and the sepulchres of Kings."[21] He goes to Egypt and to India, and his original encounter with May years before had occurred not in Rome "at the Palace of the Caesars, but at Pompeii" (XI, 354). May spoke with "the perfect straightness of a sibyl" (XI, 389) as she foretells Marcher's destiny. "'You were to suffer your fate. That was not necessarily to know it'" (XI, 391).

## A Modern Alcestis in "The Modern Warning"

A parallel to the "Dear Circe" letter of 1883 is another letter written six years later on November 6, 1889, from the Hotel de Hollande on the Rue de la Paix. James is in Paris, and his unknown correspondent is addressed as "My dear Athenian." The first paragraph of the letter repeats James's identification with an ancient, only instead of a Homeric pig, it is a striking personality from a Platonic dialogue. "For once in my life I am more Attic than Alcibiades! I am living on the honey of Hymettus while you eat Spartan broth in Pall Mall" (fig.

Figure 36.   Gustave Moreau, *Oedipus and the Sphinx,* 1864
*(The Metropolitan Museum of Art; bequest of William H.
Herriman, 1921)*

37). He continues, "I saw a million things in the exhibition, but was obliged to neglect several other millions. They did not neglect me, however, they have much exhausted me. Let this explain the reluctant brevity of your faithful fellow-owl. HENRY JAMES." A "fellow-owl" would intensify the association with Athens because the owl was Athena's bird. We do not know the reason for this sudden donning of a toga, but as in the case of the "Dear Circe" letter we can see it as an overflow from an immersion in classical literature. In this instance it is the legend of *Alcestis,* made available through Euripides and it appears in a tale published in 1888, a year before James's letter to his "dear Athenian." "The Modern Warning" (1888), was suggested to him, according to the *Notebooks,* "by reading Sir Lepel Griffin's book about America" (*The Great Republic*).[22] Griffin's book is a sharp critique of American society, and in James's tale it is translated into an equally sharp anti-American book called *The Modern Warning,* written by Sir Rufus Chasemore, an English aristocrat. It is the cause of the dilemma his American wife Agatha Grice is put into because of her beloved brother's excessive sensitivity to any criticism of the United States.

The *Alcestis* as recounted by Euripides is subtly introduced by degrees and then blossoms forth in the deathbed scene of Agatha Grice Chasemore. First, Agatha is given a Greek name, coming from the word 'αγαθός [agathos] (good). Grice could be pronounced Greece, and the connection with the three graces, a classical conceit, is made in the following pun: "and the three Grices—I had almost written the three Graces—."[23] There is also a link between this Agatha and Saint Agatha and the derivation of *her* name, as given by Jacobus de Voragine, as "a slave to Christ." Agatha says facetiously, "Oh, if one is going to be a slave I don't know that the nationality of one's master matters!" (VII, 21).

Agatha Chasemore is a slave to two men. The feud expressed between her brother, Macarthy Grice, and her husband, Sir Rufus Chasemore, resembles the struggle between Death and Herakles. There are also certain incestuous elements from Greek literature. Macarthy hoped his sister would never marry at all so that she could devote herself exclusively to him. Sir Rufus's jocularity might be related to the comic mood given by Herakles to the play *Alcestis* by Euripides. The Alcestis theme in James's tale develops after the Great Republic theme has been played out. The sources divide themselves into equal halves in this story, originally called "The Two Countries." Not only is it made up of the two books, one modern and one ancient, but it also concerns the making of Chasemore's book, *The Modern Warning.* After Agatha reads the proofs of her husband's book, she begins to act irrationally, Sir Rufus thinks. She makes him renounce "the dream of rendering a signal service to his country." She makes him promise not to publish it.

The clue that points to *Alcestis* as the underlying legend in this story can

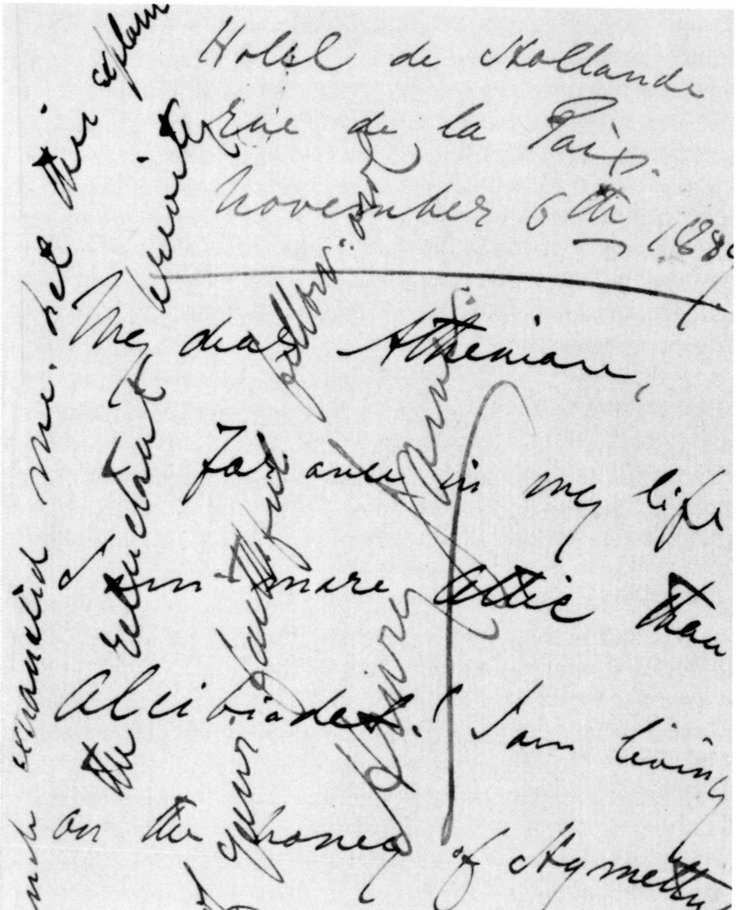

Figure 37. "Dear Athenian," Letter from Henry James to an Unknown
Correspondent, November 6, 1899

be found in the sentence retracting Agatha's decision. "Suddenly, illogically, fantastically, she could not have told why, at that moment and in that place, . . . she broke out: 'My own darling . . . I have changed entirely—I see it differently; I want you to publish that grand thing'" (VII, 81). This statement comes after her brother, whose opinion of the book she had dreaded and whom she feared personally, told her he was coming over to England. In other words, Agatha is sacrificing, or is preparing to sacrifice, herself so that her husband can have what he wishes, for in killing herself she then directs the anger of Macarthy away from her husband. "She doubtless placed her tergiversation in a more natural light than her biographer has been able to do: he however will spare the reader the exertion of following the impalpable clue which leads to the heart of the labyrinth" (VII, 82). This figure emerges from the body of classical mythology, specifically from the Theseus legend. Chasemore takes Agatha's permission to publish his book, and she can now see he is happy.

The hidden reason for her change of mind about the publication of the book is that James has made Agatha follow Alcestis's decision to sacrifice herself for her husband, since in the Euripides play her dying in her husband's place will allow Apollo to grant Admetus a longer life than he was fated to have. Agatha's sudden change in allowing Sir Rufus to publish his book corresponds to the decision that Alcestis makes to die for her husband. Agatha is also dying for her husband because she knows that Macarthy's antagonism will know no bounds when the book appears. To allow her husband to have his way, she has to disappear from the scene by killing herself. However, the end is not like the end of the Greek play, in which Herakles wins back Alcestis from Death. Agatha is forever dead, sacrificed to her brother's paranoia, at which point the Greek legend takes over the story.

We are then suddenly presented with the scene of Macarthy's entering the Chasemore house, in a replica of the opening of *Alcestis* by Euripides. Death and Herakles confront each other, for Death has come to take away Alcestis. So, too, Macarthy and Sir Rufus exchange greetings on the steps of the Chasemore house; they both stepped into "an atmosphere of sudden alarm and dismay." The servants then imitate the servants in the Greek play. "'We are afraid her ladyship is ill, sir; rather seriously, sir, we have but this moment discovered it, sir; her maid is with her, sir, and the other women'" (VII, 83). "Their faces were very white; they had a strange, scared expression" (VII, 83). Sir Rufus yells at Macarthy, "'By God, you have killed her! It is *your* infernal work! . . . Your damned fantastic opposition—the fear of meeting you'" (VII, 85). The waiting woman claims it was a faint, which corresponds to the servant in *Alcestis* saying "'she is both dead and alive.'"[24] Then Macarthy "rushed at his sister and for a moment almost had a struggle with her husband for the possession of her body," repeating the offstage struggle between Death and Herakles for the body of Alcestis in Euripides' play. Because Admetus has extended courtesies to Herakles as a traveler, in gratitude he has brought back Alcestis to the living. James has no such happy ending.

There may, however, have been another version of the Alcestis theme at work, one from the plastic arts. In 1884, on Sunday, March 29, James took Sargent around to the studios of ten artists to see the pictures just going into the spring exhibitions.[25] One of these artists was Sir Frederick Leighton, president of the Royal Academy, and it was his studio that impressed James the most, as he wrote to Grace Norton. One of Leighton's most famous pictures, which he had finished by this time, was *Hercules Wrestling with Death for the Body of Alcestis,* shown at the Royal Academy in 1871. Although snapped up immediately by a collector, this important picture, which took Leighton two years to paint, was well reproduced in photographs, and many studies of it exist. We have no evidence as to whether James saw such studies or the picture itself, but it was well known that Browning had written about the picture in "Balaustion's Adventure" (1872) and that the death of Alcestis served as an analogue for the death of his own wife. Since three years after "The Modern Warning" was written James began "The Private Life," in which he used Leighton and Browning as figures in a "conceit," as he indicated in his *Notebooks,* it seems hard to believe that he was unaware of this picture. He was very familiar with Leighton's work whenever it was shown when he was in London; we have his art critical pieces to prove it. With Leighton he was on friendly terms, though he envied his financial success, and he frequently visited his home and studio, where studies of the painting were exhibited on its walls.

Leighton has painted Herakles and Death battling to the right of the picture, with the dead body of Alcestis stretched out in the center portion (fig. 38). It provided Leighton with another one of the sleeping women themes with which he seems to have been obsessed.[26] Macarthy's eye had been caught "with a lifeless arm" (VII, 84), a prominent feature of the Leighton picture, in which Alcestis's right arm is stiff as if in rigor mortis. It seems as if James is recalling the details of the picture as well as those of the play. In his story, Death is conceived as being Macarthy himself, since Chasemore says, " 'You have killed her.' " In the picture Herakles is wrestling with a winged figure of Death who has a cloak wrapped around him with the top part muffling his face. Macarthy, too, "overwhelmed," flung himself into a chair "covering his face with the cape of his ulster" (VII, 85). This gesture is also given by Euripides to Admetus sorrowing at his wife's death: "He covers his head with his robe" (GD, 709).

The translation into modern terms of Euripides's play is an additional "modern warning," as well as being the title of the book Sir Rufus writes. Agatha's suicide is a modern warning against Anglo-American bad feelings. She sacrifices herself so that her husband can publish his book, which offends her patriotic brother. If she is dead, the antagonism of her brother, a fanatical

Figure 38.  Frederick Lord Leighton, *Hercules Wrestling with Death for the Body of Alcestis,*
1869–71
*(Wadsworth Atheneum, Hartford; the Ella Gallup Sumner and Mary Catlin Sumner
Collection)*

and paranoid American, will not be directed against Sir Rufus since the two men will no longer have any relation to each other. Their family ties and responsibilities will have been broken. The only way for Agatha to avoid incurring her brother's wrath against her and Sir Rufus, is to kill herself. The writer of the story acts as if the idea were a mystery to him as the reporter of the tale, as well as to Agatha, for hers is a decision to get rid of herself for her husband's sake.

Sir Rufus stands for Admetus, for his book with its warning to his countrymen, was his life, since he was a permanent official of England, and with Agatha out of the way he might publish his anti-American book. She has turned about and has seemed to express enthusiasm for the book now, for "by the end of a week she persuaded him that she had really come round," drawing "from him the confession . . . that the manuscript . . . had not been destroyed at all" (VII, 81). This fact seems to have been inserted to show us that his book was more important to Sir Rufus than his wife. "Sir Rufus was as happy as a man who after having been obliged for a long time to entertain a passion in secret finds it recognized and legitimate, finds that the obstacles are removed and he may conduct his beloved to the altar" (VII, 82–83). It is, finally, his very life, and like Alcestis, Agatha, the good one, gives up her life for her husband's satisfaction. The final scene, couched in the same image as Leighton's famous picture of the classical legend, seems to provide this reader with "the impalpable clue that leads to the heart of the labyrinth," the labyrinth of Agatha's morbid and irrational behavior.

Euripides was known for his interest in women and their passions, and ten of his eighteen extant plays are given over to them and bear their names as titles. But Euripides also presented the passions of two old men, and James rewrites this theme, bringing it up to modern times and modern society in *The Ambassadors.*

### Euripides, Waymarsh, and "The Sacred Rage"

"The sacred rage" is a phrase repeated nine times in *The Ambassadors,* yet we are never sure what it is. It is not defined explicitly, and it nags at us as we try to understand its full significance. Always associated with Waymarsh, the lawyer friend of Strether's, the phrase makes its first appearance when he goes on a shopping spree with Miss Gostrey, who sees him as having "struck for freedom" from puritan thrift. Lambert Strether, the hero of the novel, describes this "periodical necessity" as "the sacred rage" (AM, 34). When Waymarsh meets Miss Barrace (whose name rhymes with Paris), he goes with her "into the shops," and she claims, "'I've all I can do to prevent his buying me things.'" Strether admits "'he's much more in the real tradition that I. Yes,' he mused, 'it's the sacred rage.' 'The sacred rage, exactly!'—and Miss Barrace, who had not before heard this term applied, recognized its bearing with a clap of her gemmed hands" (AM, 198). Strether responds to her report of Waymarsh's splurges with "'*What* a rage it is!'" (AM, 198). After the lawyer establishes a relationship with Sarah Pocock, his rage is appeased and Strether now misses "the occasional ornament of the sacred rage, and the right to the sacred rage . . . he also seemed . . . to have forfeited"(AM, 354). This "rage" affects Strether himself indirectly, and he begins his wild shopping by buying "seventy blazing volumes" of Victor Hugo and lunching with Marie de Vionnet, Chad's mistress (AM, 220).

The term "the sacred rage" may have its source in Euripides' drama *The Bacchae,* where it appears defined as a divine madness that Bacchus inspires in his followers. That James was alluding to the Euripidean analogue appears probable when we consider that at this time in England Euripides (and particularly *The Bacchae*) was undergoing reinterpretation and causing great interest in general as well as in university circles. Way's translation of the entire oeuvre of Euripides in English verse appeared from 1894 to 1898, and R.Y. Tyrrell's new edition of *The Bacchae* was published in 1896. A.W. Verrall had spearheaded the interest in Euripides' plays around the turn of the century in his book, *Euripides the Rationalist* (1895). His point of view was criticized by Gilbert Murray, whose translations of Euripides' plays—including *The Bacchae*—appeared from 1902 until 1909, after he had popularized his ideas about *The Bacchae* and his view of Euripides as the exponent of irrationalism in his *History of Ancient Greek Literature* (1897). Reviewing the plot of *The Bacchae* for his 1987 *History* ("For excitement, for mere thrill, there is absolutely nothing like it in ancient literature"), Murray asks the meaning of this play in which two old men, Teiresias and Cadmus, "recognize" Bacchus as God and "feel themselves young again." He then answers, "Reason is great, but it is not everything. There are in the world things not of reason, but both below and above it; causes of emotions which we cannot express . . . which we feel, perhaps, to be the precious elements in life."[27] This interpretation of Euripides coincided with Freud and Breuer's contemporary investigations of the irrational in *Studies in Hysteria* (1895).

It is very significant in this context that James himself owned Murray's book, which was one of a series edited by his close friend Edmund Gosse.[28] But even as early as October 31, 1895, James was thinking of such a theme, for he records having received the germ of *The Ambassadors* from Jonathan Sturges ("Live all you can. . . . You have time. You are young. Live!"). "I seem to see something, of a tiny kind, springing out of it, that would take its place in the little group I should like to do of *Les Vieux*—The Old,"[29] indicating that James had perhaps read an earlier French commentary on Euripides' plays by H.

Weil, *Sept Tragédies d'Euripides,* for it was in France that this interest in the antirationalism of Euripides began.[30] "Les Vieux" would refer to Cadmus and Teiresias, the two elderly men who are rejuvenated under the spell of Dionysus.

James made only two allusions to Euripides in his critical writing. The first, at age twenty-two, shows that he read the Greek dramatist early; the last, at fifty-four, shows he was well aware of the new handling of the Euripidean oeuvre.[31] It occurs in his *London Notes* for August 1897, on the occasion of Bourget's lecture on Flaubert at Oxford, which James had attended. James pointed out the failure of the academic pundits to clarify the meaning of the classics for modern society. He noted that "the light kindled by the immense academic privilege is apt suddenly to turn to thick smoke in the air of contemporary letters" and that certain "movements of the classic torch round modern objects have the effect of putting it straight out." The classical specialists reveal "a failure of the sense of perspective," which leads often to "queer conjunctions, strange collocations in which Euripides gives an arm to Sarah Grand and Octave Feuillet harks back to Virgil."[32]

Euripides surely was in the air, and it is very likely that James was looking at the immensely readable Murray book, just published. James probably re-thought *The Bacchae* in the light of contemporary attitudes to the play. Connecting Euripides with Sarah Grand was an ironical way of making the sublime dance with the ridiculous, for Sarah Grand—the popular writer of the 1893 bestseller *The Heavenly Twins*—used classical machinery in a trivial way. However, the combination also underlines the fact that Euripides was a popular writer in his own day. James was to couple his Euripidean character, Waymarsh, with another Sarah, this time Sarah Pocock (just as Marie de Vionnet is coupled with Jim Pocock and Chad with Mamie), in a Jamesian version of a Dionysiac frolic. James's "conjunctions" would be not quite as "queer," though equally amusing.

The clue to the Euripidean element lies in "the sacred rage" that afflicts Waymarsh. It takes hold of a man who has come to Europe to forget his abusive wife, about whom he never speaks, inhabiting "a province in which mystery reigned" (AM, 21). Wrapt in a "sombre glow," he fears " 'I *may* lose my mind over here' " (AM, 23). This madness or "sacred rage" can only be appeased by bouts of shopping. James's choice of shopping as appeasement was an ironical one he had made before. He had dealt with this spectacularly American form of consolation—resorted to usually by women, perhaps in reference to the demented women in *The Bacchae*—when, during "sacred rites" in "The Pension Beaurepas" (1879), he portrayed Mr. Ruck's womenfolk taking out their "restlessness" in "shopping."[33] In 1903 the "sacred rites" of 1879 become Waymarsh's "sacred rage."

If this phrase carries the freight of the Euripidean allusion, then it is worthwhile to explore the question of whether there is more of the Euripidean concept in *The Ambassadors* considered as a whole. James would surely know from Murray's book that Euripides was the Greek dramatist who had developed most fully the "'anagnorisis' or 'recognition' as a dramatic climax," and it is possible to find an echo of this contribution in the great recognition scene in which the heretofore "blind" Strether recognizes the true relation between Chad and Mme. Vionnet.[34] Teiresias could be a model for Strether because, though blind, he sees more than Pentheus, the King, who is spiritually blinded by his prejudices. "'Blind before, and now indeed / Most mad!'" Teiresias tells Pentheus, "'Nay, I speak not from my art, / But as I see—blind words and a blind heart!'" When Cadmus asks Teiresias, "'And in all Thebes shall no man dance but we?'" Teiresias answers, "'Aye, Thebes is blinded. Thou and I can see'" (GD, 238, 239, 233). Strether learns to see while under the spell of Paris, the place that allows repressions to disappear. At first blinded by his Puritan inheritance, he eventually sees what life is all about, and Miss Gostrey, on the closing page of the novel, tells Strether that what is remarkable beyond his "'being right'" is his "'horrible sharp eye for what makes [him] so'" (AM, 458). Strether maintains his position as the seer—the Teiresias—of the drama.

**Endymion, "The Velvet Glove," and Olympus**

In 1909 Henry James published "The Velvet Glove." This short story is a mock-epic with a meticulously worked out classical mythology understructuring the imagery, language, and characterization, all mounted to launch an elaborate literary joke. At once the heroine of the mock-epic and the butt of the joke is Edith Wharton, who plays the dual role of Artemis and the scribbling princess.

Attention both to the elements and to the tone of the story will show that the word "Olympian" (occurring fifteen times in the thirty-three page story) is part of a carefully structured mock-epic that shows how absurd it is for those who are capable of living on a high romantic plane to yearn for the writer's art. Although the machinery of the mock-epic involves hyperbole and personification, it is intimately related to two of the serious recurrent themes of James's late oeuvre. First, it is necessary to live fully. Strether's advice to young Bilham in Gloriani's garden of *The Ambassadors* is repeated here, in Gloriani's studio, in the thoughts of John Berridge, the writer-hero. Second, a writer must maintain his integrity and standards no matter how strong the temptation may be to compromise them. These two themes are joined in the request made by a glamorous princess for a literary puff for her worthless novel from John Berridge, an American author of current popularity.

A new literary star "that had begun to hang, with a fresh red light, over the vast ... Anglo-Saxon horizon," Berridge is the author of a "slightly too fat" volume, *The Heart of Gold* (a self-deprecation of *The Golden Bowl*), made "into a fifth-act too long play," which unlike James's own plays, has been a great hit.[35] By compressing his tale into three dense parts or acts, James humorously corrects the prolixity of *The Golden Bowl*. He continues this self-deprecation when he travesties the effect of the writer on the young lord who approaches him on behalf of his novelist friend. "Perhaps the very brightest and most diamond-like twinkle he had yet seen the star of his renown emit was just the light brought into his young Lord's eyes by this so easy consent to oblige" (XII, 235). The exaggerated gallantry of the James of the late correspondence is expressed by this special kind of joke—a parody of snobbery. The stage is thus set for a mock-epic in which the Olympian Diana or princess descends to the earth to seek out her favorite shepherd, Endymion or John Berridge.

The tale begins its high exaggeration in the opening sentence when "poor John Berridge" (a term of endearment James reserves for the sympathetic "I"-heroes of the later stories) is placed as "the new literary star." The "red light" identifies him as an American (the Western star, Mars, is red) who is approached by a young aristocrat whom Berridge finds familiar in some way, for he "had wondered about him, had . . . imaginatively, intellectually . . . quite yearned over him" (XII, 236), but whom he cannot place. Berridge is aware of the man's superiority. "One placed young gods and goddesses only when one placed them on Olympus, and it met the case, always, that they were of Olympian race, and that they glimmered for one, at the best, through their silver cloud, like the visiting apparitions in an epic" (XXI, 238). This begins the references to Olympus and Olympians, mentioned six times in three pages. The music played at the party makes "the whole of Olympus presently open," until an unknown beauty, "Olympian herself, supremely, divinely Olympian" (XII, 240), arrives and John Berridge knows he has seen before both god and goddess together. "Who had they been, and what? Whence had they come, whither were they bound, what tie united them, what adventure engaged, what felicity, tempered by what peril, magnificently, dramatically attended?" (XII, 241). Surely this is a parody of Homeric language or at least neoclassic locutions in epic poetry, enfolding classical myths. So closes part one.

Part 2 opens with Mme. Gloriani introducing John Berridge to a great French dramatist whose use for Berridge is simply to ascertain who the "young woman might be . . . who wore the pale yellow dress, of the strange tone, and the magnificent pearls" (XII, 243). The "strange tone" of the dress is the color Diana wears in Keats's "Endymion"; it is the color of the moon and is significant here because James will soon identify the Princess with Diana or Artemis. In this part of the story, the references to Olympians, Atlas, Hebe, and Diana, thicken and accumulate. We are prepared for it by the "Atlas-back of renown" belonging to the well-known dramatist who blocks out, temporarily, John Berridge's view of the glamorous couple. The allusion to Atlas, who gathered the golden apples of the Hesperides for Hercules, is related to the princess's making her way to our hero and telling him that she has read his *Heart of Gold* three times. "If she was Olympian . . . this offered air was that of the gods themselves: she might have been . . . Artemis decorated, hung with pearls, for her worshipers, yet disconcerting them by having . . . snatched the cup of gold from Hebe. It was to him, John Berridge, she thus publicly offered it; and it was his over-topping *confrère* of shortly before who was the worshiper most disconcerted" (XII, 244). This ties Hebe's husband, Hercules, to whom the cup of gold *should* have been given, to Atlas (here, the dramatist).

In the next three pages, the word "Olympian" occurs seven times, mostly in relation to an Olympian career and what John Berridge would have made of it. "He should have consented to know but the grand personal adventure on the grand personal basis: nothing short of this . . . would begin to be . . . Olympian enough" (XII, 245). His revery is broken by the young lord's giving him a copy of *The Top of the Tree* by Amy Evans, the novelist friend he had mentioned, whose book "represented an object as alien to the careless grace of goddess-haunted Arcady as a washed-up 'Kodak' from a wrecked ship might have been" (XII, 249). Then James quotes a passage from this book, which also contains classical references to Phidias and Astarte but is written poorly, dominated by "which" clauses. John Berridge is in a daze when the princess tells him that *she* is Amy Evans and that it is her latest book, *The Velvet Glove,* which she wants him to read! In fact, if he will forego supper at Gloriani's, she will drive him home. While "the perspiration on his brow might have been the morning dew on a high lawn of Mount Ida" (XII, 254), he joins her as part two ends.

Part 3 opens with Berridge ensconced in the princess's "chariot of fire," her motorcar, with her hand on his, while "the whites of her eyes . . . gleamed in the dusk like some silver setting of deep sapphires" (XII, 258). Silver is Diana's color. She reveals her desire that he write a puffing preface for *The Velvet Glove*. The effect on him is this: "It was as if she had lifted him first in her beautiful arms, had raised him up high, high, high, to do it . . . and then . . . setting him down exactly where she wanted him to be—which was a thousand miles away from her" (XII, 259). The iron fist shows itself under the velvet glove. Amy Evans now takes over from the divinity. He who had wanted to be loved for himself is loved for a preface! If, after this revelation, Berridge should stop the car, "that would be an answer . . . only to inanely importunate, to utterly superfluous Amy Evans—not a bit to his at last exquisitely patient companion" (XII, 260). She awaits his answer: "she quite bent over him, as Diana over the sleeping Endymion," and he realizes that "she *was,* for herself . . . Amy Evans and an asker for 'lifts,' a conceiver of twaddle both in herself and in him" (XXI, 261). The enchantment is over! But she is unaware of his thoughts and kisses his hand to influence him further. He in turn kisses *her* hand, from which the glove has fallen, and tells the chauffeur to stop. He gets out and sees her through the open side window of the car, "suspended, silvered over and celestially blurred, even as a summer moon by the loose veil of a cloud. . . . It was such a state as she would have been reduced to . . . for the first time in her life; and it was he, poor John Berridge . . . who would have created the condition" (XII, 262). So he puts her back in the moon, as Diana, and eliminates Amy Evans. He bids her goodnight and refuses her the preface. " 'Nothing would induce me to say a word in print about you. I'm in fact not sure I shall ever mention you in any manner at all as long as ever I live' " (XII, 263).

The princess does not understand and thinks Berridge does not like her. He says he adores her but is ashamed for her. " 'You *are* Romance . . . so what more do you want? Your Preface . . . was written long ages ago by the most beautiful imagination of man' " (XII, 263). (Here he may be referring to Homer, the poet of mythology.) When she fails to understand, he tells her not to try. " 'Only live. Only be. *We'll* do the rest.' " And when still obtusely she urges him just to *try* the preface and he sees he cannot communicate with her, he decides on something else: "he'd, by the immortal gods, anticipate it in the manner most admirably effective" (XII, 264). He kisses her on the mouth, he breaks away from the car, and "he had no further sound from her than if, all divinely indulgent but all humanly defeated, she had given the question up" (XII, 265). The story ends "as she passed to disappearance in the great floridly-framed aperture whose wings at once came together behind her" (XII, 265), in true fairy-tale style. And the dual existence of divine goddess and silly scribbler, so admirably developed, sustained, and paralleled, is brought to a close.

The atmosphere of this wistful disillusionment of a mortal with a goddess's view of herself is densely poetic. The mythological references differ from the extended metaphors of the other late work in that they girdle the entire story from beginning to end and stem from the effect the two young aristocrats have on the writer-hero. They operate as metaphor, not simile, since the princess is a double, both goddess and Amy Evans. Gloriani's party is also an Olympian entertainment. The story is dramatic in a mock-heroic sense. It is like the Greek drama of the ancient legends in that slowly, bit by bit, John Berridge "discovers" that the princess is only a hack writer, the complete revelation not taking place until the final tête-à-tête in the motorcar, so bedazzled is he by her Olympian aura. The divine goddess prefers to become a mortal, euhemerized into a vulgar lady novelist, but Berridge refuses to help her in her base transformation. He places her "suspended, silvered over, even as a summer moon" back in her divine role. He will play Endymion to a goddess for love, but he will not betray his literary standards for the ambition of an Amy Evans.

Throughout the story, James so sticks to the classical unities of time and place that from the hints of "ten minutes" here and a "half-hour" there we can time the story at just about two hours, almost exactly the time it takes to read it, for its density precludes skipping. The place is a few feet of standing room at Gloriani's studio party (remembered as the party scene in *The Ambassadors*), and, for part three, the close interior of the princess's motorcar. It is the most theatrical or dramatic of the last seven stories of *The Finer Grain,* with the drama focusing on the activity of the hero's consciousness, which is the machine making the mythological metaphor. However, the physical actions that do take place—the personal encounters, the seating in the motorcar, the hand kissing, the leaving of the car by John Berridge followed by his kissing the princess on the mouth (an action equivalent in a James story to an offstage murder in a Greek tragedy)—are all concretely realized. But they are small, restricted actions, as befit the rococo nature of this mock-epic, and are fashioned for the stage of the mind, not of the theatre. The climax of part one is not only the arrival of the princess at the party, but also Berridge's awareness that she is the "missing connection" to the young lord, that she is equally Olympian, and that both are "preoccupied . . . with the affairs, and above all with the passions, of Olympus" (XII, 241). The small events of the plot all support the "discoveries" that Berridge makes after the manner of Oedipus, but the truth dawns slowly. It is impeded by the mythological apparatus of glamor that part two constructs after the princess's arrival and introduction. Singling out our writer, as Diana does the shepherd of her whim, the princess is the Olympian goddess tricked out by metaphor and glorified by remembered myth. In the third act, in her "chariot of fire," the intimacy of her close presence and the significance of her kissing Berridge's hand could only be staged in the privacy of the prepared consciousness's of both hero and reader. It is a light, playful drama depending on interior rather than external action, the few overt gestures contributing intensity to the ironic situation.

The manner in which the mock-epic is mounted is very carefully worked out. John Berridge is placed as a star in the heavens as the story opens. This permanently deifies him, for the gods have survived beyond classical periods in the heavenly bodies. Then the Olympian note with its "silver tone" implemented by the tenor's music—"It ruled the scene . . . while all the rest of consciousness was held down as by a hand mailed in silver" (XII, 239)—ends part one. Part two is a mythologized account of the princess's asking for John Berridge's good will; she is a snatcher of Hebe's cup and an "Artemis decorated, hung with pearls, for her worshippers" (XII, 244). She has chosen her shepherd, or so Berridge thinks, in a note of divine whimsy. Part three is the breaking of the illusion and the revelation of the true cause of the princess's favor—her desire for Berridge's preface. The divinity is bifurcated into Artemis and Amy Evans. Berridge ends the mock-epic by driving Amy Evans out of the picture and sending Artemis back to her divine role. What carries the hyperbole along is the excitement accompanying the classical apparatus, for classical references in literature, art, and architecture were the stock in trade of the turn of the century.

That James should use neoclassical tags to structure his story was much more natural then than it would be today. The World Columbian Exposition in

Chicago in 1893, dominated by so much neoclassical architecture that it was called "The White City," brought to every man's eye what had been part of a well-educated person's background of the last half of the nineteenth century. Henry James's youth had been well stocked with neoclassical impressions of all sorts. Even before his spelling out Livy, one of his first memories as a toddler was "the elegant image" of "a place called the Pavilion . . . that of a great Greek temple shining over blue waters in the splendour of a white colonnade and a great yellow pediment."[36] Classicism in art came to him through the newer revivals rather than through the old channels. "[T]he grand manner, the heroic and the classic, in Haydon, came home to us more warmly . . . than in the masters commended as 'old'" (SB, 314). It was the romantic aspects of nineteenth-century classicism that excited a young boy who liked Paul Delaroche as well as Eugène Delacroix, and the Galerie d'Apollon in the Louvre gave him a general sense of glory, fostered by Prudhon's *Cupid and Psyche* and "David's helmetted Romanisms" (SB, 350). "The beginning in short was with Gericault and David" (SB, 351). All these impressions of the romantic neoclassicism of the early nineteenth century for him were "charged somehow with a useability . . . which would keep me restless till I should have done something of my very own with them."[37]

It was not until his trip to America in 1904, with the memories it stirred up (later to be reworked by him in three autobiographies), that the details of classicism seem anything more than the clichés used by Amy Evans or followers of the Chicago White City. And it is only in "The Velvet Glove" that the trappings of classicism appear as humorously handled allegory. (In his early essay on Hawthorne, James advises against allegory except when used lightly and humorously.) In "The Jolly Corner," a story probably written just before "The Velvet Glove," we are indirectly put into a mythological setting by the suggestion of the underworld in the descent of Spencer Brydon and the discovery of his alter ego in a figure almost blind like Pluto and, like Pluto, very rich. But this perhaps unconscious identification with the king of the underworld is part of another trend in James's last stories, where certain archetypal figures emerge from folklore. Julia Bride is the heroine of a quest but fails to gain her ends. Crapy Cornelia is an aged Cinderella. Kate Cookham in "The Bench of Desolation" is a witch transformed into a fairy godmother.

Is there anything in James's life that can explain the concentration of ancient Greek references in four periods—that of 1883 to 1884, of 1888 to 1889, of 1902 to 1903 and, roughly, of 1909? As far as the period from 1883 to 1884 goes, there have recently surfaced a copy of *The Iliad* (1883) and of *The Odyssey* (1879) in English versions by Andrew Lang and others, signed by James who had recently made Lang's acquaintance.

We may also account for it by the beginning friendship between Edmund

Gosse (who is now known to have had strong homoerotic tendencies) and James, which started, as we see from letters, around 1882. We have a letter from James to Gosse dated June 9, 1884, thanking him for his appreciative note about "The Author of 'Beltraffio'" in which the writer Mark Ambient is based on John Addington Symonds. To it James adds a postscript: "Perhaps I *have* divined the innermost cause of J.A.S.'s discomfort—but I don't think I see, on p. 571, exactly the allusion you refer to. I am therefore devoured with curiosity as to this further revelation. Even a post-card (in covert words) would relieve the suspense of the perhaps-already-too indiscreet H.J."[38]

How innocent this protestation of simple divination is we can only guess. But there are a few clues in the tale itself that indicate that James may not have been so innocent about Symonds's homosexuality. The letter of introduction that the narrator has brought for Mark Ambient, the author of "Beltraffio," has come from "my friend the American poet," a "missive" sent to Ambient as a note of introduction, which he answers in the affirmative, showing a desire that "I should tell him all about the other great man, the one in America."[39] That this great man is Walt Whitman is a strong possibility, and if we concede this possibility to be a probability, then we are onto the clue of homosexuality. Also, it has been suggested to me that Mrs. Ambient would not kill a child because she thought reading the aesthetic poets might corrupt the child, but because she thought that he would become a practicing homosexual like his father, a belief widespread among Symonds's contemporaries.

One can speculate that James knew about Symonds's reputation. Early in January or February, James wrote the only extant letter he ever penned to John Addington Symonds (HJL, III, 29–31) in which he thanks Symonds for a volume of "Italian Local Sketches" which James had already owned.[40] This was in return for James's present to Symonds of his own *Portraits of Places.* James owned twenty volumes by Symonds, dated as early as 1879, and the assumption is acceptable that he bought them as they were published. In connection with the Whitman allusion in "The Author of 'Beltraffio,'" he also owned Symonds's *Life of Whitman,* published when Symonds died in 1893. Did he also "divine" that interest in Whitman on the part of Symonds in connection with the introduction of the "great American poet"? And did the fact that the young man of twenty-five, the narrator of the tale, was also a friend of Whitman's show that the young man was himself probably a homosexual? The story, "The Author of 'Beltraffio,'" seems to take place around the late 1860s. Whitman's *Leaves of Grass* had gone into its fourth edition in 1867 and William Michael Rossetti had praised it that year; in 1868, the latter published his own selection of Whitman's poems.

So much for the possibility that James's was only a pretended innocence about the homosexuality of Symonds. In the tale the plot involves the passion against the aesthetic mode of art as being sufficient reason for a mother's killing her son. Are we to read behind it or to take it at its face value? It is to be remembered that James's notebook entry claiming that "J.A.S." is the writer in his tale shows that James found Symonds's "somewhat hysterical aestheticism" sufficient reason for his wife's disapproval and a sufficient reason for seeing a story in that disapproval.[41]

As for the next emergence of the Greek form of love, there appear lurking in the more or less literary allusions to Athens, in a letter of 1899 to "my dear Athenian," definite clues to a homosexual content. "My dear Athenian" might refer to his friend, the attaché to the Greek consulate; we have a letter of James's written to the secretary of the Rabelais Club, to which James belonged, asking permission to bring with him this attaché of the Greek legation. But then it may refer to some friend who shared, in a kind of cryptic code, certain affinities with the young men of ancient Greece, perhaps of an emotional and sexual nature. The comments in the letter show a close knowledge of the homoerotic element in the Platonic dialogues, a volume of which James owned in the Jowett translation, but of a later date. He surely knew the dialogues well before he acquired the volume he later owned.

"For once in my life," the letter begins, "I am more Attic than Alcibiades! I am living on the honey of Hymettus while you eat Spartan broth in Pall Mall." James knew that being Attic meant being completely Athenian and that the mountain of Hymettus loomed over Athens. He was even more Athenian, he claims, than Alcibiades, the lover of Socrates, who himself was outlawed because of his presumed mutilation of the Hermae, those pillars crowned by the bust of Hermes, god of fertility, and containing a phallus below the bust, set up usually at the street corners of Athens. Alcibiades escaped being punished for this outrage by fleeing to Sparta, where he worked against Athens.

James seems to have known all this because he is "more Attic than Alcibiades," because he is not a traitor, whereas his friend, he imputes, is like Alcibiades, since he eats "Spartan broth," only in "Pall Mall." He would have "pressed [the] hand" of this Athenian friend, had he known, he continues, that they would not be in Paris together. When he does arrive, James himself will be too busy to see him, "but we will make it up in the dark days of London." He explains that he has been taking in the Exhibition of 1889, even though at this time he was finishing *The Tragic Muse* and also taking on the translation of the new Tartarin book Daudet was doing for Harper's. He writes, "I saw a million things in the exhibition, but was obliged to neglect several other millions. They did not neglect me, however—they have much exhausted me. Let this explain," he winds up, "the reluctant brevity of your faithful fellow-owl." As I have noted above, James is a fellow-owl because both he and his friend are votaries of Athena, the patron saint of Athens, and the owl was her bird. This closes the brief note on Athens and their both being Athenians or fellow votaries of the Greek way of life, with its possible suggestion of the Greek way of loving.[42]

James wrote of these days in Paris in the only published letter of the period, one to his brother William, about what "a great impression" the Exhibition was. In June 1888, under the title of "Two Countries," "The Modern Warning," with its Greek and classical content was published, preceding the Paris letter to the "dear Athenian" of November, 1889. The Greek element, though hidden in "The Author of 'Beltraffio,'" is expressed clearly in the story written right after it, "Pandora," to be followed by the few but clear allusions to classical mythology in "A New England Winter," with its Odysseus-Circe component, all stories published during 1884. Four years later comes "The Modern Warning," and then we wait until 1903 and *The Ambassadors* to find a classical component within the larger pattern of the novel. "The Beast in the Jungle" is another aspect of the classical emphasis during this year. "The Velvet Glove" of 1909 concludes the Greek classical strain, though the Virgilian note is taken up in "Crapy Cornelia," with its emphasis on the *lares penates,* the household gods, and *The Aeneid.* The homosexual element at this time is no longer up front; now the Endymion theme prevails in "The Velvet Glove," with Astarte as a classical focus as well as the whole panoply of gods appearing with their Greek names rather than their Roman, as in "The Last of the Valerii." The Olympians in "The Velvet Glove" are heterosexual, and the passion there is overtly normal in its most aristocratic form. Since the encoded heroine was Edith Wharton, as is now generally accepted, and she was in the midst of a passionate love affair about which James knew, the stress on heterosexuality is appropriate.[43]

We may then say that the first wave of Greek references, (omitting, that is, the two early stories dealing with the Oedipus theme and the Oresteia in *The American*) may have been stimulated by James's initiation into the society of literary homosexuals, who were beginning to be free within their own group about expressing their inversion. This influence continues until 1888 with "The Modern Warning," but now it is the theme of incest between brother and sister. The elements of the Oedipus theme occur again the "The Beast in the Jungle," and *The Bacchae* penetrates *The Ambassadors,* with the themes of destiny and fate as envisaged by the ancients. With "The Velvet Glove" we witness a parody of the Olympian scene and the fictive reinvention of the Endymion-Artemis theme in a kind of mock-epic. The Greeks have been played out.

## Virgil, "Crapy Cornelia," and a Lost World

In "The Story of a Masterpiece" (1868), filled with quotations from Browning, Gibbon, and the French poets, James quotes the words *Exegi monumentum,* from an ode by Horace, and that is all we ever get from that poet. James's greater familiarity with and use of Virgil is testified to first by his earliest reviews (two in 1867). When he reports on William Alger's *The Friendship of Women,* he is amused that the author advises us to read about Dido, but "in what guise?" It is in the category of "friendships of sisters. . . . One fancies the great Virgilian funeral-pyre flaming up afresh in one supreme, indignant flash."[44] The boyhood years in which James had "worried out Virgil" with his tutor came to fruition in the allusions to Virgil that appear now and then.[45] James remembered the figure of Venus who hid in a cloud to protect her son, which he uses in *The Princess Casamassima,* repeating it in *The Wings of the Dove* when Kate protects Densher. A Virgilian line in "The Figure in the Carpet" appears when Venus makes herself known to her son by her very walk. It is used by Gwendolyn Erme to indicate that George Corvick has cabled her that he had known Vereker's secret. "I'm sure when you see it you do know. *Vera incessu patuit dea!"* (the real goddess reveals herself simply by the way in which she steps forward).[46]

After 1900 James brings a Virgilian element into his work that is part of the Arcadian elegiac tradition, which was absorbed by Poussin, then Watteau, and especially by Balzac, through whose channel it finally enters *The Ambassadors.* Virgil contributed dissonance to the pastoral Theocritan idyll with the knowledge that death and loss of love go hand in hand in Arcady. The evening hours are part of Virgil's invention of Arcady in his Eclogues, and Strether's experience in *The Ambassadors* partakes of this quality. Virgil here is the initiator of the Arcadian mood, but it seems to have arrived for James through the agency of Balzac.[47] However, it is *The Aeneid,* in its purest and most pervasive form, that invades "Crapy Cornelia" (1909), one of James's last stories.

In the last part of the story there is a consciously Virgilian interlude located specifically by a Latin quotation from Virgil's *Aeneid,* book 1. "The few scattered surviving representatives of a society once 'good'—*rari nantes in gurgite vasto*—were liable, at the pass things had come to, to meet" (XII, 349). The complete quotation, which James has excerpted for his purposes, is: *"Adparent rari nantes in gurgite vasto / Arma virum, tabulaeque, et Troia gaza per undas"* (*Aeneid,* book 1, lines 118–19). Dryden's translation reads: "And here and there above the waves were seen, / Arms, pictures, precious goods and floating men." The line James quotes in "Crapy Cornelia" he has chosen very carefully to emphasize the thrust of his story. It comes from the part of the Latin epic in which Juno, jealous of Venus, has raised a storm that shipwrecks some of the Trojan fleet traveling to the shores of Italy intent on preserving the Trojan stock. The words omitted from the Virgilian quotation quoted above prepare the educated reader for the *tabulae* or pictures that, floating in the story, will serve as connecting links for White-Mason with his dead youth. Those *tabulae* could be considered the *carte-de-visite* photographs left over from the shipwreck of Cornelia's and White-Mason's mutual past mentioned in "Crapy Cornelia." The quotation from Virgil has been prepared for by the preceding phrase, "the origins . . . of persons swimming into their ken." It is followed by a summoning up of "shades once sacred" and mention of "the doubtless very queer spectre of the late Mr. Worthingham," all of which suggest Aeneas's visit to the underworld (XII, 349). It is buttressed by the "unquiet truths that swarmed out after the fashion of creatures bold only at eventide" (XII, 350). On the next page James sounds the shipwreck theme again, making this interlude completely Virgilian with the metaphor for Mrs. Worthingham's meeting Cornelia in Switzerland. They resemble ("castaways on a desert island and in a raging storm" [XII, 351]), both figures drawn from the *Aeneid.* The Virgilian ambience associated with Arcadia is invoked when White-Mason refers to "those spacious, sociable, Arcadian days" of his and Cornelia's youth (XII, 357). The hero and Cornelia are to do what Aeneas had been assigned by his Olympian sponsors to do, to "make over and recreate, our lost world; for which we have . . . such a lot of material" (XII, 357). The basic material which he holds in his hands consists of the *carte-de-visite* photographs, pop art debris saved from the storm of time, floating on the waves of the present and preserved by Cornelia. With the photograph of Mary Cardew, a dead sweetheart from the past, he can connect with the past. James makes the transition from the overlit, glaring movie world of Mrs. Worthingham via Virgil, and it is through the summoning up of things past that White-Mason is able to reject her and her environment, in favor of the dim world of Crapy Cornelia, a world made up of the popular relics of a sentimentally reconsidered past.[48]

# 4

# English Popular Literature

## Iconic Analogy in "The Lesson of the Master": Saint George and the Dragon

To understand better "The Lesson of the Master," one must see it as James's saint's legend—his version of the legend of Saint George and the dragon—profaned, burlesqued, and converted into a narrative analogue. As a bit of transformed hagiography, it comes off as a joke by which James presents his most deeply felt and basically unchanging attitudes to the kind of austerity he feels necessary for a serious writer's life and to the danger of marriage and the propagation of children. By taking into account the legend of Saint George (the slayer of the smoke-breathing, fire-making dragon, the converter to Christianity of pagan people and the savior of England during the Crusades) as the operational metaphor of the tale, the reader may find it easier to choose between two possible interpretations seemingly presented side by side. Was Henry St. George, the "master" of the tale, genuinely concerned with "saving" and converting Paul Overt, the budding genius, *for* the glory of England and literature, or *from* Marion Fancourt, the princesslike maiden from Asia, so that he could marry her himself when the time came? Are we to take seriously the advice that influenced Paul Overt's career, given by the master first in the smoking room at Summersoft and then in St. George's cagelike study, or are we to see it as the ironic preparation for selling the young man short?[1]

That the tale is ironical James himself has clearly told us in his preface to the volume of the New York Edition that contains "The Lesson of the Master." What the irony truly consists of appears when the story is read as a carefully clued-in reinterpretation of the life of Saint George as it appears in *The Golden Legend.* James accomplishes this by a technique in which his own viewpoint is made quite clear by certain iconic or indexical references to a work of literature. Perhaps his strategy in "Benvolio" comes closest to the one we find in "The Lesson of the Master" because the tone is comic and the resolution is left to the reader at the close of the story in a kind of do-it-yourself ending. However, a close reading or rereading consistent with the analogue leaves no room for doubt as to the ending intended by the author. *The Golden Legend,* so familiar to every English reader who had seen innumerable illustrations of the Christian warrior overcoming the dragon, from the Burne-Jones stained glass window to the coin of the realm, presents a tale of the patron saint of England rich in icons that lead a subterranean life in the texture of the story[2] (fig. 39). If followed clue by clue, it decides for us that James's point of view is not that of Paul Overt but his own. Who the dragons are and who the saint is in this story are unequivocally determined by analogy.

To reach this conclusion, one must read the story twice. James frequently stated, either through fictive characters or through his own letters and critical writings, that he expected his reader to give his prose a second reading.[3] The key to the existence of the analogue exists in section 2 of the six-part story. Paul Overt, an aspiring young writer with a successful book set in foreign lands, attends a country-house weekend at an eighteenth-century Adam house and meets Henry St. George, a distinguished "master" of English prose (whose work has deteriorated and has never fulfilled its high promise), together with St. George's wife. The latter had declared that she once made her husband burn a book because she thought it was bad, after which Paul remarks to Marion Fancourt, a beautiful young woman with whom he will fall in love, " 'St. George and the dragon, the anecdote suggests!' " James continues, "Miss Fancourt however did not hear it; she was smiling at her approaching friend."[4] (This is later changed in the New York Edition, clearly for the sake of emphasis, to " 'St. George and the dragon is what the anecdote suggests!' Miss Fancourt, however, didn't hear it; she smiled at the dragon's adversary").[5]

Although the reader may not pay attention to this statement, the analogy between Henry St. George and the Saint George of legend is a directive to the reader (who has learned from previous examples of the same iconic analogic technique) that he must, unlike Miss Fancourt, "hear it" and watch out for it. In this way James plays fair with the reader. From this point the burden is on the reader to follow the clues to decide for himself what the author meant. In "The Middle Years," a story written five years later, James will speak through the character of Dencombe, who is "amused once more at the fine full way in which an intention could be missed," for "on a first perusal" his young friend, Doctor Hugh, "had failed to guess" what Decombe has "tried for," and he had to read the story a second time.[6]

Here in fiction James makes clear his technical arcaneness and the necessity for the reader's rereading and very careful scrutinizing of the narrative strategy. The reader is cooperator in "The Lesson of the Master." Part of the fun of reading the story is skirting the danger of missing James's intention. In his preface, he exposes to us his "lively impulse . . . to reinstate analytic appreciation, by some ironic or fantastic stroke, so far as possible, in its virtually

Figure 39.   Sir Edward Burne-Jones, *St. George Killing the Dragon*, 1865
             *(Private collection)*

forfeited rights and dignities."[7] This indicates the force he sees in the "fantastic stroke," by which he may mean the analogue of the saint's legend, in making us use our heads to test "whether the very secret of perception hasn't been lost."[8]

There is a development in James's use of figurative and linguistic analogy. During the 1880s, he identifies himself as a painter, using the "brush stroke" and coloristic terms to build up his "picture." In the first paragraph of the opening section of the story, Mrs. St. George is presented as a figure "in the crimson dress which made so vivid a spot, told so as a 'bit of colour' amid the fresh, rich green" (VII, 213). James will continue to describe her and her red dress, one among her other consuming and destroying attributes, to build her up as the dragon of the legend, the devil in Henry St. George's life. In her red dress, sitting among those who did not go to church with General Fancourt, who has just returned from Asian lands and pagan ways with his beautiful daughter Marion, she greets the returned churchgoers Henry St. George and Marion Fancourt with " 'Ah, here they come—all the good ones!' " (VII, 219), and puts herself thereby on the side of the Devil. When she declares that only once did she make her husband do anything—when she made him burn a book because she thought it was bad—Paul Overt, already shocked by her worldliness, her fashionableness, her love of society, is horrified by her ability to destroy the work of a talented man. This section ends on the note of the burning of the book and the realization by both Paul Overt and the reader that Mrs. St. George, dressed in the color of the Devil, is a lady dragon who, like the city-burning dragon of *The Golden Legend,* burns books. St. George and Miss Fancourt, called "angels" (VII, 219) and "angelic" by the nonchurchgoing guests, seem invested with sanctity.

Section 2 opens with Miss Fancourt expressing her tremendous enthusiasm for Paul Overt's novel *Ginistrella,* with continued references to Mrs. St. George's nonangelic qualities, her "profane allusions to her husband's work" (VII, 244). Balancing this there is a further pressing of Saint George's historically heroic characteristics, which come out "in little installments" (VII, 224). The heart of section 2 builds up the intimacy between Miss Fancourt and Paul Overt: the presentation of Miss Fancourt as a desirable, sympathetic, artistic person with ambitions to write a novel, and the "profane observation" (VII, 231) by Paul that the burning of St. George's book by Mrs. St. George suggests the legendary Saint George and the dragon—a correspondence, as we have already noted, that Miss Fancourt "did not hear" (VII, 232). Later that day Mrs. St. George takes a walk with Paul, and the "perfect red wall [of the park] which all the way on their left, made a picturesque accompaniment" (VII, 233) seems to have been introduced as another "red" attribute of the dragon-devil, Mrs. St. George. Her conversation now is limited to the worldly aspects of the house's noble owners. Mrs. St. George again closes the section on the note of her ill health, for "her strength was not equal to her aspirations" (VII, 234).

The word "aspirations," the last word in section 2, could be considered a pun, referring also to the dragon's aspirations, which are clouds of smoke, for section 3 now opens in the smoking room at Summersoft, the weekend house. That the mood is medieval and early Christian, involving the historical period of the Saint George legend and early conversions to Christianity, is suggested in the references to the place as "rather a bower for ladies who should sit at work at fading crewels rather than a parliament of gentlemen smoking strong cigars" (VII, 234). Paul Overt is called an "insincere" smoker (VII, 235) (changed in the New York Edition to "faithless" smoker, perhaps an intensification by James of the early Christian element, which in turn stresses the Saint George icons). The men are dressed in "bright habiliments" (VII, 235), indicating the colored smoking jackets, no doubt, but the words chosen have medieval connotations. Ironically, we are told that St. George, married to a smoke-breathing dragon, is not allowed to smoke by her, and the confusion between wife and cigarette is one of the jokes of the scene. "'Have you got one yourself?'" "'Do you mean a cigarette?'" "'Dear, no! a wife.'" "'No; and yet I would give up my cigarette for one.'" "'You would give up a good deal more than that'" (VII, 236).

In this scene dominated by smoke—an icon of the dragon when it menaced the population of the Asian town—Henry St. George, having begun to discuss wives through the connection between smoking and being prevented from smoking by Mrs. St. George, proceeds to discourage Paul Overt from taking on "'The idols of the market—money and luxury and "the world"'" (VII, 239). "'Don't become in your old age what I am in mine—the depressing, the deplorable illustration of the worship of false gods!'" (VII, 239). This chapter involves many items of the saint's legend and a further identification between Henry St. George and Saint George of the Christian legend. In fact, the repetition of such words as "false gods" and "idols of the market" seems to repeat the actual language of the Saint George chapter in *The Golden Legend* by Jacobus de Voragine, which was available to James in the Caxton version and which William Morris was to publish with several illustrations by Burne-Jones, as part of a revival of interest in heroic medieval English folklore, a few years after this story was written. In it Saint Ambrose refers to the miracles of Saint George when "he destroyed the temple with all its false gods."[9] When Saint George pretends to Dacian that he will "worship the idols," his body is "burnt with lighted torches";[10] so Henry St. George makes himself a martyr by fire when he says, "'But to show you that I'm still not incapable, degraded as I am, of an act of faith, I'll tie my vanity to the stake for you and burn it to ashes'" (VII, 239). "'Look at me well and take my lesson to heart'" is the gist of this section.

" 'for it *is* a lesson' " and the lesson is multifold (VII, 238). First, do not worship false gods; then "do" England, not life abroad.

Mrs. St. George is presented again in her worldly guise—"she likes great celebrities" (VII, 239)—and Miss Fancourt is presented as " 'an angel from heaven' " (VII, 242) and "life herself," a princess from "Asia" like the princess saved by Saint George, seeing things "as if from the top of the Himalayas." She is a "woman's figure which should be part of the perfection of a novel" but which turns "into smoke, and out of the smoke—the last puff of a big cigar—proceeded the voice of General Fancourt" (VII, 243). The smoking scene ends with Mrs. and Mr. St. George, "an honourable image of success, of the material rewards and the social credit of literature" (VII, 245), leaving the scene in a costly carriage.

Section 4 opens at an art gallery where Miss Fancourt, who had seen no "private views in Asia" (VII, 247), walks off with St. George, and Paul begins to suspect the master of having more interest in a personal connection with the girl than he had admitted. Paul's visit to Miss Fancourt's apartment, colorfully decorated with "pottery of vivid hues" and "with many water-colour drawings from the hand . . . of the young lady" (VII, 249), included a discussion of Mrs. St. George's relation to her husband and of her lack of "care for perfection." On the other hand, Miss Fancourt felt " 'one ought to go in for it! I wish I could' " (VII, 251), and Paul Overt cannot "get used to her [Miss Fancourt's] interest in the arts he cared for; it seemed too good to be real" (VII, 253).

Section 5 is laid in St. George's study, built by his wife for his maximum production. "[S]tretching from the door . . . was a large, plain band of crimson cloth, as straight as a garden path and almost as long" (VII, 258), another way of saying that this is how Mrs. St. George leads her husband "down the garden path" and another way of presenting her with her dragon's red color, reminding us that she had also led Paul down the garden path at Summersoft with the red wall "on the left." The role of Henry St. George advances from the scene in the smoking room, where he claims he is a martyr to the worship of false idols, to this scene, where he is the savior saint proposing to " 'save' " Paul Overt, who is "overt," "open" to being saved or not, as only he may decide, for the literary glory of England. By this time Henry St. George has read Overt's work and sees him as strong enough to become a great writer. He says, " 'you *are* strong' " (VII, 260)—a figure of speech, introduced seemingly only to remind the reader of the master's martyrdom. Overt's reply, " 'Don't say that. I don't deserve it; it scorches me,' " recalls the saint in *The Golden Legend,* whose body was "burnt with lighted torches."[11] He confesses that he married " 'the mercenary muse whom I led to the altar of literature' " and that his life has been " 'a kind of hell.' " So " 'let my example be vivid to you,' " he adds. When Paul claims that the master's work has not been as bad as that, St. George declares that it is made of *carton-pierre,* combustible cardboard (VII, 262).

The Saint George parallels continue as Paul mentions how satisfactory it must be to have a son at Sandhurst and the master declares, "'Oh, I'm a patriot,'" as befits the warrior patron saint of England. But the "tragic secret that he nursed under his trappings" ("trappings" recalling the armor of Saint George, the"soldier's trappings" mentioned in *The Golden Legend*)[12] was St. George's sense of his own failure. Paul again brings up the incident of Mrs. St. George's burning of the book, a book that was about the master himself, a book that he wishes Paul to do over, and which, one feels, is actually being done in this story. When the master tells Paul that even the sympathetic Miss Fancourt could not really understand his mission and that actually the artist is a corruption in society but is committed to his "'consuming ache'" (VII, 269), Paul finally chooses his fate, that of the artist, as life on the highest terms, higher even than being married to Miss Fancourt. St. George then pledges himself with his "'sympathy'" and his "'help,'" with his "'highest appreciation, my devotion,'" to help Paul "'stick to it—see it through'" (VII, 270).

Section 6 shows that Paul has learned St. George's lesson by heart—"to have tested and proved its doctrine" (VII, 272), that of concentration and elimination of all but work. News that Mrs. St. George has died and that her husband mourns her deeply is followed by his suspicion that "if Mrs. St. George was an irreparable loss, then her husband's inspired advice had been a bad joke and renunciation was a mistake" (VII, 273). This still does not prevent Paul from reading over his manuscript and from seeing that he could make it better. He remembers the master's "'Stick to it—see it through'" part of the lesson, and he does see it through for two years. On his return from the Continent, St. George appears to Paul no longer as a savior but as someone who is imposing martyrdom on him. "His face was red and he had the sense of its growing more and more crimson . . . his cheek burned at intervals as if it had been smitten" (VII, 277) when he learns that the master is to marry Marion Fancourt. By leaving for Europe he felt he had made what he considered St. George's treachery "too easy—that idea passed over him like a hot wave" (VII, 278).

When St. George, for Paul now the "mocking fiend," appears at the party, he stands "before the fireplace" (suggesting the fires the dragon had started). Paul's confrontation with the master also takes place before the fireplace, from which the master had moved away but to which he returns ("they had met in the middle of the room. . . . Then they had passed together to where the elder man had been standing"). James arranges this in detail to place the conversation against the blazing fire. After Paul indicates that he feels the master had not "'acted fair,'" St. George explains that he did this because "'I wanted to save you, rare and precious as your are'" (VII, 282) and that he himself has stopped writing and that Paul should consider "'the warning I am at present'" (which to Paul means "he *was* the mocking fiend," since the warning seems to be that while Paul was away St. George took his girl). The final turn of the screw would be that St. George after marriage "should put forth something with his early quality."

> Greatly as he admired his talent Paul literally hoped such an incident would not occur; it seemed to him just then that he scarcely should be able to endure it. St. George's words were still in his ears, 'You're very strong—wonderfully strong.' Was he really? Certainly, he would have to be; and it would be sort of revenge. *Is* he? The reader may ask in turn. . . . The best answer is that perhaps he is doing his best but that it is too soon to say.

When Paul's new book appeared, the master found it "magnificent." "The former has still published nothing, but Paul Overt does not even yet feel safe. I may say for him, however, that if this event were to befall he would really be the very first to appreciate it; which is perhaps a proof that St. George was essentially right and that Nature dedicated him to intellectual, not to personal passion" (VII, 284). The ultimate lesson of the master is that the artist must sacrifice everything. He must become "'a mere disenfranchised monk'" (VII, 269). In functioning at one's highest level of creativity, one must give up "'personal passion.'"

How does this incorporated legend and how does the manner in which it has been incorporated help the reader choose one of two possible interpretations of St. George's role? Does he save the young writer from destroying his talent, or does he cheat Paul Overt out of his young woman? Having followed through thus far the icons of Saint George, the savior of England and of the fire-aspiring dragon, Mrs. St. George, who burns his book, whose spirit presides over the smoking room, who represents the devil and the idols of the market, whose color is red, whose soul is worldly, who loves celebrities and the show of society, the reader, to make up his own mind, must go back and review the story. Was St. George right in predicting what marriage to Marion Fancourt would lead to? The reader must now pay closer attention to the manner in which James has presented Marion Fancourt.

The master had warned Paul away from Marion in section 5 in his study, for simply by being a wife and a mother she would necessarily force the young writer to earn money for the protection of her young. But a strong part of the argument that St. George is being crafty in steering Paul Overt clear of Miss Fancourt depends on the fact that she seems to be presented as "angelic," as contrasted to Mrs. St. George. She seems to be, by her own word, sympathetic to the arts; she has attempted to write a novel, and her clothes are "aesthetic drapery" (VII, 226) as opposed to the "aggressively Parisian dress" (VII, 218) of Mrs. St. George. Miss Fancourt's dress is of a "pretty grey-green tint" (VII, 220) in contrast to "the red dress" of the trinketed lady (VII, 216).

However, even in the very first section of the story the rereader will see that James is beginning to break down the angelic version of Miss Fancourt, but in a muted and recessive way. It is noteworthy that she "has magnificent red hair," a color that bodes no good. Red hair is not always a sign of evil in James's fiction. Milly Theale's hair color is a token of her being a symbolist, fin de siècle heroine—thin, dressed in black, diseased—as are so many other Continental heroines of the time, but in no sense evil. Although Miss Fancourt's clothing is something "in which every modern effect has been avoided," because of this it has "therefore the stamp of the latest thing" (VII, 220). In other words, she is as fashion-conscious as Mrs. St. George, perhaps more so, since her "aesthetic drapery" of section 2 is seen again as "conventionally unconventional, suggesting tortuous spontaneity," which Overt excuses because he is attracted to her (VII, 226).

In fact, at the very opening of section 2 Miss Fancourt is described as being "insatiable" in the eyes of her father, both as to her reading matter ("'She reads everything—everything'") and as to her appetite for people: "'He introduces everyone to me. He thinks me insatiable'" (VII, 223). So was the dragon of the saint's legend threatening "the indifferent maiden" (the Asian princess with whom we are at first to connect Miss Fancourt, hence the allusions four times to Asia, twice to India, to indicate her exotic provenance), for he ate up all the livestock in Libya and then was fed a maiden chosen by lot each year to hold his insatiable appetite at bay.

A guide to the technique for assessing the real personality of Miss Fancourt is presented in the impression Paul gets from St. George's face. "The text [of the man] was a style considerably involved—*a language not easy to translate at sight*. There were shades of meaning in it and a vague perspective of history which receded as you advanced" (emphasis mine). Paul's conclusion that the "story came out as one read, in little installments" (VII, 224) might be a microcosm of what we must do as we read this story. As Paul talks with Marion we see her beyond *his* seeing her. *He* is caught by her sense of life and her beauty; *we* are struck by the meaninglessness of her comments. When Paul says she should not bother to write a novel since "'It's so poor being an artist'" as compared with being "'a person of action,'" she answers, "'But what is art but a life—if it be real? ... I think it's the only one—everything else is so clumsy!'"—a cliché underlined by her next comment, totally unrelated to it: "'It's so interesting, meeting so many celebrated people'" (VII, 228). This comment aligns her with the story's obvious dragon, Mrs. St. George, who "likes great celebrities" (VII, 239). Nor does Marion get the bon mot Paul had made about Saint George and the dragon or apparently "did not hear it," in spite of the illusions Paul has about her intelligence (VII, 232).

In section 3, the smoking room scene, the two men rave about the beauty and vitality of Marion, and, though Paul calls her "'an angel from heaven'" and St. George agrees, the latter also describes her as having "come back from Asia with all sorts of excited curiosities and unappeased appetites" (VII, 243), repeat-ing the attribute of insatiability of the dragon of the legend, an attribute never even given to Mrs. St. George. Then her figure emerges in Paul's fancy and turns into smoke, another attribute of the dragon. But it is section 4, which takes us to Marion's drawing room, that her environment is pictured as the dragon's lair. Her room is "painted red all over" (VII, 249). Whereas the obvious and so far only acknowledged dragon, Mrs. St. George, only *wears* red, Marion *lives* in a red environment. James mentions the color of this room three times, calling it also "the bright, red, sociable, talkative room" (VII, 252) and "the personal red room" (VII, 256), so that the reader will remember it was red, the same color as Mrs. St. George's dress and the color of Marion's hair. In fact, it is very hard to figure out why for aesthetic reasons a woman with red hair would choose a red room, and this underlines another fact about Miss Fancourt: her undeniable poor taste and her provincial dependency on fads. Whereas Mrs. St. George was trinketed and furbelowed, she took her cues about dress from Paris, the acknowledged arbiter of such things. Miss Fancourt is influenced by the "artsy-craftsy" taste of the moment in London for pseudo art. Her room was "draped with the quaint, cheap, florid stuffs *that are represented* as coming from south-ern and eastern countries, where they *are fabled* to serve as the counterpanes of the peasantry" (VII, 249) (emphasis mine), in other words, fakes. The author speaks of her "aspirations" as he had of Mrs. St. George's, in this case being both "noble and crude, and whims for whims he liked them better than any he had met" (VII, 253). After all, had not the master fallen genuinely in love with *his* dragon (VII, 262)?

In section 5, in St. George's study, St. George goes into greater detail about how and why marriage is a trap for the serious artist committed to his work. Paul, thinking of Marion, asks St. George whether the case is not differ-ent "'when his wife is in sympathy with his work?'" The master answers that "'often, they think they understand, they think they sympathize. *Then it is that they are most dangerous'*" (emphasis mine) (VII, 264). This is the first time that the reader can see Marion's sympathy as something to be avoided, some-thing far worse than Mrs. St. George's worldliness. When Paul admits to being in love with Marion, St. George claims he has done a few favors for him in that direction. However, Paul, who wants to live on the highest plane, is convinced finally that he should give her up if he seriously wants to realize his talent.

In her final appearance, at her engagement party, Miss Fancourt is totally changed. The reader can see her complete transformation into the "mercenary muse" whom Henry St. George (who has ceased to think of himself as a writer) is about to marry. Here "she was in white, there were gold figures on her dress, and her hair was like a casque of gold" (in the New York Edition James eliminates the word "like" and makes "her hair a casque of gold" [NY, XV, 89]). She is now the personification of the gold standard. Person has become symbol. Her red hair is no more, having turned into the gold of money, and her happiness has now a "kind of aggressiveness, of splendour" (VII, 279). Paul, of course, does not see her change; she simply looks marvelous to him, but the *re*reader (if not the reader) can see she is a tableau of money. The money motif is carried out in the words "it cost her nothing to speak to one in that tone; it was her old bounteous, demonstrative way." It occurs to Paul that she "was so happy it was almost stupid—it seemed to deny the extraordinary intelligence he had formerly found in her" (VII, 279).

At this point we see that Paul's apprenticeship in hard work has really begun to divest Marion of her angelic qualities. But although he may not be ready yet for the bitter acknowledgment of Marion's mediocrity, we are. It is quite clear by the end of the story that the worst dragon of all is the girl he might have married; she is worse than Mrs. St. George, who at least had the ability to create the circumstances propitious for the kind of writing St. George could do. Marion has no sense of business; she has none of the virtues of organization that St. George mourned when his first wife died. The only kind of life St. George or anyone could lead with this provincial "culture-vulture" would be a totally uncreative one. When St. George says to Paul, " 'Consider, at any rate the warning I am at present' " (VII, 283), he not only was dead serious but he was right.

I think that by taking this iconic voyage through the story the reader convinces himself that St. George was the true savior of the young writer, that he preserved him for the glory of England as the patron saint of England should, that his strictures to keep to the English scene, to avoid encumbrances, to concentrate, to " 'stick to it, to see it through' " were worth the necessary sacrifice of personal happiness. " 'Well, you can't do it without sacrifices; don't believe that for a moment. . . . I've made none. I've had everything. In other words, I've missed everything' " (VII, 265). When Henry James put two alternatives before the reader, as he had done in "Benvolio," the choice really had already been made. When Paul Overt rereads his manuscript and stays another year-and-a-half in Europe when he might have gone home to claim Marion, he has already made his choice, since "Nature dedicated him to intellectual, not to personal passion" (VII, 284). The device of the legend of Saint George and the dragon which pervades "The Lesson of the Master" underlines the perils that James saw the contemporary artist as facing, and it is therefore clear that Henry St. George speaks for Henry James.

It is this way of reading the story that resolves the alternative interpretations that the story poses on first reading. The comic descent of the early English Saint George into the confines of Ennismore Gardens creates a Victorian saint's legend, fraught with mild profanity and impertinence, much like James's mock-epic, "The Velvet Glove." Both stories illustrate his continuing interest in making his own variations on literary forms to create analogues for contemporary behavior. Perhaps the transformation of Paul Overt into a saint himself, a martyr of art, which, in the late nineteenth century, had taken the place of religious dedication and self-deprivation, may illustrate a further expansion of the analogue. We may conclude with James in his preface to the New York Edition that "the logic of such developed situations" had indeed "imposed itself all triumphantly."[13]

## Baroness Tautphoeus's *The Initials*: A Small Boy and a Grown-up Novel

Even before the age of twelve Henry James was an acute literary critic—only at that stage he could not offer reasons for his judgments. Although he "fondly hung" over *The Lamplighter,* a juvenile novel by the American Maria Cummins, he also knew it was not a "grown-up" book, though he "had only" his "secret reserves" about that judgment. It was his interception and reading of a present his father had bought for his mother, *The Initials,* which made him see "how right I had been. The Initials *was* grown up and the difference thereby exquisite; it came over me with the very first page."[14] *The Initials,* written by the English novelist Baroness Jemima Tautphoeus (1807–93), a book of over four hundred pages in very small print, was published in America in 1850. It is pretty rough going, for the plan of the book is episodic, though there do occur (with the suddenness of a home run and the reality of true life) crises which have no real build-ups to warn us of their arrival.

The hero of the novel is a young Englishman, Alfred Hamilton, the second son in an English noble family, who has come abroad to learn German. In Germany he boards with a family in which there are a stepmother and her husband, Madame and Mr. Rosenberg, with their two daughters, Crescenz and Hildegarde. Alfred falls in love, first with the first daughter and, second (and presumably forever), with the second. The first daughter is the prettier but the sillier one, and she is soon affianced to Major Stultz, over twenty years her senior, for she must marry or be a governess. There are innumerable encounters between Crescenz and Alfred, flirtatious and bickering in nature, before her engagement, her little dangerous flirtations after the engagement, an outbreak of cholera, and the cholera death of Mr. Rosenberg.

The most charming part of the book, however, is that part of the story which functions as a frame. The "Initials" of the title refer to a letter the young English traveler receives, signed by the initials A.Z., a letter that intrigues him and that has been sent by a Countess Zedwitz, an old friend of his father's, with promises to introduce him to her friends and to lodge him while in Germany. The countess is a charming woman who has a titivating, if not exactly flirtatious, relation with him. But his main emotional entanglements are with the two Rosenberg girls. There are literary references to Schiller's ballad "The Glove," used analogically to the girls' relation to Hamilton, and there is mention of Weber's *Der Freischütz*. Hildegarde reads a censored novel by George Sand, and, though Hamilton insists she stop reading it and she promises to return it, she is found reading it the next day.

Did this novel, *The Initials,* play any part in the way James worked his reading into his own fiction? It made a strong enough impression to have him record it as crucial to the growth of his imagination. We know that his memory was extraordinary, so we are not surprised to see reappearing similar situations in many of his stories that were written in the 1860s and 1870s. The tone of the novel is something that we can find in almost undiluted form in James's *The Europeans,* a novel that apparently James did not "take very seriously."[15] The tone of the conversation among the young people in *The Initials* finds its way into James's novel in the trio of the young man, Felix Young, and two sisters, Gertrude and Charlotte Wentworth, one pretty and the other, who becomes Felix's bride, plainer but more spirited; Felix corresponds to Alfred Hamilton. But, in addition to this tone, there is the added background of Felix's sister, the Baroness Münster, the morganatic wife of the Prince of Silberstadt-Schrecken-stein, a background that is very close to that of the author of *The Initials,* for Jemima, Baroness Tautphoeus, was the wife of the Baron von Tautphoeus of Marquartstein, who was chamberlain to the King of Bavaria. When James wrote *The Europeans* his familiarity with Anglo-Saxon women married to highly placed German aristocrats was perhaps only through his early reading of *The Initials* and his knowledge of the author of that book.

The relation between A.Z., the count in the book, and Alfred Hamilton is repeated in the relation between Eugenia, Baroness Münster, and Clifford Wentworth, the very youngest male member of the Wentworth household, which Eugenia and her brother visit when they journey from Europe to America. However, there is nothing that is equivocal about A.Z.'s character, and she never shows a tendency to lie, which Eugenia does and which prevents her from making a good marriage with Robert Acton.

The books read in *The Initials* were among books that James read, if not as a boy then at least as a very young man. Count Raimund, cousin to the Rosenberg girls' dead mother, reads the poems of Heine, which James's father gave him on his fifteenth birthday. The young men and the girls discuss the Schiller ballad, "The Glove." We know that in his youth James read Schiller when he studied in Germany, a few years after he read *The Initials,* and George Sand's novels were James's favorite reading as a very young man. The concentration on flirtation and its varying positions in different European societies reminds us of "Daisy Miller" but even more of *Confidence* (1879), that novel written the year after *The Europeans* and "Daisy Miller," in which flirtation itself, as in *The Initials,* is used to screen a young girl's true feelings and to mask her love for someone who is not suspected of being the object of her attentions. The German background is somewhat similar to that of an earlier story, "Eugene Pickering" (1874), where *Der Freischütz* of Weber is brought in early in the story, and probably with symbolic intentions. So it is also brought into *The Initials* when Hamilton is reminded of the "wild huntsman" just before he is lost in the mountains while he himself is hunting.[16] Major Stultz, who marries Crescenz, is paralleled by the major who marries Mme. Blumenthal in James's tale. The title of an early James story, "Travelling Companions," may have come from a phrase in *The Initials* as well as from Goethe's *Italienische Reise*—Hamilton "found his travelling companions seated"—for the term was not too common at this time, and the young James may have absorbed every phrase and element of his first "grown-up" book.

Although the stories by James that seem to reflect an influence of *The Initials* were mostly written by 1879, in 1884 in "Pandora" there is an echo, especially in the imbedded references to "Daisy Miller" that Count Vogelstein makes when he watches Pandora Day on shipboard. When Alfred Hamilton arrived in Germany he had the intention of training to become a diplomat, and he had confided to the lady with the initials "his intention of writing a book" (I, 32) whose subject would be "Germany, and the Domestic Manners of the Germans, or something of that sort" (I, 32). So too Count Vogelstein of "Pandora" is a young diplomat, "appointed to the secretaryship of the German legation of Washington."[17] He also keeps a journal, since his object is to know everything about America: "he inquired with his eyes . . . with his ears, with his nose, with his palate, with all his senses and organs" (V, 358), and like Hamilton he ends up by paying attention to at least one pretty girl. Count Raimund, Hildegarde's aristocratic cousin who is insanely in love with her though he is engaged to marry Marie, knows everything about England, but it is "information . . . altogether acquired from reading." Count Vogelstein also shows this tendency when his reading of "Daisy Miller" helps him to place Pandora. Raimund, though, gives *The Initials* its sensational character by committing suicide on the eve of his wedding to Marie because of his hopeless love for Hildegarde. This shooting, in addition to cholera's striking twice in the novel, to Hamilton's being banged up, and to a couple of girls's being tossed out of sleighs, manages to cut into the monotonous, even tenor of the pursuit of pleasure in which the young men and women tediously engage. What James may have gotten from *The Initials* was a sense not of style or art but of an easy kind of relationship in Continental society—ironic between A.Z. and young Hamilton and comic between young Count Zedwitz and Hamilton. Dialogue and direction among a group of four or more characters while going on picnics and mountain climbing, while attending masquerades and balls, all presented in a light but not a frivolous manner, was perhaps a good way of having the international theme introduced to the greatest practitioner of that kind of story while he was yet a child.

There is a curious similarity between another novel of Baroness

Tautphoeus's, *Quits,* written in 1857, seven years after *The Initials,* and James's first novel, *Watch and Ward* (1871). The two books begin with similar incidents in the plot with merely a slight variation, a fact that suggests some intimate association and proof that James read it. *Quits* was the next most popular novel by the baroness. A young woman and her father are on a steamer when the father suddenly dies and the girl must be taken care of by someone. The young English lord, who is also a passenger and who protects her, turns out to be a distant relative. He brings her to his family in England, but his mother feels annoyed because an even closer relative, an uncle in London, ought to be responsible for her, for she worries that her son will become romantically involved with the girl. The girl's name, Leonora, is shortened to Nora by everyone in the novel, and we remember that James's heroine is also called Nora. James's initial episode is different but still quite close. His Nora is left an orphan when her father commits suicide in a hotel, also the first episode in the book, and the hero adopts her and brings her home to become his wife. Here she is only a child, not a nubile young woman, but in *Quits* Nora becomes a responsibility just as if she were a child. Her uncle, who reluctantly takes her in, also becomes very devoted to her, though he does not try to make her his wife. This is another one of the books James read early in life in which an orphanage and the lack of protection of the young, as well as their corruption by sinister and selfish adults, dominate the text. It was literally the first fiction he read and of a purely pop nature that his reconstructive genius saw fit to redo within limits.

## James and Miss Braddon: "Georgina's Reasons," *The Portrait of a Lady,* and the Victorian Sensation Novel

*"Georgina's Reasons"*

Because "Georgina's Reasons" (1884) was written to order in three installments for *The New York Sunday Sun,* a sensational newspaper, it has been dismissed as a potboiler. Because Georgina, the heroine, does things for which there seems little motivation, the story has also been judged one of "the least attractive of James's fictions," and merely an opportunity for James to develop one of his passive heroes.[18] A more rewarding way of reading it, however, is to see it as Henry James's pure "sensation" story, unique in his oeuvre. The demands of this genre James himself described in his 1865 review of Mary Elizabeth Braddon's *Aurora Floyd.*

In "Georgina's Reasons" James met those demands, but also enhanced the genre by applying to the central character his understanding of contemporary experimental psychology. Commissioned by the newspaper even before James had worked it out, the story was aimed at an audience of readers eager for sensationalism. Three weeks after James wrote to Thomas Sergeant Perry that he had agreed to write it, he recorded in his *Notebooks* an anecdote he heard from Mrs. Kemble about a young woman who married an army officer, had a child, and remarried without dissolving the first marriage.[19] The legal husband was then faced with the problem either of revealing the marriage and getting a divorce or of leading a bigamous life as his wife was doing. James wrote in his notes that "it was not made clear to me . . . what the heroine did."[20] Aside from the resolution, the plot was all arranged for James in the anecdote, and he proceeded to work it out. The way in which he did so shows that he had as models two of the most successful sensation novels of his time, *Lady Audley's Secret* and *Aurora Floyd,* both by Miss Braddon.

In his review of *Aurora Floyd,* he gives Miss Braddon credit for having created the sensation novel with plots noted for bigamy, arson, murder, and insanity. Several points in the review, especially remarks about the influence of Wilkie Collins on these "domestic mysteries," make it seem probable that James had read Mrs. Oliphant's unsigned essay on sensation novels in *Blackwood's Magazine* of May 1862.[21] Mrs. Oliphant had questioned the success of Dickens's horror stories written for a popular periodical: "To combine the higher requirements of art with the lower ones of a popular weekly periodical, and produce something which will be equally perfect in snatches and as a book, is an operation too difficult and delicate for even genius to accomplish."[22] This is the kind of challenge James would take up. Why should a story written for the people not be good?

Given the germ from real life (Mrs. Kemble's anecdote), James wrote about a "singular" young woman who keeps her first marriage secret, abandons her child who then dies, harasses a woman companion to death, commits bigamy, and reduces a man of honor to misery for the rest of his life. Bigamy, murder, and insanity, if not arson, are thus the components of his "sensation" story. Georgina Gressie, his baleful heroine, has characteristics drawn from both Lady Audley and Aurora Floyd, although the latter was a victim of passion rather than a cold-blooded criminal like Lady Audley. Georgina borrows from Aurora her imperial air and her height and from Lucy Audley her cold smile and her incapacity to love anyone but herself. It is clear from a reading of these stories of bigamy that James's tale borrows heavily from their machinery. From two recently published letters which James wrote to Miss Braddon in 1911 we learn that he considered her books deserving of his close attention. He not only called her "a magnificent benefactress to the literary estate,"[23] but he recalled, "I used to follow you ardently, and track you close, taking from your hands deep draughts of the happiest of anodynes."[24] It becomes clear when we read Miss Braddon's novels along with "Georgina's Reasons" that James did indeed track her close, for he borrowed extensively from her narrative techniques, while still containing his drama within the international framework of his fiction of the 1880s.

James presents his heroine with several echoes of the works of Miss Braddon. Georgina's bigamy is discovered in the same fashion as the heroine's in *Lady Audley's Secret*. As George Talboys, Lady Audley's first husband, recognizes his wife in a portrait and learns thereby that she has married someone else of great wealth, so Raymond Benyon, after his wife has sworn him to secrecy about their marriage, learns that the portrait of a Bourbon princess in the Royal Palace in Naples is a double for Georgina Roy, née Gressie, who is also now married to a very rich man. Georgina's resemblance to a princess and her possession of queenly attributes also harken to *Aurora Floyd,* whose heroine is "queenly" and "taller than most of the throng." The suggestions of royalty about Georgina continue in her new name, Roy, and in the description of her New York house as a travesty of the Royal Palace in Naples. In contrast to the palace, with its "high saloons, where precious marbles and the gleam of gilding and satin made reflections in the rich dimness,"[25] Georgina's parlor is "an immense, florid, expensive apartment, covered with blue-satin, gilding, mirrors and bad frescoes" (VI, 75). The technique of travestying an interior by repeating its elements in a parallel but downgraded structure was first used by Miss Braddon. Lady Audley's room was presented as filled with "cabinet pictures and gilded mirrors" and "the looking-glasses, cunningly placed at angles and opposite corners by an artistic upholsterer, multiplied my lady's image."[26] Lady Audley is finally immured in a *maison de santé* where her rooms are a grotesque version of her boudoir. "The wan light of a single wax-candle . . . was multiplied by paler phantoms of its ghostliness . . . in those great expanses of glimmering something which adorned the rooms, and which my lady mistook for costly mirrors but which were in reality wretched mockeries of burnished tin," while she sat amid "all the faded splendor of shabby velvet and tarnished gilding and polished wood" (L, 255). James, the art critic, would have especially noted and been impressed by the clever technical use of paintings and décor by Miss Braddon, a method which he was to use many times himself.

The heroine of *Lady Audley's Secret,* Lucy Talboys, is the twenty-year-old wife of a poor young man who leaves her and their newborn infant to make his fortune. Lucy, dissatisfied with her lot and without regard for anyone else but herself, changes her name, becomes a governess, abandons her child, and commits bigamy when she marries an older nobleman. When her husband returns, she throws him down a well. After her husband's nephew recognizes her activities and her real identity, she burns down a hotel to kill him. Bigamy, arson, and attempted murder end in her own confession of insanity. James's heroine—a "fair girl, with a beautiful cold eye, and a smile of which the perfect sweetness, proceeding from the lips, was full of compensation" (VI, 13)—resembles lady Audley, the "blue-eyed" charmer with "flaxen curls" and "a smile of fatal beauty, full of lurking significance" (L, 143). From Lady Audley's loveless nature ("I do not love anyone in the world") comes the heartlessness of Georgina, who also wants to be married to money and power. James translates Lady Audley's "strange laugh" (L, 18) into Georgina's "short, liquid, irrelevant laugh" (VI, 15), her "unanswerable laugh" (VI, 24). Finally, like Lady Audley's, Georgina's chief reason for her peculiar behavior is her quarrel with her parents.

The queenly heroine of *Aurora Floyd,* in contrast to the pert little Lucy, is infatuated with her father's groom, marries him as a schoolgirl and, thinking him dead, remarries. She is accused of murder when her husband's body is found, but she is proven innocent and all ends well. James has also borrowed the physical characteristics of Aurora—her resemblance to Cleopatra mentioned more than once, her imperial effect, and her great height—for his Georgina, as well as her "absurd infatuation" (VI, 22). Georgina, the "insolent queen of his [her husband's] affections" (VI, 14), "perceived a certain analogy between herself and the Empress Josephine. She would make a very good empress. . . . Georgina was remarkably imperial" (VI, 16). When Georgina is called "the Twelfth Street Juliet" who "dismissed her Brooklyn Romeo" (VI, 25), we recall that Aurora Floyd's mother, a former actress, had fascinated her husband in the role of Juliet. In addition, Raymond, James's hero, has been given a stammer, a conversion of Aurora's first fiancé's limp.

However, beyond the resemblances in plot and character, beyond the bigamy, murder, and madness common to the sensation novel, the common denominator in Miss Braddon's two famous novels and James's story is "the secret" on which all of the tensions are based. It is twofold in both *Lady Audley's Secret* and in James's story. The first secret is bigamy; the second is the heroine's insanity. The first secret lies back of Benyon's dilemma in James's tale, for Georgina decides that "if I choose to keep it [her marriage] a secret," so must Raymond. This he must do because of his innate sense of integrity, on which Georgina depends, but since he refuses to commit bigamy as his wife has done, his life is ruined. The great correction made by James of Miss Braddon's novels is to show how Georgina's willfulness operates in Benyon's consciousness and how it converts him into one of James's "poor young gentlemen," straddling the two worlds of Europe and America.

The second secret, insanity, is a touchier problem. In Miss Braddon's novel Lady Audley finally confesses to her own insanity and is locked up. Indeed, her behavior seems quite consistent and reasonable; her confession sounds like a sane description of her disease and not like the report of an insane person. Georgina's insanity, on the other hand, never admitted by her, is perceived from her unbalanced behavior by two of her intimates, Mrs. Portico, a family friend, and her husband, Raymond Benyon. Yet a full understanding of Georgina's insanity escapes them. Raymond simply blurts out, "'You are insane,'" when the cold-blooded heroine tells him cheerfully that she is now the mother of another man's son, even though she admits that she has allowed Raymond's son, their child, to die. Mrs. Portico, "frightened . . . into compliance" by this "demented" girl's behavior, dies from not being able to deal with her contradictory personality.

In his review of *Aurora Floyd* James had written that Lady Audley was "without a heart, a soul, or a reason." It is the last word, "reason," that he takes up to use as the title of his story, for Georgina presents many reasons for her eccentric behavior, all of which are irrational and self-contradictory. As Lady Audley's chief "secret" is that of her insanity, so Georgina's "reasons" are the evidence for her irrationality. In fact, they represent a casebook representation of the psychopathic personality, characterized chiefly by a lack of stability and continuity of motives. James reveals Georgina's own "secret" by lining up the most preposterous, contradictory, and cold-blooded "reasons" a woman might conjure up to explain her actions.

Her erratic behavior, as well as the reasons she gives for it, classifies her as a psychopath, suffering from a nervous disorder that was just being recognized in the early 1880s. The *Oxford English Dictionary* records a use of the word "psychopath" that appeared in 1885 in the *Pall Mall Gazette* and that emphasized a moral side to the medical definition: "Besides his own person and his own interests, nothing is sacred to the psychopath."[27] The British psychiatrist J.D. Pritchard had earlier separated moral disorders and moral insanity from other forms of insanity, though it was not until 1888 that Koch categorized distinct psychopathic infirmities and Kraepelin listed the different variants.[28] William James, studying nervous disorders in France from 1882 to 1884, must have been concerned with this form of "moral insanity," though we have no evidence in his letters that he and Henry discussed the subject, which was in the air. This moral issue would also be the way in which James, writing twenty years after Miss Braddon, would bring his interpretation of the sensation story up to date. Actually William James used the term in 1890 in his *Varieties of Religious Experience* when he described George Fox as "a psychopath or *détraqué* of the deepest dye," a man whose "mind was unsound."[29] In 1896 William James is quoted as defining a psychopath as someone with "an inborn aptitude to immoral actions in any direction."[30] In handbooks of medicine today the term psychopath has disappeared, though it can still be found in the textbooks of the 1930s. In Cecil's *Textbook of Medicine* (1937), the psychopathic personality is defined as follows:

> *Condition of Mental Instability* (Psychopathic Personality, Constitutional Psychopathic Inferiority). . . . There may be undue, disturbing prominence of instinctive demands, perverse instinctive tendencies; peculiar lack of responsiveness to ethical standards with a consequent disconcerting tendency to lie and steal; or lack of the stability and continuity of motives which are so helpful for a productive life.[31]

Psychopaths, or those suffering from what are now termed antisocial diseases, frequently exploit their own personal attraction and are often quick to take advantage of other people's weaknesses; Georgina and Lucy used their charm to the hilt.[32] If James was writing a contemporary sensation story he would have to bring contemporary medical attitudes to a depiction of insanity. Whereas Lady Audley proclaims her insanity and is removed from society through her own diagnosis, Georgina's self-evident psychopathological personality ruins Raymond Benyon and Mrs. Portico.

James attempted two things in his tale that are too frequently thought contradictory. One was to hold the interest of the reader of a Sunday sensation paper; the other was to maintain the rigorous standards he set for his fiction. He succeeded remarkably well by fusing the conventions of the sensation novel with the growing contemporary scientific interest in abnormal behavior. Georgina, whose "singularity" Stevenson recognized when he called her "that far-different she,"[33] appears to hold her own with Lucy Talboys and Aurora Floyd. At the same time, as an American character and a product of the mind of Henry James, she is presented within the frame of reference of the experimental psychology of the 1880s.

## *Miss Braddon's* The Doctor's Wife *and* The Portrait of a Lady

If, as I have argued elsewhere, *Madame Bovary* acted as a seminal model for the character of Isabel Archer, linking her to Emma Bovary, whose author, according to James, had represented "the state, actual or potential, of all persons like her, persons romantically inclined," then Miss Braddon, too, probably influenced *The Portrait of a Lady* via her Bovary novel, *The Doctor's Wife,* for in those days James did "track" her "close." "Miss Braddon is brilliant, lively, ingenious, and destitute of a ray of sentiment." So James in 1866 describes the author whose two sensation novels had acted as such a spur to his own sensation story for a sensation newspaper, the *New York Sun.*

In 1864, the year after *Aurora Floyd,* Braddon published *The Doctor's Wife,* a clever and obvious translation of the basic situation in *Madame Bovary* and one of the first such to appear. Isabel Seaford is a young woman bred on romantic novels who identifies with Edith Dombey among others, and she expects a glorious aristocrat to meet her and make her his wife. She is courted and won by a young country doctor, George Gilbert, and she therefore becomes Isabel Gilbert, the two first names, incidentally, of the heroine and hero, if one may call him that, of James's *The Portrait of a Lady.* A friend of the young doctor is Sigismund Smith, author of sensation novels and pieces for the press. (Isabel reads an author called Algernon Mountfort.) Also like Isabel Archer, Isabel Gilbert has a "pale face" and "black hair" and "tawney yellow" eyes. "There was no one like her." She had picked up her novel—reading it in a day school in the Albany Road, Albany the town being also the place, only in America, where Isabel Archer had formed her tastes in reading, although her reading was more of historical than romantic novels. "Sigismund sold his imagination and Isabel lived upon hers," for the "impalpable tyrants" she read about "ruled her life." In this sense she is close to Emma Bovary. "She wanted her life to be like her books; she wanted to be a heroine, unhappy, perhaps, and dying early."[34]

Isabel Seaford acted "as if she resided in a balloon," the figure James was to come to use always as a symbol of romance (DW, 15). "She's waiting for a melancholy creature with a murder on his mind" (DW, 15). Her father is a villain, but his villainy is concealed until it is needed to bring this novel into the sensation pattern. She marries Gilbert because "she wanted the drama of her life to begin," and by doing so "Isabel forgot she had a Destiny" (DW, 36, 42). This reminds us of Isabel Archer, a young woman, as James wrote, "affronting her destiny." She follows Emma's pattern completely by marrying a country doctor and becoming bored. She also, like Emma, falls in love with the heir to a large house and fortune, Roland Landsell, who corresponds to Rudolphe.

The plot begins to diverge when Roland tells of an adventure in which a man who threatens him with murder the next time he sees Roland will eventually turn out to be Isabel's father. Like Emma, Isabel Gilbert does not marry her ideal. James's Isabel does marry her ideal based on her notions of the beautiful and of the value of an aesthetic life. Roland in this novel seems to lead the kind of life that Ralph Touchett leads, with a large house and a picture gallery which he explains to Isabel. He has two nieces the way Lord Warburton has two sisters. Lady Ottendolyn, a young widow, seems to be the wife prepared for Roland, but she marries someone else. Since Roland is a poet, Isabel now walks around with Shelley's poetry and, like Isabel Archer, she is given things to read by her lover. This Isabel, like Isabel Archer, "was fond of everything that was beautiful, . . . pictures, and flowers . . . and wonderful foreign cities."

Isabel Gilbert is silly, like Emma Bovary, and in that sense, Isabel Archer is an improvement over the unimportant heroines. Isabel Gilbert is impressed by a fraudulent Raphael (DW, 83). When Roland takes her in hand, he changes her reading matter, introducing her to Robespierre and Carlyle's *French Revolution* (DW, 89). Ten years older than she is, he starts her off on a new course of reading, and his role is therefore here very much like Gilbert Osmond's in *The Portrait of a Lady*. Like Osmond, he was "capricious in his moods" (DW, 95). He gives a picnic in his home, Waverly Castle, and it looks as if Isabel is going to repeat Emma's disasters. Roland reflects both Ralph Touchett's point of view, which, in Ralph's case, is justified by his being ill, and Osmond's failure to amount to anything though he pretends he does not care about such matters. "'I might have been good for something in this world,'" Roland mutters on his picnic, "'if!'" (DW, 98). A friend tells Roland he should stop romancing Isabel, acting here like Ralph Touchett, and that he should leave, which he does; but he returns while Isabel Gilbert is selecting books in his library, of which he has given her the permanent use while he is in Corfu and other places. Suddenly she sees that he has come back. He seems to love her the way she wants to be loved. Her husband, just at that moment, contracts typhoid fever and dies. That should leave her free to marry her aristocratic lover, but soon Roland also dies in his country home, and he does the courteous thing by leaving her his considerable fortune (DW, 194), recalling the way Isabel Archer became rich.

The imitation of *Madame Bovary* is accurate up to a point, and that point is the character of Rodolphe-Roland. In the French novel, Rodolphe ditches Emma, but here he falls in love with her. The subject of the father's threatening Roland in his "adventure" is a Braddon touch, and Roland dies, very much the way Ralph Touchett does, because of her father, a conventional irony. The end of this novel might have set James thinking: "Let's take Isabel from here and see what happens to her when she becomes rich and how she conducts her life." But Isabel Archer, though mistaken in her ideals, is a cautious person and a responsible one. Isabel Gilbert's life exhibits her childishness, whereas Isabel Archer learns through her marriage and through her experience. Roland's leaving Isabel Gilbert a fortune is, in essence, like Ralph Touchett's leaving Isabel Archer his fortune, or rather his getting his father to leave her one. In these ways *Emma Bovary* seen through Miss Braddon's eyes may as well have had its effects on James's variation of Flaubert's heroine.

### Literary Ancestors of "The Turn of the Screw": *Temptation* and *Jane Eyre*

Temptation

In addition to the ghost-story told him by the archbishop of Canterbury, in which servants corrupt the children living in an old country house, the models furnished by Mrs. Radcliffe and Charlotte Brontë, referred to in "The Turn of the Screw" itself, and the choice of the journal in which James published his story all played a role in the genesis of the tale. *Collier's* not only represented for Henry James a wide audience, but it may have reminded him of the reading of his Manhattan childhood and of such a journal as its widely read Victorian predecessor, *Frank Leslie's New York Journal of Romance, General Literature, Science and Art*. One of the *Frank Leslie's* stories, called *Temptation,* printed anonymously but probably written by Tom Taylor, an editor of *Punch* best known for his melodramatic plays, readily identifies itself as the distinctly imitated source of "The Turn of the Screw." The story was serialized between January and June 1855 (New Series, vol. 1, part 1) and comprised six parts in sixty-five chapters. Since James does mention within the pages of "The Turn of the Screw" itself that the ghost story, told before Douglas's tale, had been "incomplete and like the mere opening of a serial," we truly are alerted to a serial story being somewhere in James's consciousness.[35] Following the format of a serial, James has divided his story into twenty-four parts.

*Temptation* was printed in two parts every month, and the division in "The Turn of the Screw" perhaps was to give the reader the sensation of reading a serial in a magazine over the period of a year, with short chapters of great dramatic tension. The central theme of *Temptation* involves a struggle for possession of an inheritance; and after the fashion of Victorian cliff-hangers it uses a series of subplots especially involving children who are victims of abuse and lack of caring—with a main villain called Peter Quin which James changed to Quint. Peter Quin's hatchet man is called Miles, "trained in the school of Peter Quin," just as little Miles in James's story learned from Peter Quint. In the *Frank Leslie's* tale the chief house is located in Harley Street. James, it is apparent, did not take the trouble to choose another suitable street—this one had been fixed in his mind for almost half a century. In the earlier tale, there are a brother and sister, Felix and Fanny, whom we may read as the originals of Miles and Flora, and it is Felix who dies, like James's other little boys, victims of family and adult coercions and cruelties. Peter Quin is dead when James's story begins because he had been hanged by his henchman Miles in the New York journal's series forty years before, a scene vividly illustrated with Quin hanging from the ceiling of his room (fig. 40).

Although there are other places where James may have found individual names, like Miles in an unimportant role in *Jane Eyre* or Quint as a name in a psychical research case record, *Temptation* has such a constellation of names that appear all together in one place—Peter Quin (both given and family name together, minus the final t), Miles, Harley Street for the chief residence, Griffiths if not Griffin (one of the storytellers in the frame of "The Turn of the Screw")—that the contextual simultaneity simply argues itself as the source.[36] The other isolated instances had to be pled for.[37] What supports this coincidental accumulation of names almost identical with the Tom Taylor serial is the carryover of the portentous evil created in the serialized novel—the insidious power of Peter Quin over the lives of more than one set of child victims. It is the fate of the children in this story that really forms the substance of "The Turn of the Screw."

James seems to have asked for a masthead for "The Turn of the Screw," and his old friend John La Farge responded with a picture of the frightened little Miles and a governess who was endowed with two right hands, one of them a dark one, cupping Mile's head as if influencing (or coercing) his imagination, an action perhaps related to her unconscious deviltry.[38]

This rehandling of so many elements in the Tom Taylor cliff-hanger unfortunately does not solve the problem of whether or not the ghosts in "The Turn of the Screw" are real or the products of the disturbed governess's anxieties,

# FRANK LESLIE'S NEW YORK JOURNAL,

### Of Romance, General Literature, Science and Art.

NEW SERIES.—VOL L.—PART 4.　　　　　APRIL, 1855.　　　　　16 3-4 CENTS.

## TEMPTATION.

Continued from page 141.

"I never knew that!" replied the ruffian, lowering his voice, and endeavoring to hide his confusion. "He was as bold a fellow as ever lived—and that's why his pals gave him the name of the captain! Some said he was the son of a gentleman—others of a lord; but no one ever knew the real truth, unless it was your grandfather."

His listener reflected for some moments in silence.

"I hope," added the speaker, "that you won't turn me and Bet out of the house—it is our bread!"

"On one condition," answered the heiress, "I will suffer you to remain!"

The countenance of Miles began to brighten.

"Which is, that you endeavor to gain the bread you speak of by honest means!"

"Honest means! continued the man, in a tone of contempt; "and who would give me credit for them—trust me, or employ me? No one! There is nothing so difficult to convince the world of as a rogue's repentance! I tried it! I had only committed one crime then: and not a creature would find plenty to employ me in evil; amongst the rest, your grandfather, and—there—you know the rest!"

"I will employ you!" observed Martha. The eyes of the fellow flashed with a momentary expression of triumph. If he could only worm himself into her secrets, he thought—obtain some hold upon her—he might defy the future.

"But not in the manner you suppose, and probably would wish!" continued the speaker, who had noticed and perfectly comprehended his secret thought. "From the nature of your past life, the haunts of the reckless wretches who live by violating the laws both of heaven and earth must be well known to you?"

"Well, miss, what if they are?"

"I will supply you with the means of visiting them. Use all your cunning to obtain some clue

MADAME GAMBLE ... OF THE DETECTION ... AND ... GOSSET.

fears, and frustrated passion for the "master" who resides in Harley Street. There are no ghosts in *Temptation*. There is only an evil governess in *Temptation,* not an insane one. It was left for James to render the ingredients of the tale—children rejected by their parents and left to the mercy of villains—in a late nineteenth-century way but still purporting to belong to the generation of Taylor and Brontë; this was an archaistic attempt not only to revive the terror that informed the popular literature of the periodicals of the 1850s but to bring it up to modern times.

*Temptation* as a story hinges on the copies of the will of Edward Trevanian, to a large estate. Edward dies on his twenty-first birthday, leaving his inheritance to the infant Fanny Maitland, the heir of his best and only friend. The plot concerns itself with the multiple abductions of the infant girl, who grows up in successive homes to be a marriageable young woman. The matter of the book is a struggle between two sets of opponents: on one side, a series of surrogate mothers who love and protect this little girl, as well as the young man who will marry her, and on the other, evil forces marshaled by Edward's father, Sir Richard Trevanian, who wants Fanny destroyed so that the inheritance can go to his son by his second wife. Sir Richard's chief "agent" is "his instrument of evil," Peter Quin, the owner of a center for refugee thieves and villains. Quin in turn directs and influences a man called Miles. Shift this function to Peter Quint and make Miles the innocent victim and we have the scenario for "The Turn of the Screw." Like James's Miles, the Miles of the *Frank Leslie's* serial is caught between Peter Quin, the evil "boss," and Quin's granddaughter, Martha, the good boss, who is one of the benign mother substitutes. After she takes Miles as *her* menial (in order to find Fanny) and wields power over him because she possesses documents that deal with his guilty past, Miles is tempted to break into her house and steal these documents but loses his life in the process.

The important factor about the thriller *Temptation* is the striking appearance all at once of names that occur in "The Turn of the Screw." Peter Quin, the villainous employee of Sir Richard Trevanian's, reappears in James's story as Peter Quint, both first and last names almost identical. Miles, also appearing in *Temptation,* is in a relation to Peter Quin that is very reminiscent of Miles's relation to Peter Quint in James's tale. Miles has been corrupted by Peter Quin and is used as his victim and "ready instrument of hatred to the innocent child."[39] And who is the innocent child? The small infant who grows up to be the heroine of the story, although a very passive one, is named Fanny; she suggests the eight-year-old Flora of James's tale, because she is always compared to a flower or is seen in relation to a plant. Martha's love for Fanny "was like one of those rare plants that bloom but once, producing but one solitary flower—her love for Fanny was that flower" (TE,144). Fanny not only takes the part of a "fairy flower" in a pantomime, but she is a "flower untimely forced

. . . a tender plant transferred to its native soil!" (TE, 264). After one of her surrogate mothers, Mrs. Du Bast, dies, she is succored by a Mrs. Watkins and becomes an actress. The atmosphere in the theatrical boarding house "is like that of a hot house—it forces the growth if not the vigor of the plant" (TE, 196).

Much of the action takes place in Harley Street (when it is not taking place in Martha's country house, Brierly Grange) and, when Martha Quin is legally parted from her evil grandfather and moves to a luxurious house, we are as much aware of it as the seat of power as we are in "The Turn of the Screw." We remember that when Mrs. Grose and the governess want to refer to the master they allude to the street where he lives rather than to him (in a kind of synecdoche). It is by his "Harley Street" residence that we know him. The residence of Martha Quin is also mentioned as "Harley Street," and always by the street rather than the house, as in "The Turn of the Screw" (fig. 41).

The name Griffiths is echoed by Griffin, the name of one of the storytellers in the frame to "The Turn of the Screw." Griffin is that particular one who is outdone by Douglas's tale; Griffin's tale had only *one* ghost, which a child, and the mother after him, see; but Douglas will have two ghosts. The remarks made by both Mr. and Mrs. Griffin in "The Turn of the Screw" show that they seem to have suffered a certain amount of defeat in this respect. Mrs. Griffin claims she can only understand in "a literal, vulgar way" something such as the love that the governess experienced. Griffiths, in *Temptation,* is a resentful old man, who resists with much noise his being directed in the law office by Clement Foster, a lad of tender years, his employer's son. Because of this resentment, Griffiths can be considered one of the evil characters in *Temptation.* Miles, Flora's ten-year-old brother in "The Turn of the Screw," is seen to be both the victim and the instrument of Peter Quint's evil devices, much as the Miles in *Temptation* is the victim and the "instrument" of Peter Quin's evil activities. Quin, however, takes his hire and cue from more powerful evil-doers like Sir Richard Trevanian, the arch-villain of the Taylor serial. However, even Tom Taylor, whose terror does not depend on ghosts, also suggests the effect on the human personality of violence and cruelty. Unlike James, who wanted the reader to let his imagination supply the sense of evil, Taylor specifies and comments on the effect of this evil. When Mrs. Grose uses "'Horrors'" (X, 122), we remember its appearance in *Temptation.* "'Poor thing! When I recollect the horrors she has gone through I don't wonder at it.'" (TE, 140). Peter Quin has no conscience, but like most men who are criminals "he had many terrors," and "it was not his conscience which disturbed him but his terrors" (TE, 144). We must remember that Miles in "The Turn of the Screw" is killed ostensibly by terrors. Taylor is a sophisticated writer and knows that "solitude breeds strange fancies," which may be the essence of what happens to the governess in James's story in the solitude of Bly. Taylor is also fully aware of

SCENE IN THE DRAWING-ROOM IN HARLEY-STREET.

Sally and Fanny were conversing in one of the strawberries.

Impelled by a curiosity she could not resist, she cautiously approached. The first words she heard rivetted her attention.

"It was the same gentleman, I am sure," said the dancer, "who, when your dear mamma died, paid for the funeral, and gave the five guineas for you! He said that he had discovered your family, and that, in a few days, a lady—a real lady, rich and good—your own mamma—would claim you!"

The child looked at her doubtfully: she remembered the two separate attempts that had been made upon her liberty and life. She feared that the fine promises of the stranger concealed some new danger.

"What are you thinking of, Fanny?" continued the speaker?"

"My mamma was good," replied the orphan; "but she was poor! Young as I was when they took me from her, I remember our solitary home—so poverty and misery! I think I see her now," she added, "with her dark, sad eyes, as she used to gaze upon me, and call me her only treasure! It cannot be my mamma!"

"Perhaps she has become rich!" observed her companion.

The child shook her head doubtingly. She remembered the cold, unsympathising manner of the brother of Madame Du Bast, and had no confidence in any change of fortune of which she was the herald.

"What motive can he have?"

"I don't know!" exclaimed the orphan; "I cannot suppose a reason why cruel men should seek me out—and yet they have done so! Sally—dear Sally," she added, throwing her arms around the neck of the dancer, "do not—for pity's sake, do not tell him where I am! They will kill me—I am sure they will! Have you told Mrs. Watkins?"

"No!"

"Barry?"

"Oh, yes!" replied the girl; "I have no secrets from him. You know we are to be married soon! He cannot endure that I should appear in public! He is earning a great deal of money! You are to live with us then, and we shall be happy—oh, so happy!"

The orphan gently laid her head upon her shoulder, and wept in silence. Her adopted sister started as she felt the warm tears of the desolate little creature trickling down her neck.

"Are you not happy, now?" she asked.

"I was happier with you!" replied the child; "for you loved me."

"And does not madame?"

"She is kind to me—very kind to me! But her love is not like yours! I have fine clothes—but I hate them; masters—they weary me! I would rather have a kiss or a kind word from you and our dear old landlady, than all the new frocks and lessons in the world!"

"But does madame never kiss you?" demanded Sally, who could not comprehend why so much bounty should be lavished without a corresponding amount of affection.

"She praises me!"

The reply drew tears into the eyes of the listener. She felt that her purpose, whatever it might be would be defeated, unless she contrived to interest the heart of her pupil in the task to which she had devoted her: the extreme sensitiveness which rendered Fanny so susceptible of coldness or kindness, might else defeat her object.

Unobserved by the children — Fanny was little more than a mere child — she hastily withdrew. Her mind was made up. She at once determined to fly from England, and bear her pupil with her. Barry soon afterwards joined the speakers in the garden. Miss Mellon had sent him to seek them. Again the visit of the mysterious stranger, his conversation with Sally, and the fine promises he had held out, were discussed. It was agreed that in the event of his making a second visit, she should refer him to Mrs. Watkins and the painter.

"You can trust to our prudence!" said the young man; "for affection is ever cautious! Besides we will call the poor blind lieutenant, who is always asking after you into our councils! We shall soon be able to judge whether he means honestly or not by you!"

With this understanding they returned to the house, and shortly afterwards took their leave for town in the carriage of Miss Mellon.

That same evening, when Fanny, as usual, offered her pale cheek to the kiss of Madame Garrachi—as she bade her "Good night," the unhappy woman caught her in her arms, and drew her gently towards her.

"I must speak with you, Fanny!" she said "you are young—very young; but I think you will understand me!"

Her pupil regarded her with surprise: she had a grateful as well as a sensitive nature, and feared she had offended her.

"Are you angry?" she asked.

"Angry!" repeated madame; "and with you—whose patient sweetness might disarm even merited reproach! No, Fanny—no! I have been to blame! A heart like yours requires more than fine clothes!"

The child looked up in her face and quietly smiled.

"You love Sally!" continued the speaker.

"Dearly, madame!"

"Dearer than I did Felix?" demanded the lady. "Should you lose her, it would be long—very long—before another supplied her place!"

At the name of her former playfellow, the eyes of Fanny filled with tears.

"You will fill it!" observed the singer, with a sigh; "be dear to me as he was! My only hope of peace in this world depends on you! I would see you happy, brilliant, and admired as I once was! Do you comprehend me?"

Young as she was, her pupil did comprehend her; not the purpose which the speaker had in view—but that the wound she had received was too recent to admit another to supply the place of her lost boy.

"I have been thoughtless—very thoughtless!" she murmured; "but it is so sweet to feel that we are loved!"

"You are, Fanny!" exclaimed madame; "you are beloved!" We will quit this place! You shall have companions of your own age—the bloom will return to your cheeks—mirth to your eyes! I have been selfish in my sorrow—but I did not intend to be unkind! I have another motive for having been here!" she added, thoughtingly; circumstances have convinced me that your enemies have not yet abandoned their designs upon you—nay, do not look so terrified—my affection shall guard you, and defeat their projects!"

This was said in order to prepare Fanny for the flight she meditated: it accorded but too well with her own terrors and the information she had received from Sally.

"Yes—let us go!" she eagerly answered; let us leave this place!"

"You will accompany me, then?" exclaimed Madame Garrachi, in a tone of triumph.

"Anywhere with you," was the reply, "If you will only love me!"

The very next day, the late prima donna of His Majesty's Theatre began to make arrangements for her departure, which she announced to Miss Mellon, who felt both surprised and hurt at a resolution which she was powerless to oppose. The prepara_ the corrupting influence on the dislocated and abandoned children in his novel. "'I begin to think Peter Quin has corrupted your heart'" (TE, 132).

The atmosphere of the world of parent substitutes and their charges, of those who would be good influences and those whom they fight against and who are out to destroy the children for money, entered into the imagination of James early. It is very different from the sentimental treatment of the similar subject in Dickens. Taylor seems aware of what happens to the character when neglected and abandoned. Oliver Twist remains pure in heart and is affectionate, but not Edward. It takes the loving attention of a number of foster mothers to keep Felix and Fanny happy, and Felix dies as did Edward. It is significant that the boys die and the girls escape being totally victimized in both Taylor and James. Peter Quint in "The Turn of the Screw" might be considered the tool of the Harley Street master, since the master has allowed him control over the children. If James's main job was to make a "little tragedy" to show up "the exposure . . . the helpless plasticity of childhood that isn't dear or sacred to *some* body," then the master can be considered just as evil in James's terms as the ruthless Sir Richard, who not only abandons his eldest son Edward (by his first wife) to a cruel clergyman but who wants the heiress (who will divert Edward's fortune from Walter, Sir Richard's son by his second wife) to be drowned.

In addition to the names, *Temptation* contains plot structures very similar to those in "The Turn of the Screw." There are sets of brothers and sisters, biological or sentimental, who act in unison against others. One set includes Walter and Emily Trevanian, who, when small, are preferred by their father to Edward, the abandoned child. They adopt a conspiratorial attitude toward Edward when they return to England, reminding us of the similar conspiratorial stance that James's governess thinks Miles and Flora take against her. Here are Emily and Walter Trevanian conning their virtuous half brother, Edward: "Emily . . . played a song to him—Walter read; in short he was surrounded with those nameless attentions so consoling to the invalid. Gradually they made the intended impression upon his naturally grateful and susceptible nature. There was something inexpressibly shocking in the calculated hypocrisy of being so young, like twin serpents, stealthily twining themselves around the heart of the youth whose death they watched for" (TE, 5). This reminds one of the way Miles and Flora handled the governess, or the way the governess thinks they handle her.

The second set of siblings consists of Felix Garrachi and Fanny, after Madame Garrachi, the fourth surrogate mother, takes the little abducted girl into her household. Her son Felix gets along like a brother with Fanny without any feelings of jealousy because he sees that she is only "the object of benevolence" and not "the real rival for his mother's affections." The description of the two children reads like the description of Miles and Flora in the governess's eyes:

"It was beautiful to watch the two children, the boy, his hair and eyes dark . . . the girl, fair . . . her features radiant with the holy innocence of childhood—her hair floating in masses of natural curls over her head and shoulders" (TE, 207). James's governess saw the boy Miles as "incredibly beautiful" (X, 32) and as for Flora, she "was the most beautiful child I had ever seen," and she comments on "the golden glow of her curls" (X, 72). She was, in fact, "dazzled by their loveliness" (X, 41). Felix actually dies like Miles in "The Turn of the Screw," suddenly, as his mother holds him, for Alberto Garrachi finds him dead. His wife says, "He died upon my bosom"; Fanny survives as Flora will.

The last set of siblings consists of Clement Foster, three years younger than Miss Harriet Wyndham, *Temptation's* governess, the girl he grew up with, hired not to take care of children but to assist the grown woman, Martha Quin, now rich. Deprived of an education by her evil grandfather, Peter Quin, she is to be taught as if she were still a child. Miss Wyndham is the "bad" governess, who wishes to exploit her employer, first by discovering her secret if she has one, and, second, by worming her way into her confidence so as to inherit her fortune. But, in addition, Miss Wyndham wishes Clement, a youth only sixteen years old, to propose to her, which he almost does before they both are interrupted by a visitor. This may be the model for James's governess's erotic behavior with Miles. Poor Edward Trevanian, severely beaten at school, learns to be "cold and apathetic in manner." Introduced to his half siblings, he sees that "they have never known what it is to miss parents' care" (TE, 4). When asked whether his mother is still alive, he answers that "not having heard directly or indirectly from her ladyship for the last ten or twelve years, I may be excused the question" (TE, 5). At school they tried to "debase and brutalize my mind with blows" (TE, 5) and "to break my spirit." Here the school corrupts, whereas in "The Turn of the Screw" Miles is sent down for corrupting the school. The day that Edward dies, on his twenty-first birthday, three men think they see his ghost, but it is actually Edward himself, still alive. He is killed actually by a "fatal aneurism, brought on by the harsh treatment he was subjected to in his youth" (TE, 33). Miles, in James's tale, dies in like manner, "his little heart, dispossessed, stopped" (X, 138). An aneurism is one medical possibility here; Miles may have had an undetected and neglected heart injury. The other maltreated child, Edward's heiress, Fanny, whose mother died at her birth, after a series of hair-raising adventures is found finally by Martha Quin, who has sought the one person she could love. When Martha finds Fanny has been taken away again, she secures the documents giving Fanny the right to her mother's fortune. From this act stems the interesting relation between two people, the granddaughter of the villain, Peter Quin, and his "slave" Miles, the "ruffian." It reminds one vividly of the relation between the governess and Miles in a power battle behind which looms the figure of Peter Quint, the "base menial" who was in the governess's eyes the real master of the household and the real master of Miles's imagination. Just as Miles is Quin's chief slave, so Miles in "The Turn of the Screw" is the ready tool of Quint's crimes.

The recurrent word "master" in "The Turn of the Screw," the name by which we know the irresponsible parent figure in Harley Street, is equally recurrent in *Temptation* and has a very special force. Mr. Griffith, the dastardly clerk in his employer Foster's ofice, must eat humble pie before Clement Foster, the master's young son. The appellation "master" is painful to the resentful and jealous Griffith and for this reason becomes a word to which the reader pays attention. Martha tells Griffiths that she shall " 'see your master in the morning,' " to which the author adds, "It was not intentional that the heiress employed the word 'master'—but in ignorance of the *usage du monde"* (TE, 143). When Martha inadvertently uses the term "master" to the sensitive Griffiths, he "colored deeply" (TE, 143). As Foster's head clerk he feels humiliated at referring to a youth as his "master," and he inadvertently addresses him as such. "He who had dreamed of a partnership with his boss has a youngster lord it over him: 'Master—Mr. Clement, I mean' " (TE, 323). His is asked by a visitor, "Where is your young master staying?" and Griffiths answers "bluntlly, 'He is no master of mine, I am his father's managing clerk' " (TE, 323). The servant George has *his* master, Clement Foster. Mrs. Everett has *her* master in Sir John Mordaunt (TE, 101). But the chief character to be victimized by *two* masters, Peter Quin and Martha Quin, is Miles in *Temptation.* After Miles finally hangs his master and fixes the corpse's dress to make it look like suicide, he apologies for the bad job by saying, "I am not a regular *valet de sham"* (TE, 141). This recalls to us that Peter Quint was a valet to the master in "The Turn of the Screw" or it is at least a conversion of this; "Peter Quint—his own man, his valet, when he was here!" (X, 47).

Martha's mastery of Miles is carefully analyzed: "It is not supposed that Miles, who had been trained in the school of Peter Quin, would leave any means untried to discover the abode of Martha whom he both hated and feared. Hated, for having subdued and humbled him—and feared from the power which her knowledge of his crimes had armed her with" (TE, 260). Martha, after Miles's murder of Quin, begins to become masterful, and Miles feels the pressure. "The assassin . . . began to feel that, in compassing the death of the agent, instead of obtaining his liberty, he had merely changed masters." This is important for understanding Miles's relation to the governess in "The Turn of the Screw." Miles in James's story is pressed between the ghost of Peter Quint and the governess, who takes charge of the children after Quint has left, just as Miles of *Temptation* is caught between Peter Quin and Martha Quin, after he has hanged the first.

The climax of the relationship between Martha and Miles is when Miles, shot as an intruder, is dying. Martha calls to him: " 'Tell me, child. Confess!

. . . implore for mercy'" (TE, 262). He answers, "'There is no mercy for me. No sooner was I out of the clutches of the *old devil,* your grandfather, than I fell into yours. I tried to release myself—and here I am!'" (TE, 262) (emphasis mine). This is strikingly close to Miles's last words in "The Turn of the Screw"; for this last confrontation between Miles and Martha Quin corresponds quite closely to the situation in which the young Miles of "The Turn of the Screw" finds himself just before *he* dies. He, too, is caught between Peter Quint and the governess, one of which is "'you devil.'" The latter word, the situation between two masters, and the name of the victim, Miles, seem to argue that James, whether unconsciously or consciously, was reliving the serial thriller of his boyhood.

After Miles dies, Martha has a relationship with Clement Foster, who will marry Fanny. Whereas her relation to Miles was like the diabolic one between the governess, Miles, and Quint in "The Turn of the Screw," Martha's relation to Clement is like the other aspect of the relation between the loving governess and the young boy in her charge in James's tale. There are a series of interviews between Clement and Martha which are very different from her interviews with Miles. Clement is young, like James's Miles. "'He is truth and honor itself,' she thought, 'ingenuous as a child, he will neither refuse his confidence nor deceive me.'" She says to him: "'There was a time when you used to confide to me all your boyish griefs . . . the struggles between duty and inclination . . . but now you have a sorrow which you brood over in silence.'" There is a passage in *Temptation* when Martha confers with Clement that corresponds very closely to James's governess's trying to get Miles to confess to her. "'I fear I have lost your confidence,' he attempted to argue away her suspicions." She responds, "'You have not replied to my question—you have merely evaded it. . . . Speak to me freely as you would to a dear friend—an elder sister or a mother!'" The entire dialogue reminds one of that between the governess and Miles in James's tale: "'Don't you remember how I told you . . . that there was nothing in the world I wouldn't do for you?'" and he answers her, "'you wanted me to tell you something.'" He tells her finally that he took her letter to the master from the hallway table on which she had put it (X, 131–33). The difference is that everything works out well in *Temptation,* and there are happy endings all round.

There is an important similarity between Miss Wyndham, the governess in *Temptation,* and the governess in "The Turn of the Screw." They both believe in ghosts! When Mrs. Everett, the housekeeper at Brierly Grange, and equivalent figure to Mrs. Grose, shows Martha the room where the "ghost of the murdered king was supposed to appear to Cromwell" (TE, 261), Martha asks her governess, "'Do you believe in presentiments?'" "As a matter of course, the governess did" (TE, 261). Clement, a realist, makes fun of all this. The governess is also jealous of the feelings Clement and Miss Quin share. Clement says to Martha, " 'My own dear good mother could not be more kind. But of course . . . you are much younger than she.' "

For those who argue that the governess in James's tale is unconsciously creating "demons" in order to get the indifferent master in Harley Street to react to her, the following descriptive passage about Miss Wyndham will indicate how anyone, including the younger (or older) James, would admire the astuteness and verbal dexterity of the author of *Temptation,* for the very conscious Miss Wyndham is a "very clever young lady, whose powers of mental calculations would not have disgraced a senior wrangler" (TE, 330). We are assured that "love with the governess was a calculation, scarcely a feeling—certainly not a passion. . . . Like a true mathematician, she only calculated the additional power of perseverance necessary to overcome an unexpected amount of indifference" (TE, 330). At nineteen, she attempts to force the sixteen-year-old Clement to propose marriage to her, relying for success on his innocence, and on the fact that they were like brother and sister when children. She flirts with Walter Trevanian "to excite the jealousy of her boyish lover" (TE, 322). Would not both these suggestions recall, first, the governess's relation to young Miles in the James tale, where, in the presence of the maid at dinner, they "feel shy in the presence of the waiter," just "like some young couple . . . on their wedding night" (X, 128), and, second, her unconscious desire to make the master pay attention to her by an extreme and desperate situation of her own contrivance? Miss Wyndham acts consciously, James's governess, unconsciously.

In addition to the structure of Martha's relation with both Miles, the hired ruffian, and with Clement, the young hero, Martha shares certain other characteristics with James's governess. She is obsessed with the search for Fanny, of whom she had grown fond because Fanny gave her "something to love and live for" (TE, 133), "someone to love and protect" (TE, 133). If the psychoanalytical theory demonstrates that the governess's hallucination is the result of her fear of not being loved by the master through her failure to get the children to love her, then there is another similarity between her character and that of Martha in *Temptation.* "The defect in Martha's [character] was the morbid fear that Fanny would cease to love her" (TE, 98). The very word "morbid" establishes Martha as belonging to the same personality type as James's governess. So James's governess, equally obsessed with her desire to protect the children and to counteract Quint's effect "on innocent little precious lives" (X, 51), combines Martha's and Miss Wyndham's traits. Both James's governess and Martha are therefore concerned with the evil done to children. Martha's chief worry is that Fanny will be corrupted, although the young "flower" and Clement resist all "temptations." After having been told where Fanny is, but finding her already gone, Martha says, " 'She must be sadly changed! They have corrupted her young heart' " (TE, 266). We are told of "the inability of Mrs. Watkins to protect" Fanny when Madame Garrachi wants to take her, but Madame Garrachi loves her and teaches her (TE, 267).

Madness, a recurrent theme in the sensation novels of the nineteenth century, is always present in "The Turn of the Screw," and as such it paves the way for the modern interpretation of the governess's hallucinations, a form of madness resulting from hysteria caused by sexual repression. The governess makes seven references to madness, six of them referring to herself, sometimes in an exaggerated sense; one she applies to the children. Madness or insanity is mentioned in *Temptation* a dozen times, more often than in James's tale, for both the good woman, Martha, and the bad guy, Walter Trevanian, the son for whom his father had hired all the crooks to see that Edward's will became invalid, are both considered mad. Edward himself had first been thought mad, to disqualify him from inheriting, and had been so maltreated that the author grants that his so-called madness was "the madness of sensibility newly awakened" (TE, 3). Whatever Martha does is considered madness by at least one other character. Martha is forty and Clement seventeen. Foster says, "She can never be mad enough to think of him for herself!" (TE, 267). This age difference would be equivalent to the difference between Miles's and the governess's ages in James's tale, though here it is actually twice as much. The atmosphere of madness is also at Brierly Grange, for there Sir John Mordaunt, the owner, who is still alive, is described by his housekeeper as " 'MAD—he must be mad!' " (TE, 101).

There are two situations where madness can refer to the actual states of *being* mad in *Temptation*. The first occurs when cruelty drives Edward to return the violence he suffered at the hands of his tormentors at school. The second occurs when Walter Trevanian's madness is referred to as a real thing, though we do not see it in his behavior, for there is more *calculated* deviltry in this novel than madness as such. But since so many characters are thought so often to *be* mad and so many references are made to their possible madness, James, if he read this novel, could have been given the idea of using madness for his own tale.[40]

Although Harley Street, Martha Quin's London home when she becomes rich, is the main site of the action of the serial, Brierly Grange, the house she rents in the country, is the site of the death of Miles when he is shot while house breaking. The presence of an uneducated housekeeper, Mrs. Everett, may have suggested Mrs. Grose, and the presence of a master, Sir John Mordaunt, who is distinguished by never being in residence, makes the resemblance to Bly and the circumstances surrounding the appearance of ghosts in "The Turn of the Screw" very strong. The household goes on, as at Bly, with no master and no mistress, until Martha arrives, and Miles is the intruder (like Bly's ghosts) when Clement fatally shoots him. Mrs. Everett is as happy to talk to Martha as Mrs. Grose was to talk to James's governess. "The female cicerone demanded nothing better than to reply to her. It was so long since she had found occasion to use her tongue, that the opportunity was a relief to her." The atmosphere at Brierly, therefore, is close to that at Bly: a house with an absentee owner, ghostlike suggestions, a down-to-earth housekeeper, and an intruder who breaks the peace and dies himself, after attempting to victimize Martha, now in charge of him.

Jane Eyre

William S. Petersen has devoted much ingenuity to a reconstruction of Henry James's opinion of *Jane Eyre* by digging it out of Mrs. Humphry Ward's introduction to that novel in the Haworth Edition of 1899–1900.[41] It seems more pertinent to determine the effect of Charlotte Brontë and of *Jane Eyre* in James's own fiction, since the act of criticism was for James, in the last analysis, the possession of a work and its incorporation into a newly created form. "To criticise is to appreciate, to appropriate, to take intellectual possession, to establish in fine a relation with the criticised thing and make it one's own."[42] I believe that it can be shown that in "The Turn of the Screw" James took possession of the persona of Charlotte Brontë and of certain basic structures in her novel *Jane Eyre*.

　　While the figure of Charlotte Brontë has been commented on (as implied in "The Turn of the Screw" as a prototype of the governess), the actual stuff from *Jane Eyre* has not been followed through. In the first place, just before or even while James was writing "The Turn of the Screw," he reviewed Clement Shorter's book on Charlotte Brontë. On February 6, 1897, James wrote of Shorter's book, "the decisive word about the unhappy family it commemorates has still to be written."[43] Perhaps James saw "The Turn of the Screw" as the decisive word. We know that James thought that the mixture in the public's mind of the lives and of the works of the Brontës was "the most complete intellectual muddle . . . ever achieved, on a literary question, by our wonderful public."[44] However, in 1897, at the end of the year when working on "The Turn of the Screw" (which, as he himself wrote, was simply a "shameless potboiler"[45] and for which he would make use of any techniques for creating horror that he could control), it seems that he went to *Jane Eyre* for some materials out of which to make his story and for techniques by which to tell it.

　　From Mrs. Gaskell's *The Life of Charlotte Brontë* James could learn that Charlotte's "finished manuscripts were copies . . . in clear, legible, delicate traced writing, almost as easy to read as print."[46] James's governess's manuscript in The Turn of the Screw" was "in old faded ink, and in the most beautiful hand" (X, 17). From Mrs. Gaskell's *Life* he could have read, "I will show you a heroine as plain and as small as myself, who shall be as interesting as any of yours."[47] James's governess makes herself as interesting as any heroine to the young man who was in love with her and who preserved her manuscript. Mrs. Gaskell tells us and James that Charlotte was thirty years old when she wrote *Jane Eyre,* and the governess in "The Turn of the Screw" is thirty years old, as Douglas indicates by some simple arithmetic, since he was twenty and she ten years older. Even though the presence of Miles in *Temptation,* along with Quin and Harley Street, argues for the main source of the name in "The Turn of the Screw," still Mr. Miles, the schoolmaster whom we meet on the first few pages of the Brontë novel and who then disappears, could be a supporting reminder to James of such a name. We know James was reading *Jane Eyre* because he had a discussion with Mrs. Humphry Ward about it just as he was writing "The Turn of the Screw" in 1897. We are not surprised to find that there is an episode in *Jane Eyre* which looks very much like the very heart of "The Turn of the Screw." In chapter 17 of *Jane Eyre,* when the world comes to Thornfield Hall for a party, Blanche Ingram engages in a venomous conversation with Rochester, designed to undermine his faith in Jane as governess. "'You should hear mamma on the chapter of governesses,'" Blanche says. Half of those "'she had had,'" she continues, were "'detestable, and the rest ridiculous, and all incubi.'" [48] Then, whispering in her mother's ear to indicate that a governess was within earshot, Blanche goes on to enumerate the governesses in her life and their vagaries. One of them had a relation with a tutor, a Mr. Vining.

> "He and Miss Wilson took the liberty of falling in love with each other—at least Tedo and I thought so; we surprised sundry tender glances and sighs which we interpreted as tokens of 'la belle passion,' and I promise you the public soon had the benefit of our discovery; we employed it as a sort of lever to hoist our dead-weights from the house. Dear mamma, there, as soon as she got an inkling of the business, found out that it was of an immoral tendency. Did you not, my lady mother?"
>
> "Certainly, my best. And I was quite right; depend on that: there are a thousand reasons why *liaisons between governesses and tutors* should never be tolerated a moment in any well-regulated house; firstly—"
>
> "Oh, gracious, mamma! Spare us the enumeration! Au reste, we all know them; danger of *bad example to innocence of childhood; distractions and consequent neglect of duty on the part of the attached—mutual alliance and reliance; confidence thence resulting—insolence accompanying—mutiny and general blow-up.* Am I right, Baroness Ingram of Ingram Park?"
>
> "My lily flower, you are right now, as always."
>
> "Then no more need be said; change the subject."[49] (Emphasis mine)

This passage showing the evil effects of a liaison between a tutor and a governess on innocent children can be said to be part of the central theme of "The Turn of the Screw," even though Quint is not technically a tutor.

James wrote in a letter that what he wanted to do "was to give the impression of the communication to the children of the most infernal imaginable evil and danger—the condition, on their part, of being as *exposed* as we can humanly conceive children to be.... I evoked the worst I could."[50] In other words,

James took the liaison, which would be, in Blanche Ingram's paraphrase of her mother's reasons, "the bad example to innocence of childhood," the "neglect of duty," "alliance," and "general blow-up" of the two lovers, and made it the work of ghosts in order to fashion an influence as bad as it possibly could be. Even if these ghosts are just the projections of the thwarted desires of the governess who takes the place of Miss Jessel and Peter Quint, her imagination has provided the typical liaison of socially inferior household employees with satanic overtones.

Before Blanche Ingram mentions the two lovers, Mr. Vining and Miss Wilson, she reminisces with her brother, Theodore, Lord Ingram, about all the governesses they could remember, "'What tricks Theodore and I used to play on our Miss Wilsons, and Mrs. Greys, and Madame Jouberts.'" Whereas Miss Wilson was "not worth the trouble of vanquishing," Mrs. Grey "was coarse and insensible; no blow took effect on her." Mrs. Grey may have suggested Mrs. Grose, gross and coarse. "Poor Madame Joubert," they had "driven to extremities."[51] She might be a kind of model for Miss Jessel.

Additional material from the novel filters through in significant manner. Early in "The Turn of the Screw" James alludes to the possible presence of "an insane, an unmentionable relative kept in unsuspected confinement" (X, 38). Does he not here give us the clue? Even before that reference the governess is introduced as "the youngest of several daughters of a poor country parson" (X, 19), reminding us of Charlotte, who was, however, the eldest daughter. When the real struggle begins to take place in "The Turn of the Screw," the weather changes into autumn. "The summer had turned, the summer had gone; the autumn had dropped upon Bly and had blown out half our lights" (X, 86). In *The Lesson of Balzac* in 1905, James wrote, "Why is it that in Charlotte Brontë we move through an endless autumn?"[52]

James has folded into "The Turn of the Screw" very clear-cut reminders of both Charlotte Brontë and of *Jane Eyre:* the manuscript in a fine hand; a heroine of thirty who is one among the many daughters of a poor parson and who enters into service as a governess; two mischievous children who have been exposed to the corrupting influence of a liaison between a former governess and tutor, both employees of the household as the valet Quint and Miss Jessel had been, and a heroine who wishes to make herself interesting to "the master," a term that reminds us immediately of *Jane Eyre,* all set in the autumnal world of Charlotte Brontë.

Another technical device in "The Turn of the Screw" may have been derived in part from a chilling story by Charlotte Perkins Gilman, "The Yellow Wall Paper," published in *The New England Magazine* in January 1892 under the pressure of William Dean Howells. Refused by the *Atlantic Monthly* because it was "so terribly good it ought never to be published," the story anticipates a specific feature of the first-person narrative of the governess in "The Turn of the Screw." In Gilman's story her first-person narrator is a sick woman who reveals herself gradually to the reader to be insane, though she tells her story as if she were completely rational. The difference between the insanity of James's governess and that of the doctor's wife in "The Yellow Wall Paper" is that the latter's is made clear to the reader at the end. She thinks she is a woman trapped in the yellow wallpaper on the walls of her bedroom which the reader learns from its details is in a room in an insane asylum. The full recognition of the narrator's mania blossoms forth only at the end of the tale, where it emerges from the complete rationality of the narrator's report.

James's technique never openly reveals that the governess's tale is really a hallucination, either in the story itself or in its frame. In "The Turn of the Screw" the reader must do at least "half the work" himself. But the precedent for treating the report of an insane person as if it were a statement of fact, which is the basis of James's technique, was undoubtedly "The Yellow Wall Paper." It is quite probable James knew about and read the tale because he was at this time in close contact with Howells. The latter reports that he "could not rest until I had corrupted the editor of *The New England Magazine* into publishing it."[53]

## The Dickens Imprint: "Julia Bride" and *Oliver Twist*

James maintained all his life what he called his "private altar" to Dickens (AU, 372). Scattered through his critical writings there are over fifty occasions when James brings Dickens in as an example or uses him as a comparison, rivaled only by the number of his critical references to Balzac and Shakespeare. He recounts his debt to Dickens in detail in his autobiographical volumes. Beginning very early with seeing Dickens on the stage before he could read him, "the force" of what he called "the Dickens imprint . . . however applied, in the soft clay of our generation" was first created by "the immense authority of the theatre," an imprint which "was to resist so serenely the wash of the waves of time" (AU, 68). This imprint seems to have become more legible as time went on, because James, as his work written after the age of sixty shows, dug down deeply into his youthful memories. It was the "authority of the theatre" again that late in life brought back *Oliver Twist,* which James had enjoyed so much as a boy. A letter to Antonio Navarro, November 1, 1905, refers to "when we met that evening [*Oliver Twist*] under Tree's fantastic influence,"[54] for Herbert Beerbohm Tree had in his dramatized version of the Dickens novel entertained James in the company of the husband of Mary Anderson Navarro, the actress. Three years after he saw *Oliver Twist* staged, James published "Julia Bride"

(1908), a short story utilizing his childhood memories. Elements snatched from Dickens's *Oliver Twist,* the beloved novel of James's boyhood, are tucked into it.

Julia Bride, the ironically named heroine, a much engaged, never-to-be-married beauty, vainly strives to obtain guarantees for her one great matrimonial chance, that of marrying Basil French, a member of a socially prominent New York family. Her various clandestine encounters in New York's great public rooms—the Metropolitan Museum of Art and Central Park—and her desperate behavior are like Nancy Sikes's meetings on the streets of London. In a close conference conspiring with an exfiancé in the New York out-of-doors, she exposes her plans "quite as if they had been Nancy and the Artful Dodger, or some nefarious pair of that sort, talking things over in the manner of 'Oliver Twist.' "[55]

This metaphorical use of the Dickens novel most closely associated with James's youth is the one and only specific reference to a Dickens classic in all of James's fiction. The fact that "the Dickens imprint" would not be legible for him until James became a sexagenarian is probably to be explained by James's late return to his childhood home after twenty years of expatriation. We may speculate that there is something of both Nancy Sikes and Julia Bride in Henry James, who plotted to attract his country's favor with the New York Edition of his collected works and who never lived to see that he was not to remain the virtual failure he seemed to be in the years that saw the publication of that unsuccessful edition as well as the publication of "Julia Bride." Julia relates to *Oliver Twist* in that she is a New York version of a streetwise urchin, just as Fagin's boys and girls are the London originals, for corrupted by him they scrounge and steal for him. In Julia's turn she has been corrupted by her mother and brought up by different fathers, as Oliver had also been.

In "Julia Bride" there are two definite references to *Oliver Twist* that reinforce each other. The first one describes Julia's meeting with Mr. Pitman, her much-divorced mother's second husband, so that she can get him to lie about her mother and tell the French family she wishes to marry into that *he* was the wrongdoer, not her mother: "it took them but three minutes to turn out, on either side, like a pair of pickpockets comparing, under shelter, their day's booty, the treasures of design concealed about their persons" (XII, 162). The great story about pickpockets is of course *Oliver Twist,* and the second reference, already mentioned, establishes this fact. It occurs when Julia Bride is to meet her other accomplice, her exfiancé, Murray Brush, "when she once more fairly emptied her satchel quite as if they had been Nancy and the Artful Dodger, or some nefarious pair of that sort, talking things over in the manner of 'Oliver Twist'" (XII, 181). By naming both the novel by Dickens and Nancy, its heroine, James specifically points to his consciously invoked literary analogy.

In looking at the parallels between "Julia Bride" and *Oliver Twist,* one must realize that Dickens permeates James's late tale only on a metaphoric level and that James planted the metaphor exclusively in Julia's consciousness. It is on this level that Murray Brush, in his destruction of Julia's matrimonial plans, her social death, and his self-centered exploitation of her connections, can be viewed as a parallel to Bill Sikes and Fagin. For being "patronized" by Murray Brush operates on Julia just as if he is killing her; he will indeed destroy her social life. Even when he calls her "Julia," his "'Julias' were somehow death to her" (XII, 184). Like Nancy, who has been offered a new life by the Maylies but who is destroyed by Sikes, so Julia reads "an immense fatality" in Murray's "face" (XII, 185). Nancy is maltreated by Fagin as well as by Sikes, for, after using her as a confederate, Fagin betrays her. Murray Brush is in this respect like Fagin as well as like Sikes, for he wants to use Julia to advance himself and his fiancée in society through Basil French. Julia feels Murray Brush will destroy her in using Basil French, just as Sikes had destroyed Nancy.

Sike's murder of Nancy is repeated figuratively in James's tale. Julia "had ceased personally, ceased materially . . . to exist for him, and the whole office of his manner had been more piously and gallantly to dress the dead presence with flowers" (XII, 187–88). This is a conversion by James of the sordidness of Nancy's life and murder into the rich upper-class life of these New Yorkers. Julia's desperation is the same as Nancy's. An echo of the most startling scene in *Oliver Twist,* Nancy's murder by Sikes ("The sun—the bright sun . . . burst upon the crowded city. . . . It lighted up the room where the murdered woman lay. It did. He tried to shut it out, but it would stream in. . . . God, how the sun poured down upon the very spot!") reappears transformed into a thought in Julia's mind.[56] She "saw as clear as the sun in the sky the exact manner in which, between them, before they had done, the Murray Brushes . . . would dish, would ruin, would utterly destroy her" (XII, 189).

Julia's mother, Mrs. Connery, bears some relation to Mrs. Corney—the workhouse mistress in *Oliver Twist* who marries Mr. Bumble, the beadle— beyond the mere resemblance of her name. Mr. Connery is Julia's mother's third husband, with whom she is now fighting, for like Mrs. Corney she has fought with all her husbands. To quote Dickens, "Now, Mrs. Corney that was, had great experience in matrimonial tactics, having, previous to the bestowal of her hand on Mr. Corney, been united to another worthy gentleman" (OT, 325). Mrs. Connery (like Mrs. Corney) criticizes her former husband, Mr. Pitman, for his "business slackness" (XII, 155). Mr. Pitman is a true Dickensian character, "like some pleasant eccentric ridiculous but real gentleman, whose taste might be of the queerest" (XII, 166), and so is his fiancée, Mrs. David E. Drack, exhibiting "a large complacency, a large sentimentality, a large innocent elephantine archness," and wearing "black brocade, with enhancements . . . that twinkled and tinkled, that rustled and rumbled" (XII, 171).

The slang of New York City is aimed to function in James's tale as does the slang of the gutter in Dickens's novel written in 1837, with reminders of the latter in such words as "dodge" (twice), "dish" (twice), and "pounce," "trap," "reeled." "Dodging" is a constant exercise in *Oliver Twist:* Fagin sends Bolter "to dodge a woman" (OT, 404) and to follow Nancy when she meets Brownlow. The "Court" in "Julia Bride" appears as the court also does in *Oliver Twist,* and although in James's story it is a divorce court, the child Julia has been forced to perjure herself just as if she were one of the juvenile criminals in *Oliver Twist.*

There are, moreover, images recalling those in *Oliver Twist.* Like Nancy, Julia was "condemned . . . to sit, to walk, to grope, to flounder" among "the lies, the perversities" surrounding her, like those that beset Nancy (XII, 114). When Julia thinks how she and her mother are treated "as if they had been antelopes or zebras, or even some superior sort of performing, of dancing, bear," we are reminded that Nancy is treated like an animal in *Oliver Twist* (XII, 159). " 'She's kept tolerably well under, ain't she?' he asked . . . in the tone of a keeper who has tamed some wild animal"; and again Sikes says, " 'I thought I had tamed her, but she's as bad as ever' " (OT, 384, 400). Julia meets Murray Brush during "a morning hour in a sequestered alley of the Park" (XII, 176). This corresponds to the dark alleyway of that part of London inhabited by Fagin and his associates. Julia's "untrammeled past" haunted "those devious paths and favouring shades" in the park (XII, 177). The place "reeked" with "old associations." She "had knocked about," and she would have to "dodge" memories. She tells the very much improved Murray what she wants, "in spite of feeling herself slip, while she did so, to some doom as yet incalculable" (XII, 180). This reminds us of how Fagin, when he knows Nancy has met someone outside his group, pretends to be nice to her, but he is like Murray Brush, for he is doing it only to betray Nancy to Sikes, who he knows will kill her. Murray even begins to sound like Fagin, with his "my dear child" repeated three times (XII, 183, 190); Fagin calls everyone "my dear" or "my dears." Like Nancy, Julia "knew inevitable submission," and she "had to surrender to the great grey blankness of her doom!" (XII, 185–86). The foreknowledge of Julia's ruin subjects her, when she arrives in her bedroom and flings herself on her face, "to the full taste of the bitterness of missing a connection, missing the man himself" [Basil French] (XII, 191). This scene imitates the one in *Oliver Twist* when Nancy, after her interview on the steps of London bridge, had "sunk down nearly at her full length upon one of the stone steps, and vented the anguish of her heart in bitter tears" (OT, 416).

From Dickens's novel we know that his real heroine is Nancy. She is not only the most complex character, but she is also the only person of Fagin's crew who is basically good, always loyal to her lover but also protective of those good people not doomed like herself. Julia, based on Nancy, is a correlative figure transposed into New York of 1908, and she is beaten, like Nancy, by those who might have helped her if they themselves had not been steeped in the money-loving society that had both horrified and amazed James when he experienced it in his 1904–5 trip to the United States. Julia is like Nancy, a keeper of stolen goods, because she has not returned to their original givers her six engagement rings. " 'I've kept them all, and they tell my story' " (XII, 167). The pathos of this statement unites her very language with that of Nancy Sikes. Julia's character resembles Nancy's in that she, too, cannot "turn upon" the selfish members of her own circle, like Mr. Pitman and especially her exfiancé, Murray Brush. When Mr. Brownlow asks Nancy to turn Fagin in, she refuses because " 'I'll not turn upon them, who might . . . have turned upon me, but didn't, bad as they are' " (OT, 412). So Julia vouches for Mr. Pitman's character to his fiancée although he cannot be made to " '*lie* for me' " (XII, 164), that is, for Julia, to favor her relation to her desirable possible fiancé, Basil French.

The opening scene of "Julia Bride," set on the steps descending from the upper painting gallery of the Metropolitan Museum (fig. 42), has a curious resemblance to a Cruikshank illustration for *Oliver Twist* also featuring a flight of stairs which the figures have descended. It is "The Meeting," one of the four scenes "intended to comfort and cheer" (OT, 410) but which, as James tells us in his childhood memories, "present themselves under his hand as but more subtly sinister, or more suggestively queer, than the frank badnesses and horrors. The nice people and the happy moments, in the plates, frightened me almost as much as the low and the awkward" (AU, 69) (fig. 43). This fear and sense of doom also invade the tale of the failed Julia Bride, who loses her chance for a decent life, as had Nancy Sikes, because of the exploitative people surrounding her.

Almost obliterated by the Dickens imprint in "Julia Bride" are the fainter marks left by the work of Mrs. Humphry Ward, whose *Robert Elsmere* was the most popular of the mid-Victorian novels dealing with the loss of Christian faith. When James wrote to Mrs. Ward in 1902, answering some of her questions about *The Wings of the Dove,* he remarked, among other things, that "Mrs. Stringham is a charming idea not carried out" (HJL, IV, 243). Here he possibly is referring to the portrait of Mrs. Annie Fields, whom he remembered with so much enthusiasm, and her relation to her "adoptive daughter," a relation which he seems to be enclosing within *The Wings of the Dove.* Although one is not aware of Mrs. Ward's appearing as a person in his novels, we know from established scholarship that James thoroughly edited and revised *Miss Bretherton,* her novel about an actress, and that *The Tragic Muse* shows clear signs of plot influence and scene similarity.

There is, however, a curious parallelism between *Marriage à la Mode,* Mrs. Ward's very popular novel published in 1908, and James's short story of 1908, "Julia Bride." Both are about the popularity and ease with which Americans get divorced and the effect of divorce on the happiness of the individuals

Figure 42.   W. T. Smedley, Frontispiece to *Julia Bride* by Henry James
(New York and London: Harper's, 1909)

Figure 43.   George Cruikshank, *The Meeting*, 1837–39
             Illustration for *Oliver Twist* by Charles Dickens.

involved. In Mrs. Ward's novel, Daphne Floyd, an American heiress, falls in love with a handsome young Englishman, Roger Barnes, who is penniless. Although he is not in love with her when he marries her for her fortune, he learns to love her and to adore their little girl. Daphne sees him innocently holding the hand of a young woman he had been engaged to before he met his wife and, in a fit of jealousy, divorces him with no evidence that he has been or plans to be unfaithful to her. He responds to the break-up of his family by deteriorating completely. Roger's little girl, whom Daphne has taken away, dies without his seeing her, and he himself is dying from tuberculosis when a friend, a Mr. French, convinces Daphne to go back to him to save him. Notwithstanding her offer, Roger refuses to go back to her and dies miserably.

Although demonstrating the mores of divorce, the too-speedy separation among rich Americans destroying the lives of the couple involved, *Marriage à la Mode* makes its points very differently from James's tale "Julia Bride," which shows, in a humorously oblique way, how the marital future of a young woman has been damaged without possibility of repair by the many divorces of her mother, for her own multiple engagements are simply a reflection of her mother's habits and neglect of her child's moral education. A further, seemingly random, association exists in the presence of a Mr. French in each work. In "Julia Bride" this is the name of Julia's aristocratic fiancé, who will never become her husband. It seems highly likely that either Mrs. Ward's novel influenced the short story or vice versa, and, unless we know more about the details of their appearance, we cannot say whether Mrs. Ward's book or James's tale came first. In a letter written to Mrs. Ward in 1906, James wrote that "I can't read new fiction" but, he continues, "I find the reading of other things [including some old fiction] a greater boon than ever" (HJL, IV, 415). This reminds us that *Oliver Twist* is behind "Julia Bride," just as Poe's "The Fall of the House of Usher" is behind "The Jolly Corner," both stories of the same date.

## Mrs. Oliphant and "Broken Wings"

Victorian England produced an interesting flock of women writers who led independent, difficult lives and supported themselves by journalism and by writing novels. Among them, besides Miss Braddon, was Sarah Grand, who is credited with having invented the term "The New Woman" and who had a bestseller with her novel *The Heavenly Twins* (1893). There was also the prolific Margaret Oliphant (1828–97). After Mrs. Oliphant's death in 1897, James wrote in his August letter for *Harper's Weekly,* "I know not if some study of her remarkable life and still more of her remarkable character, be in preparation, but she was a figure that would on many sides still lend itself to vivid portrai-ture."[57] In the story "Broken Wings" (1900), James appears to be paying, in the character of Mrs. Harvey, a graceful tribute to the touching and gallant figure of Mrs.Oliphant, the prolific, hard-working Victorian novelist, popular short-story writer, essayist, and contributor of a monthly "London Letter" to *Blackwood's Magazine.* But before we go on to that portrait, let us see what James's attitude was to her before 1900.

James, in his *Harper's Weekly* letter, expresses his wonder that "her love of letters . . . would be so great without even . . . on a single occasion, being even greater." Working "largely from obligations," she showed "in it all a sort of sedentary dash" (NN, 453). James ends his note on Mrs. Oliphant with "wishing that the timid talents were a little more like her and the bold ones a little less" (NN, 455). Even as early as 1883 James had, in his essay on Trollope, remarked that the quality of improvisation was as great in Trollope as in "the delightful Mrs. Oliphant."[58] In 1897, when A.C. Benson spent the night at Lamb House, James told him that, after Mrs. Oliphant's death, Henley had implored him to read her novel *Kirsteen* (1890), after James had confessed that he had not read it.

> Henley said, "That you should have any pretentions to interest in literature and should dare to say that you have not read *Kirsteen?*" I went back to read it, and was at once confirmed, after twenty pages, in my belief—I laboured through the book—that the poor soul had a simply feminine conception of literature: such slip-shod imperfect, halting, faltering, . . . down-at-heel work. . . . Yes, no doubt she was a gallant woman . . . but an artist, an artist![59]

He probably never knew that the article in *Blackwood's,* "Sensation Novels," which made such an impression on him as a young writer, was by the same writer of "slip-shod" work. James's "London Notes," written after Benson's visit and his reading of *Kirsteen,* takes account both of Mrs. Oliphant's lack of artistry and of her gallant working habits, and the last words of James's "Broken Wings" ("and now to work") show how, in spite of her neglect of rigorous art in her numerous creations, Mrs. Oliphant shared with James the habit of constant hard work.

The outline of the story "Broken Wings" occurs in James's *Notebooks* in his entry for February 16, 1899 (N, 282): "Don't let me let go either the idea of the 2 artists of some sort—male and female—I seem to see them—as a writer and a painter—who keep a stiff upper lip of secrecy and pride to each other as to how they're 'doing,' getting on, working off their wares, etc." (N, 282). Since Mrs. Oliphant was working probably harder for a market than any other woman novelist of her time in England, and since her husband had been a painter, also working at odd jobs, like making designs for stained-glass windows, one sees from James's preliminary note that he probably had already read her *Autobiography* that had appeared in 1899. By September 17, 1899, during a time when James was producing a story a week—very much the same speed with which Mrs. Oliphant herself got her stuff out—he had written "Broken

Wings," as well as an article on the future of the novel, a travel piece, and other varied literary assortments, very much in the manner of Mrs. Oliphant, who worked at any and every literary turn for the money.

In his preface to volume XVI of the New York Edition, in which he included "Broken Wings," James wrote that he could not "disinter again the buried germ" of the story. The admonition of "such adventures as poor Mrs. Harvey's [the heroine who corresponds to Mrs. Oliphant], the elegant representative of literature at Mundham," and "the appeal of mature purveyors obliged, in the very interest of their . . . marketable freshness, to dissimulate the grim realities of shrunken 'custom'" awaited, James wrote, the proper moment for his dramatizing a situation recorded in his notebooks; and under "some forgotten touch, however, at its right hour, it was to round itself."[60] The "forgotten touch" probably was the publication of the *Autobiography* of Mrs. Oliphant in 1899, when James's stirred memories were reinforced by a record of her activities and her own statements about her predicaments, so close to Mrs. Harvey's.

There are certain other factors that clearly indicate that Mrs. Harvey was the "vivid portraiture" of Mrs. Oliphant that James's 1897 "London Notes" had suggested she deserved. Perhaps in addition to the *Autobiography* James had read his friend J.M. Barrie's introduction to Mrs. Oliphant's posthumously published *A Widow's Tale and Other Stories* (1898), in which we read that at the end of her life, after the death of all her children, her dwindling popularity and loss of income, Mrs. Oliphant "was less the novelist now than a pathetic figure in a novel," a figure that would lend itself to "vivid portraiture" in a short story.[61] Perhaps James and Barrie had discussed Mrs. Oliphant over a meal at the Reform Club, for James surely indicated in his 1897 "London Notes" that he agreed with Barrie's judgment that every one of her more than one hundred books "could have been improved by the comparative duffer" (WT, vii). However, Barrie concluded his introduction with, "Mrs. Oliphant wrote so many short stories that she forgot their names and what they were about, but readers . . . will not soon forget this one"—that is, her own story (WT, viii).

James owned Mrs. Oliphant's *Autobiography,* which appeared a year after her death and his tribute to her in *Harper's Weekly*. We know from Benson's testimony that he "laboured through" *Kirsteen* and what he thought of it. In addition, there existed on the shelves of James's Lamb House library a copy of *Miss Marjoribanks* (1866) by Mrs. Oliphant. In 1875 James had reviewed in the *Nation,* anonymously, Mrs. Oliphant's book of stories, *White Ladies*. He also owned Lawrence Oliphant's *Piccadilly* and had reviewed in 1878 that author's *The Tender Recollections of Irene MacGillicuddy*.[62] The Oliphant kinship and association, to say nothing of the "puffing" of her friend Stuart Straith's costumes in her *Blackport Banner* articles, bring Mrs. Harvey of "Broken Wings" close to Mrs. Oliphant, who had used her column in *Blackwood's* to "puff" Lawrence Oliphant's work.

"Broken Wings" is the story of Mrs. Harvey and Stuart Straith, two practitioners of literary and artistic wares who mistakenly believe each other and are believed to be more successful and more remunerated than they actually are at the moment they meet. Disillusioned, they console each other for having failed at the game of pretending to be highly paid celebrities, and they wind up eschewing the country-house circuit, which turns out to be too expensive for their purses, and finally get down to their own work. The literary *improvisatrice,* Mrs. Harvey, like Mrs. Oliphant, is known only by her last name: Mrs. Oliphant's books were signed "Mrs. Oliphant," not Margaret Wilson Oliphant. Mundham, the country house that represents the "world," is the kind of great house Mrs. Oliphant's biography shows her to have visited early in her career.

Stuart Straith, the painter who abstained from courting Mrs. Harvey after her husband's early death (like that of Mr. Oliphant), is forced to supplement his income by designing dresses for theatrical pieces, as Mrs. Harvey is forced to write a monthly London Letter for the *Blackport Banner,* a chatty newspaper. They accompany each other, after having renewed their friendship following their weekend at Mundham, to a play called *The New Girl* (so named, possibly to emphasize the fact that they themselves are an "old" girl and boy, and that the fashion for their wares has changed). Mrs. Harvey volunteers to write up Straith's art in her column in " 'The *Blackport Banner.* A 'London Letter'—The new books, the new plays, the new twaddle of any sort—a little music, a little gossip, a little 'art.' You'll help me—I need it awfully—with the art. I do three a month.' '*You*—wonderful you?' He spoke . . . and could no more help it than Mrs. Harvey had been able to help it in the stalls. 'Oh, as you say, for the fee!' "[63]

Mrs. Harvey's moonlighting sounds as if it has been paraphrased from a letter Mrs. Oliphant wrote to Mr. Blackwood, a letter of November 1884, which is included in her *Autobiography,* suggesting to him that she would like to do a monthly London letter for his magazine, *Blackwood's* (the similarity to the *Blackport Banner* is clear). She writes,

> "By the way, a notion has been coming and going in my mind . . . of a monthly article on 'Things in General.' Should you be at all disposed for anything of the kind? Short of politics, I should be included to take in everything that was going on—theatres, pictures, books, even a taste of gossip when legitimate. What do you think? It might be made very interesting, though whether I can do it or not remains to be seen."[64]

She not only could do it but did it, if not every month, at least every few months, as she had been doing it since the 1850s. James had written of the *Blackwood* articles in 1897 that "her biographer, if there is to be one, will have no small task in the mere drafting of lists of her contributions to magazines and journals in general and to *Blackwood's* in particular. . . . I should almost suppose in fact that no woman had ever, for half a century, had her personal 'say' so publicly and irresponsibly" (NN, 454). Indeed, Mrs. Harry Coghill who arranged and edited the *Autobiography and Letters,* lists more than two hundred and seventy entries from 1852 through 1898, some published posthumously, in *Blackwood's,* and a recent bibliography lists over seven hundred items.

In "Broken Wings" Stuart Straith concludes—after going over the whole history of their vanished early success in their respective arts and the false impression that their, especially her, amazing productivity creates in the fashionable world of the country house—that "we're simply the case . . . of having been had enough of" (XI, 236). We can trace Mrs. Harvey's and Straith's unfashionableness to Mrs. Oliphant's statements about her role in literature in the opening pages of her *Autobiography:* "I am behind the fashion. . . . I have no longer the place or fashion I had" (AL, 4). She continues, "One may love me (i.e. in a sort of way), but by none am I enough beloved." She considered herself "rather a failure all round. . . . I acknowledge frankly that there is nothing in me to impress anyone, and yet there is a sort of whimsical injury in it which makes me sorry for myself" (AL, 8).

The candor and conflicting emotions of these statements seem to have gone into the creation of the fictive Mrs. Harvey and into the projection of her and her friend's peculiar relation to their own reputations. When at the end of "Broken Wings" the lady writer and gentleman painter vow to give up the great country-house world because they cannot afford the rich ("everything costs that one does for the rich"), we see that James may have learned in the *Autobiography* that Mrs. Oliphant's fortune "has never been very much, never anything like what many of my contemporaries attained" (AL, 70). Although she admits that "I have done very well for a woman," she adds, "though I did very well on the whole, I never did anything like so well as the others. (George Eliot and George Sand make me half inclined to cry over my poor little unappreciated self)" (AL, 8).

Mrs. Harvey's husband, like Mrs. Oliphant's, had died "over ten years ago," early in their marriage. It is true that James does not give to Mrs. Harvey the rearing and education of three children (all of whom predeceased Mrs. Oliphant) as the compelling motivation for the prolific production of the "numerous . . . admired volumes," for perhaps he winced when he read in her *Autobiography* that "the men who have no wives, who have given themselves up to their art, have had an almost unfair advantage over us" (AL, 5). Perhaps he wished, as Leon Edel believes, to identify himself with her as a worker.

Like Mrs. Oliphant, whom J. M. Barrie thought looked like "one who wore rare caps and fine lace," and was a gentlewoman who "loved beautiful things," Mrs. Harvey had only "two frocks"; ("I couldn't stay another day," she told her fellow guest Lady Claude at Mundham). "The gracious, fine Scots gentlewoman," (WT, v) Mrs. Oliphant, turns into Mrs. Harvey, whom "Straith

. . . could see . . . was as handsome as anyone, . . . and also as 'smart' as the evening before" (XI, 220).

There is an important theater image in *Kirsteen* where the young noble-woman, whose poverty keeps her from the social world to which she belongs, measures her first ball: "She looked round her as if it had been 'the play.' Kirsteen knew nothing at all of the play, and had been brought up to believe that it was a most depraved and depraving entertainment, but still there had never been any doubt expressed for its enthralling character. The ball, she had decided from the first day it had been mentioned, would be as good as going to the play."[65] James puts into Straith's mind a similar image, for when he first sees the "fine hazes of August" at Mundham he is reminded of "the artful gauze stretched across the stage of a theatre" (CT, 219). James prepares us by this image for the judgment of both his spectators of the theatrical piece *The New Girl,* which illustrates Kirsteen's observations that the ball would be as good as the theater. To Mrs. Harvey and to Straith, Mundham is better than the theatre; "whatever the piece might be, the real thing as they had seen it at Mundham, was more than a match for any piece. For it was Mundham that *was,* theatri-cally, the real thing; better for scenery, dresses, music, pretty women, bare shoulders, everything . . . a much bigger and braver show, and got up, as it were, infinitely more 'regardless'" (XI, 226).

When Mrs. Harvey and Stuart Straith join forces and vow to cut the Mund-hams out of their lives, they say in concert, "'And now to work,'" an attitude James not only admired in Mrs. Oliphant but emulated himself. As James had written about her earlier in his 1897 London Notes, "Her capacity for labour was infinite—for labour of the only sort, that, with the fine strain of old Scotch pride and belated letterless toryism that was in her, she regarded as respectable." He adds, "She was really a great *improvisatrice,* a night-working spinner of long, loose vivid yarns." He concludes, "There is scant enough question of 'art' in the matter, . . . there is a friendly way for us to feel about so much cleverness, courage and humanity" (NN, 454–55). These are the qualities that her fictive correlative, Mrs. Harvey, also displays and that James admired.

### The Etonian in *The Portrait of a Lady:* A Blend of Whyte-Melville, A. C. Benson, and a "Beautiful Blameless Knight"

There is one character in Henry James's *The Portrait of a Lady* whose name, with its definite meaning, has somehow avoided the critical eye. It belongs to Bob Bantling, the suitor of Henrietta Stackpole, the young American journalist. The O.E.D. gives as the definition for *bantling* "a young or small child, a brat (often used depreciatively, and formerly as a synonym of bastard)." In the 1881 version of *Portrait* there does not seem to be any specific reason, stated or inferred, why James should choose that particular name for the character. It is only in the revised version of the novel, published in 1908, that James inserted a few sentences that seem to shed light on his choice of the word.

Henrietta has just told Isabel that she is going to marry Mr. Bantling, but she cannot explain her choice. Isabel tells her that explanations are not necessary since "'Mr. Bantling isn't a riddle.'" Henrietta answers, "'No, he isn't a bad pun—or even a high flight of American humour.'"[66] It is this last phrase in the sentence that seems to give away the reason for James's choice of the name. He has indeed attempted a pun and has followed it closely with an allusion to a phrase from Washington Irving's *Knickerbocker's History of New York*. That allusion is to "a tender virgin accidentally and unaccountably enriched with a bantling," a phrase so well known as a "high flight of American humour" that the O.E.D. gives it as an example of how the word *bantling* is used. The joke of the matter is that Henrietta Stackpole is clearly meant to be "the tender virgin" who has, by the accident of having met Bantling at Ralph Touchett's London house and by the seeming unaccountability of their being attractive to one another, been "enriched" by such a husband.

That seems to be the reason why James has in his own "high flight of humour" borrowed from that of his predecessor. It is possible that in the first version of *The Portrait of a Lady* he hoped the reader would fill in the quotation from Irving for himself, but James's experience in regard to his readership during the previous twenty-five years had taught him that his reader must be told what to look for. For that reason, perhaps, we have been given the reference by Henrietta in the revised novel just as the book is about to end.

The enrichment that Bantling brings to Henrietta is clear from the way James has built up the character even in the 1881 version of the novel, which is further embroidered in the revision. The character of Bob Bantling, whom Henrietta Stackpole does marry, is that of a typical Eton graduate—good natured, dependable, a man of the world, and a seemingly perpetual bachelor until he meets Henrietta. In 1881, when James conceived him as a counterweight to the other Englishman, Lord Warburton, and as the one character not an egoist among a band of egoists, he had to go to literature to build up his typical Etonian since his acquaintance with such men of classically bred but elegant leisure was limited. Our evidence for this comes from another insertion in the revised edition, where, as it were, he gives away his technique. It consists of one hyphenated word introduced in a sentence where Bantling's background for enjoying the ruins of Rome is itemized. He "had been bred at Eton where they study nothing but Latin" (PL, 261), to which now has been added, "and Whyte-Melville" (R, 283).

George John Whyte-Melville (1821–78) was a novelist unfortunately forgotten today who, known as "the laureate of fox-hunting," might also have been called the laureate of the turf and of Eton. He died just before James began to write *The Portrait*. Whyte-Melville's first novel and perhaps his best known and most widely read was *Digby Grand: An Autobiography* (1853). Although Whyte-Melville wrote over twenty novels, this particular work seems to have given James most of his material for what a typical, Eton-bred gentleman, bachelor, and man of the world would be like at forty. Whyte-Melville was an Etonian himself and, therefore, his hero is a reliable product of the college.

If we review Bantling's character, we can see in it borrowings from Whyte-Melville's masterpiece, even in the 1881 version of *The Portrait,* though James does not reveal his source until the revised version of the novel. Bantling is first introduced as an "amiable bachelor, . . . a stout fair, smiling man of forty who was extraordinarily well-dressed" (PL, 131). In *Digby Grand* a gentleman is also described as "an agreeable, pleasant fellow."[67] Bantling in this introductory passage also tells Henrietta about his sister, Lady Pensil, who writes poetry, and her name, too, is a pun. Bantling is not one for poetry " 'unless it's Byron. I suppose you think a great deal of Byron in America' " (PL, 132). The only poet Digby likes is also Byron, for he mentions him four times. Digby owns a bronze replica of the *Dying Gladiator,* " 'the most valued of all the works of art I possessed,' " because of Byron's lines about him in *Childe Harold.* "On the pedestal that supported his god-like figure, relaxing, drooping, failing, but unconquered still, were inscribed those glorious stanzas that will survive even the mighty creation of the sculptor's art" (D, 183). Is it an accident that not only is Byron mentioned but that the *Dying Gladiator* also makes an appearance in *The Portrait* just after Isabel has rejected Warburton?

James gives the title of Baron to Bantling's brother-in-law, just as a baron was Digby's ancestor. "Baron" strikes the right kind of note for this Jamesian Etonian, for, as Bantling tells Henrietta, it is a " 'convenient sort of rank. You are fine enough, and you are not too fine' " (PL, 133). When he meets Warburton, with whom he stands on equal ground, he only "took occasion to nod to his lordship," which impressed Miss Stackpole. He is also amazed by the Touchetts' disapproval of hunting. " 'The old man thinks it's wicked to hunt, I am told' " (PL, 132). In this Bantling resembles Digby, and when he comes back from his trip to the States he immediately joins a hunting party. In the States he exhibited the same interest in rivers and steamboats that Digby had shown in Canada.

However, Bantling's chief similarity to Whyte-Melville's character is that like Digby he has been and is now a retired guardsman. (Whyte-Melville himself was a Coldstream Guard who retired early from active duty.) When young Digby is to be launched on a career, he tells his father, " 'most Eton fellows got into the Guards.' " The " 'summit of my ambition,' " said "Dandy" Grand, was " 'an appointment to the Guards' " (D, 101). So James, following his source, makes Bantling an exguardsman. Being well dressed is a sine qua non for the Etonian guardsman or Whyte-Melville gentleman. Bantling becomes a captain in the Guards as does Digby and, like Digby, is also "well dressed and possessed of considerable knowledge of the world." For a Whyte-Melville aristocratic hero it "is as indispensable for him to be well-dressed as it is for a man of middle station to be dressed at all" (D, 115).

Henrietta says about Bob Bantling, "'He's not intellectual but he appreciates intellect; on the other hand he doesn't exaggerate its claims.'" This seems to come from the kind of comment Digby makes in *Digby Grand:* "'Reflection is not a matter of hours in a dark room with a dry volume. Self-communion may take place in a second of time, surrounded by all that can enchant the eye'" (D, 66). Like Digby, Bantling is a bachelor until the end of the book, and as his model had made an original marriage to a poor girl, so Bantling's marriage is also an original gesture, a sign of his curiosity and a free mind. Although Isabel was disappointed that Henrietta had not been original, that is, consistent with her professed independence, at least Bantling was. "There was a want of originality in her marrying him. . . . A little later, indeed, she reflected that Mr. Bantling, after all, was original" (PL, 522). He too thinks, like Isabel, that his marriage is odd. "'But I've always rather liked striking out a line'" (PL, 568).

*Digby Grand* is more or less an encyclopedia on what activities were considered gentlemanly for an Eton-bred member of the aristocracy, usually a younger son, someone who would not be saddled with the responsibilities of having inherited a title, like Lord Warburton, and someone who could enjoy the liberties of his class without paying the penalties. Like Digby, Bantling is entranced by something he cannot control. For Digby it was "the mysteries of the turf" (D, 238); for Bantling "the mystery" was Henrietta. "'I really believe that's what he wants to marry me for—just to find out. It's a fixed idea—a kind of fascination'" (PL, 523).

There is a chapter in *Digby Grand* on all the regiments a young man would like to join, and when Digby gets into debt he is forced to exchange his commission in the Guards with a member of a lesser group. From Rifles, Highlanders, Lancers, Fuseliers, Hussars, Light Infantry, Horse, Foot, and Dragoons (D, 251), Digby chooses the cavalry division of Dragoons. It is interesting that in the 1908 version of *The Portrait* James makes Bantling also a guardsman, in his case an "ex-Lancer." Ralph Touchett remarks, in fact, that Henrietta is "'doing very well . . . going over to Paris with an ex-Lancer! If she wants something to write about she has only to describe that episode'" (R, 250). But like Whyte-Melville's heroes, Bantling is as pure and innocent as is Henrietta, and, actually, as Whyte-Melville himself seemed to be. That writer seems to have been as modest and self-effacing as Bantling; both were called "simple."

An Etonian and the grandson of a duke, Whyte-Melville "appeared to under-value his literary faculty," for he "ignored literary society; he almost exclusively cultivated the sporting," we are told by his historian, Frederick Locker-Lampson.[68] "He was one of the pleasantest people I ever met" (C, 382). Ironically, he died in the hunting field taking a jump. It is interesting that James owned a copy of Locker-Lampson's *My Confidences,* published posthumously in 1896, and in that book he might have found in the following anecdote told by the author a characteristic of his own invented Etonian, Bob Bantling. "I once encountered Whyte-Melville as he was ringing the Q____s' bell. We exchanged a word or two, and on parting, I said, 'You like the Q____s?' 'Yes,' said he, and his answer was characteristic: 'Yes, very much. I like *him* better than she does, and I like *her* better than he does'" (C, 384).

Actually, Whyte-Melville was a moralist and was supposed to have "exerted a considerable and wholesome influence on the manners and morals of the gilded youth of his time." Bantling, too, comes across in both versions of *The Portrait* as a man not only of great worldly experience but of great kindness and dependability in helping Isabel in her crisis, as well as shepherding Henrietta throughout her grand tour. He also is the great example in the book of an unprejudiced mind, the complete opposite of Isabel's husband, the cold-hearted aesthete, Osmond.

In 1881 James knew no Etonians intimately and had to go to the literature of Eton and to the novels of the man who was the specialist on the Etonian gentleman about town. Twenty-five years later, when it came to revising the novel, he was able to put into Bantling's portrait some new facts based on his first-hand friendship with a bona fide Etonian. This friendship seems to be the reason for the rather numerous insertions in the revised *Portrait* that flesh out Bantling's character and behavior. In James's revision of *The Portrait* certain major characters are refined, expanded, made more concrete in their attributes and more subtle in their perceptions. Yet even a character very important to the novel, Madame Merle, is left more or less alone, whereas Mr. Bantling is further developed. The "genial" exguardsman of the 1881 version of the novel has been paid more attention by the American novelist, now a quarter of a century away from the first version, than Edward Rosier, Pansy Osmond, Mr. and Mrs. Touchett, and the Countess Gemini, for their lines have been left more or less the way they were. But Bob Bantling has had his gallantry stressed, his Etonian ties emphasized, the pun in his name called attention to, his honourable celibacy underlined (together with his willingness to take on a totally foreign type of woman to be his wife in a class-structured society), his affinity for the novels of the "laureate of fox-hunting," Whyte-Melville, and his kindness to Isabel when Ralph is dying. He is now even finally iconified by a popular picture also associated with Eton.

Why did James pay so much attention to what is, after all, an accessory character? Bantling in no way affects the action of the book, other than to have Henrietta Stackpole, the young woman journalist and nonconformist patriot, engage in an action, by marrying him, that makes her entire history of protestations ironically self-contradictory. The emergence of Bantling as a more rounded character may depend on the fact that James in the late 1890s had met and felt very responsive to a real life Bantling, Arthur Christopher Benson—Etonian, sportsman, and belletrist closely connected with Eton and of the same age, when James got to know him, as his own character, Bob Bantling. Arthur Christopher Benson was born in 1862 and thus was one generation younger than James. He was in his early forties during the middle part of their correspondence, which spanned the years from 1892 until 1915. The most intense period of their friendship occurred just before James revised *The Portrait of a Lady,* in the first years of the new century. The eldest of the four sons of the archbishop of Canterbury, Arthur spent a good part of his life at Eton—first as a student, then as a master there in 1885 and not resigning until 1903–4. He, therefore, personified the Etonian ideal for James.

On February 26, 1895, James wrote a chiding letter to Arthur Benson, criticizing his book *Lyrics* and telling him that "art should be as hard as nails." The artist is, he wrote, "an absolutely Roman father. Don't to your bantlings, be too much the mere 'governor.' "[69] It is curious that the word *bantling* should appear here. We can only speculate that Arthur reminded him consciously or unconsciously of his own Bob Bantling, invented ten years before James ever knew the Bensons. In 1907, when James revised *The Portrait,* Arthur was forty-five years old, approximately the same age as Mr. Bantling, who is described in the 1881 version, as we have seen, as "a stout, fair, smiling man of forty" (PL, 131). James had before him his own character, invented in 1881, who must have struck him as a skeleton compared to real-life Arthur Benson, who, with further embellishments, might easily take on the lineaments of a youngish man, of the same age and in the same state of bachelordom, involved with gentlemanly interests, and enjoying a total commitment to the Etonian way of life. James had discovered in life someone very close to one of his own puppets, and the appearance of the word *bantling* itself in the letter quoted above seems to argue some connection between the two.

Bantling is now made a contemporary Etonian. When he comments on the state of health of the dying Mr. Touchett, James changes the 1881 diagnosis that Bantling makes of the illness, which he judges is " 'dropsical as well, he has a lot of water' " (PL, 132), to a much more knowledgeable and scientifically accurate statement: " 'to my certain knowledge he has organic disease so developed that you may depend upon it he'll go, some day soon, quite quickly,' " which Mr. Touchett promptly does do (R, 142)! James now augments Bantling's bits of conversation to make him less foolish and more worthy of a man of the world. He describes his sister more specifically, calling her "plain," but recognizes that she "makes up awfully well" (R, 142). Arthur Benson never married, and the revision of the Bantling material emphasizes the seemingly asexual relationship between Henrietta and her British courtier. Whereas they are first called "harmless confederates" (PL, 202), in the revision they are called "groping celibates" (R, 218). In addition, the "good Mr. Bantling" changes to "the perfect man of the world" (R. 219). The "intellectual flirtation" (PL, 260) between Henrietta and Bob Bantling changes to "intellectual adventure" (R, 282).

To the specification about Bantling's background a few evocative words are now added to fill out his portrait. In 1881 Henrietta points out how convenient it is that Mr. Bantling will go to Rome with her because " 'he had been there before, as he was a military man, and he had had a classical education—he was brought up at Eton, where they study nothing but Latin . . .'" (PL, 261). In 1908, as we have already noted, she extends this to " 'he had been bred at Eton where they study nothing but Latin and Whyte-Melville'" (R, 283). In Rome in 1881 Henrietta gets engrossed in Mr. Bantling's "Latin reminiscences" (PL, 265). In the revision the Etonian connections are reinforced, for it was "delightful" to Henrietta "to hear him [Mr. Bantling] speak of Julius Caesar as a 'cheeky old boy.'" Now the Roman leader is subsumed under Etonian terminology (R, 288).

In 1897 James wrote to Arthur Benson, "Perfect indeed your arrangement—the conditions of your big shoot" (B, 44), which calls attention to the fact that like Bantling who cannot understand why Touchett is opposed to hunting, Benson liked the traditional English sports. James liked Arthur's *Diary,* which Benson sent him. With "my voracity for personal introspections, I find in your existence a great deal to feed upon" (B, 46). James adds, "I welcome it as a document, a series of data on the life of a young Englishman of great endowments, character, and position at the end of the nineteenth century" (B, 46). He calls him one of the "heirs of all the ages" (B, 35), which makes us think of the freedom with which Mr. Bantling welcomes the new experience of the somewhat eccentric Henrietta Stackpole. We remember that he "always rather liked striking out a line" (PL, 523–68).

*"A Figured Objectivity"*

There is a third ingredient that went into the making of Bob Bantling, one that appears long after the 1881 version, and one that would appeal to what James called, in a letter to Arthur Benson in 1904, "my documentary passion, reducing everything to a figured objectivity" (B, 63). The particular "objectivity" that reinforces the "figure" of Bantling occurs in the insertion in the revision of the novel in which Isabel (made comfortable by Bantling's concerns for her when, tired and anxious, she arrived in the London railway station to be transported to Gardencourt), "thought of him extravagantly, as a beautiful blameless knight" (R, 563). The association here is Etonian, but it could only be such after 1897. In that year for the June the Fourth celebration, a yearly event at the college, George Frederick Watts gave to the school a version of his popular painting *Sir Galahad,* which he had especially painted for Eton, on the request, repeated over the years, of one of Eton's most revered masters, Henry Elford Luxmoore.

Hugh Macmillan, in *The Life-Work of George Frederick Watts, R.A.,* wrote that this picture, based on a portrait of Arthur Prinseps, "cannot fail to be an inspiration to the young minds that are trained there for the high places of the field, teaching them like the famous hero to wear in all temptations the white flower of a blameless life."[70]

The "beautiful blameless knight" to whom Isabel compared Bantling could only refer to Sir Galahad and Watt's portrait of him, placed conspicuously in the chapel that every Eton boy had to attend regularly. Thus Watt's *Sir Galahad* is the "figured objectivity" behind Isabel's simile. And James knew the picture; he had see the first version of *Sir Galahad* painted in 1862; it had been shown at the Grosvenor Gallery in 1877 in an exhibition that James reviewed for the *Galaxy.* There he called attention to the many portraits by Watts and to an allegorical picture, but he made no comment on *Sir Galahad.* The fact that he had nevertheless seen it and had respected Watts as "the first portrait painter in England" made him undoubtedly susceptible to the version Watts painted especially for Eton.[71]

In addition, we have letters that indicate that when James visited Eton in May 1900, he met Mr. Luxmoore, the man responsible for the gift of *Sir Galahad* from Watts; James most likely was taken by him to the chapel, for as James wrote to Benson, "I had never got so romantic an impression of Eton," and it "made me think more things that I can say now"; what is more, it "enriched my mind. It lashed up my imagination" (B, 55). This is just a few years before he drops the Etonian material into *The Portrait of a Lady* revision. Watts had felt that "art would be a most valuable auxiliary in teaching, and nowhere can lessons that may help to form the character of the youth of England be more important than in the great school where statesmen and soldiers and leaders of thought receive their first impressions."[72]

Sir Galahad is represented in profile in full armor and is accompanied by his horse (fig. 44). Presumably if any Arthurian knight could have made Eton it would have been Galahad, for he represented the male ideal of the school—courtly, pure, and persevering, and, of course, horse-loving. Watts tended to do knights in armor often, and in addition he made four versions of his *Sir Galahad,* the last in 1903. Watts was fond of using horses in his pictures, since, according to his wife, he was genuinely fond of riding and of anything to do with horses, as were Etonians and Whyte-Melville's heroes. The average Etonian, trained to lead a life in which horses, riding, and hunting would play a paramount part, would be ready to enjoy and respect such a painting. Watts also painted himself in armor, and his interest in identifying with knights of chivalry reflected his idealistic personality.

Bob Bantling, too, was a combination of worldly interests, joined to a certain purity of point of view. He was willing to take on the risks and the challenges of the unknown like Sir Galahad, and yet unlike Sir Galahad he was

Figure 44.   George Edward Watts, *Sir Galahad,* 1862
Copy in the Eton College Chapel.
*(Private collection)*

fully equipped with a knowledge of the world. Fortified by his new, appropriate pictorial icon, Bantling is now in the revision "brave," he is "celibate" as was Galahad, and he risks traveling alone with a pretty young woman in the 1870s without any thought or care about what people might say, "'Because my heart is pure,'" he might declare with Tennyson's Sir Galahad. Henrietta did very well for herself! The association between Bantling and Sir Galahad is made not through Whyte-Melville but through Arthur Benson.

It becomes clear from James's letters to Benson that the image of Galahad and the image of Arthur were somehow united. James wrote to Arthur, "Farewell, fine ornament of a mighty order, I shall look out for you in the courts of heaven" (B, 36), and he refers to Arthur's "gallant and graceful note" (B, 54) when finally in 1900 James gets to Eton properly and sees the college. Arthur Benson also had a habit of using the names of Arthurian knights to decorate his own prose. In his book of essays about scholastic life, called *From a College Window* (1907), he reminisces about criticizing one's friends as "not leaving Lancelot brave nor Galahad pure!"[73]

The atmosphere of the Eton of James's visit is admirably caught in *Shades of Eton* by Percy Lubbock, a young member of James's circle of friends centering around Howard Sturgis's home, "Qu'acre." Benson was Lubbock's tutor at Eton, and the pages devoted to the quality of the temper encouraged by Benson and Luxmoore, the cultivation in that nursery for "scholars of taste" of a special "manner and tone," make us see what essence James was striving for in his retouched portrait of Bob Bantling in the revision of *The Portrait*. Lubbock describes the Eton of the 1890s in which the classics and the legacy of Ruskin, the perfection of a sense of taste, plus a "touch of worldly conversation," reigned.[74] What we recognize as a quality of Bantling is described by Lubbock as the life-time necessary equipment of an Etonian, the keeping of an independent point of view always, for "a free spirit, out of school, was supreme."[75] Benson and Sir Galahad "lashed up" James's imagination to further embellish his portrait of Bantling, his only graduate of Eton (that "palace of pedagogy," as James called it) and the only exguardsman in all of his fiction. The brew of Bantling can thus be seen to have been blended from literature, life, and art, a mixture as before, in the Waring blender of James's mind.

# 5

# American Popular Literature

## Maria Cummins, *The Lamplighter,* and James's Early Fiction

*The Lamplighter,* by Maria S. Cummins, is a book James read when a "small boy," and the circumstances of his reading it he gives in vivid detail in his *Small Boy and Others*.[1]

> *The Lamplighter,* over which I fondly hung and which would have been my first "grown-up" novel—it had been soothingly offered me for that—had I consented to take it as really and truly grown-up. I couldn't have said what it lacked for the character, I only had my secret reserves and when one blest afternoon on the New Brighton boat I waded into The Initials saw how right I had been. The Initials *was* grown up and the difference thereby exquisite; it came over me with the very first page, assimilated in the fluttered little cabin to which I had retired with it. (AU, 46)

James had brought back the book which his father had bought for his mother,

> a gift of such happy promise as the history of the long-legged Mr. Hamilton and his two Bavarian beauties, the elder of whom, Hildegarde, was to figure for our small generation as the very type of the haughty as distinguished from the forward heroine (since I think our categories came to no more than those). I couldn't have got very far with Hildegarde in moments so scant, but I memorably felt that romance was thick round me—everything, at such a crisis, seeming to make for it at once. (AU, 47)

Although he protested that he never considered it "my first 'grown-up' novel," he does admit he "fondly hung" over it. It was a very popular novel, beaten only by *Uncle Tom's Cabin* and *The Scarlet Letter*. Over one hundred thousand copies of it were sold up to 1902. It was written by a judge's daughter not much more than twenty years old, and she died before she was forty.

The early tragic life and gradual rise of the little orphaned girl for whom there are a series of surrogate parents, mostly fathers, are the dominant notes. The entire story is governed by moralistic aims for young people, and it illustrates an attempt to lead them into religious ways of thinking, for the book was to be part of Sunday-school libraries. The little girl, picked up from the streets, sick and ill bred, gradually learns virtue and good manners, marries her childhood sweetheart, finds her real father, and sees that her blind surrogate mother and protector becomes the wife of her real father, who had been the surrogate mother's stepbrother. There are also in this book "sets" of children of different sexes, as in "The Turn of the Screw." The little orphaned girl, Gerty, has a little friend, Willie Sullivan, who will return from India a rich man, and, though there is a threat that he may be interested in the "bad" and vain stepsister of Gerty's blind protectress, he really loves Gerty and all ends well. And now a resumé of the plot.

Little orphaned Gerty, aged eight, is maltreated and turned out of the house while she is sick by an angry woman, Nan Grant. The lamplighter, Trueman Flint, called Uncle True, takes Gerty into his own house and takes care of her. She is dressed properly and her expenses are paid by Miss Emily Graham, the blind lady. "The child's language expressed unmitigated hatred."[2] In "The Turn of the Screw" Flora, too, is eight years old, and when she is put upon she, too, emits "horrors." " 'On my honour, Miss, she says things—!' "[3] " 'Really shocking. . . . About you, Miss. . . . It's beyond everything, for a young lady; and I can't think wherever she must have picked up—' " (X, 122). Even before that episode, after the governess claims Miss Jessel is out there and tells the child, Flora " 'was hideously hard; she had turned common and almost ugly. . . . 'I think you're cruel. I don't like you!' Then, after this deliverance, which might have been that of a *vulgarly pert little girl in the street* [emphasis mine], she hugged Mrs. Grose more closely and buried in her skirts the dreadful little face" (X, 116), which seems to have lost its beauty—"her incomparable childish beauty had suddenly failed" (X, 116).

This might be a recollection of the lines from *The Lamplighter* when Gerty, who has suffered so at the hands of Nan Grant, alarms Uncle True by her language: "The child's language expressed unmitigated hatred, and even a hope of future revenge," for she had been "uttering the most bitter invectives against Nan Grant, making use of many a rough and coarse term, such as she had been accustomed to hear used by the ill-bred people with whom she had lived" (L, 38).

But the theme of *The Lamplighter* is the "neglected orphan" and her surrogate parents, in this case, first, True Flint, who adopts her, then Emily Graham, the blind young woman who supports her and who with her father, Mr. Graham, takes her on after True dies. The lady next door has a son, Willie Sullivan, just a few years older, and he and Gerty grow up together with great affection. Gerty for a while gets into rages when she thinks of Nan Grant, to the point that she throws a stone into Nan's window and breaks it. Moreover, she claims that she did it on purpose. "She did not understand herself, or her own sensations; we may not say how she was responsible for them, but this much is certain, her face alone betrayed that; as evil took violent possession of her soul, peace and pleasantness fled away. Poor child! how much she needs to learn the truth! God grant that the inward may one day become as clear to her as now the outward light!" (L, 57).

Gerty meets the blind lady, Emily Graham, and loves her. She feels she herself is ugly, and when Emily tells her that people *like* ugly children, if they are good, Gerty answers, " 'I'm real bad' " (L, 63), reminding us of Miles who wants to do something "bad" and gets up in the middle of the night to show the governess he is bad, saying to her, " 'When I'm bad I *am* bad!' " (T, 80). Like Miles, Gerty, who as soon as she gets older is called Gertrude, is an "excitable but interesting child" (L, 64). Miss Emily, who lives in the dark of her blindness, prays that the child's temper will be cured. Her "undying purpose" was to "cure that child of her dark infirmity" like the governess's self-appointed job in "The Turn of the Screw" (L, 72). Miss Graham teaches Gerty the "difference between honesty and dishonesty" and what "duty" means (L, 83). When the Grahams go on a trip to the South, Dr. and Mrs. Jeremy then care for her and act as foster parents. She is now a "doubly orphaned girl" (L, 204). During the trip Mr. Graham meets and marries a "handsome, showy, woman," and life becomes hard for his blind daughter. Mr. Phillips, the man of mystery who has white hair but is not an elderly person, yet who has a sorrowful face and a grieved unhappy air, turns out to be Gerty's natural and long-lost father, and the stepbrother as well of Emily Graham, whose blindness he had accidentally caused, and whom he finally marries. That "strange and inconsistent man" saves them all from a burning ship.

The novel seems to be another one of those contemporary pieces of fiction dealing with children who are not loved by parents, who are cast off by evil guardians and finally claimed by their loving real parents after a number of surrogate parents. In the case of *Temptation,* mothers are the surrogates, but here in *The Lamplighter* the emphasis seems to be on fathers. Thus the cold, tortured days of their youth are atoned for. First, True Flint, the lamplighter, picks up little barefoot Gerty, who almost dies from exposure; then Emily and her father, Mr. Graham, adopt her; and then, finally, the real father, Phillip Taylor, claims his child. The childhood beau, Willie Sullivan, also comes back, true to his love, Gerty, even though for a while she thinks he loves Mr. Graham's silly, vain stepdaughter.

There is also the symbolism of light, first that of the lamplighter, whose occupation, lighting people's lamps, gives Gerty a view of other people's family happiness through their windows. Then there is the light that animates the soul of Emily Graham, even though the world exists for her in darkness because of her blindness. It is the light of the Lord, however, that lights up all their lives with a quotation from the Bible that brings the book to an end. "Thy sun shall no more go down, neither shall thy moon withdraw itself; for the Lord shall be thy everlasting light, and the days of thy mourning shall be ended" (L, 485).

The intensity with which the "small boy" read *The Lamplighter* allows us to take the liberty of investigating where and how this four-hundred-and-eighty-five-page book left its mark on the fiction of the larger boy. It is curious how many names of the characters in Cummins's best-known novel appear in James's first few stories. Gertrude, heroine of *The Lamplighter,* becomes Gertrude Whittaker, heroine of "Poor Richard," a story by James published in 1867 when he was twenty-four years old, and she also appears as Gertrude Wentworth in *The Europeans,* 1878. The Graham family lends its name to the suicide, Robert Graham, whose friend, the hero, Philip Osborne, also takes his name from Phillip Taylor who is first known as Mr. Phillip in *The Lamplighter.* James's story, "Osborne's Revenge" appeared the next year, 1868. Ben Bruce, the Mr. Bruce who flirts with Gerty, appears in the Mr. Bruce of "The Story of a Year" (1865), written when James was only twenty-two, his first story published under his own name.

### Edward Everett Hale's "My Double; and How He Undid Me" and the Undoing in "The Private Life"

There is a remarkable resemblance between James's story "The Private Life" in the April issue of the *Atlantic Monthly* (1892) and the anonymous tale "My Double; and How He Undid Me," in the September issue of the *Atlantic Monthly* (1859), later revealed to be the first successful story by Edward Everett Hale (1822–1909), whose name has been remembered chiefly for "The Man without a Country." Both stories involve a double very different from the threatening double usually found in fiction, notably in "William Wilson," *Dorian Gray,* and "The Jolly Corner," where some elements of the uncanny (which Freud described enter. These two stories separated by thirty-three years exhibit doubles invented to allow a writer privacy for study and creation, while his alter ego takes care of the social life and administrative details that distract him from what he wants to do. Their tone is humorous, and there is much room for invention.

It seems hard to believe that in English no tale had been written before Edward Everett Hale's "My Double; and How He Undid Me" in which a double is created to take care of "the duties . . . which one performs as a member of one or another social class or subdivision, wholly distinct from what one does . . . by himself."[4] We are presented with the Reverend Ingham of Naguadavick, Maine, the narrator, who found he was "living two lives for two sets of people, one real and one merely functional—one my parish, whom I loved, and the other a vague public for whom I did not care two straws" (GM, 4). Becoming "crazed by this duality of life," he finally "resolved to look out for a Double" on his wife's suggestion (GM, 5). He finds an Irishman, Dennis Shea, who looks just like him; he changes Shea's name to his own and dresses Shea like himself. "Whenever he was out, I should be at home," so no extra clothing is needed (GM, 6). His master equips Shea with four cover-all speeches which he learns by rote. They are: (1) "Very well, thank you. And you?"; (2) "I am very glad you liked it"; (3) "There has been so much said, and, on the whole, so well said, that I will not occupy the time"; and, finally, (4) "I agree, in general, with my friend the other side of the room" (GM, 6). When these are misapplied, the effect is hilarious.

When it is a question of attending a boring party, Dennis becomes the guest, while Reverend Ingham continues reading in Pfeiffer's "Mystics." When Ingham wants to stay at home and write to learned German professors, Dennis goes to vote in his place. Ingham quotes instances of other friends who had doubles, one who has him preach his "afternoon sermons for him," so that "some of the most well-defined men, who stand out most prominently on the background of history, are in this way stereoscopic men, who owe their distinct relief to the slight differences between their doubles" (GM, 15). His own contribution "is simply the great extension of the system, so that all public machine-work may be done by it" (GM, 16). For a year all goes well, and while Dennis does the socializing and committee attending, Ingham concentrates on his private duties, "my intimate and real duties" (GM, 5), and polishes up on his ancient and modern foreign languages to make up for "how little I had done with them while I attended to my *public* duties!" (GM, 16).

Finally, Dennis is sent to one meeting where his four sentences will not take care of the situation. The crowd gets angry, Dennis loses his temper and breaks forth angrily into an Irish brogue, making the crowd think the Reverend Ingham is an inebriate. Although he is driven out of his town, and exiled, he continues to work steadily on his *Traces of Sandemanianism in the Sixth and Seventh Centuries*[5] (GM, 21). Although the public thinks he is undone, he is happy. During his first trip to England Henry James, Senior, had been attracted to the gospel of Robert Sandeman (1718–71), though he soon abandoned Sandeman's theology. The reference to Sandeman in "My Double" may have remained in the younger James's memory long after reading Hale's story, because of his father's interest in Sandeman. The resemblance between the fictive Reverend Ingham and Sandeman is strengthened by the latter's migration to New England in 1764.[6]

In "The Private Life," James has given his tale a name that describes the kind of private life Clare Vawdrey, a great writer based on Robert Browning, can lead, while his double carries on his social and public life for him. James presents Vawdrey's double with the same limitations of capacity as Ingham's double, Dennis Shea, only on a more complex and sophisticated level. Vawdrey's double "struck" the narrator "as having neither moods nor sensibilities nor preferences." He liked "one subject . . . precisely as much as another," and "I never heard him utter a paradox or express a shade or play with an idea."[7] He would march "into the flat country of anecdote, where stories are visible from afar like windmills and signposts," and "of his perceptions it was too mystifying to think" (VIII, 192). He is a brother to Dennis Shea who does what Ingham tells him to do as long as he is charged not to be "in any way original in his discharge of that duty" (GM, 10).

The conditions are the same for both doubles. When Dennis "appeared in the front of the house, I [Ingham] retired to my sanctissimum and my dressing-gown" (GM, 6). Just so does the real Vawdrey, the writer of brilliant plays, retire to the bedroom of the hotel where the entire cast of characters who inhabit "The Private Life" are staying. His concentration puts the Reverend Ingham to shame, for *he,* the real Vawdrey, works "in the dark" and refuses to answer the narrator, who begs his pardon when he enters to get the manuscript the public Vawdrey had given him permission to take from his room. This tactical error on the part of the double is like those of the "shiftless" Dennis and reveals the truth to the narrator; so Vawdrey the writer is also "undone." The dumbfounded narrator wonders, "Why was he writing in the dark and why hadn't he answered me?" (VIII, 205). Since the double is as handsome as Dennis Shea ["Dennis is goodlooking" (GM, 9)], he is attractive to Blanche Adney, the actress in search of a great part.

The public Vawdrey is put into a predicament when he tells Blanche that he has written " 'before dinner . . . a magnificent passage' " in the third act of the play which she has been begging him to write for years. When he is told by each member of the group that during that time he was "holding us all spell-bound on the terrace," he answers, " 'I don't think I really know when I do things' " (VIII, 199). Since they challenge him, he claims he " 'could repeat the scene,' " which he contracts to do later. When the group convenes with Lord Mellifont (a figure based on Lord Leighton, the painter) acting as chairman and making "our grateful little group feel like a social science congress or a distribution of prizes" (VIII, 200), we have an echo of the kinds of meeting at which Dennis represented Ingham, such as the exhibition of the New Coventry Academy (GM, 8) and various commencement dinners (GM, 9). The figure of speech James uses to describe Vawdrey's predicament, "Suddenly, instead of beginning, our tame lion began to roar out of tune" (VIII, 200), corresponds to the situation when the double "undoes" Ingham and returns home "wild with excitement—in a perfect Irish fury" from the meeting of a society "for keeping children from taking hold of the wrong end of knives when they eat" (GM, 18).

Vawdrey in *his* tight situation was "imperturbably and merrily natural" (VIII, 200). This was true also of Dennis's aplomb at the party where no one bothered to notice that the four speeches learned by rote were inappropriate to the occasion. Vawdrey admits to the narrator in James's tale that " 'there *is* no manuscript'" (VIII, 201) but that he will "'write it tomorrow.'" He adds that if "'there *is* anything, you'll find it on my table'" (VIII, 201). Giving the narrator permission to go to his room, the public Vawdrey gives away the plot there and then, as irresponsibly as Hale's double had done. When James's narrator goes up to Vawdrey's room to get the manuscript, he recognizes that the real, the private Vawdrey himself is sitting at his table, writing. Meanwhile Vawdrey's double is enchanting Blanche on the terrace, having finally received the script from the writing alter ego. "'Oh, the eccentricities of genius!'" she exclaims, and the narrator answers, "They seem greater than I supposed." He tells her his discovery of the real Vawdrey, "the author of Vawdrey's admirable works" (VIII, 209), and he explains the principle of the double to Blanche. "There are two of them. One goes out, the other stays home. One is the genius, the other's the bourgeois, and it's only the bourgeois whom we personally know. He talks, he circulates, he's awfully popular, he flirts with you!" (VIII 210). And he advises her to see for herself.

But the ingeniously told notion of a double invented to get some kind of private life for a man overwhelmed by his worldly responsibilities was not enough for James. At this peak period of his writing life, when he was composing for the theater, his private creativity could only be channeled into his brilliant short tales. His public writing life consisted of writing plays to make "a fast buck," as we now say; his private writing life consisted of constructing short tales in which all his creative ingenuity would be taxed to the limit to atone for writing down to a mass audience. This brilliant story shows how he took the notion of the double, which many years before had created a sensation for the same audience to which he was now appealing, and elaborated it into the story of a *double* double, only the other double, paradoxically, is not even one; it is merely half of one.

He invents this partial man (also from a real-life character), the painter, Lord Mellifont, to balance the double, Vawdrey, creating a man who "isn't even whole. . . . [I]f there are two of Mr. Vawdrey, there isn't so much as one, all told, of Lord Mellifont" (VIII, 211). "He was all public and had no corresponding private life" (VIII, 212), just as the real Clare Vawdrey "was all private life and had no corresponding public one" (VIII, 212). Therefore, James created a balance between the two, developing an original conceit, but one which, without the more limited double from Hale's story, might never have been thought of. In fact, in "The Private Life" James's inventive imagination concerns itself chiefly with the seductive but only partial man and his effect on the gathered group of creative artists of the stage, literature, and music who are on holiday in Switzerland. It is he who saves the day when the public Vawdrey is unprepared to recite from his play because the real Vawdrey has not yet written it.

However, James is most explicit in his evaluation of the real Vawdrey, who, in spite of his seclusion, makes Blanche fall in love with him after she visits him in his dark workroom. James thus shows the power of genius to enchant where the stupid though handsome and flirtatious substitute finally fails. During a storm the public Vawdrey talks idle gossip with the narrator who entertains "the irritating certitude that for personal relations this admirable genius thought his second best good enough. . . . The world was vulgar and stupid, and the real man would have been a fool to come out for it when he could gossip and dine by deputy" (VIII, 225).

The writer who excludes the world and writes in his "sanctissimum," like the Reverend Ingham, is the true hero. If his work keeps him from the world, the world will come to him, as Blanche did. It is, in essence, a justification of the ways of Henry James to himself and to the reader. Here the writer works "in the dark" literally, though James was to use the same phrase metaphorically the next year in a story, "The Middle Years," whose hero, Dencombe, is a portrait of himself. In 1889 James himself was reported by Joseph Pennell to have been seen in his flat working "at a high writing desk in a dark room."[8] The actual "writing in the dark" (VIII, 205) is repeated in a figure of speech in Dencombe's definition of the writer's commitment. "We work in the dark—we do what we can—we give what we have." The "frustration" that "doesn't count" is "only life," and life is what the double takes care of in "The Private Life."[9] The man who lives only for the world like Lord Mellifont disappears when no one is around; he leaves no mark at all.

Given the difference in the input and appeal of both tales separated by more than a generation, one must ask how it is that James used this tale by Hale as part of his mature "rank fantasy," as he called it. The tale appeared in the September 1859 *Atlantic Monthly,* shortly before the sixteen-year-old James was taken along with the rest of his family to Europe to improve his education, and to be sent to a pre-engineering school so that "he might benefit from less reading and more mathematics."[10] But reading he was going to continue to do, just as it is highly likely that before he sailed or perhaps during his sea voyage he read Hale's story in the journal to which his father undoubtedly subscribed, since Mr. and Mrs. Fields, the editors, were the Senior James's close friends. Henry James would contribute thirty-five pieces of prose to the *Atlantic Monthly* from 1865 to 1875; *Roderick Hudson,* his first published novel, would also appear in its pages.

In Europe a few months after his arrival James writes to his friend, Thomas Sargeant Perry, that since his reading time is limited "I have read mostly little bits from Magazines, Newspapers, & the like."[11] His younger brother, Garth Wilkinson James, wrote to "Sargey" on May 28, 1860, "Harry has become an author, I believe, for he keeps his room locked all day," and when Wilky looked in he "saw some poetical looking manuscripts lying on the table, & himself looking in a most author-like way." Older brother William "shows his productions while the more modest little Henry wouldn't let a soul or even a spirit see his."[12] Henry is annoyed at "Wilky's foolhardy imprudence in disclosing, as he did, my secret employment."[13]

We know from other sources how good Henry's memory was for his boyhood reading, so well demonstrated in his *Autobiography,* especially in *A Small Boy and Others,* as well as in the repetition of certain key situations and names of characters found in the books he mentions as being influential in his life, such as *The Lamplighter,* a novel that we have seen gave names to characters in his first novel, *Watch and Ward,* and to some in his earliest tales. He wrote to Mrs. Braddon (the author of famous sensation novels): "I used to follow you ardently, . . . taking from your hands deep draughts of the happiest of anodynes," something he confessed only in 1911, but we have already traced the specific influence of *Lady Audley's Secret* on "Georgina's Reasons," James's sensation story of 1884.[14,15] In 1892 his memory has gone back to the tale he read in 1859 to make use of in a story he is to present to the same readership, that of the *Atlantic Monthly.* Whether that memory was conscious or unconscious we may never know, but hitting on the same type of double, unique in literature, suggests dependency on Hale's tale.

As for Edward Everett Hale (1822–1909), his career as a writer was launched by the extraordinary popularity of "My Double; and How He Undid Me," his first published story. The descendent of distinguished ministers and editors, a great-nephew of Nathan Hale, and a nephew of the orator, Edward Everett, he inherited the inability to juggle many balls—the complex duties of a minister of a big church, the talent and urge to write, the moral impetus to reform, the patriotic urge to propagandize during a national crisis. He spoke from the pulpit and wrote for many causes. His leadership expressed itself in his membership on the Harvard Board of Overseers, as well as in his presidency of the New England Emigrant Society. In addition to contributing to many periodicals, he founded and organized the Lend a Hand programs. Lend a Hand was an organization which grew out of a short story, "Ten Times One is Ten" with a hero, Harry Wadsworth who exemplified the motto "Look up and not down, look forward and not back, look out and not in, and lend a hand." Another story, "In His Name," gave birth to other organizations for religious work. His many works include philanthropic essays, biographies, and practical books like *How to Do It.*

One work that has lasted, along with a score of poems, travel pieces, and feminist essays, is "A Man without a Country" (1863), which also appeared in the *Atlantic Monthly.* The tale of Philip Nolan was written as a piece of propaganda just at the outbreak of the Civil War to create intense feelings of patriotism in the young men of the time. The charm of the tale, however, has extended far beyond its purpose. The man who said " 'Da__n the United States! I wish I may never hear of the United States again!' " every high school boy or girl in the United States recognizes even today and knows through realistic details the refined torture of a punishment for such traitorous words, which ended by making Nolan love his country "as no other man has ever loved her." The improbability of the situation is countered by the reality of the setting, and the story reads like one of the annals of our history.

This same dose of realism attached to a fantastic idea characterizes the story which now has been forgotten, "The Double; and How He Undid Me," though its success at the time started Hale on his career of writing short stories. William Dean Howells, the future editor of the *Atlantic Monthly,* relates in his introduction to his anthology *The Great Modern American Stories* the story's effect on a generation of young men just turned twenty-one like himself. He read it on a sick bed in Columbus, Ohio, "and laughed myself back into health over it." This was "the first of many readings of it and laughings over it with all the friends who then inhabited Columbus to the sum of the little city's population of 20,000. These were all people of my own age, say of twenty or twenty-one" (GM, vii), and one can readily believe that the ideal audience for that story would be young people from sixteen to twenty-one. Henry James would fit into that audience neatly.

Hale, himself a lifelong Bostonian, conceals his identity only by making the locale of his story a town in Maine, for it is clear from his biography that he himself is the Reverend Ingham and that the number of societies and organizations with which he was involved, in addition to his chores and responsibilities as a Congregational minister, particularly that of the South Congregational (Unitarian) Church of Boston at the time when he wrote the story, would make him fantasize a double for himself to make his load lighter. So popular was the tale that it determined much of his later fiction. Hale's powers of invention seem to have been extraordinary, and the many Inghams who appear as characters in his other books seem to be doubles, or clones of the original, but always in new situations.

In the vast critical and memorial material he left behind him, James never mentioned Hale as a writer or a personality, nor do any of Hale's books appear in the list of books in the Lamb House library. But given the time when the story took the readership of the *Atlantic Monthly* by storm and given James's age on the eve of his trip to England, there seems to be little doubt that James was one of the young men who enjoyed the tale. What he did with the notion of the double invented to relieve a writer of social burdens is a testimony to an ingenuity even greater than Hale's. He made the conceit into a justification of the writer's isolation and dedication, as well as a brilliant piece of sophisticated humor in the style of Wilde's paradoxical "Decay of Lying," in which James himself had been critically noticed.

In his 1909 preface to the New York Edition volume that included "The Private Life," James had either forgotten where he had picked up the notion of a double or concealed it, for actually his originality consisted in the *"pair* of conceits" (emphasis mine). He intended to "Play them against each other."[16] There he seems to give himself credit for "the whimsical theory of two distinct and alternate presences, the assertion of either of which on any occasion directly involved the entire extinction of the other: our delight in our inconceivable celebrity was *double,* constructed in two quite distinct and 'water tight' compartments. . . ."[17]

Yet in his *Notebooks* James did not make a detailed account of the double for the Browning figure but instead concentrated on Mellifont. He merely wrote,

> the idea of rolling into one story the little conceit of the private identity of a personage suggested by F.L. and that of a personage suggested by R.B. is of course a rank fantasy, but as such may it not be made amusing and pretty? It must be very brief—very light—very vivid. Lord Mellifont is the public *performer*—the man whose whole personality goes forth so in representation and aspect and sonority and phraseology and accomplishment and frontage that there is absolutely—but I *see* it: begin it, begin it![18]

Clearly for him, then, as he was about to write the story, the conceit consisted of the *combination* of both the double of one man and the mere half of another man conjoined and played "against each other." That combination he seems to have considered *his* idea; the double part was the one he had undoubtedly inherited from Hale.

## Louisa May Alcott and James: A Literary Youth and a Little Woman

Although the conjunction of Louisa Alcott, "the Thackeray—the Trollope of the nursery and the school-room," and Henry James who called her that and who was himself the recorder of adult consciousness in its most complex states, seems at first glance somewhat ridiculous, actually it is not, for when the twenty-two year old James reproved Miss Alcott, nine years his senior, in his 1865 review of *Moods,* he did so as one member of a literary community to another. His father had close relations with Louisa's father, although their famous contretemps did not take place until after the younger James had written his two reviews ten years apart. Louisa has recorded meeting the family, including Henry Junior himself after he had written his very critical review of *Moods,* when his father attended one of Bronson Alcott's lectures in Boston.[19]

What had Henry Junior done to justify his impertinent stance to the more seasoned writer of fifty-four publications, including *Hospital Sketches* (1863), which James Senior had read and liked, as well as *Moods?*[20] Surely Henry Junior's six publications at this time put him in a minor league, especially since he had published his first signed tale, "The Story of a Year" (March 1865), in which certain details indicate that he may have been reading *Hospital Sketches.*

"The Story of a Year" is based on the reality of the Civil War, which James never experienced directly, although he did visit his brother Wilky in the hospital. The atmosphere of wounded and dying soldiers visited by their mothers is similar to that found in Alcott's record of her war experiences. James's early tales contain many borrowings from literature and in his own words show "an admirable commerce of borrowing and lending, . . . not to say stealing and keeping."[21] Alcott's fairy tale, "A Modern Cinderella" (1860), may also have given James the notion of using a classic fairy tale as an analogue. James wrote his own Cinderella tale, "Mrs. Temperley," in 1887, the year he wrote his essay on Emerson, in which he considered Fruitlands, Bronson Alcott's experiment, a "Puritan Carnival."[22]

Perhaps the most amusing comment in James's review of *Moods* is "we are utterly weary of stories about precocious little girls," considering how his own were to appear thirty years later in "The Turn of the Screw" (1898) and *What Maisie Knew* (1897). His youthful priggishness emerges when he accuses Sylvia of "impropriety" in camping "in company with three gentlemen" even though dressed as a boy. James is not ready for the "new" girl, who made a precocious appearance in Alcott's novel. He will face up to her in "Pandora" and *The Bostonians* twenty years later and again as late as 1909 in "Mora Montravers," whose heroine goes further than Sylvia in defying conventions. But James's heroines are basically of different stuff from the very American tomboy whom Alcott was the first to record, her Jo becoming the classic example and Katharine Hepburn her contemporary embodiment.

This twenty-two year old dares to tell an experienced writer who has actually been to the front and saved her family from starvation that he is struck by her "ignorance of human nature and her self-confidence in spite of this ignorance." That is because he does not understand Alcott's material. The problem that Sylvia's "moods" create for her is resolved by her choosing to be a friend rather than a wife. Since the novel is one in which the problem of marriage, of deep concern to Alcott, is threshed out in an original manner (marriage should be "out" for "odd" women), we can understand why Henry James was not at all impressed by the novel's dilemma. James makes the mistake of confusing a very American novel with the typical French novel; the heroine's wishful disguise as a boy is the Yankee mode of the tomboy. Alcott's view of marriage is closer to modern mores than to James's.

When James reviewed *Eight Cousins* ten years later, his position in the literary world had changed. He was the author of *A Passionate Pilgrim* (a collection of tales), *Transatlantic Sketches* (a group of travel pieces), and *Roderick Hudson,* a novel serialized during the year and brought out in book form one month after his review. During 1875 James had published seventy-one articles, the fruit of two trips to Europe. After finishing *Roderick Hudson,* he decided to go to Europe for good. Three days before he left for London, on

October 17, his review of Alcott's book appeared in the *Nation*. For Alcott he would no longer be "a literary youth" but an example of the "young men . . . growing up here of high promise" whom Emerson wrote about to Carlyle in 1883.[23] She would pay attention to his comments.

James's second literary judgment about Alcott's work had to take into consideration two things: first, her new position as the leading writer in America *about* young people, but not necessarily *for* them, a role R. L. Stevenson would also play for the English a decade later; and second, his own Europeanization. James's opening sentence confirms these two changes. His is now a European attitude which notes that American children have lost "the sweet, shy bloom of ideal infancy." He sees Alcott as "the reason for it"—for she "is the novelist of children. . . . She is extremely clever and, we believe, vastly popular with infant readers." Alcott may have recorded the loss of bloom, but how could she be the cause of it? James still is priggish, for, while admiring her as a "satirist," he thinks the book "a very ill-chosen sort of entertainment to set before children. . . . The smart satirical tone is the last one in the world to be used in describing to children their elders and betters and the social mysteries that surround them."

In finding this anomaly in her work, James has put his finger on Alcott's peculiar straddling of the two worlds of childhood and adulthood. It had created the problem in *Moods* for Sylvia, who felt happier in a pal-like relation to men, rather than a sexual one, and it no doubt reflected Alcott's permanent role as a successful child to her parents and as the tomboy in a family of girls. She has distressed generations of girls who cannot forgive her for not letting Jo marry Laurie ("I *won't* marry Jo to Laurie to please anyone"), but rather a middle-aged professor.[24] Today one can understand that Jo was happier as a friend to Laurie, and, if she had to marry to become the heroine of *Jo's Boys,* her husband would have to be some father symbol, based on Bronson Alcott, probably the only man to whom Louisa Alcott could relate.

It is this androgynous characteristic a hundred years before its time that disturbed the young James. Twenty years later his Maisie and Mrs. Wix would repeat some aspects of the conspiracy between an adult and a child against the "others" in which Rose and her Uncle Alec engage and that annoyed James. But in 1875 he yearns for the "'Rollo' books of our infancy . . . as an antidote to this unhappy amalgam of the novel and the storybook." He failed to recognize in this "amalgam" a new genre of American literature because his eye was turned eastward; he was troubled by the need to choose between America and Europe. To placate his uneasiness he now wrote many adult fairy tales, one, "Benvolio" (1875), just a few weeks before his review. Careful to include "the glow of fairy-land" he was to miss in *Eight Cousins,* he nevertheless had no happy endings. Because of his irritation at the precocious children he found annoying even in *Moods,* a novel for adults, he failed to see the fairy-tale underpinnings in *Eight Cousins,* the seven boy cousins obvious equivalents for the Seven Dwarfs, and Rose, a modern Snow White. Each boy is individualized, as the dwarfs are, and all fall in love with their cousin in the sequel, *Rose in Bloom.* The ideal family structure for a girl with three sisters like Alcott would be to have many brothers or male cousins, as does Rose, who is happily surrounded by sexually harmless males. *Eight Cousins* thus shows a fantasy world in which marriage has no place.

In 1865 James had predicted that Alcott could someday "write a very good novel, provided she will be satisfied to describe only that which she has seen." In *Eight Cousins* she has described certain true aspects of family life, yet James deplores her "private understanding with the youngsters she depicts, at the expense of their pastors and masters." The knowingness of the little heroine shows that she "reads the magazines, and perhaps even writes for them." He objects to Alcott's having transposed the romanticism of *Jane Eyre* to present-day conditions and to her Rochester's using the waterspout to descend from her room: "Why not by a rope-ladder at once?" Here it amuses the reader of James to remember that, while he criticizes Uncle Alec for dancing a polka with Rose for getting the best of her aunt, Sir Claude in *What Maisie Knew* would conspire even more deeply with Maisie against the adult women involved with him.

James's strong feelings about Alcott's novel seem to have affected his own fiction. The "knowing" air of Randolph Miller, Daisy's younger brother, might be a reflection on American children not so much observed as read about in Alcott's novel. In 1878 James was not sympathetic to this kind of child, and we are not in any way to love or admire little Randolph. We are simply to recognize the truth of his portrait, which may depend on James's initiation into the psychology of children in America through Alcott's novel. Randolph Miller can be seen as a tribute from James to Alcott for providing him with seven variations of the type among Rose's cousins.

In spite of the immeasurable difference between the consciousness of Alcott's and James's characters, the two writers may have given each other useful hints in constructing their fiction. Their interaction was probably more important when the young James was learning to write. Alcott's prototypes may have served as a source for the young Americans James needed in his first international tales. And even in his fin de siècle stories about English children it is possible he fell back on his earlier impressions of Alcott's family groups. But in Alcott's books the adults are never evil in relation to the youngsters; in James's fiction they almost always are, and the few adults who protect "the plasticity" of youth, like Mrs. Wix and Mr. Longdon, are outnumbered by such equivocal guardians as the oppressive governess in "The Turn of the Screw" and Mrs. Brookenham's corrupting circle, so different from Rose's.

Certain relationships between James and his family circle and Alcott's and hers unquestionably left their mark on the structure of James's invented characters' family relationships. We see it especially in the unfinished novel *The Ivory Tower*, where Rosanna Gaw and her father can be viewed as existing in a framework similar to that of Louisa and Bronson Alcott, only Rosanna has eaten of the tree of knowledge and her relationship to *her* Laurie, Gray Fielder, is fraught with the dangers and evils of a more frightening world. The cousinship of Alcott's world has become poisoned, but at this later period in James's life, after his trip to America and its reminders of his youth, the basic family formulations and individual responses gathered from Alcott's books early in his life undoubtedly reappeared in his fiction, as did the fairy tales and Greek legends that were the fruit of his early reading habits.

## A Surprising Parallel: Clara Sherwood Rollins's "A Burne-Jones Head" and "The Beldonald Holbein"

"A Burne-Jones Head" is a short story written by an obscure American writer, Clara Sherwood Rollins. It relates the social rise and fall of Mrs. Rogers, a young woman who greatly resembles the type of beauty invented by Sir Edward Burne-Jones, the English pre-Raphaelite painter. With that distinction the young woman is launched into society by the favorite beau of a social leader, who sponsors the "Burne-Jones head" in her circle only to expel her when she becomes jealous of her success. The young woman is shipped back to the American provinces whence she came as if she were a painting. The society that first embraces and then rejects her refers to her in the terminology of a masterpiece of portraiture; the metaphor embraces the whole story.

What is interesting for us about this story is that Henry James wrote a story with a similar title, "The Beldonald Holbein" (1901), in which there is a similar identification of a woman with a portrait of a master. She, too, is brought into a social circle by a lady who then ejects the "Holbein" out of jealousy and ships her back to America. There is the same recourse to the terminology of painting by which the author presents his heroine, who differs from the Rollins heroine only insofar as she is old and not considered a conventional beauty until an artist's eye recognizes her "type."

One might ordinarily assume that the author of "A Burne-Jones Head" used "The Beldonald Holbein" as a model, until a glance at the copyright date shows quite clearly that the Rollins story was published in 1894, seven years *before* the James story. The resemblances are so close as to seem to be not a matter of accident. We are forced to conclude from the evidence gained from an analysis of both stories that the fifty-seven year old James seems to have been influenced by a story written by a twenty-year-old girl of limited production and even more limited reputation. However, although Clara Rollins was young and apparently without reputation, her precocious gifts must not be underestimated. Born in St. Louis in 1874, she later moved to Boston and wrote poems, articles, and short stories that show a sophisticated wit. She had written *Three Pieces for Amateurs* under her maiden name of Clara Harriet Sherwood. Her stories appeared in magazines and in 1894 were collected in *A Burne-Jones Head and Other Sketches*. In 1897 appeared another group, *Threads of Life,* but after that it is difficult to find further information about her.

The channel by which Mrs. Rollins's story probably reached James was through its publisher, Lovell, Coryell and Company, a subsidiary of the United States Book Company, whose agent in London was Woolcott Balestier. Until his untimely death in 1891, Balestier was both James's agent and his friend. James wrote a preface to Balestier's posthumous book, *The Average Woman* (1892), also published by the United States Book Company. In 1891 James wrote prefaces to two collections of stories by Rudyard Kipling (who married Balestier's sister), also published by Lovell, Coryell and Company. Therefore, it is likely that in 1894 the publishers sent James, now one of their authors, a copy of Mrs. Rollins's book, perhaps even for his critical comments. Since James never mentioned the book, this, of course, is conjecture.

The resemblance between the basic situations in both the Rollins story and the James story is striking enough to warrant the supposition that James had read "A Burne-Jones Head" and, in his characteristic fashion, challenged perhaps by the obvious "ladies' journal" quality of the story, spritely and literate though it is, "redid" it by improving upon what was for him its interesting structure. What, no doubt, interested him in "A Burne-Jones Head" was the jealousy felt by a society woman when a man she likes pays more attention to an "intruder" woman of great beauty, identified with a famous painter's type (fig. 45). For that reason the society woman is moved to make the rival a social outcast in her set, ending in the rival's banishment from the locale.

James attached the mechanics of the basic plot in the short story by Clara Rollins to a real-life situation, related to him by Maud Howe in May 1899, about her mother Julia Ward Howe, who had enjoyed, in her seventies, a *succés de beauté* in Rome while visiting her daughter because the artists in the American set saw her as a Holbein portrait. (Hitchcock's illustration for the periodical appearance of James's story bears no resemblance to a real Holbein [fig. 46]). The function of the heroine in James's story is exactly that of the "Burne-Jones Head." She is imported to embellish her patron's social career but banished when she outshines her. In Clara Rollins's story, Mrs. Rogers, the "Burne-Jones head," takes singing lessons from a Signor Padronti, in whose studio she meets Peyton, who launches her at a dinner party. Mrs. Tillbury, the social leader in love with him, "raved over her, claimed her for her own, placed the Tillbury arms upon her, and christened her a 'Burne-Jones.' "[25] "And thus it was that the Burne-Jones head, after being approved at the private view was exhibited to the world—that is, to Mrs. Tillbury's world" (B, 26).

Mrs. Rogers's downfall takes place because, as an admired masterpiece of

Figure 45.  Frontispiece to *A Burne-Jones Head*
by Clara Rollins (New York:
Lovell, Coryell & Co., 1894)

Figure 46.  Lucius Hitchcock, *The Beldonald Holbein*, 1901
Illustration for the appearance of Henry James's story "The
Beldonald Holbein" in *Harper's New Monthly Magazine*.

Burne-Jones's art, she "was almost too much of a success to please Mrs. Tillbury. She liked to have her taste approved, but Peyton had always been at *her* elbow more or less. Now it was decidedly less. . . . However, she concealed all feeling of discontent beneath her most fascinating smile" (B, 30). At the opening of an operetta in which "the Burne-Jones was to sing the leading part," the invited guests gossip about Peyton's relations with her and her failure to produce her husband for the concert. The conclusion of the story is "that the Burne-Jones head is turned" (B, 35). Peyton not only overhears this gossip, but he realizes that "the Burne-Jones" does so, too. Wounded and disillusioned with society, she returns to her provincial home with her husband. "So the Burne-Jones went back into the rustic frame where she belonged. And the little world that had admired and criticized and gossiped forgot all about her." Peyton consoles himself with a real Burne-Jones head, which he buys in Paris and "which Padronti insists resembles his lost pupil" (B, 49).

Let us look at James's story, published seven years later. The basic anecdote of the aged Julia Ward Howe's success as a Holbein portrait, "her coming out . . . at the end of her long, arduous life and having a wonderful unexpected final moment—at 78!—of being thought *the* most picturesque, striking, lovely old (wrinkled and *marked*) 'Holbein', etc., that ever was" is maintained as the core of the story which first appeared in *Harper's New Monthly Magazine* for October 1901 (N, 290–91). The success of James's heroine, Mrs. Brash, depended entirely upon her looking old and stylized, yet completely within the tradition of German Renaissance portraiture. Mrs. Rollins's heroine, conforming to the romantic requirements of a "ladies'" magazine of the period, is rescued from a romantic escapade injurious to her reputation. James's superior irony resides in his use of the paradox of an old, not a young, woman *becoming* a beauty because of her resemblance to a work of art. James focuses on the vanity of Lady Beldonald, who uses her aging relative Mrs. Brash as a foil for her own conventional beauty. (James makes Mrs. Brash fifty-seven, to correspond to a real portrait by Holbein.) Since the artist by whom she herself wishes to be painted prefers Mrs. Brash, Lady Beldonald sends her back to America.

Although James has made an entirely different, much richer, and immeasureably better story out of the original structure, we continue to find parallel bits of plot. The heroes of both stories discover the lady-into-painting through another friend. In James's story, the painter's friend, Paul Outreau, like Mrs. Tillbury, names the painting that the heroine has, metaphorically, turned into. " 'She's the greatest of all Holbeins,' " and a " 'Holbein head' "—" '*c'est une tête à faire.*' "[26] Another correspondence occurs when Lady Beldonald wants to be painted to achieve social success, and she pretends to love her elderly rival and "faced the music of Mrs. Brash's success." She "never attempted to hide or to betray her" (XI, 303). In the parallel story, Mrs. Tillbury also "concealed all feeling of discontent beneath her most fascinating smile" (B, 30). Mrs. Brash herself refuses to be painted because she is aware of how Lady Beldonald feels, just as Mrs. Rogers knows, by having overheard the conversation about her at the concert, how nasty and jealous everyone is of her success.

Moreover, James seems to have paraphrased two sentences from the Rollins story. The first, "And thus it was that the Burne-Jones head, after having been approved at the private view, was exhibited to the world" (B, 26), becomes elaborately amplified in James's story. There "dropped into my memory a rich little gallery of pictures. . . . I see Mrs. Brash . . . practically enthroned and surrounded and more or less mobbed; see the hurrying and the nudging and the pressing and the staring; see the people 'making up' and introduced, and catch the word when they have had their turn; hear it above all, the great one—'Ah yes, the famous Holbein!' " (XI, 301–2). The rich embroidery of the language and the images does not conceal the fact that the Rollins sentence may have been the foundation on which the colorful construction was built.

The second sentence in the Rollins story that James reworks mentions that the Burne-Jones head always wore either "a white gown . . . which she had evolved" (B, 25) or a black one. In like manner Mrs. Brash, in James's story, "had developed her admirable dress . . . always either black or white." As the painter-narrator of James's story has made a woman into a work of art, "She was, in short, just what we had made of her, a Holbein for a great museum. . . . The world—I speak of course mainly of the art world—flocked to see it" (XI, 298), so Mrs. Tillbury, in the Rollins story, the taste-former of her group, has made a young woman into a work of art, which she regrets since it threatens her with the loss of her own admirer.

James concludes his story with the reverse of Clara Rollins's image of the picture leaving its frame. The nasty gossips at the musicale concluded that "the Burne-Jones head is turned." The "masterpiece," knowing that people think she is Peyton's mistress, "went back into the rustic frame where she belonged. And the little world that had admired and criticized and gossiped forgot all about her" (B, 49). "I know nothing of her original conditions," the painter-narrator in "The Beldonald Holbein" tells us, "save that for her to have gone back to them was clearly to have stepped out of her frame" (XI, 306). What happens to them is different, but the relation of a person to a frame is the same. Not surviving, like the Burne-Jones, his Holbein is crushed. Instead of her "head being turned," the picture actually "turns its face to the wall: It wasn't—the minor American city—a market for Holbeins, and what had occurred was that the poor old picture, banished from its museum and refreshed by the rise of no new movement to hang it, was capable of the miracle of a silent revolution, of itself turning, in its dire dishonour, its face to the wall" (XI, 306). Poor Mrs. Brash, the rejected and deacquisitioned picture, went out "like a snuffed candle." In retribution, the painter will take his revenge on Lady Beldonald by painting her as she really is, not as she wants to be.

The end of "the Holbein" therefore, is different from that of "the Burne-Jones head." The latter, surviving but forgotten by all, now concentrates on her baby. The Holbein, on the other hand, "stood, without the intervention of the ghost of a critic, till they happened to pull it round again and find it mere dead paint" (XI, 306). The narrator-painter in the James story refers to Mrs. Brash as if she had indeed been a real painting, a thing and not a person. "Well, *it* [emphasis mine] had had . . . its season of fame, its name on a thousand tongues and printed in capitals in the catalogue" (XI, 306). "The Burne-Jones head" regains her place as an actual person, since Peyton buys a Burne-Jones painting to replace the living one. In fact, the Burne-Jones figure that serves as a frontispiece for the book might be considered by the reader as Mrs. Rogers's replacement, while the original resumes her life as a mother and wife on an Iowa farm. What is a metaphor in Mrs. Rollins's story becomes a reality in James's, in which a person is totally transformed into an analogue. The incisive painter-narrator in "The Beldonald Holbein" gives the story its final irony by suggesting he will do the portrait of Lady Beldonald without flattery. The cruel image James uses gives the reader some idea of what his portrait will reveal: Since " 'she *will* have the real thing—oh well, hang it, she shall!' " A box of sardines " 'is only "old" after it has been opened. Lady Beldonald never has yet been—but I'm going to do it' " (XI, 290).

In 1894, the stylish painter of beauties was Burne-Jones, and Oscar Wilde wrote that women were now beginning to look like his figures. Henner, too, produced women whose features could be found in pretty young contemporaries. Mrs. Rollins mentions Henner as another painter who would "have delighted in her [the heroine's] copper hair and warm flesh tints" (B, 7). This idea of youthful beauty that could be appreciated only by the trained eye of the artist is probably what held James's interest when he read the Rollins story, though in his own tale he uses a type that is caviar to the general. " 'I don't say your friend,' " the narrator tells Lady Beldonald, " 'is a person to make the men turn round in Regent Street' " (XI, 293). What appeals to the painter in the story is that he had never "before seen that degree and that special sort of personal success come to a woman for the first time so late in life" (XI, 296).

After Mrs. Brash is "shipped" back to America, she is totally transformed into a painting. She is referred to as "the masterpiece we had for three or four months been living with," which had made us "feel its presence as a luminous lesson and a daily need." It "had been the gem of our collection," and we "found what a blank it left on the wall" (XI, 304). In James's vision, the metaphor has become the reality; it exhibits the transformation of a rhetorical analogue into a material entity. What happens to Mrs. Brash is that she dies, not as a person but as a work of art, for "it turns its face to the wall" and becomes "mere dead paint."[27]

Referred to as an *it* and not a *she,* James's heroine exhibits through paradoxical irony another extension of the high value art had over life for James, a value appearing more and more in his work after *The Tragic Muse* (1890). It occurs in great concentration in the group of stories about artists written around the turn of the century, of which "The Beldonald Holbein" is one.[28] The combination of the paradoxical lady-into-painting with comic exaggeration, which becomes savage when involved with the silliness of the art-loving social world, might give away James's desire around this time to contradict Wilde's judgment of him in *Intentions:* "Mr. Henry James writes fiction as if it were a painful duty." In "The Beldonald Holbein," James gives the lie to Wilde's "crack."[29]

In 1902, James's friend, Mrs. Cadwalader Jones, had sent to him for his opinion a couple of volumes of short stories by a young, then fairly unknown writer, Edith Wharton. James's reaction, as he wrote to Mrs. Jones, was to want to do over at least one of the stories that had interested him. "If a work of imagination, of fiction, interests me at all (and very few, alas, do!) I always want to write it over in my own way, handle the subject from my own sense of it. *That* I always find a pleasure in." He continues, "But I can't speak more highly for any book, or at least for my interest in any. I take liberties with the greatest." James could find something to redo *his* way in Shakespeare, in Edith Wharton, or even in Clara Sherwood Rollins. The clever but typical ladies' magazine story like "A Burne-Jones Head" probably intrigued him by the atmosphere instantly established on its first page. We here reprint the opening lines:

> Mrs. Tillbury called her a Burne-Jones Head, and Mrs. Tillbury was a woman who possessed a vast knowledge of art in general and the world in particular.
> She gave dinners for her protégé, to which she invited the indolent dilettante Bohemian New York circle of which she was perhaps the centre. And as the Burne-Jones head was attached to a very beautiful body the men raved over her. Women thought her stupid, but she became the fashion all the same, for she was a novelty and her voice was wonderfully sweet. (B, 7)

The tone is that in which James pitched his own clever story, and it is clear that, though James took "liberties with the greatest," if any "work of imagination" interested him, he "always want[ed] to write . . . it over in [his] own way, handle the subject from [his] own sense of it."[30]

## Annie Fields and Sarah Orne Jewett: Susan Shepherd Stringham and Milly Theale

In the summer of 1898 Mrs. Annie Fields, the widow of James T. Fields of *The Atlantic Monthly,* who had given James his early start in publishing his stories, came to visit the author during the first summer of his occupancy of Lamb

House. With her came Sarah Orne Jewett, a talented writer fifteen years her junior and, since Mr. Fields's death, Annie's constant companion. Both women were known to be related in a "union" like the then well-known "Boston marriage," and, beginning in 1882, had made European trips together. Sarah Orne Jewett had as a young girl of twenty entered the Fields' circle in Boston with the publication of the first of her stories of Maine life, which today are considered the classic representation of that region. The effect on James of the original character of Sarah Jewett's writings was to receive its final statement in his piece, "Mr. and Mrs. Fields" (1915), in which he commemorates the impressions of the publisher's Charles Street salon remembered from his early years. Like a pearl within its shell is included an appreciation of the Maine author. He speaks of Mrs. Fields as "bringing with her a young friend of great talent whose prevailing presence in her life had come little by little to give it something like a new centre." He feels that "to speak in a mere parenthesis . . . is to do myself the violence of suppressing a chapter of appreciation that I should long since somewhere have found space for."[31] He apologizes for not having already done that chapter to commemorate Sarah Jewett's stories of New England.

"She had come to Mrs. Fields as an adoptive daughter, both a sharer and a sustainer" (LAE, 174). He refers to the "association of the elder and the younger lady in . . . an emphasized susceptibility" (LAE, 175). No matter that the so-called younger woman was really forty-nine, only six years younger than James himself and fifteen years younger than Mrs. Fields, and that she died at sixty, tragically, from complications resulting from "a fall in a carriage accident," a "premature and overdarkened close of her young course of production" (LAE, 174).

But thirteen years before this 1915 essay James had paid tribute to both women in *The Wings of the Dove*. It was the "sustaining" character of the relationship and the dedication of Mrs. Annie Fields to the unusual character of the younger woman that one easily recognizes in the relationship between Mrs. Susie Stringham and Milly Theale, once we are cued in. In his book on Sarah Orne Jewett, F. O. Matthiessen describes her as "a tall slender girl, never very strong, but full of bursts of energy"[32] whose parents and relatives had all died early. In Annie Fields's edition of Sara Orne Jewett's letters (1911), she also mentioned that Miss Jewett's parents died young and that Miss Jewett herself was sickly all her life, as we know Milly Theale was bereaved and stricken by disease. In 1882 Annie Fields and Sarah Jewett made their first trip to Europe together, a trip blessed by Whittier, who wrote a sonnet to their travels called "Godspeed," just as Susie Shepherd (as Milly called Susan Stringham) and Milly made their first joint trip together. James, in his essay, comments on Miss Jewett's "remarkable distinguished outward stamp" as well as her "elegance of humility or fine flame of modesty" (LAE, 174), characteristic of Milly Theale as seen by her friends.

In his major phase novels James began to introduce cameos of his friends, recognizable, he probably hoped, by those involved. In *The Ambassadors,* behind Miss Barrace was Henrietta Ruebell; and in *The Golden Bowl,* Mr. Crichton of the British Museum is undoubtedly Sir Sidney Colvin, as Fanny Assingham is Fanny Sitwell. These cameos are self-contained portraits with the recognizable characteristics of James's friends, and yet those characteristics do not add anything to the story; they operate as little gifts, little portraits of friends. James had done it before in "Pandora," where he created a portrait of his friends Mr. and Mrs. Henry Adams in the Bonnycastles of Washington, D.C.

Here, in *The Wings of the Dove,* there is the double portrait of Annie Fields and Sarah Orne Jewett. We recognize that in Mrs. Stringham he has planted some of the characteristics of Sarah Orne Jewett as well as those of Annie Fields, which we have already noted: first, her trio of names, Susan Shepherd Stringham, usually called Susie Shepherd by Milly Theale to make a vague, concealed correspondence to Annie Fields; second, she is from "Burlington, Vermont," an attempt to approximate South Berwick, Maine, Miss Jewett's home, yet to conceal it while still making it north of Boston. Again, Susan Stringham "wrote short stories" and "was a contributor to the best magazines," like Sarah Orne Jewett, and like her "fondly believed she had her 'note,' the art of showing New England without showing it wholly in the kitchen," a just appreciation of Jewett's art.

The depth and extent of Mrs. Stringham's attachment to the young woman, Milly Theale, is expressed in their relationship "that might have been afloat . . . in a great warm sea that represented . . . an outer sphere, of general emotion and the effect of anything in particular was to make the sea submerge the island, the margin flood the text. The great wave now for a moment swept over. 'I'll go anywhere in the world you like'" (XIX, 199). Merton Densher's remark on Susie's "'little dry New England brightness'" is a good description of Sarah Orne Jewett's talent (XX, 38). Susie calls Milly "'dearest'" and "'my own'" (XX, 102). and she would have "drowned her very self for her" (XX, 142).

The trip Susie is making with Milly, as we noted, corresponds to the trip made by Annie Fields and Sarah Orne Jewett in 1882 right after Mr. Fields's death, a trip everyone within the group applauded and sanctioned. Their love was a relationship recognized, respected, and approved by Aldrich, Whittier, and Longfellow. James includes material we know relates to Sarah Orne Jewett's background and education. Susie's opinion that "To *be* in truth literary had ever been her dearest thought" is characteristic of Miss Jewett. "There were masters, models, celebrities mainly foreign . . . in whose light she ingeniously laboured" (MA, 107), and from Matthiessen we learn that "perhaps the greatest spur to her [Miss Jewett's] work was Flaubert." But there the transposition ends. The rest of her character, behavior, and relation to Milly stems from Annie

Fields, in regard to her "sustaining" relation, to her age, and to her role of mother or even lover. When they were not together, they "jotted notes of love" (MA, 72).

The personality and physical appearance, as well as the relation to a senior female companion, is that of Sarah Orne Jewett set within the character of Milly Theale. The continual black dress and robes worn by Milly imitate Sarah Jewett's costume, noted in newspaper reports, such as when Miss Jewett poured tea at a Sargent exhibition dressed "in black with a large effective black hat with many nodding plumes." As the two women were absorbed into a "union" after Mr. Fields's death "that endured as long as their lives," so we see Susie Shepherd working out of love for Milly to get Densher to love Milly also, and Susie is with Milly at her death. It is interesting that years after *The Wings of the Dove,* in his memorial sketch of the new England author and her patron, James uses the figure of outstretched wings to characterize "their reach together." He refers to the "stretch of wing that the spirit of Charles Street could bring off" (LAE, 175). James had visited Jewett's house in Maine as well as the Fields's house on Charles Street, and he was thoroughly impressed with their personalities. The "impression" made by Milly on Susie Stringham was as passionate and as akin to romantic love as the relation of the two prototypes had been, and James describes it with intensity. Susie stops writing stories "as soon as she found herself in the presence of the real thing, the romantic life itself. That is what she saw in Mildred—what positively made her hand tremble a while too much for the pen," and Milly shared her impression, for "she had never seen anyone like her either" (XIX, 107–8). Milly's "high dim charming ambiguous oddity" corresponds to Sarah Orne Jewett's "slender dignity of . . . bearing . . . sparkling charm and piquant grace" (MA, 72).

Beyond these biographical elements applied to both fictional women, James referred to Sarah Orne Jewett in his borrowing from Jewett's fiction itself. There is the striking fact that in Miss Jewett's first book, *Deephaven,* the heroine's name is Kate Lancaster. In the *Wings of the Dove* Kate Croy lives with her aunt at Lancaster Gate. The juxtaposition cannot be purely accidental. In this instance, the personalities and the relation of the two women energize the relation of the two women in the novel, as well as indicating that James had read *Deephaven* and knew the name of its heroine and the place where she was living. Also, James's notebooks testify to his having received the germ for his 1902 tale *Flickerbridge* from "A Lost Lover," one of the stories in *Tales of New England,* Sarah Orne Jewett's 1879 volume of short stories. When Miss Jewett and Mrs. Fields visited James in 1898, Miss Jewett presented James with an inscribed copy of this book in its 1894 reprint.

On February 19, 1899, a few months after the two women's visit, James noted,

Struck an hour ago by pretty little germ of small thing given out in 4 or 5 lines . . . of Miss Jewett—*Tales of N.E.* A girl on a visit to new-found old-fashioned (spinster gentlewoman) relation, 'idealized her old cousin I've no doubt; and her repression and rare words of approval, had a great fascination for a girl who had just been used to people who chattered and were upon most intimate terms with you directly, and could forget you with equal ease'. That is all—but they brushed me, as I read, with the sense of a little—a very tiny—subject. Something like *this*. I think I see it—*must* see it—as a young *man*—a young man who goes to see, for the first time, a new-found old-fashioned (spinster gentlewoman) cousin. He has been ill—is convalescent—so doesn't get well very fast—has had infernal influenza.

We know from the rest of his notes the additional changes he made in "Flicker-bridge," the story based on the germ and published in 1902, but the source is, as he writes, in "A Lost Lover" in Miss Jewett's volume of tales (N, 286–88). The tale itself has no further relation to the Jewett tale, and James goes off on his own on the horrors and dangers of publicity and the destruction of authentic characters by the public passion for ruining originals. Both *Deephaven* and "A Lost Lover" were among Miss Jewett's early fiction, which James especially praised in his essay on Mr. and Mrs. Fields (LAE, 175–76). So in his own way James had "found space for a chapter of appreciation" of both Annie Fields and Sarah Orne Jewett in *The Wings of the Dove* and "Flickerbridge."

### Edgar Fawcett's *A Romance of Old New York* and *The Wings of the Dove*

A most interesting and curious puzzle exists in the relationship between the popular novel by the American writer Edgar Fawcett (1847–1904), *A Romance of Old New York,* published in 1897 and presented by him to his friend Henry James in February of that year, and Henry James's *The Wings of the Dove* published in 1902 (fig. 47). On the flyleaf is written, "To Henry James, Esq. from his friend and devout admirer, Edgar Fawcett. New York. February. 1897" (fig. 48). In Fawcett's book a young man is encouraged by his fiancée and her father to make love to a dying young woman much in love with him to bring her some happiness before she dies. Fawcett, in what seems to be a parodic version of James's novel, has the young woman recover, a state that furnishes the plot with a situation never encountered in James's serious work. As a comedy, almost a farce, the work has a relation to the plight of Milly who does die and who covers with her outspread wings Merton and Kate, who, unlike Fawcett's pair, are out to despoil her.

Yet what seems a straightforward effect of Fawcett's book on James's plot is complicated by the fact that James had sketched out the basic elements of his novel for himself in his *Notebooks* of 1894–95, two years before Fawcett's book appeared. Even more curious is the fact that James in his notes had himself rejected the possibility that his heroine might turn the tables by recovering from her illness as "vulgarly ugly" (N, 171). J. I. M. Stewart takes up this variant in

Figure 47.  *A Romance of Old New York* by Edgar Fawcett (Philadelphia: Lippincott, 1897)

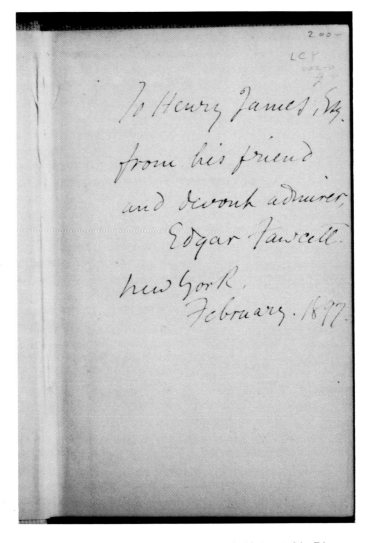

Figure 48.    Inscribed Flyleaf of *A Romance of Old New York* by Edgar
Fawcett
"To Henry James, Esq. from his friend and devout admirer,
Edgar Fawcett. New York, February, 1897."

his Jamesian novel of 1954, *Mark Lambert's Supper*. He writes, after having read the entry in Matthiessen's 1947 edition of the *Notebooks* in which James asks himself what the sequel to the young man's agreeing to marry "the poor girl" might be in the certitude that she will die and leave the money to him, "I can scarcely imagine any—I doubt if I can—that isn't ugly and vulgar: I mean vulgarly ugly. This would be the case with the girl's not, after all, dying—and that's not what I want or mean." Stewart puts into the novelist Lambert's Memorandum Book this recollection of his invented friendship with Henry James: "James once confessed to me having toyed with the idea of giving Milly Theale's story this twist in *The Wings of the Dove:* The designing young man— rather the *designed-for* young man—would marry the mortally sick heiress, who would promptly recover as a result. James dismissed the notion as vulgarly ugly."[33] Fawcett's novel makes a comedy out of the situation and, although it is vulgar in that it is a pop novelette, it is not ugly because there is no money involved, and since the sick girl has her own lover, the two couples are happily paired off at the end.

What James, three years after his notebook entry, must have thought or felt when just such a vulgar if not "ugly" solution to the novelistic problem was presented to him by his friend Edgar Fawcett in his *A Romance of Old New York,* we can only fondly speculate about. That the two men were friends is evidenced by a letter in 1898 to Gailliard Lapsley from James.[34] James refers to having seen "E. Fawcett yesterday." The second and more relevant proof that the two writers were in close touch just when James had begun to write *The Wings of the Dove* "in the middle of July, 1891" is a notation in the *Notebooks* for July 28, 1901 (EP, 197).[35] James makes note of "the suggestion, equally vague, conveyed by passage in recent letter to me from E.F." (identified by Edel and Powers as Edgar Fawcett (1847–1904), American novelist, poet and playwright). This letter, James continues, "I've destroyed—passage character-istically advising me—and in the strongest good faith—to go to the U.S. and give readings from my work—for the money and the boom," a notion he then discards.

But the interesting statement that he has "destroyed" the letter suggests some kind of contents other than the suggestion to give public readings in the United States. What that can have been we do not know. It might have had something to do with the simultaneous treatment of a similar theme in their two novels. James might probably want to "destroy" any evidence that Fawcett had treated comically a situation that he was beginning to treat so seriously. Surely James would not want his subject, handled so consciously and tragically in his tribute to his dead cousin Minny Temple, to be confused with the pop novel by his friend Fawcett which had handled the raw theme comically and superficially in a novella easily read in an hour. James would have been right if his fears on that score were the cause of the destruction of Fawcett's letter, because

Fawcett's novel has been totally forgotten. Fawcett's handling, one must point out, never involved the money angle so important to James's plot. Fawcett has the deception engaged in only for the sake of a dying girl's happiness.

In Fawcett's novel a young man in the first decades of the twentieth century is encouraged by his fiancée, Charlotte Verplanck, and her father to make love to and become engaged to her fatally ill sister in order to give her some happiness before she dies since she was in love with him. Although horrified by the "hypocrisy," the hero, Mark Frankland nevertheless reluctantly carries out his fiancée's wishes. Her father suffers greatly for the sick girl, "'I violate my promise to her,'" of keeping the secret of her love and by doing so "'I am telling the first actual lie of my whole life.'"[36] "'Yet it is a lie told in the passionate fatherly hope of easing her final hours on earth'" (R, 42). Charlotte "'is willing to join with me in the request I am now about to make'" (R, 43). Charlotte also entreats him, but Mark refuses. "'It would be hypocrisy.'" The father accepts his refusal, but Charlotte threatens to break off their engagement if he refuses. He consents but ventilates his feelings to Aaron Burr, who tells him, "'Charlotte will love you all the more.'" The sin, clearly, in this novel, is lying.

The possible effect that Fawcett's book had on James can be seen in the resistance of Fawcett's hero, Mark, to the suggestion that he pretend to love the dying girl against his will. The lies told in the Fawcett tale begin with Mr. Verplanck's lie that violates his sick daughter Pamela's oath of secrecy about her feelings for Mark Frankland. In the same fashion Merton Densher also resists realizing what Kate is asking him to do, that is, to marry a dying girl so that he and Kate will be rich when he becomes a widower. But James has demonstrated this resistance in a most subtle manner. Densher refuses to see what Kate means when she asks him to be nice to Milly. He almost refuses to see why Maud Lowder wants him to attach himself to Milly, although he realizes it means that it will leave the way clear for Kate to marry Lord Mark. There are one hundred and twenty pages of Densher's *not* understanding what Kate and the others (Susan and Maud) have planned *for* Milly. He finally, after he is paid by Kate's visiting him in his rooms, *postpones* his "horror" and his "shame."

This resistance of Densher's to all of Kate's build-up of how he, Densher, must involve himself with Milly, is seen even in the prior treatment by Fawcett. Mark does not wish to understand what Pamela's father is trying to tell him and resists the idea as Densher does, since he, too, prefers the other girl, in this case, Charlotte. In fact, when Mr. Verplanck brings up the subject, Mark thinks he is talking about his other daughter, Charlotte, the girl to whom Mark is engaged. As the older man proceeds, Mark "was pierced by a peculiar dread, which he could not explain and could only feel," echoing Merton Densher's dialogue with Kate. After Verplanck's request, Mark answers in the way that has been obvious all along to the reader, "Oh, no, no! Believe me, sir, I could not possibly consent!" (R, 44). He resists, but his fiancée, Charlotte, with a face that "hardened a little," says that what Mark calls "the falsehood of the situation" would be justifiable. "You could do it for my sake . . . as a sacrifice" (R, 46).

> "I would make, for you . . . almost any sacrifice."
> "Make this, then," said Charlotte. . . .
> "Soil my honor," faltered Mark . . . "by asking her for my wife whom I do not love and whom I have no intention of marrying?" (R, 47)

Charlotte, who persists after her father withdraws, threatens "to break our troth" (R, 50), and when she refuses Mark's caress, he breaks down. Densher's bargain is effected by Kate's consenting to be his mistress, the sacrifice of her virtue which meant an oath of fidelity eighty years ago.

In *A Romance of Old New York,* "the thing he had consented to do," however, "filled him with sorrowful dismay" (R, 55). Aaron Burr encourages him to do it. "'Charlotte will love you all the better in years to come for having served her with so splendid a loyalty!'" But we know that Aaron Burr's character was a mixture of both loyalty and deceit. From now on the plot becomes that of a farce. Pamela, instead of dying, gets well. Mark tells Pamela's rejected suitor, Gerald Suydam, what he has consented to do. "'I'm horrified'" is his response (R, 68). When Charlotte accuses Mark (whose name, Frankland, is supposed to connote his honesty) of telling falsehoods about herself, Mark responds that he is "'not used to this sort of dreadful deception. . . . I warned you that I'd make a botch of the whole abominable affair. . . . And instead of getting encouragement from you, the arch-conspirator [like Kate] I receive reprimands and reproaches'" (R, 74–75). She answers, "'For my sake, persevere!'" "'Remember, it will be only for so short a time!'" She "won't even let [him] kiss [her] while it continues!"

We recognize a difference from the sexual submission as a reward for the pretense of loving the other girl that exists as the crux in *The Wings of the Dove.* There, however, Densher had first thought that the attention he was to pay Milly was to direct Aunt Maud's attention away from Kate and Merton because Aunt Maud wants Kate to marry into the aristocracy. In like fashion, Charlotte says the pretense of love could be done "'for my sake, if you chose, as a sacrifice'" (R, 46). However, there is never the venial addition of marrying for money. When Pamela becomes healthy, Mark refuses to go on with the lie. "'It's lying as I've never dreamed I *could* lie'" (R, 95). Then there appears a figure that reminds us of *The Golden Bowl* when it is broken. Mark says that Pamela is trying to break his heart as she had broken Gerald Suydam's heart. "'But she will never succeed. . . . It was broken before. You've got one piece, and I retain the other.'" Charlotte answers, "'Then I'll never give it back to you, so that you can mend the fragments and live a contented life . . . unless you stand firm for a while longer in this trying and most unforeseen difficulty'" (R, 96). The pressure on Mark is relieved by Aaron Burr's sending him to Boston on business.

The opposition between the "tall, sturdy rose-tree, conscious of its strength," which is how Burr describes Charlotte, and the sickly Pamela, is quite like that between the two girls in *The Wings of the Dove*—the healthy, sexy Kate and the ethereal, delicate, moribund Milly. Mark writes a "passionate love letter" to Charlotte, and we see that the expression of his feelings resembles greatly Merton Densher's for Kate Croy. Pamela reacts to learning about her family's plan from Gerald, her boyfriend, so she flirts with Aaron Burr as her revenge. Aaron Burr has lost a daughter, Theodosia, who had died young. "'I was the lover of my own sweet daughter,'" confesses Burr to Mr. Verplanck. "'I never meet a young woman . . . that I don't feel it in me to make her fond of me'" (R, 174). Familiar with love, he confesses that when Mark told him, "'Colonel, here I am, the sworn and loyal sweetheart of one sister while bound by charitable falsehoods to another'" (R, 176), he decided to save him. Theodosia (R, 172) suggests the Byzantine court and its empress, brought by James into *The Wings of the Dove* as an appropriate metaphor for Milly's court. Burr wants the gift that Mark proposes to him for having helped him out of an embarrassment to be focused in the naming of his first child either Theodosia or Theodore (the latter is the last word of the little novel). We see it in the final treatment of the novel. The name of Lord Mark, the development of the Byzantine material, possibly suggested by Theodosia Burr's name, and the prolonged resistance of Mark Frankland to swallowing what Charlotte and her father wish him to do, never appear in James's *Notebook* memoranda, where Lord Mark is only Lord X.

Since James wrote his novel after Fawcett's novel had appeared, we can see that what was popular in the theme attracted James but attracted him as material for a remodeling into a tragic novel about moral behavior. He would not do the vulgar thing, as Fawcett had done, by making a serious commitment to a dying girl a subject for comedy, in which she does not die and in which she has a lover of her own waiting in the wings. Mark Frankland's horror at a situation in which he has to lie sets the tone for Merton Densher's more horrible task. The pop theme becomes the underpinning for one of the most tragic novels of the twentieth century since it deals with the confronted consciousness of two people engaged with each other for selfish ends, a novel that so taxed the emotions of Virginia Woolf that, as she wrote to Lady Ottoline Morrell, she felt "very ill for some time afterwards."[37]

Another novel, *New York* by Edgar Fawcett—who was so prolific with his thirty-five novels and his many plays that Henry Stoddard is supposed to have remarked "Won't somebody please turn this Fawcett off?"—is of interest to us because he dedicated it to Henry James: "To Henry James: With the touch of a

Velasquez you have painted many portraits. No living Briton or American ranks above you in your art. And so with reverence for the depth and reach of it, I venture to make you my modest offering, as one to whom your gifts have been for years a delight, and by whom your fame, now strengthening with time, was long ago foretold." It is dated Venice, April 1898 and signed E. F. One assumes that James received this as a gift in a copy of his own, although no such volume seems to have turned up in the library lists itemizing his books. However, the only volume extant that he owned by Fawcett is *The Romance of Old New York.* Fawcett's novel of 1898, *New York* (and there is another called *A New York Family,* which shows how obsessed he was with his town), came out just when James was moving to Lamb House in Rye, at which time he wrote his one dream story, "The Great Good Place," although it did not appear in print until 1900. When we look into Fawcett's novel, we can see how it is possible that it entered in part into the tissue of James's story.

The hero of Fawcett's novel is George Oliver, a young man who was conned into a crime as a very young man and who spent three years in prison. On his release he finds his former middle-class world closed to him. He meets a group of people called "The Clasping Hand," a charitable organization that purports to "aid through moral stimulus of counsel . . . friendliness, comradry, sympathetic warmth."[38] Crevelling is the leader, and to go along with him would be like "going with a brother." We remember the order of Brothers who take over George Dane in "The Great Good Place." He is a man who is also overcome by the world's cares and who has the same first name as Fawcett's hero. Crevelling, who is called "most benevolent," reminds the reader of one of the Brothers in James's benevolent order, although the main source for the story seems to be *L'Envers de l'histoire contemporaine,* the novel by Balzac devoted to a charitable and benevolent organization. The one thing in favor for also considering *New York*'s contribution to the depiction of a charitable, benevolent society is that James probably read it just when he was writing his own version of such an order in his dream of the perfect sanctuary. What James does with Fawcett's icons is to transform them into one of the most beautiful prose poems of a writer's wish for a perfect retreat, but the relationship is negligible compared to that of Fawcett's *The Romance of Old New York* with *The Wings of the Dove.*

We are not sure at all whether James kept to himself his plot for *The Wings of the Dove,* sketched out in its main lines in 1894, or whether he discussed it with Fawcett, but we have seen that such popular tales as Fawcett's attracted him and made him want to imbue them with his own life. The absurd Fawcett novelette, *A Romance of Old New York,* seems a vulgar parody of *The Wings of the Dove,* but knowing of its having been written prior to (and also presented to James prior to) James's tremendous epic of greed and love, knowing of its presence in James's library, and aware of the friendship between the two men while *The Wings of the Dove* was being written, we cannot help but speculate that there was some kind of interrelationship.

### *The Ivory Tower* and F. Marion Crawford's *The Three Fates*

James's relation to F. Marion Crawford (1854–1909) was somewhat complicated by his understandable resentment of the younger Crawford's personal beauty and immediate success with a first novel, *Mr. Isaacs* (1882), written when the author was only twenty-eight. Living until fifty-five, having provided Mrs. Isabella Gardner with her great love affair, Crawford produced more than forty novels and three historical works, which helped him make a fortune and enabled him to buy Sant'Angelo, a luxurious villa in Sorrento, which James visited in 1899. At that time James wrote that Crawford was "a prodigy of talent—and of wealth! It is humiliating."[39] This clearly showed his envy, although he considered Crawford pretty much of a lightweight.

That year James wrote to Morton Fullerton that although Fullerton's half-sister was supposed to write like Henry James, he advised her to have sooner "written like Anthony Hope or F. Marion Crawford. . . . Let her apply my yearning, my inclination, as I can't apply it."[40] Whether here he is being ironical or being truthful is hard to verify. Yet other facts seem to contradict this picture of a serious author annoyed by the success of a much lesser talent. One is that James admits in a letter to the Countess Rosebery, to whom he writes from Boston in June 1883, that "we have all read Mrs. Carlyle, and 'Mr. Isaacs,'" Crawford's first novel based on his experiences in India.[41]

As we have already seen in chapter 2, it is significant that within five months after writing this letter James published a story, "The Impressions of a Cousin," in which the main character, Mr. Caliph, is partially based on the Persian hero of Crawford's novel. In addition to this fact of the incorporation of one of Crawford's characters, there are evidences of a change of attitude to Crawford, the man himself, that takes place in James after Crawford's fairly early death at Sorrento on April 9, 1909. One place this occurs is in passage of praise for Crawford in *A Small Boy and Others* (1913), which James began to write in 1911. "The most endowed and accomplished of men Frank Crawford, so that I have scarcely known another who had more aboundingly lived and wrought, about whom moreover there was singularly more to be said, it struck me, than at all found voice at the time he might have been commemorated" (AU, 531). But a stronger piece of evidence is James's combined tribute to and correction of *The Three Fates* (1892), Crawford's novel laid in New York. The tribute made by James takes place in *The Ivory Tower,* begun tentatively in December 1909, about eight months after Crawford's death, when James wrote some notes about a book he would later turn into *The Ivory Tower,* one of his two last unfinished novels. The plot is different from the published fragment in James's preliminary "colloquy" with himself, but the names of the characters will be carried over from it, and the plot contains certain suggestions that seem to have been inspired by *The Three Fates*.

In Crawford's novel, as in James's, there are two old men who hate each other, for in *The Three Fates* Jonah Wood has been financially ruined by Thomas Craik, who has become a multimillionaire at his expense. Craik repents on his deathbed, and, changing his will, he leaves his fortune to George Wood, a writer, the son of the man he had ruined, not to his own sister, Totty Trimm. The relation between the two old men is somewhat like that of Gaw and Betterman in *The Ivory Tower*. Betterman does not die immediately, and his temporary improvement sends Abel Gaw off to his end sooner. The same thing happens in *The Three Fates*. George Wood's beginning career as a writer probably struck James as being close to his own, though it actually is Crawford's. The young man starts by writing criticism for the journals, but Constance Fearing, whom he loves, encourages him to write a novel which is a great success.

Totty's drawing room is like Rosanna's, with an elegant writing table "with its perfect appliances," and there is on it "a box of those cigars."[42] We recall "the embossed . . . superfluities, a blotting-book covered with knobs of malachite, a silver box . . . a gold cigar case" of James's Newport mansion.[43] The plot begins to thicken when Totty Trimm fraudulently opens the safe box in her husband's vault and steals the will in which Thomas Craik had left everything to George Wood and not to her.

The clincher for the relationship between the novels lies in the important role that an Indian cabinet plays in both as a place of concealment for a will or a letter relating to an inheritance. In *The Three Fates* Totty Trimm hides Craik's will in a

> small Indian cabinet which her brother had once given her in which there was a hidden drawer of which no one knew the secret but herself. This cabinet she had brought with her and had kept all through the summer in a prominent place in the drawing room, justly deeming that things are generally most safely hidden where no one could ever think of looking for them. On returning to New York the cabinet was again packed in one of Totty's own boxes, but the will was temporarily concealed about her own person, to be restored to its hiding place as soon as she reached the town house. (3F, 343)

In James's novel too a central role is played by a strange Indian cabinet, an ivory tower which gives the novel its name. In it is placed the letter from Abel Gaw, Rosanna Gaw's grasping father, which Gray fears to open and yet cannot destroy, since it deals with the fortune he is to inherit. The place of concealment in *The Ivory Tower* is "a remarkable product of some eastern, probably some Indian, patience, and of some period as well when patience in such cases was at its greatest. . . . It consisted really of a cabinet of easily moveable size, seated in a circular socket of its own material and equipped with a bowed door . . ." (IT, 143).

Craik visits Mrs. Trimm's home when she is out and notices he is standing "before a table on which among many other objects was placed the small Indian cabinet he had once given to his sister." He decides it would be "an excellent practical joke to take out the object it probably concealed in the secret drawer" and carry it off. "The idea was in accordance with that part of his character which loved secret and underhand dealings." Mamie hears him, and George says, "'He is opening that Indian cabinet as though he did not want to be heard'" (3F, 372). Meanwhile, Craik takes out the envelope and glances at the contents. At that point, Totty enters the room, and Craik denounces her, cursing her and revealing her deceit. George wants to know what the meaning of it is, and he is told, "'Here is my will. There is the cabinet. And there is Charlotte Sherrington Trimm. . . . The only way she could get the money into the family was through you'" (3F, 376).

But beyond the striking similarity of the role each "Indian cabinet" plays in the two novels, "the black things" behind the fortunes that are at stake pervade them as well. Crawford writes, "[And] yet in another place, in a magnificent chamber where the softened light played upon the rich carvings and soft carpets, an old man lay dying of his last fit of anger" (3F, 393). James builds a whole situation, as every reader of his novel knows, out of such a sentence. For both authors, the dying old men hope and believe that they can receive absolution by giving away their ill-gotten wealth to the two young sensitive men who will know how to make better use of it. Jonah Wood feels that Thomas Craik has made restitution to him by leaving to his son, George, "anywhere from twelve to fifteen millions of dollars" (3F, 405). George "detested everything connected with money, and had only a relative idea of its value," yet "he was staggered by the magnitude of the fortune suddenly thrown into his hands" (3F, 405). This attitude is implicit throughout *The Ivory Tower,* for it is Gray Fielder's response to his forthcoming vast inheritance. "'A million is nothing nowadays,'" says Trimm, but George decides that he "'shall go on writing books because that is the only thing I can do approximately well. . . . I believe I shall be ridiculous in the character of the rich man'" (3F, 408). The latter is a point of view we recognize as Gray Fielder's. The story ends with George's loving Grace but expecting not to be loved by her; "the eyes of the lonely man closed with an expression of intense pain" (3F, 412). Whether Gray Fielder will ever achieve happiness is also problematical in *The Ivory Tower.*

# 6

# The Footprints of Kipling

## "Sir Edmund Orme" and "The Phantom 'Rickshaw"

With Kipling's early publications, his reputation, that of "the Infant Monster," as Henry James called him in a letter to Stevenson, and his enormous popular success astounded the literary world and particularly James. He was shortly to give Kipling away in marriage to Carolyn Balestier, the sister of the young Wolcott Balestier, who had also, in a "Napoleonic" fashion, taken over the publishing world of America by printing popular volumes. James's preface to the American edition of Kipling's tales, *Mine Own People,* shows how James especially admired the stories of military life as well as envied their author. Mr. Cleever, in Kipling's tale "A Conference of the Powers," seems to be a portrait of Henry James, the James who was shocked to hear about the Anglo-Indian wars and the suffering that young men endured but who seemed to be charmed by them as well.[1]

As Kipling continued to write, James continued to complain about the violence in his tales. He expressed this in 1893 in a letter concerning *The Jungle Book:* "The *violence* of it all, the almost exclusive preoccupation with fighting and killing is also singularly characteristic."[2] In 1892 James had written a story called "The Pupil" to show Stevenson, with whom he had inaugurated a friendship over a correspondence based on their responses to Walter Besant's essay on "The Art of Fiction," that a tale of adventure would not have to be a "boys' book" of the kind that Stevenson had so admirably written in *Kidnapped* and *Treasure Island.*[3] The next year James wrote "Owen Wingrave." Though considered by Leon Edel, along with "The Pupil," as a story affected by Alice James's death and by consequent memories of James's childhood and family life, I see it, like "The Pupil," as an answer to this successful author, Kipling, who had such an extraordinary effect on James. Since the latter was then so deeply involved with producing his own tales, James wrote the preface to *Mine Own People* only because Balestier (who was devoted to Kipling) asked him to. But he would have to rewrite him *his* way: "That fiction which I can read I can only totally rewrite." Kipling's violence was the one thing James did not like about Kipling's tales, and so he sought to demonstrate how a tale of bravery, furnished with military icons, could be *without* violence. Thus "Owen Wingrave" (1892), as an antiwar story, came to be.

But before that, in 1891, James wrote his first ghost story, "Sir Edmund Orme," in which there is a real ghost, a palpable one, a visible person, yet seen only by a limited number of people. Mrs. Marden is haunted by Sir Edmund Orme, whom she had rejected as a suitor when she was young. The narrator, in love with Mrs. Marden's daughter, also sees the ghost, and just before Mrs. Marden dies, the daughter, too, sees Sir Edmund, but only to be comforted in her lover's arms. Sir Edmund's work is done, and he need not reappear. In James's preface he asks himself, "what put . . . such a fantasy as 'Sir Edmund Orme' into my head? The habitual teller of tales finds these things in old notebooks—which however but shifts the burden a step, since how, and under what inspiration, did they first wake up in these crude cradles? One's notes, as all writers remember, sometimes explicitly mention, sometimes indirectly reveal, and sometimes wholly dissimulate, such clues and such obligations."[4]

"Sir Edmund Orme" takes its place as "the bright thought of a state of *unconscious* obsession or, in romantic parlance, hauntedness, on the part of a given person, the consciousness of it on the part of some other, in anguish lest a wrong turn . . . shall determine a break in the blest ignorance" (EW, 1263). James was to write three stories in which a ghost actually appears and is seen by another person. The first was "Sir Edmund Orme." The story seems to have been inspired by Kipling's "The Phantom 'Rickshaw," and the plot is so close that James must have been challenged to redo it his way. James wrote "Sir Edmund Orme" during the period of his reading the early Kipling stories that had bowled him over with their uncanny skill. In fact, the only thing that James had remembered in connection with his own tale was something we can interpret as being challenged by another writer. "For as I meditate I do a little live it over, do a little remember in connexion with it the felt challenge of some experiment or two in one of the finer shades, the finest (*that* was the point) of the gruesome. The gruesome gross and obvious might be charmless enough; but why shouldn't one, with ingenuity, almost infinitely refine upon it?—as one was prone at any time to refine almost on anything?" (EW, 1263). Was he refining on Kipling's theme?

"The Phantom 'Rickshaw," written a few years earlier, was published in India in a blue paper pamphlet as *The Phantom 'Rickshaw and Other Eerie Tales* (1888), the fifth in a series sold for one rupee each by the Indian Railway Library, and was described as not being exactly a "real ghost story . . . but rather a collection of facts that never quite explain themselves" (fig. 49). In his preface to the story, Kipling referred to "The Phantom 'Rickshaw" as inhabited by a hero who "insisted on dying because he believed himself to be haunted." The

Figure 49. *The Phantom 'Rickshaw & Other Eerie Tales* by Rudyard
Kipling, A. H. Wheeler & Co.'s Indian Railway Library No.
5, 1888

story concentrates on the obsession of Jack Pansay, part of the British establish-
ment in India, who, after a year of conducting an affair with a married woman,
Mrs. Keith-Wessington, gets bored, jilts her, and becomes engaged to Kitty, a
young woman in the resort town of Simla, frequented by British personnel. The
rejected woman dies as a result of his treatment of her; the guilt felt by Jack is
conscious when, dying, he tells his story to the reader, but it is unconscious
during the time of the visitation of the jilted woman. This unconscious condition
of guilt creates a ghost of Mrs. Wessington, who appears in her rickshaw as a
phantom only to his eyes and only during important moments of his life. She
keeps repeating, "So I hear you're engaged, Jack dear. . . . I'm sure it's all a
mistake—a hideous mistake."[5] The hauntings begin when Jack is buying an
engagement ring for his fiancée. He believes the phantom of Mrs. Wessington's
rickshaw is real, but Kitty sees nothing, and he watches Kitty and her horse ride
directly through the rickshaw. The situation worsens, and finally Jack begins
to live only in the world of his jilted lover and her rickshaw. His engagement
is broken, and he loses touch with the real world.

"Sir Edmund Orme," on the other hand, is about a rejected suitor who
appears within perfectly conventional surroundings, as a guest at a party or a
worshipper at church. By his presence he warns the lady who rejected him (and
who is therefore obsessed by his existence) that he is out to make sure that what
happened to him will not happen to the young narrator of the tale, who is in
danger of being rejected by the woman's daughter. The obsession is that of
Mrs. Marden, not of the young suitor, though he too has become sensitive to
the ghost, enough to see him and to like him. In James's tale the ghost of Sir
Edmund Orme forces Mrs. Marden to confess to having jilted him years ago to
the young man who really loves her daughter, but when the daughter shows
signs of trifling with her lover, Sir Edmund's ghost appears in order to warn the
young man. James's ghost is benevolent; he helps the suitor, who is allowed to
see him because he really loves the girl. The lover and the mother both fear that
the young woman will see the ghost, but she does so only when her mother dies,
and she accepts it, since she does not reject the narrator as her husband. The
ghost sees that the girl is not going to put her fiancé through the paces through
which her mother had put him, and the mother has paid him back with her life.
So the ghost is satisfied and disappears forever.

Let us look back at "The Phantom 'Rickshaw." The peripety of Kipling's
tale of action occurs when the hero goes over completely in his haunted state
to the land of Mrs. Keith-Wessington. This peripety seems to be repeated mildly
in James's "Sir Edmund Orme." Both young men, Jack Pansay in the Kipling
tale and the narrator in the James tale, enjoy being drawn into the world of the
ghost. They are not afraid and know that the ghost in each tale is benevolent.
Jack stops Mrs. Wessington's rickshaw and drags Kitty to it while he tells Kitty
of "my old relations to Mrs. Wessington," at which point she cuts him across

the face with her riding whip. After that Kitty writes to say that if a man behaves as he had to Mrs. Wessington he ought to kill himself (PR, 29), at which point his "two selves joined." The two selves are a combination of the self who lives in reality and the self who has the hallucinations of Mrs. Wessington's rickshaw. The rickshaw and Kitty pass him as if he does not exist, and now his two selves are joined, in the world of Mrs. Wessington's rickshaw. "It was a ghastly and yet in some ways a marvelously dear experience" PR, 35), and the rickshaw, "save that it cast no shadow," looks like "the real thing" (PR, 35). "I hungered to be among the realities of life; and at the same time I felt vaguely unhappy when I had been separated too long from my ghostly companion" (PR, 36).

Yet James's use of "The Phantom 'Rickshaw" makes it his own, for, as he told Wells in regard to a novel of his that James had "appropriated," *The First Men in the Moon,* "the superstructure I reared upon it had . . . nothing in common (*but* the subject!) with, yours."[6] So here, too, James's appropriation of "The Phantom 'Rickshaw" has in common with the model chiefly the subject, the "unconscious obsession" that produces a hallucination for a guilty person in a love relationship. James's hallucination is far different since the ghost materializes not only for the woman guilty of jilting but also for the young man threatened with a repetition of the situation by the woman's daughter. In the story by Kipling, the hallucination in Jack's mind is accounted for by the stress of overwork and the disastrous climate of India. It can all, also, be attributed to the deteriorated condition of a man stricken with a fatal disease. In the case of James's story, the appearance of the ghost of Sir Edmund Orme not only to the mother, but to the fiancé and briefly to the daughter, can be accounted for by the idea of sympathetic feelings for the guilty party, Mrs. Marden. Like Jack Pansay, Mrs. Marden also pays with her life for having caused the death of a fiancé through fickle behavior.

Though that ghost in James's tale is palpable and can be seen by all the three participants in the drama, James makes it clear that he is only a construction of Mrs. Marden's guilt, compounded by her daughter's awareness of the monster her mother's guilt had evoked. The narrator, who saves the girl, is protected or warned by the ghost, but with his love he in turn protects the daughter from the ghost when she accepts his proposal. James seems to have fashioned a complex tale from the simple one by Kipling, in which the guilt of having jilted a woman and having caused her death creates a ghost, but only in the mind of the guilty man.

The forms of the stories are similar. In the Kipling tale there is a first ghostly appearance in front of Peliti's bar, an appearance Jack Pansay thinks is real until Kitty rides through the ghostly group. Then he learns that the coolies who carry the rickshaw had died as well as Mrs. Wessington and that the rickshaw "had been broken up." "So there *were* ghosts of 'rickshaws after all and ghostly employment in the other world! How much did Mrs. Wessington give her men? What were their hours? Where did they go?" Even the young man, haunted by his guilt, not only because he jilted Mrs. Wessington but because he caused her death, thinks in these realistic terms. But the amusing additional fact is that the apparition does also. When Dr. Heatherlegh, who had been treating Jack for his delusions, drives home with his patient and tries to cure him of a nervous breakdown, the apparition, "in what seemed devilish mockery of our way," appeared (to Jack only) "with a lighted headlamp" (PR, 21). In a sense, Mrs. Wessington's ghostly group is protective of the narrator as Sir Edmund Orme will be of James's narrator. Since the rickshaw suddenly stops as it appears in front of Jack and the doctor, Jack reigns in his horse, and the doctor's horse halts as well. Thus the rickshaw prevents a fatal accident to the two men.

Jack then undergoes a cure for what the doctor thinks is a "spectral illusion . . . implicating eyes, brain and stomach." After he feels he has been cured, Jack goes for a ride with Kitty, who, like James's narrator, knows nothing about the apparition. Suddenly he sees "the yellow-panelled 'rickshaw and Mrs. Keith-Wessington" (PR, 26). He finds himself lying on the road, and he asks Kitty, " 'Has it gone, child?' " Then occurs perhaps the most brilliant piece of narrative strategy in the entire story. Kitty says, " 'Has what gone, Jack dear? What does it all mean?' " And then from Kitty's mouth we hear the words that make up the constant refrain of Mrs. Wessington, " 'There must be a mistake somewhere, Jack. A hideous mistake.' " This means that Mrs. Wessington has usurped reality completely and now inhabits even Kitty. From now on she will be the only woman. Jack tells Kitty to speak to "It," as he calls the apparition, and also reveals to her his "old relations with Mrs. Wessington" (PR, 27). Kitty then cuts him with her whip and breaks off the engagement, but the real break with Kitty and with reality took place when, out of Kitty's mouth, came Mrs. Wessington's words.

From then on Jack's relationship to reality changes, and "it seemed that the 'rickshaw and I were the only realities in a world of shadows" (PR, 31). He strives against this at first by rapidly repeating the multiplication tables. When the doctor asks him to choose between epileptic fits or temporary insanity, he divides into "two selves" (PR, 29–30). He finds that he "had experienced some permanent alteration," for he has passed into the ghost world. Now, for the first time, he engages in conversation with Mrs. Wessington's ghost and finds that it was "in some indefinable way a marvelously dear experience." And even though he makes "no change in his mode of life," he is "unhappy when . . . separated too long from my ghostly companion" (PR, 36).

It may be here that James got the idea to make the narrator in "Sir Edmund Orme" happy to see Orme's ghost, but for different reasons. He's "a splendid presence," the narrator tells Mrs. Marden after the first appearance.[7] So far from "dreading another encounter with the 'perfect presence' . . . I was filled with

an excitement that was positively joyous. I had desired a renewal of the sensation" (VIII, 136). James fully develops this attitude to the ghost. "I was ready,"
declares the narrator, "to generalize on the sinister subject, to declare that ghosts
were much less alarming and much more amusing than was commonly supposed" (VIII, 137). The relation of Kipling's narrator to his ghost seems to be
a precedent for James to develop this idea for himself. What is more, the Kipling
connection is fortified by the appearance of James's ghost in "the Indian room"
at Tranton, and the words "Indian room" are mentioned five times.

James's remodeling of Kipling occurs again during this period of the height
of Kipling's success and friendship with James, though not so much in detail
as in a general attitude to children. James not only owned the entire set of
Kipling in the Scribner's edition, but recently a copy of *Wee Willie Winkie &
Other Child Stories* has surfaced with James's signature. Published by A. H.
Wheeler and Co. in Allahabad, it was the sixth in the one-rupee series of Kipling
books published in 1887 and 1888, just before Kipling made his reappearance
in England (figs. 50, 51). We can see James reading the preface to it:

> This is the last book of the series, and it naturally ends with the little children who always trot
> back to the tail of any procession. Only women understand children thoroughly, but if mere
> man keeps very quiet, and humbles himself properly, and refrains from talking down to his
> superiors, the children will sometimes be good to him and let him see what they think about
> the world. But, even after patient investigation, and the condescension of the nursery, it is
> hard to draw babies correctly.

There are four stories in the volume that appear in the following order:
"Wee Willie Winkie," "Baa-baa Black Sheep," "His Majesty the King," and
"The Drums of the Fore and Aft"—and three of them clearly left their mark of
James's fiction. In his 1891 essay on Kipling, James tells how he was touched
in "The Drums of the Fore and Aft" by "the history of the 'Dutch Courage' of
two dreadful, dirty little [drummer] boys who, in the face of Afghans, scarcely
more dreadful, save the reputation of their regiment and perish, the least mawk-
ishly in the world, in a squalor of battle incomparably expressed."[8] We see how
James digests this in his fiction, for on the first page of chapter 1 of *What Maisie
Knew* James describes the role of his small heroine during the divorce proceedings of her parents: "Only a drummer-boy in a ballad or a story could have been
so in the thick of the fight." Here was her "squalor of battle," and her predecessors, those drummer boys, are to be found in "the dirty little boys" who die to
be an example of dauntless courage to the demoralized troops, who are shamed
by the boys' playing their drums and leading them to success in battle, the battle
in which the boys die as a result of their heroism.

Beyond that oblique reference to the Kipling tale of two boys who die so
that their battalion can win, and beyond the fact that Maisie herself may have

Figure 50.  *Wee Willie Winkie & Other Child Stories* by Rudyard Kipling,
A. H. Wheeler & Co.'s Indian Railway Library No. 6, 1888

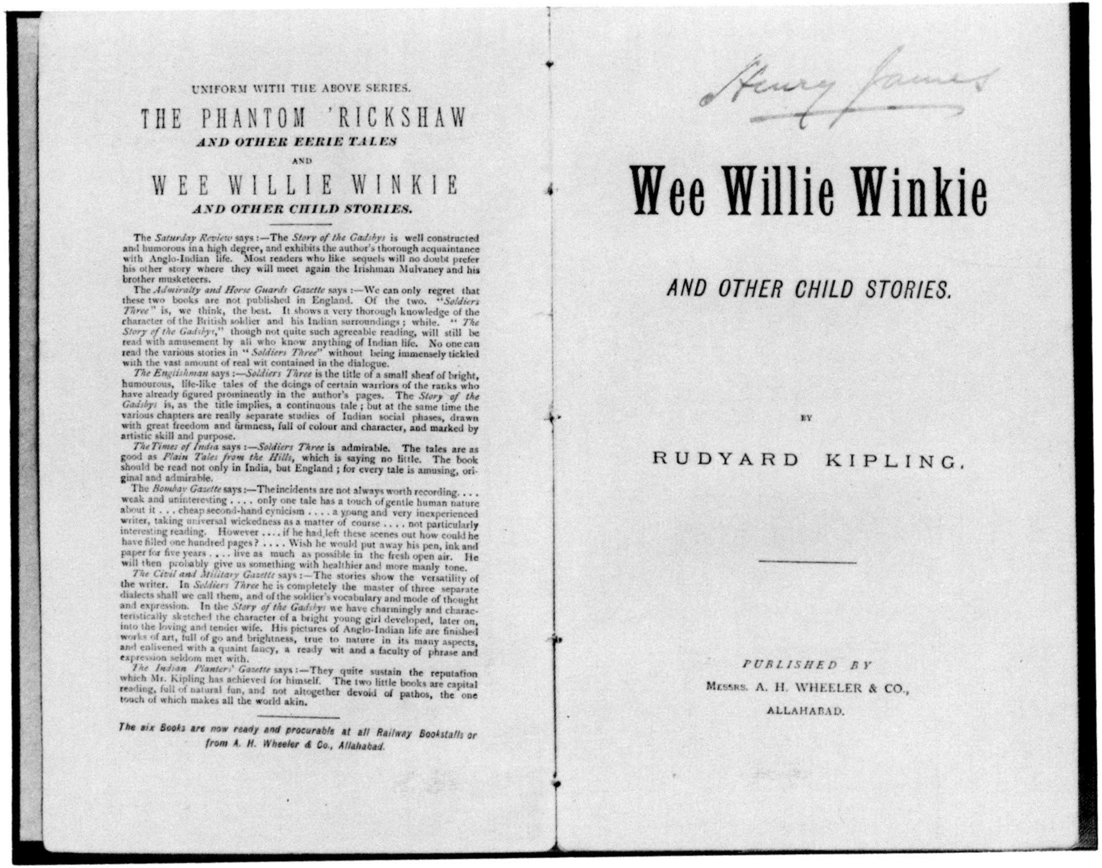

# Wee Willie Winkie

### AND OTHER CHILD STORIES.

BY

RUDYARD KIPLING.

Messrs. A. H. WHEELER & CO.,

ALLAHABAD.

*Henry James* [signature]

---

UNIFORM WITH THE ABOVE SERIES.

## THE PHANTOM 'RICKSHAW
### AND OTHER EERIE TALES

AND

## WEE WILLIE WINKIE
### AND OTHER CHILD STORIES.

The *Saturday Review* says :—The *Story of the Gadsbys* is well constructed and humorous in a high degree, and exhibits the author's thorough acquaintance with Anglo-Indian life. Most readers who like sequels will no doubt prefer his other story where they will meet again the Irishman Mulvaney and his brother musketeers.

The *Athenæum and Horse Guards Gazette* says :—We can only regret that these two books are not published in England. Of the two, "*Soldiers Three*" is, we think, the best. It shows a very thorough knowledge of the character of the British soldier and his Indian surroundings, while in "*The Story of the Gadsbys*" though not quite such agreeable reading, will still be read with amusement by all who know anything of Indian life. No one can read the various stories in "*Soldiers Three*" without being immensely tickled within the vast amount of real wit contained in the dialogue.

The *Englishman* says :—*Soldiers Three* is the title of a small sheaf of bright, humorous, life-like tales of the doings of certain warriors of the ranks who have already figured prominently in the author's pages. The *Story of the Gadsby Six*, or the title implies, a continuous tale : but at the same time the various chapters are really separate studies of Indian social phases, drawn with great freedom and furnished, full of colour and character, and marked by artistic skill and purpose.

The *Times of India* says :—*Soldiers Three* is admirable. The tales are as good as *Plain Tales from the Hills*, which is saying no little. The book should be read not only in India, but England ; for every tale is amusing, original and admirable.

The *Bombay Gazette* says :—The incidents are not always worth recalling, ... weak and uninteresting ... only one tale has a touch of gentle human nature about it ... cheap second-hand cynicism ... a young and very inexperienced writer, taking universal wickedness as a matter of course ... not particularly interesting reading. However ... if he had left these scenes out how could he have filled one hundred pages ? ... Wish he would put away his pen, ink and paper for five years. ... five as much as possible in the fresh open air. He will then probably give us something with healthier and more manly tone.

The *Civil and Military Gazette* says :—The stories show the versatility of the writer. In *Soldiers Three* he is completely the master of the speech and expression. In the *Story of the Gadsby* we have charmingly and characteristically described the character of a bright young girl developed, later on, into the loving and tender wife. His pictures of Anglo-Indian life are finished works of art, full of go and brightness, true to nature in its many aspects, and enlivened with a quaint fancy, a ready wit and a faculty of phrase and expression seldom met with.

The *Indian Planter's Gazette* says :—They quite sustain the reputation which Mr. Kipling has achieved for himself. The two little books are capital reading, full of natural fun, and not altogether devoid of pathos, the one touch of which makes all the world akin.

*The six Books are now ready and procurable at all Railway Bookstalls or from A. H. Wheeler & Co., Allahabad.*

---

Figure 51.  Title Page of *Wee Willie Winkie & Other Child Stories* with Henry James's Signature

been named after the young heroine of Kipling's early novel *The Light That Failed*—highly criticized by James and also dealing with childhood wounds— we see another Kipling story in the volume James owned that seems to have found its way into *Maisie*. The main idea behind "Wee Willie Winkie," a child roughly the same age as Maisie, is that even Wee Willie's limited knowledge of life in the world was enough to save his hero's fiancée from disaster when she rides out of bounds into the badlands surrounding the army compound in which they live. As with Maisie, the very limitations of the child's knowledge may have been an advantage; his information was basic and not cluttered by nonessentials. The story ends, "'She belongs to you, Coppy,' ... indicating Miss Allardyce with a grimy forefinger, 'I *knew* she didn't ought to go across ve wiver and I *knew* ve regiment would come to me if I sent Jack home.'" The child refers to the abduction by bandits of Miss Allardyce, Coppy's fiancée, and Willie's attempt to rescue her ending in their capture; they are both saved by the clever child's sending Jack, his riderless pony, back to the regiment.

The story might have been called "What Wee Willie Winkie Knew." Getting to the essential situation, in spite of tender years and an innocent view of the relations between people, is what Wee Willie gives to James's Maisie. Maisie contemplates, however, a much more complicated set of human interrelations. In his journalistic fashion, Kipling also indicates that for Wee Willie Winkie the relations between Brandis or Coppy, his officer hero, and Miss Allardyce, are something he cannot comprehend. "Three weeks after his youthful bestowal of affections on him . . . Wee Willie Winkie was destined to behold strange things and far beyond his comprehension," but his sense of loyalty, like Maisie's, is never questioned: "He would not betray promises," Coppy felt. "Thus the secret of the Brandis-Allardyce engagement was dependent on a little child's word."[9]

The second story in the volume, "Baa-Baa Black Sheep," shows how five-year-old Punch and his three-year-old sister Judy are farmed out by their parents, who return to India, and how their caretakers exert evil influences on them. This makes the boy lie about his report card as a reaction to his fear of reprisal if the reports are bad. The small boy and girl are not dear to someone, but they are finally rescued. The situation of these two children and that of the two in "The Turn of the Screw" are very close, for Miles, in "The Turn of the Screw," also tells lies, and perhaps it is for this reason that he was sent down from school. His behavior, as well as Flora's, is a result of neglect by the people who should be caring for them. James was so impressed by Kipling, "the Infant Monster," that we must expect some imprint to be left on him, especially by the earlier works; "Baa-Baa Black Sheep" may be an additional popular tale that fed with many others "The Turn of the Screw."

Another aspect of Kipling's presence can be found in James's short story "Owen Wingrave." *The Light That Failed* was a novel that James did not rate too highly, but it is a novel that involves Kipling's interest in the military and in battle scenes. James was drawn to the veridical detail in Kipling's military stories. He felt that certainly the pictures of the soldiers were among the best work Kipling did. But he objected to the violence of the bloodshed. We will now deal with two tales by James that indicate the strong presence of Kipling's world drawn into his own, and we begin with "Owen Wingrave," written at the highest point of James's friendship with Kipling along with James's deepest immersion in the young man's fiction.

## "Owen Wingrave" and the Antimilitary

In May of 1891, James had published his foreword to Kipling's *Mine Own People,* in which "A Conference of the Powers" presented a caricature of James himself, about which, however, James had made no comment. On November 28, 1892, "Owen Wingrave" appeared, and its antimilitarism may be seen in the context of the heavy presence of Kipling, inaugurated in 1890 when James had met him. Although James had praised Kipling in his foreword to *Mine Own People* for the volume's "most brilliant" stories, those "devoted wholely to the common soldier," he preferred these soldiers in their off-duty activities.[10] He is against the gruesome aspect of the fighting. Given this pressure from Kipling's material, "Owen Wingrave," the story based on James's own antimilitarism, seems a natural consequence of the close friendship existing by this time between James and the promilitary Kipling. James mentions among his sources his reading of General Marbot's memoirs which, as he wrote in his *Notebooks* for March 1892, gave him the idea of the *"soldier,* the type . . . as a transmitted . . . presence, in the life and consciousness of a descendent . . . of totally different temperament."[11] But he is put off by "the ugliness, the blood, the carnage, the suffering," which had also put him off much of Kipling.

James makes his soldier, Owen Wingrave, reject a military career, yet at the same time expose himself "to the possibility of danger and death . . . even in this very effort of abjuration." James wants to show "just *how* he has been a hero even while throwing away his arms" (N, 119). As James in 1891 had shown Stevenson that he could write an adventure story that is an adventure of the mind rather than of the body but yet, as "The Pupil" shows, can be created by the vocabulary and icons of the outdoor "boys' story," so the following year he showed Kipling that he could write a story against warfare as a profession, a story that could still be created by the vocabulary and icons of the military life. The result, according to Leon Edel, is "the only 'pacifist' story" in all James's fiction (TY, 104). Yet, ironically, it is also the only story built from cellar to attic by military terms, references, and allusions. James is showing Kipling that he could handle the same kind of material "the Infant Monster" handled, but in his own way for the end of peace, not war.

Kipling himself was aware of James's contradictory attitudes about war and the extent to which James loathed violence and yet was stirred by the tales told by young military men. The very volume for which James provided a foreword contains the story "A Conference of the Powers," in which a great writer of subtle, genteel fiction is charmed by the company of a group of young military men who have been through the horrors of war. Eustave Cleever is the novelist introduced to three young men of the 45th Bengal Cavalry; they welcome him, thanking him for his book. He does not mind talking, "for he was a golden talker" (MO, 199). He is bearded, like James, but the interesting thing for us is that he is puzzled by the boys, for he has never "come into contact with the thing which is called the Subaltern of the Line" (MO, 200). He admits, " 'I live chiefly among those who write and paint and sculp and so forth. We have our own talk and our own interests.' " When the young men talk about the bloody warfare they have seen, Cleever softly answers, " 'The whole idea of warfare seems so foreign and unnatural, so essentially vulgar . . . that I can hardly appreciate your sensations' " (MO, 201). But then he asks them to " 'tell me everything about everything.' " He is very interested in the slang of the army, and, when the infantry sings barracks-room verses, Cleever responds, " 'Oh gorgeous. . . . And how magnificently direct! . . . It is epic' " (MO, 204). But he is shocked to hear that the young men have all killed other men. Cleever is clearly Henry James, and, though James made no reference to this tale in his foreword to the book, he must have known that he himself was Cleever.

The fact of his creation of the character of Owen as an antiwar defender within a year of his foreword argues for "Owen Wingrave" as a response to Kipling's caricature of James in "A Conference of the Powers."[12] James has created a young hero who dies on a battlefield of traditional hauntedness by defying his military ancestors, rather than on a bloody battlefield in which there is carnage perpetrated by himself on others. Owen engages in heroics without involving bloodshed. He dies while fighting an invincible force, family tradition, and therefore avoids the problem of cowardice. The story itself is a masterpiece of James's habitual way of stoking his furnace with tags and allusions to the theme, that of the military, to posit the dilemma such a tradition of military life creates for a young man who prefers poetry to military tactics.

The terms of warfare begin very early in the tale. Spencer Coyle, the army coach, the "celebrated crammer," and Owen were "evidently in no condition to prolong an encounter in which they each drew blood."[13] In this tale of a young man who is brought up in a family consecrated to the military and who, because of his aversion to bloodshed, refuses to become part of its history, the terms of the military continue to abound, which scholarship has long noticed. What has not been paid attention to, however, is that Sir Philip Wingrave, who lives at Paramore, has had "a crowded Eastern past" (IX, 20), reminiscent of Kipling's matter, and the housekeeper at the house is a widow of a man who had "fallen in the Indian mutiny." The resemblance of the young couple to Paul and Virginia, mentioned twice, is not irrelevant to the military content because Bernardin de Saint-Pierre, the author of the natural idyll of 1787, *Paul et Virginie,* was also a military engineer and was, as well, pensioned off and decorated by Bonaparte, undoubtedly the greatest military tactician of all times. But Bernardin de Saint-Pierre was also a malcontent, hating society as it then existed; he had a vision of a life lived in nature, not in warfare. Coyle notes that Owen is a "fighting man" (IX, 43), although not a military one. " 'Let him prove it,' " answers the difficult young woman. Challenged to sleep in the haunted room by his fiancée, Owen is found dead, looking "like a young soldier on a battlefield" (IX, 51).

## "The Beast in the Jungle" and *The Jungle Books*

By 1893 James felt Kipling's powers as a writer had diminished. "He charged himself with all he could take of India when he was very young, . . . but I doubt if he has anything more of anything to give. . . . But what he *did*—in two or three years—remains wonderful."[14] When, the following year, James read *The Jungle Book* (1894), he wrote, "The *violence* of it all, the almost exclusive preoccupation with fighting and killing is also singularly characteristic" (TY, 52–53). James's great complaint about *The Jungle Book* is that the violence in the story is too much for him. In a letter to Grace Norton, at the time that Kipling bought his place near Rottingdean, James deplored Kipling's lack of any question of *"shades"* and "his evolution from the less simple . . . to the more simple," from Anglo-Indians down to "the engines and screws."[15] To Jonathan Sturges James wrote of Kipling's *Seven Seas:* "It's all *violent,* without a dream of a *nuance.*" When we review the letters he wrote earlier on Kipling's work, we see that he was overwhelmed by Kipling's energy: he called him "that little black demon of a Kipling" (LIII, 360).

In the summer of 1902 James began "The Beast in the Jungle" and dropped it. On October 12 he took it up once more. Kipling lunched with James the next day, October 13.[16] Three days later, on October 16, James finished his own story, according to Miss Wells, James's secretary at that time. Since we know James had read both *Jungle Books,* it is hard not to see that they must have had some effect on his own tale. This effect may have been primarily to give James the metaphors he needed for the strange poem of despair that "The Beast in the Jungle" is, for it was *the* metaphor for the unique fate that was to overtake John Marcher. "Something or other lay in wait for him, amid the twists and turns of the months and the years, like a crouching beast in the jungle. It signified little whether the crouching beast were destined to slay him or to be slain. The definite point was the inevitable spring of the creature. . . ."[17]

In *The Jungle Books* all the characters, except Mowgli, the man child brought up by wolves, are the beasts in the jungle, and the story is theirs: one of them, the tiger that "springs from behind and turns his head aside as he strikes," seems to slink through James's story. Marcher's and May Bartram's shared imagination had "its incalculable moments of glaring out quite as with the very eyes of the very Beast" (XI, 372). When, after May's death, Marcher realizes the desert his life has become, his search for the meaning of his experience is presented in the transposed metaphor of *The Jungle Book;* "poor Marcher waded through his beaten grass, where no life stirred, where no breath sounded, where no evil eye seemed to gleam from a possible lair, very much as if vaguely looking for the Beast, and still more as if missing it" (XI, 394). Finally, his realization of the futility of his life and his failure to love May is felt in the last appearance of the basic metaphor. "He saw the Jungle of his life and saw the lurking Beast . . . perceived it . . . rise, huge and hideous, for the leap that was to settle him" (XI, 402).

The other powerful metaphor that Kipling's *Jungle Books* gave James is the figure of "the Law of the Jungle," which appears on almost every page of each of *The Jungle Books.* For Kipling's ferocious, instinctive, and cruel hereditary Law "never orders anything without a reason, forbids every beast to eat Man, except when he is killing to show his children how to kill, and then he must hunt outside the hunting-ground of his pack or tribe."[18] The dominant force that held the animal world together was fear of the Law of the Jungle. Marcher too felt his life was in the hands of a law. In contrast to the law of the tribe or pack of the anthropomorphized animal world of Kipling, Marcher's law, as James translated it, was an idiosyncratic individual matter but just as immutable. "One's in the hands of one's law—there one is. As to the form the law will take, the way it will operate, that's it's own affair" (XI, 370). That the Law and the Beast are related in James's mind, is clear, for in the same speech just quoted, Marcher had referred to the beast as if he were waiting for the beast to leap at him. "For the beast to jump out? . . . It isn't a matter as to which I can *choose.* . . . It's in the lap of the gods" (XI, 370).

However individual and mysterious the law that was to dominate Marcher's fate, its force in his life had the strength of the force of Kipling's jungle Law. "Since it was in Time that he was to have met his fate, so it was in Time that his fate was to have acted. . . . They were subject, he and the great vagueness, to an *equal and indivisible law*" (XI, 379) (emphasis mine). Just so Mowgli had learned from Baloo, the Brown Bear, "that the Law was like the giant creeper . . . and no one could escape. . . . All the jungle obeys at least one Law" (JB, 153), and again in verse, "Now this is the Law of the Jungle—as old and as true as the sky; / And the wolf that shall keep it may prosper, but the wolf that shall break it must die" (JB, 169). Marcher "had justified his fear and achieved his fate; he had failed, with the last exactitude, of all he was to fail of. . . . He saw the Jungle of his life and saw the lurking Beast" (IX, 402).

# 7

# Popular Scandals and the Press

Although James expressed his distaste and horror of the prying publicity of the press of his time, denouncing both the private "publishing scoundrel" of "The Aspern Papers" and the rapacity of contemporary journalists in *The Reverberator* and "The Papers," he privately enjoyed public scandals. He encouraged Edmund Gosse to fill him in on the progress of Wilde's trials. He wrote to Grace Norton in August 1885 of his interest in "the great Dilke scandal": "no very edifying chapter of social history. It is, however, by no means without a certain rather low interest, if one happens to know (and I have the sorry privilege) most of the people concerned, nearly and remotely, in it."[1] After revealing the details he knows of Sir Charles Dilke's simultaneous liaisons, James goes on: "The whole thing is a theme for the novelist—or at least for *a* novelist. I, however, am not the one, though you might think it, from the length at which I have treated the topic!" (EL, III, 99). Perhaps the Dilke scandal was not for James, yet some of the effects of other contemporary private scandals and the great public one of "l'affaire Dreyfus" did, translated and transmuted, enter his fiction.

## Royal Models: The Real Thing behind "The Real Thing"

On February 18, 1891, James wrote to Robert Louis Stevenson the following: "Our public news is small—unless you count in the 'Card Scandal;' the imputed cheating at Baccarat of Sir William Gordon Cumming of the Scots Guards, while playing with the Prince of Wales" (EL, III, 337–38). This was the famous Baccarat or Tranby Croft Case, when the Prince of Wales was forced to testify in court. What seems significant is that four days later, on February 22, James recollected the anecdote for "The Real Thing," told him by George Du Maurier, and he was "struck with the pathos . . . the little tragedy of good-looking gentlefolk, who had been all their life stupid and well-dressed, living, on a fixed income, at country-houses, watering places and clubs . . . and were now unable to *do* anything . . . could only *show* themselves."[2]

Many factors seem to indicate that royalty itself was the real thing behind Major and Mrs. Monarch, the two aptly named principals in this drama of two upper-class, well-dressed, and handsome people who, fallen on hard times, are now out of work and are looking for an illustrator to use them as models of "the real thing" in his work since they *are* the real thing. However, in the James tale they cannot stir the imagination of the artist in black and white, who finds that the low-class male and female models serve his purpose better than the Monarchs.

Calling the two "Mr. and Mrs. Monarch" alerts the reader, surely of that time, that his own future monarchs were right then in pretty much the same position as the models in James's tale. In the first place, the tale was published right after the public scandal involving the heir to the throne of England as a witness for one of the plaintiffs in the Baccarat case. J. B. Priestley notes that it was Edward's behavior as Prince of Wales that was "one of the arguments against continuing the monarchy," especially during the 1890s.[3] During these years Edward had been criticized for having no regular employment. His mother had to look around for something for him to "do" (ED, 23). "As Prince of Wales he did whatever was demanded of him. . . . It was not his fault that he was not offered greater responsibilities" (ED, 25). This is echoed in the story when Major Monarch says " 'we've go to *do* something,' " and their idea of doing is posing in their fashionable clothes.

Mrs. Monarch is described as a typical society lady, as Du Maurier drew such ladies based on Queen Alexandra: "She was . . . essentially and typically 'smart.' Her figure was . . . conspicuously and irreproachably 'good.' For a woman her age her waist was surprisingly small; her elbow moreover had the orthodox crook. She held her head at the conventional angle."[4] Princess Alexandra, born in 1844, was forty-seven years old when James wrote the story, and the model for fashionable women. When the Major says, " 'I've always kept her quiet,' " the reader can think of Alexandra's life compared to her husband's, spent usually sitting for her photograph. "It was certainly an age that prided itself, under royal patronage, on its beautiful women. They are always being photographed" (ED, 69). The descriptions of Mrs. Monarch as "stiff" because "she had been photographed often" (VIII, 243) with a figure with "no variety of expression" seems to recall especially Du Maurier's versions of the female figure based on Princess Alexandra, especially when the artist-narrator finds he makes his versions of her "too tall," a characteristic of Du Maurier's ladies (VIII, 244). "When she stood erect she took naturally one of the attitudes in which court-painters represent queens and princesses; so that I found myself wondering whether . . . I couldn't get the editor of the *Cheapside* to publish a really royal romance, 'A tale of Buckingham Palace' " (VIII, 245–46). In the New York Edition revision, in addition to "her usual anxious stiffness" (VIII, 247), there is added Mrs. Monarch's antagonism to Russian princesses ("I could see that she had known some and didn't like them") which suggests Princess Alexandra's feud with the Russian-born Duchess of Sutherland.

Major Monarch was like Edward since he, too, had "left the army" (VIII, 232) and, like Edward at the time of the story, was fifty years old. The "advantages" of the couple in sum, strike the artist as being "preponderantly social; such for instance as would help to make a drawing-room look well" (VIII, 232). If Major and Mrs. Monarch are meant to suggest the Prince and Princess of Wales, they have been filtered through the pen of Du Maurier who, in his *Punch* illustrations, concentrated on giving for his ladies the figure of Princess Alexandra as the model. We are directed to that by Mr. Monarch, indicating that as far as their figures, their strong point, went, " '*She* has got the best' " (VIII, 232). The Prince of Wales was not permitted by his mother, Queen Victoria, to be in on any cabinet secrets until the mid-1890s. Therefore he had no occupation at the time James's story appeared (ED, 20).

In the story it becomes quite clear that the narrator's "majestic models" (VIII, 252) have ruined his work. The "colossal" figures also "bored" him a good deal; they sat "like a pair of patient courtiers in a royal ante-chamber" (VIII, 253) (fig. 52). The Monarchs lack the faculty of representation, whereas Miss Churm, the Cockney model, has the ability to "allow for the alchemy of art" (VIII, 241). James is clearly making a thrust at the useless life led by royalty which had now penetrated London life and perhaps had, by the presence of the Prince and Princess of Wales, made the social life of the upper classes in the metropolis more lax in moral behavior. From James's letters we see that his opinion of royalty was not very high. He wrote to James Russell Lowell on July 20, 1891, that "when the German emperor arrived the other day I fled before the exhibition of such abysmal platitude" (EL, III, 347). Yet he knew certain members of the Court circles, for during this period James saw a lot of Mrs. Mahlon Sands, an "American beauty" who "was a friend of the Prince of Wales" (EL, III, 358). James had brought Edward into his earlier tale, "The Siege of London," as the Prince of Wales who enjoyed the originality of Mrs. Headway, the American adventuress, and in James's final completed novel, *The Outcry* (1911), the Prince arrives at Dedborough in the manner of an Elizabethan comedy such as *As You Like It*.

At the time James was deep in the works of his friend, Alphonse Daudet, for he had collected in his *Partial Portraits* in 1888 his 1883 essay on that writer. He owned and knew well Daudet's *Les Rois en exil* (1879). In his *Memories of a Man of Letters,* Daudet told how he wrote that novel, and how the Parisian public, after a play was based on it, "remained profoundly insensible to the sufferings of royal personnages." He adds, "Monarchy posed for me: as always I wrote after nature," and "I am not the first to call attention to the deterioration of royal minds in exile." The sentence, "Monarchy posed for me," may have given James the idea of using royal-looking personages posing for

Figure 52.    Edward VII and Queen Alexandra, 1898
*(Courtesy of BBC Hulton Picture Library)*

"The Real Thing," and if Daudet was not the first to write about dethroned kings, he surely was not the last to do so.

As "a pendant to the *Real Thing*," James recorded in August 1896 (N, 125) that a

> painter (Pasolini) in Venice said, after painting the Empress Frederick: "It is only Empresses who know how to sit—to *pose*. They have the habit of it, and of being looked at, and it is three times as easy to paint them as to paint others."—Idea of this—for another little "model" story; pendant to the *Real Thing*. A woman comes to a painter as a paid model—she is poor, perfect for the purpose and very mysterious. He wonders how she comes to be so good. At last he discovers that she is a deposed princess!—reduced to mystery! as to earning her living. (N, 125–26)

After his ingenious encoding of his attitude to royalty in "The Real Thing," James could not and did not develop such an obvious subject for one of his necessarily more complex fictions. It would not have taxed his ingenuity, and he had already done it.

On the shelves of James's Lamb House library there exists a curious commentary on his interest in deposed and useless kings. He seems to have had in his possession a book by a Dr. Doran called *Monarchs Retired from Business* (1857), a serious history of when and how certain kings went out of business, as it were, and what they did with themselves thereafter. The pages of the two-volume history have been cut and show signs of having been read, even though the pages of the index have not been cut. The fact that in the essay "The Grand Canal," written right after James published "The Real Thing," we find two passages concerned with kings in exile indicates that he had them on his mind.

> From the same high windows we catch without any stretching of the neck a still more indispensable note in the picture, a famous pretender eating the bread of bitterness. This repast is served in the open air, on a neat little terrace, by attendants in livery, and there is no indiscretion in our seeing that the pretender dines. Ever since the *table d'hôte* in "Candide" Venice has been the refuge of monarchs in want of thrones—she wouldn't know herself without her *rois en exil*. The exile is agreeable and soothing, the gondola lets them down gently. Its movement is an anodyne, its silence a philtre, and little by little it rocks all ambitions to sleep. The proscript has plenty of leisure to write his proclamations and even his memoirs, and I believe he has organs in which they are published; but the only noise he makes in the world is the harmless splash of his oars. He comes and goes along the Canalazzo, and he might be much worse employed. He is but one of the interesting objects it presents, however, and I am by no means sure that he is the most striking.[5]

It is not only once but twice that James mentions royalty in exile in this essay, and in the first paragraph he is quoting from the title of Daudet's book. He finds "interesting bits" in the "recurrent memories of royalty in exile which cluster about the Palazzo Vendramin Calergi" in Venice. Major and Mrs. Monarch represent the uselessness of all the training in ceremonial and glamorous kingship that contrasted with the virtuous and profitable reign of Queen Victoria.

### "A Banal Divorce Hearing": Jury Duty and "The Given Case"

On August 7, 1897, Henry wrote to his brother, William that he had had "to serve, at Court of Queen's Bench, on a long, two-days British Jury—for which, here, even the alien is impressed after ten years of residence."[6] Although the rest of the letter involves family affairs and reports of the visits of friends, the final "P.S." includes an interesting remark. "P.S. Doing British Juryman threw lights—and glooms!" Leon Edel comments that "the case, apparently a banal divorce hearing, lasted only two days at the Court of Queen's Bench, and all we know of the experience is recorded in Henry's remark to William . . . which would suggest that the novelist was not bored. He had discussed a divorce in the opening instalments of *What Maisie Knew*—but by the time he went to court he was at work on the final pages of the novel."[7]

The "lights" that the jury duty experience shed for James seem to have appeared in a short story published the next year. "The Given Case" (1898), one of the stories James had difficulty in selling, is a tale even Leon Edel considered unworthy of comment in his *Life* of James. In his introduction to the volume of tales in which it was reprinted, he sees it merely as a going back "to James's early themes dealing with supposedly fickle or flirtatious women."[8] However, once we understand its "little law of composition," a lot can be said for it. Its tight form and witty dialogue then appear as a legalistic exercise on a "given case." The event that happened to Henry James within the year of his writing the tale helps to explain its form. He had served as a member of a London jury deciding a divorce case, and this experience, added to the original "germ" for the tale, gave him just the push as well as the underlying analogue he needed. It is that of a "given" premise in legal terms from which two different conclusions are reached by two women who have become emotionally involved with two men, even though one of them is married and the other engaged to another man.

In his *Notebooks* for May 13, 1894, James recorded having read an article in the *Fortnightly* on "'English and French Manners'" which he felt provided him with "something of a 'subject.'" French people "consider that 'flirting' is a dishonorable amusement and that a woman who has once listened to the overtures of a man considers it an act of justice to console him." Not, however, the English. "Make the 2 women—with their *opposed views of 'conduct.'*" (N, 164). A year later, on December 21, 1895, he returned to the article "about the opposition of view of the *Française* and the *Anglaise* as to the responsibility incurred by a flirtation." Although both women think it serious, they take "the opposed conclusion from that premise. . . . I shall come to the treatment—the subject, at any rate, *y est*" (N, 234). Two years later the jury duty seems to have provided him with the virtual "courtroom" procedure in which the two women protagonists are cross-examined by the two men.

James now had his treatment. Written during the next few months, from being the French versus the English point of view in regard to what a woman owes a man when she flirts with him, the story became a case of two English men against two English women who have given the men reason to believe they love them. Each woman has a prior commitment. Mrs. Despard is married to an unfaithful, absent husband, for whom she and the house in which she lives exist only as property. The other, Margaret Hamer, has been engaged for three years to an absent fiancé. She will finally break her engagement, since her commitment is less serious than that of her friend, Mrs. Despard, whose legal duty is to remain with her husband and to reject her new love.

"The Given Case," as Philip Mackern, the man who finally marries Miss Hamer, expresses it, is "'the only thing I have to do with and on the situation it has made for me I don't yield an inch.'" If the reader does not know what he means by "the given case" he is in good company, for Margaret's sister does not know either. "'You're *always* speaking of it . . . and I don't know what you mean by it. . . . The case is like any other case that can be mended if people will behave decently'" (X, 376). Refusing to leave the house, Philip uses legal terms: "he took his stand . . . upon admirable facts." The discussion of the situation in quasi-legal terms is the key to the pattern from which the tale is cut.

The story is treated as if it were constructed from the session of a court of law where the two men who feel their lady friends have a moral responsibility to them engage in cross-examinations composed of a battery of questions fired at each woman, who answers as a witness for her friend. The cross-examination, except for the two final sections of the story, takes place not between each set of lovers, but between the woman's friend and the woman's lover. Barton Reeve, who loves the married woman, Mrs. Despard, is, in fact, a lawyer by profession. His face "expressing penetration up to the limit of decorum . . . was full of the man's profession—passionately legal" (X, 353).

The terms, which in both strict and loose references to the law and to law court procedure number over seventy, begin to be distributed in the first section of the seven-part tale when the lawyer, Barton Reeve, begins his cross-examination of Margaret Hamer, Philip Mackern's beloved, which is designed to make her plead his case with Mrs. Despard. His series of questions are virtually an attack on women's treatment of men. It is countered by Margaret's statement that she will dine alone and read Gardiner's *Civil War,* an indication early in the tale that a state of civil war exists between the participants. As early as the second page of the tale the courtroom terms begin to occur: "innocence," "charge," "point" and "affair" (X, 352), followed by the information that Reeve is a lawyer, a man "concerned with advice, but not with taking it" (X, 353). Such terms as "prejudiced" and "a right to say" continue. "Cruelty" occurs twice in this section and constitutes the background for Mrs. Despard's "divorcing" her husband (X, 354), which Reeve pleads with her to do. The second section involves a return cross-examination of Philip Mackern by Kate Despard, but though she "opened fire" to ask him to let Margaret alone, Philip again places his protestations of love in the form of questions. The women are clearly being tried in absentia. Kate Despard again resorts to terms used in divorce cases and their courtroom connotations, in particular, "persecute a girl," "injured innocence," and "shamefully used her."

In the third section Reeve has another questioning session with Margaret Hamer, this time in the park. We recall that when James wrote to his brother that "doing British Juryman threw lights" he also added "—and glooms!" Husbands and wives battling each other in the scandalous divorce courts were responsible for those "glooms," though the procedure of the court seems to have created for James a method for mounting this tale, which method would constitute "the lights." The first words from the mouths of both young men in each section until the last are put into the form of questions. In the last section Philip Mackern makes a prose statement as a speech "in defence," we are told, since he establishes that he will not "yield an inch" on his stand of "the given case." We as readers see this final section as the summing up of "the case," and it is here that "the given case" is presented as a term taking care of all the evidence that the cross-examination of the main contestants and the chief witness, Mrs. Gorton, Margaret's sister, has elicited. The word "case" appears five times in this recapitulation.

"The given case" touches "'on what I hold that a woman is, in certain circumstances . . . bound in honour to do. . . . It isn't always, it isn't often, given, perhaps—but when it is one knows it. And it's given now if it ever was in the world'" (X, 378). Mrs. Gorton, shocked by the situation which has developed, in the sordid terms of the divorce court says that she should "'have declined . . . to lend my house again to any traffic that might take place between you'" (X, 378). Although when Margaret enters Mackern is aware of "a process" that might be spoiled by "a gesture," the mood of their personal unity is broken into by Mrs. Gorton's continuing sordid accusations in divorce-court invective (accusations of Mackern's intentions to "bully and browbeat" Margaret), finally calling him "a brute and a coward" (X, 379).

But Margaret Hamer settles her "given case." Now that she has accepted her responsibility in loving not her publicly announced fiancé but her young Treasury expert, there was no "burden nor need" for an "appeal." They are left "without speech or touch" (X, 379) after the accusations of Mrs. Gorton. For the first time in this tale, feeling "their moment . . . throb in the hush" (X, 380), there is no need for Philip to ask questions, for he has won. The case has been settled out of court, as it were. There is thus ample evidence in the story of the emphasis on law and courtroom procedure, the title itself being quasi-legal. We have noticed that one of the men, the advocate of his friend, is a lawyer, and the seven sections are mock courtroom cross-examinations, conducted by the two men against the two women, who are on trial for their refusal to accept responsibility in "the given case."

S. Gorley Putt thinks the story too mechanical, undoubtedly because of the scenes that are very close to the machinery of nineteenth-century French plays, like those by Hervieu and Lavedan, in which two characters engage in a dialogue devoted chiefly to one suitor and the friend of the woman with whom he is involved, with variations in patterning and a change of settings, the outdoors alternating with the indoors. But the machinery is here for a reason. It mimics the questioning by advocates of a witness in the stand. James so intensifies this form that it seems almost ludicrous until we penetrate his reasons for creating it.

The legal system seems to be the only dominant machinery operating in this story. The essential form of the constituent elements is created in the dialogue, resulting in a barrage of questions and answers. Since the passionate couple lose their happiness because of the legal lien on Mrs. Despard's person and property, and since divorce is not to be considered by that lady, their anger, irritation, and uncontrolled invective are suggestive of the temper of couple who have actually gone into the divorce courts, including the one on whose jury James served. Divorce itself is specifically mentioned twice. The word first occurs in the first section of the story when Margaret Hamer says that Kate's husband, Colonel Despard, "'has given her . . . nothing whatever—for divorcing him, if you mean that—to take hold of'" (X, 354). The word occurs again in the third section. "'She can't divorce. And if she can't, you know, she can't!'" (X, 364). "Compromise," "accuse," "scandal" (X, 375), "condemned" (X, 377), "brutality" (X, 377), and "bound in honour" (X, 378) are not only legal terms, they also convey the atmosphere of a divorce case. Although no divorce actually takes place in this story since Mrs. Despard refuses to sue for one and Margaret Hamer disrupts only an engagement, not a marriage, still the hostile atmosphere of the divorce court dominates.

Divorce as a subject will occur only once again in James's work, in his tale "Julia Bride," published ten years later, in which he alludes to the machinery of the divorce process, though off-stage, when he refers to "the Court" (with a capital letter). Julia, the six-times engaged young lady "had always heard . . . so much about the Court" because she had been used for her "horrid little filial evidence in Court."[9] She had committed perjury, "repeating words earnestly taught her and that she could scarce even pronounce" (XII, 157) to enable her mother to win at least one of her three divorce suits. But these details made possible by James's first-hand experience in 1897 simply make richer the central situation of "Julia Bride," which does not center on divorce as an issue but on the unsuccessful attempt of a desperate girl to win over, as a sponsor of her own matrimonial plans, one of the divorced husbands of her mother. Although it evidences a familiarity with procedure in court during a case of divorce, its aim is to show how the multiple divorces of a mother and the multiple broken commitments of her daughter contribute to social disgrace. This is not so in "The Given Case," whose very form of presentation is determined by the procedure in an actual divorce case in which James had served as a juror during the year the tale was written.

## The Dreyfus Case

*"L'Affaire" in* The Ambassadors

When it came down to what people's feelings for the Jews were, the great test of European thinking in the nineteenth century was the Dreyfus case. When the chips were down, Henry James took the side of the Dreyfusards. His stand broke up his friendship with Paul Bourget (Edith Wharton, his compatriot, continued her friendship with Bourget and his wife), for the Dreyfus case was the litmus test that revealed the anti-Semite in the last years of the century. One was, or rather had to be, either a Dreyfusard or an anti-Dreyfusard, and many friendships were broken on the wheel of the trial. In January 1898, Zola addressed to the president of the French republic an open letter, beginning "J'accuse," demanding a "revision" of the case based on the true facts. The reaction to the letter made Zola himself flee to England in July of that year, and its publication was the occasion of a letter from James to Zola supporting him. On October 15, 1898, James was writing to Elizabeth Cameron, Henry Adams's friend, "I eat and drink, I sleep and dream Dreyfus. The papers are too shockingly interesting" (EL, IV, 83). Within six months James was at work on *The Ambassadors*.

These events increased the tension developing between James and Bourget. On December 23, 1898, in reporting to Bourget about the death of their mutual friend, Ferdinand de Rothschild, James could not help referring to their differences of opinion regarding the Jewish question. "What strikes me more than anything else in connection with his death, is the difference marked between English and French nerves by the fact that the Crown Prince (by whom I mean of course the P. of W.) assisted yesterday, with every demonstration of sympathy, at his severely simple Jewish obsequies. And no one here grudges the Synagogue a single of its amusements—great as is the place which it and they occupy" (EL, IV, 90).

A few months later, James wrote to his brother William, "I treat the 'Affaire' as none of my business (as it isn't), but *its* power to make one homesick in France and the French air . . . is not small. It *is* a country *en décadence*.

Once one *feels* that nothing—on the spot—corrects the impression" (EL, IV, 101). This was written from the Bourget house at Hyères, where James spent about ten days. By this time the discovery of Esterhazy's forgery, together with his subsequent suicide and the Army cover-up, had revealed France's corruption, and public opinion had forced a new trial scheduled for September. The month before his April stay with the Bourgets, James had written to Mrs. Gardner that he was not looking forward to his trip to Hyères. "The odious Dreyfus affair is rather in the air between me & that retreat—I don't feel about it as I gather our friends there do. But it is everywhere—in that queerer & queerer country—and one must duck one's head and pass quickly."[10]

However, this feeling did not prevent him, while lingering in Paris, from enjoying the city, "the biggest temple built to material joys and the lust of the eyes" distinguished by *"such* a beauty of light." Both the light and the decadence appear in *The Ambassadors,* the writing of which followed that trip to Paris, and, though it is well known to what extent the Paris of the fin de siècle penetrates that novel, the presence of the "Affaire" has not been tracked down. It is there, hidden in the way characteristic of James when he throws into his fictional pudding the plums of some other dense iconic situation. Here we see terms from the press releases about the "Affaire," from the statements of Zola, the terminology of the law courts in relation to the trials, and especially *le petit bleu* (a form of rapid postal delivery) which, fished out of the wastebasket, provided the clue to the truth of the case that the French army staff wished to keep from being revealed. For the Dreyfus case produced for a period of twelve years (1894 to 1906), its own new vocabulary which, when used at the time and for many years after in any other connection, summoned up the atmosphere of the most disturbing public scandal of the nineteenth century. (It could not then be known how much worse anti-Semitism could get in the so-called enlightened twentieth century, producing a scandal based on the same subversion of truth but operating on a mass scale.) The very mention of the words "case" or "affaire" at the turn of the century pointed directly to the Dreyfus case, as did any mention of a *petit bleu.*

Before we begin to trace the marks hidden within *The Ambassadors* of the case and its function as well as its terminology, we must realize what James's intentions were. He used the case to create an analogy not only between Chad as the accused guilty party and Dreyfus himself, but one between Strether and Zola as the other guilty party who champions Chad's cause. The identification of Strether with James following that of James with Zola depended at this time on the great effect Zola was having as a heroic person. For though James considered Zola's novel *Paris,* published in 1898, an example of "more or less wasted energy," the Zola with whom he felt great sympathy was the one who wrote "J'Accuse" and who put himself in jeopardy for the truth. The heroic part

Zola was playing in connection with the "Affaire," we shall see, was to be mildly reflected in the "heroic" stand Strether takes in regard to the Madame de Vionnet-Chad Newsome "affaire" in *The Ambassadors*.

In the novel of 1903, the word "Dreyfus" is never mentioned, and it was not until 1909, three years after the close of the case, that James felt free to write another turn on it in a short story, "Mora Montravers," where *"á la Dreyfus,"* words now on the printed page, is the clue to lead us to the embedded analogy. It is with a more concealed ingenuity that the suggested parallel between Strether's mission and the "Affaire," which was rocking Europe at the time the book was written and published (1899–1903), is dropped into *The Ambassadors*. It runs as an undercurrent. To the careful reader of the time, it must have carried its message more clearly than it does to our forgetful generation. By its inclusion, James makes the point that the truth of Chad's transformation, which all his friends have noticed as the result of Marie de Vionnet's influence, is denied by the Woollett contingent, just as the truth of Dreyfus's innocence was denied by the courts.

The reason, I believe, James plants in *The Ambassadors* allusions to the Dreyfus case is that the evidential innocence of a suspect was denied because of power politics; the truth was deliberately suppressed. Strether echoes this same kind of frustration at the subversion of truth in Chad's case, since the family will not admit Chad's change for the better. " 'The difficulty is . . . that I can't surprise them into the smallest sign of his not being the same old Chad they've been for the last three years glowering at across the sea. They simply won't give any, and as a policy, you know—what you call a *parti pris,* a deep game—that's positively remarkable.' "[11]

The Dreyfus material begins to appear in certain catchwords everyone would respond to as part of the trials. In part 8 of the novel, way past the middle of the book, when the Pococks are arriving for the showdown, Strether tells Maria Gostrey, " 'I came out to find myself in presence of new facts, facts that have kept striking me as less and less met by our old reasons' " (AM, 246). "New Facts" was a phrase used frequently in the press to indicate the events that would prove Dreyfus's innocence. Strether sends a cable to Mrs. Newsome. "Judge best to take another month but with full appreciation of all reenforcements." "Wouldn't the pages he still so frequently dispatched by the American post have been worthy of a showy journalist, some master of the great new science of beating the sense out of words?" (AM, 247). This sounds like a description of the kind of journalism spawned by the press war being fought between the Dreyfusards and the anti-Dreyfusards. Strether adds that "he needed no proof," that Mrs. Newsome would not answer. The word "proof" which appears at least three times, and Strether's being "challenged or accused" recall the language of the *L'Aurore* letter of Zola and his subsequent trial. The taking of "sides" is part of the language of the "case." Strether refers to "my testimony" and the fact that "my letters . . . have spoken freely." Strether says to Jim Pocock, in the terms of the Dreyfus case, " 'But nothing is concluded. The case is more complex than it looks from Woollett' " (AM, 275). Later in the novel, in Part Ninth (chapter 22), we read, " 'It's my own little affair' " (AM, 280), " 'In Paris it's in the air,' " and " 'I'm studying the case' " (AM, 286, 287). Although the word "case" is a frequent one in James's novels, its appearance in *The Ambassadors* is significant not only because of its greater frequency but because it appears along with so many other key words and icons of the Dreyfus affair.

The novel is thus divided in half. The first half is free of the mood of a trial, but the second half is dominated by the atmosphere of "J'accuse" and the Dreyfus case. It is in chapter 28, which begins the second half of the novel, that the terminology of the "Dreyfus case" starts to infiltrate its pages. Of Chad, Strether says to Maria Gostrey, " 'He's not in the least the case I supposed; he's quite another case. And it's as such that he interests me' " (AM, 203). Strether then says he will face the Pococks, who will be coming because of Chad's cable. " 'I want to play fair' " (AM, 246). This decision on the part of Strether mimics the history of Zola's involvement in the Dreyfusard press.

The French novelist had jeopardized his future by such a commitment. He "ran the risk of upsetting his life and alienating the larger part of his readers. . . . He realized as well that he would have to relinquish the ambition, which he had long coveted, of entering the Académie Française."[12] But, once convinced of Dreyfus's innocence, "he plunged into the struggle," following Esterhazy's acquittal and Dreyfus's second conviction. Zola began by sending two letters, one to "the youth" and the second "to France," and his attack climaxed on January 13, 1898, when *L'Aurore* published "J'accuse" (a title contributed by Clemenceau) (fig. 53). It consisted of eight paragraphs of specific accusations, against six generals, three handwriting experts, and "the offices of War" for having conducted "an abominable campaign designed to mislead public opinion and to conceal their wrongdoing."[13] In his last paragraphs Zola invites a verdict against himself for slander, for his act which he states is "a revolutionary means of hastening the explosion of truth and justice."

"J'accuse " was the new missile in the war of the press over the case, and its reverberations and powerful effect are reflected in James's novel in the behavior of Strether who, at the point in the narrative we have reached, has also taken his stand and is inviting the onslaught of the Woollett contingent. He, too, has a lot to lose by championing Chad's liaison: a safe berth with a rich widow, a continuation as editor of Mrs. Newsome's journal, and peace and prosperity for the rest of his life. His attitudes to the Newsomes are now flavored by the temper and terminology of a law case, particularly and specifically the Dreyfus case. He had tasted of such a challenge in "The Given Case," where divorce hearing terms determined the language.

The atmosphere of the trial begins to occupy more and more space as the

Figure 53.   Felix Valotton, *L'Age du papier* in *Le Cri de Paris*, January 23, 1898

"relations" are "altered" between Strether and Mrs. Newsome, and, as his "relation with Maria Gostrey" becomes "not quite the same: this truth had come up between them," and since "truth" is the catchword of the "Affaire" it echoes gradually through the early sections of the second half of *The Ambassadors* (AM, 249). Maria claims she will bolster him if the "smash" between him and Woollett takes place, and he kids himself into thinking it will not, by reasoning "incorrectly" about the Pococks' arrival. "He accused himself by making believe . . . that Sarah's presence . . . would simplify and harmonise; he accused himself of being so afraid of what they *might* do" (AM, 252). The reader coming upon the repetition of "accused" would not have to be supersubtle to hear the detonations of the "Affaire."

The cable Strether sent is now referred to as an "incident," the word "justice" appears, followed by a paragraph that puts us with all the other readers of the daily press in the committee rooms of the lawyers and judges of the case: "If he had been challenged or accused, rebuked for meddling or otherwise pulled up, he probably would have shown . . . all the height of his consistency, all the depth of his good faith. Explicit resentment of his course would have made him take the floor and the thump of his fist on the table, would have affirmed him as consciously incorruptible" (AM, 255). Here Strether sees himself as a Zola during his memorable hour. He is "testifying to the variety of his ties" in connection with Chad, and Strether is "not otherwise concerned with it than as to its so testifying." Since he is not to be trusted, he would prefer to "postpone the trial," for he is afraid of Sarah Pocock (AM, 257). He has already "burned with the blush of guilt" and "already consented" before it all began "to the instant forfeiture of everything," as if he himself were Dreyfus with his decorations stripped and forfeited, before a public viewing. But in talking about his "letters" to Chad's mother and his "testimony" there contained, he is again Zola.

When the Pococks arrive, Sarah is subsumed under Army terms, for the Army was the villain of the Dreyfus case. She is expected to "open fire on the spot" (AM, 273). Strether tells Jim Pocock that "nothing is concluded. . . . The case is more complex that it looks from Woollett," mimicking the Dreyfus case, which in 1903 was not in any way concluded (AM, 275). But the central connection with the case is that the Pococks will not acknowledge the evidence that Chad has changed; they refuse to accept the truth when it appears, and it affects Strether "as a policy . . . that's positively remarkable," just as the refusal to recognize Dreyfus's innocence was a remarkable policy on the part of the Army and the judiciary.

A peculiar imitation of the trial in which innocence masquerades as villainy, as in the Dreyfus case, takes place when unwittingly Mme. de Vionnet hands over Strether to the camp of the enemy by exaggerating, in a comic vein in no way intelligible to the provincials from Woollett, the relation between herself and Strether, and that between Maria Gostrey and Strether. She condemns Strether to what seems to be a manifestation of guilt. In fact, later he is afraid that his admiring Mamie will continue to deepen his guilt, for "admiration was of itself almost accusatory" (AM, 328). When Strether says " 'it's my affair' " about something unconnected with his own trial, the reader is still put into the press jargon of the day. Miss Barrace sees Strether " 'as the hero of the drama, and we're gathered to see what you'll do' " (AM, 346). What he will do is presented as an opportunity, when the showdown with Sarah takes place, in the memorable interview that apes a trial. Sarah says her instructions from her mother are " 'my affair.' " He expected her to be won over by Mme. de Vionnet as if by a "revelation" of her distinction, but Sarah thinks just the opposite. When they discuss "proof" (another Dreyfus case term) of Strether's admiration for her mother, he adds that the " 'proof' " of the pudding, Mme. de Vionnet's virtue, " 'is in the eating,' " which makes "the chill deepen" between the two (AM, 364). She climaxes the interview by saying that Chad's " 'development' " is " 'hideous,' " not " 'fortunate' " (AM, 364–66). Strether realizes that what he had missed was all "an affair of the senses."

Everyone has a "case" of his or her own. Maria Gostrey's is referred to as "the compensation of her case" (AM, 386), her case being her love for Strether, and she refers to his "case" (" 'what degree of ceremony properly meets your case' ") when referring to Chad and Marie's going off together during the summer months (AM, 390). When Strether explains Mrs. Newsome to Marie, he describes her as if she were one of the Army staff officers withholding justice in the Dreyfus case: " 'She doesn't admit surprises ... she's all fine cold thought. . . . She had . . . worked the whole thing out in advance. . . . Whenever she has done that, you see, there's no room left . . . for any alteration' " (AM, 392). The great injustice of the Dreyfus case was that proof of Dreyfus's innocence in no way "altered" the verdict of his guilt in the trial before 1906. Maria Gostrey finds her "case" is also "settled" (AM, 394). When the revelation of Chad and Marie's intimacy in the countryside takes place for Strether, the language of the "case" leaves the text, only to return when he returns to Paris, for it had been a "case," and, after his disillusionment about the carnal innocence of Chad and Marie, the terms of the Dreyfus affair become climactic.

This is done by the introduction of the *petit bleu* into the novel, not once, not twice, but three times. The reference is to the Paris *pneumatique,* known as *le petit bleu* since it is a small, pale blue, gummed postal note hand-delivered within an hour or two by a messenger, an object that broke the Dreyfus case and became the wedge to the truth of the affair and Dreyfus's innocence. It makes its appearance in the novel when Strether receives "a communication from America, in the form of a scrap of blue paper folded and gummed . . . delivered at his hotel by a small boy in uniform" (AM, 230). He reads it and crumples it in his fist. He later reads "his compressed missive which he smoothed out carefully as he placed it on the table" (AM, 231). The next day "the little blue paper of the evening before plainly an object the more precious for its escape from premature destruction, now lay on the sill of the open window" (AM, 232). Chad sees it, and it is his mother's "ultimatum." It is as crucial here as *le petit bleu* is in the Dreyfus case. It sets everything in motion.

The "Chad Case" begins as the deputation from Woollett is announced. In Part Twelfth, Strether accepts from the concierge a second and now focal *petit bleu*. It is not from Chad, as he had expected, but from Marie de Vionnet, "the person whom the case gave him, on the spot, as still more worthwhile." As he goes to the post office to send one back to her, accepting, he feels like a real Parisian "mixed up with the typical tale of Paris" (AM, 342). Strether's second *petit bleu,* like the one in the case, represents for him the climax of Marie's and his intimacy. For the icon most laden with the emotions of the Dreyfusards was the little blue paper found in the wastebasket of the embassy which provided the information that broke the case. How Colonel George Picquart, who was assigned in 1895 to following the Dreyfus trial, found the *petit bleu* that in 1896 would change the picture of Dreyfus's guilt is one of the most dramatic incidents in nineteenth-century history. Madame Bastian was the agent who, hired as a charlady for the German embassy, collected torn or crumpled documents from waste bins and gave them to the French intelligence service. Among many documents in March of 1896, Picquart's aide reconstituted "the numerous fragments of a letter-telegram, on blue paper, known in Paris under the name of *petit bleu*. He gathered thirty or forty pieces . . . assembled them as in a puzzle, then glued them together."[14] This was the famous *petit bleu* that implicated Esterhazy and showed that Dreyfus was innocent. It linked the spy Esterhazy to the German military attaché, Maximilien von Schwarzkoppen, and the public stormed the newsstands for information about it when it exploded in the now-powerful press (fig. 54).

The climax to the plot of *The Ambassadors* is the last interview between Strether and Marie de Vionnet, and it is marked by her summons to him through her sending him a *petit bleu,* the third in the novel: "he saw the concierge produce . . . a *petit bleu* delivered since his letters had been sent up" (AM, 417). He thinks it must come from Chad after the country episode; his "curiosity, however, was more than gratified." It is from Madame de Vionnet, asking him "the very great kindness of coming to see her that evening at half-past nine," and of course he answers her, "also in the form of a *petit bleu,*" that he will come (AM, 417).

The upshot of the whole interview is that the real victim of the "case" is neither Chad nor Strether but, ultimately, Marie de Vionnet: "that a creature so fine could be, by mysterious forces, a creature so exploited" was what Strether saw, and he saw, in addition, that she was afraid "for her life." At least the Dreyfus case itself finally, after years of suffering for the victim, came out all right, three years after *The Ambassadors* was published. In James's versions,

Figure 54.   L. G., *Petit Bleu Verdict*, ca.  1898
*(Bibliothèque Nationale, Paris)*

drawn from models whose material and substance he uses to remake his own fantasy, it is usually a customary "case" for the outcome of his new fiction to be worse than that of the original model. But in this instance, in 1903, Dreyfus was still on Devil's Island and had not been vindicated. If Marie de Vionnet at the end is seen as the true analogic repetition of the "case," she ends as a perpetually condemned person. There was to be no "revision" for her.

Maria Gostrey still continues to provide information in the terms of the Dreyfus case: "she had a fresh fact for him before the week was out" (AM, 435). Strether says of the whole matter, " 'But the great fact was that so much of it was none of my business' " (AM, 440). The final chapter ends with "the case" presented now as that of Mrs. Newsome after it has been throughout the novel given to most of the other principals. Strether says to Chad, " 'Your mother's appeal is to the whole of your mind, and that's exactly the strength of her case.' " Mrs. Newsome is right about her son; he is ready to come home and live the life she has planned for him; Strether is not ready to do so.

The "Affaire" clings to the novel to the last page. After Maria Gostrey offers herself to Strether, he says that, in spite of her tempting offer, he must leave Paris: " 'But all the same I must go.' He had got it at last. 'To be right.' 'To be right?' " He adds, " 'That, you see, is my only logic. Not, out of the whole affair, to have got anything for myself.' " That is then the Zola role in him, for Zola had jeopardized his whole career and his security on French soil simply to have been right, to have had the right and truth triumph. *The Ambassadors* could have been called *The Chad Affair,* part of "the typical tale of Paris."

*"Some 'New Fact' à la Dreyfus" and "Mora Montravers"*

After twelve years of public turmoil, on July 12, 1906, "L'Affaire" was over. The Rennes verdict which, in 1899 (even after Esterhazy confessed to his role in the Bordereau paper), had found Dreyfus still guilty was finally annulled. Dreyfus was reinstated in the Army and Colonel Picquart, his first champion, became a brigadier general. Two-and-a-half years later James wrote a story in which the elements of the case could now be put on the surface of the tale, and the key words usually resorted to in a short tale as a technique of setting off the alarm, to alert the reader to encoded analogic material, could appear as a guide to its detection. When *The Ambassadors* had been written, it had not looked as if Dreyfus and the truth would ever be recognized, and so Woollett and the Newsomes never do recognize Madame de Vionnet's transforming power, and the virtuous liaison has to end in conformity with Woollett's wishes. But in 1909 "Mora Montravers" could reflect the happy outcome of the Dreyfus case in which truth finally does prevail. Until 1906 James would not mention the "Affaire" overtly in a novel; it was too incendiary and too devisive. In 1909 the wound of the country had begun to heal.

The plot of the tale involves a young woman, Mora Montravers, the niece of the Traffles, a respectable suburban couple from Wimbledon, who involves them in a scandal by moving in with her artist friend, Walter Puddick. It turns out that it is a platonic relationship and that a legal wedding ceremony is carried out only because Mora wants to secure for the young man her annuity. Since Mora is on her way after the ensuing divorce to another relationship and to an exciting life, the uncle, (actually Mora's half uncle, since she is the child of Mrs. Traffle's half sister) from whose point the story is told, realizes that a scandal has to be gone through when someone who "has tremendously the sense of life" breaks free from the constraints of respectability.

James indicates the presence of such a personality, who has a life-style so opposed to the safe pattern of Wimbledon respectability, in terms this time emerging from the Dreyfus case. The clue to the reader to see it that way is written into the narrative. The half uncle, Sidney Traffle, thinks, " 'I've only to go, and then come back with some "new fact" *à la Dreyfus,* in order to make her [his wife, Jane] sit up in a false flare that will break our insufferable spell' " (XII, 302). But before that open statement of comparison, which occurs exactly halfway through the story (repeating the relationship we saw in the second half of *The Ambassadors),* we see the terms of the "Affaire," in words suggesting especially the last stage of the case which finally vindicated Dreyfus, pepper the entire tale. First presented as a villainess in terms of the scandal she has created, Mora is described as "their unspeakable niece" (XII, 268), distinguished by "the treacherous fact of her beauty," a perpetrator of "dishonour," and "one of the most curious of 'cases' " (XII, 269). Traffle has never been able to do her "justice," and he has to accept Walter's vision of Mora as "a rum case" (XII, 270). The "innocence" of Mora's relation to Puddick is the big question. The aunt considers Mora "a monster" (XII, 278), just as Dreyfus, in the first stages of the trials, had been so considered. Traffle alone feels the truth of the situation: "there was, happily, nothing like the truth—*his* truth" (XII, 285). To solve the problem of what the situation is, the Traffles resort to using the "telegraph" to get Puddick to their house, thus aping the type of communication of the Dreyfus case.

At this point the word "fact" begins to appear. Certain "new facts" brought into the Dreyfus case, which aided the final vindication, came into the trials after 1904 and determined the outcome; so their multiple appearance in this tale speaks for their association with the final stage of "L'Affaire." They appear a dozen times, the first as a "little fact" of information (XII, 291). Traffle, who sees that he and his wife play the role of the Army in their equivalent of the Dreyfus case, expresses that feeling as their having to " 'live so under arms, against prying questions and the too easy exposure of our false explanations.' " Indeed, so used have they become to the scandalous nature of the situation that knowing of Mora's sexual innocence in her relation to Walter, Traffle finds that "never was a scandal . . . less scandalous" to their world and that Mora and Walter really have no connection after all with "lurid facts."

"Proof," that die-hard Dreyfus-case word, reappears (XII, 302), repeated two pages later; "truth," its "betrayal," and "facts" come frequently now, climaxing in the parodic interpretation that " 'the new fact' all Wimbledon was waiting for" was nothing more than her "genius of felicity" for dressing well (XII, 307). The material Traffle has been collecting about Mora's life gets summed up in a bundle of "truths" and "facts" accumulated in continuous fashion. Mora finally makes a statement. It is not "I am innocent" like Dreyfus's statement, but "I want to be free." She is the new woman, but at the same time she did not "want" Walter "to suffer" (XII, 312).

The eighth time "fact" is mentioned we realize that, as far as "new facts" in this case are concerned, they are innumerable, and that the "truths" required are so many that they finally constitute "the full truth." After his immersion in Mora's experience, Traffle sticks by his "original and independent measure that the whole case had become interesting and been raised above the level of a mere vulgar scandal," although he himself was "excluded" (XII, 328). Among the dozen references to "fact" or "facts" of some kind, we find the most Dreyfusard use of the term in the sentence, "It was hard . . . to be able neither to overlook her *new facts* without brutality nor to recognize them without impertinence" (emphasis mine). Traffle is in a dilemma, for he does not understand the "new woman," although he envies her her immersion in life (XII, 307). These references all derive from the use of the term "new fact" or "new facts" that had been widely used in the drive for the reopening of the Dreyfus case, and the words become part of the lingo spread out before the reading public of the world in the daily numbers of a French press that had, during the twelve years of the "case," multiplied in the universal demand for news of it and in the continuing battle between the Dreyfusards and the anti-Dreyfusards.

A random opening of Guy Chapman's book, *The Dreyfus Case,* one of the many books on the affair will disclose the special use of "new fact" for designating the fresh evidence that made a retrial possible—"the unliklihood of the Dreyfus family finding a new fact which might lead to the reopening of the case." The "great difficulty lay in the fact that, to secure a retrial of Dreyfus by his peers," their lawyer "must produce a new fact which threw doubt on the verdict of 1894. When that lawyer gave an exposition of the case in May 1899, he "turned to the 'new facts' on which he was calling for the case to be sent back for retrial. . . . He did not ask the court to find Dreyfus innocent, but to find that a new fact of a character to establish innocence had arisen. The audience could not restrain their applause, and Mazeau did not attempt to check it."[15] In other words, the reopening of the Dreyfus case depended on the finding of "new facts," or "facts too long withheld."

Like most of James's fiction, the "germ" material is so complex and the strands from life, literature, or art so manifold that we must mention another matter contained in "Mora Montravers" that lends itself also to Dreyfus associations. Edith Wharton may be another implant in this tale in a reflection of her independence and certainly of other characteristics. James's habitual use of the language of the Dreyfus case entered into a letter regarding the Edward Wharton–Edith Wharton relationship, as well as the Mora Montravers–Walter Puddick relationship. James wrote to Gaillard Lapsley in 1911, asking "whether there is any definite 'new fact' . . . any new proposal" in regard to Edith and Teddy's marital difficulties.[16] But throughout "Mora Montravers," the insistent repetition of "new fact" is always to be read *"à la Dreyfus."*

# H. G. Wells's Discovery of the Future
## and *The Sense of the Past*

Notwithstanding H. G. Wells's many predecessors, it was when he combined his enthusiasm for the saving role of science for mankind with the consoling idea of the future that he virtually created "science fiction." James's literary friendship with Wells, which began so enthusiastically that James looked forward to collaborating with him ("I hope you are thinking of doing Mars—in some detail. Let me in *there* at the right moment"), was bound to end in a profound misunderstanding, for one can hardly imagine two writers who looked more differently at history.[1] James was concerned with the concrete details of "the visitable past," anxious to get the real sense of the sense of the past, whereas Wells said in the words of one of his characters, "I flung myself into futurity." Yet since Wells fed James's imagination, we see James in his characteristic way continue to use his more popular and successful contemporary's material. Of *The First Men in the Moon* James wrote that the book tended to "make me sigh, on some such occasion to *collaborate* with you." By giving Wells "the benefit of my vision" James wants to become his "faithful finisher" (HGW, 82). This is clearly high comedy, but in a serious way James was affected by Wells's visions of the future. James turned them backward, however, so they appear reversed in *The Sense of the Past*.

The relation between H. G. Wells and Henry James is vital to the meaning of *The Sense of the Past*. It has usually been assumed that *The Time Machine* by Wells was the one work of fiction that influenced the plot of *The Sense of the Past*. But from the chronology of James's letters to Wells we learn that James had not read *The Time Machine*, published in 1895, until Wells sent it to him in 1900, after he had worked on *The Sense of the Past* in the autumn of 1899. However, in the summer of 1899 James had received Wells's *When the Sleeper Wakes*, published in May 1899, and in the fall he received a copy of Wells's *Tales of Space and Time*, published in November 1899. James thanked Wells for the second book on November 20, 1899 and claimed then that he had already absorbed it: "These new tales I have already absorbed and, to the best of my powers, assimilated." Although he did not agree with Wells about what would constitute the appearance of the future—"Your spirit is huge, your fascination irresistible, your resources infinite"—James seems to have been greatly affected by these stories (HGW, 62). As for *The Time Machine*, he did not receive it from Wells until the last days of January 1900, after he had asked for a copy— "after I had so *un*gracefully sought it at your hands"—by which time he had clearly already begun his own novel (HGW, 63).

Edel tells us James had a title for the book "from the first. He would call it *The Sense of the Past*."[2] But why so sure so early? Because, one speculates, *Tales of Space and Time*, read and absorbed in the summer 1899, had spread before him Wells's imagination of the future, his adventure into the concept of futurity, his flights into the unchartered. In fact, recently there has emerged from James's library Wells's *The Discovery of the Future* (1902), a pamphlet reprinting a speech "delivered to the Royal Institution on January 24, 1902" (fig. 55). James began his novel early in January and by the end of the month he had, Edel writes, abandoned it. The novel at this time, January 1900, stops after the third chapter, but in it we have the interview between Ralph Pendrel and the American ambassador to England in which Ralph tells him that for the man in the portrait with whom he will exchange places he, Ralph, is the future. "'Why I *am* the future . . . that is, for *him;* which means the Present, don't you see—?'"[3] These words were written before the end of January, and James received *The Time Machine* sometime before January 29, 1900, the day he thanked Wells for the book. Some other fiction by Wells must have been the initiating influence on James's novel of the past. In this novel the future does appear, but it is reserved for the man in the portrait, "the man from 1820." The *Sense of the Past* through chapter 3 was all done before the receipt of *The Time Machine* but done right after James had absorbed *Tales of Space and Time*, one of which is "A Story of the Days to Come." These and the novel, *When the Sleeper Awakes*, which Wells had included in his gift during the summer of 1899, have their time in the twenty-second century.

What are these stories James absorbed? Almost all are about the future and ingenious ways of seeing into it. The only story about the past is a story of the Stone Age which exists before and without history and is so unknown that it might just as well be about the future, the essence of the unknown. "A Story of the Days to Come" is about the near past, the Victorian period, but only as it is resurrected by people of the future, those of the twenty-second century. All the other tales are focused on the future, that is, on Wells's territory for adventure, and as soon as James received *The Time Machine*, (and in his letter of January 29 he shows he has read it) he adds, "I rewrite you, much, as I read—which is the highest tribute my damned impertinence can pay an author" (HGW, 63). He had, however, probably rewritten his chapters based on his response in the extreme opposite direction to the works he had received in the summer.

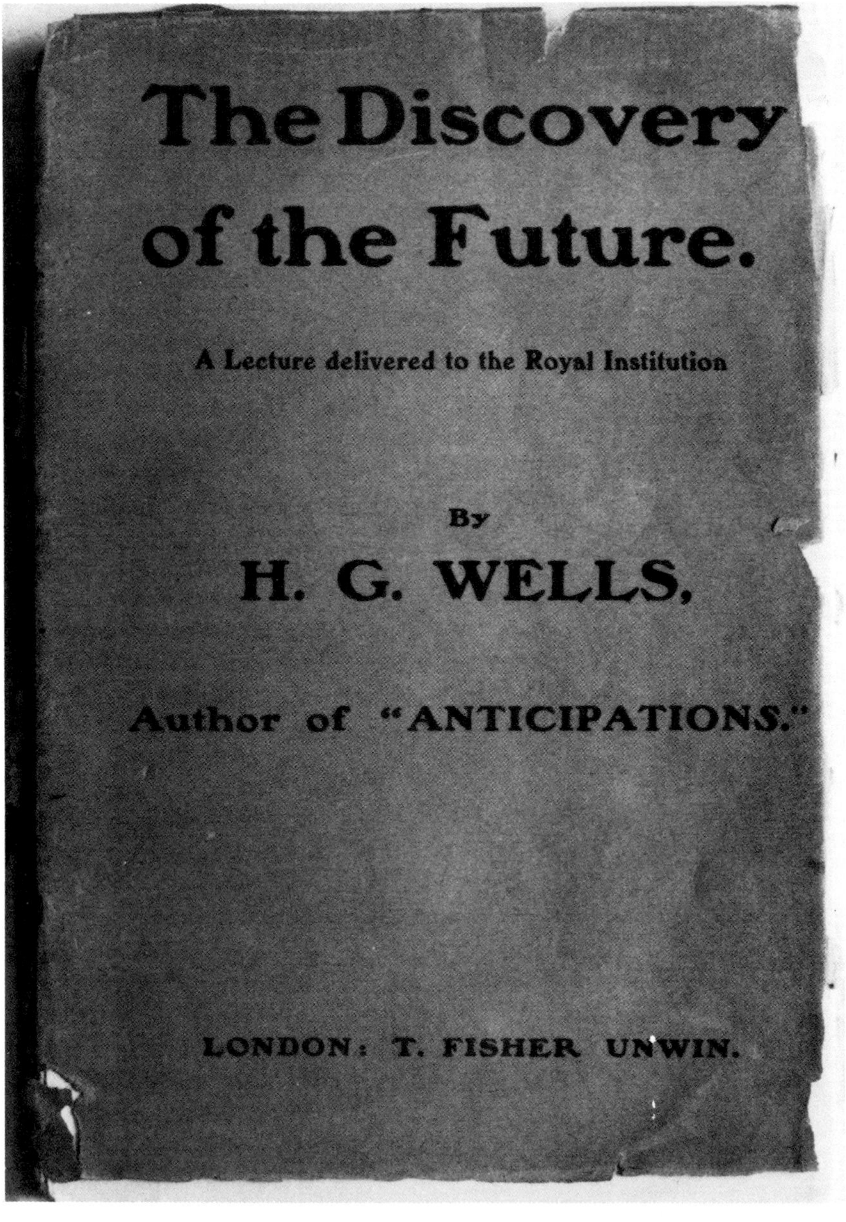

# The Discovery of the Future.

A Lecture delivered to the Royal Institution

By

# H. G. WELLS,

## Author of "ANTICIPATIONS."

## LONDON: T. FISHER UNWIN.

Figure 55.   *The Discovery of the Future* by H. G. Wells, 1902
Contains the inscription, "Henry James from H. G. Wells."

In *When the Sleeper Awakes* and "A Story of the Days to Come," the past is viewed by men of the future. In *Tales of Space and Time* there is one story, "The Crystal Egg," in which the narrator looks through such an egg and sees another world wherein someone is at the same time looking through a similar crystal, at which point the spectators from the two different worlds get into rapport with each other. This certainly suggests James's concept of a reciprocal sense of time, involving the man in the portrait who wishes to investigate his future (which is Ralph's present) and Ralph, who wishes to investigate the man in the portrait's past (which is situated in 1820). In "A Story of the Days to Come," people who live in the future get themselves hypnotized in order to find themselves back in Victorian times. "They played their little romance in the past as vivid as reality, and when at last they awakened they remembered all they had seen as though it were the real thing." " 'Think of all that opens out to us—the enhancement of our experience!' "

What James is trying to do in *The Sense of the Past* is to open up the actuality to experience and not just make it a statement of fact, as expressed here by Wells. Denton and Elizabeth in Wells's story express their desire for the past: " 'If only we had lived in the past!' " They exile themselves to the country, where the ruins of the nineteenth century still, in part, exist, but in the end it is an unsatisfactory way of life. They go back to the "highly developed cities in which they live in 2100," but "in that world they yearn for the past."[4] The hero and heroine of Wells's story compromise by decorating their house with Victorian furniture. It is very likely that James received his idea from that story about going to the past and coming back to the world of the present, only his world is that of 1910 and the world of his imagined past is 1820, a time historically resonant for James.

As Wells had had for his source Bellamy's *Looking Backward* and Kipling's "The Man Who Would Be King," James had his in Wells, for surely those two-and-a-half chapters James finished in 1900, which bring the story up to the point where the ambassador walks Ralph Pendrel to his house, No. 9 Mansfield Square, argue for this. The hero is to be a source of terror to others. In the first two-and-a-half chapters of *The Sense of the Past*, the conversations between Ralph and the ambassador indicate the effect of Wells's imagination. Ralph says, describing his ancestor of the portrait, " 'I've been ridden all my life, I think I should tell you . . . by the desire to cultivate some better sense of the past than has mostly seemed sufficient even for those people who have gone in most for cultivating it. . . . So you can fancy what a charm it was . . . to catch a person and a beautifully intelligent one, in the very act of cultivating . . . his sense of the future, don't you see. . . . I've brought him, I've given him, I've introduced him to, the Future. So there we are!' " The ambassador says to him, " 'How could you bring him what you didn't have yourself?' " Ralph answers,

" 'Why, I *am* the Future. The Future, that is, for *him;* which means the Present, don't you see—?' " (SP, 104).

When the ambassador thinks that they have merged personalities, Ralph answers, " 'I didn't say . . . that we have *merged* personalities, but that we have definitely exchanged them—which is a different matter' " (SP, 105). " 'He has given me his chance for this while I have given him mine for that' " (SP, 106). Ralph also says that the figure from the portrait is waiting in the cab so that he can start immediately to live in his future—that is, Ralph's present; the man of 1820 is waiting to go off into 1910. A kind of adventure that Aurora Coyne has dared her young man to make begins when Ralph goes into the doorway of his house, where he encounters "an increasingly thick *other* medium; the medium to which the opening door of the house gave at once an extension that was like an extraordinarily strong odour inhaled—an inward and inward warm reach that his bewildered judge would literally have seen swallow him up; though perhaps with the supreme pause of the determined diver about to plunge just marked in him before the closing of the door again placed him on the right side and the whole world as he had known it on the wrong" (SP, 115). In this sense, he is entering a new atmosphere, just as the time traveler enters a new atmosphere as he gets into his time machine, for it is possible that James wrote the last part of book 3 after he had devoured *The Time Machine*. The way he describes a nineteenth-century young man waiting in his cab ready to see his future, having "begun to beat fine wings and test brave lungs in the fresh air of his experiment," sounds like the driver of the time machine in Wells's novel (SP, 112). Ralph, in turn, feels he has been "launched" himself, since his counterpart has already been. But the story does not in any way belong to the man of 1820 who is on his way to his future. It is totally Ralph's experience, his journey to the past.

As time went on James and Wells became closer. In 1902 Wells gave his talk *The Discovery of the Future,* published in pamphlet form and inscribed, "To Henry James from H. G. Wells." In his correspondence with Wells, James wrote often about *The First Men in the Moon* (fig. 56). First, he continued to refer to the book as "Your Two Men," since he paid attention to the fact that there are two characters, like his own two male characters in *The Sense of the Past*—the ancestor in the portrait and Ralph Pendrel, the man of the present. He wrote that Wells's book tended to make him "hope you are thinking of doing Mars—in some detail. Let me in *there* at the right moment." Continuing with the book, he says he wants to "write it over, I mean *re*-compose it, in the light of my own high sense of propriety and with immense refinements and embellishments. I took over so, for instance, in my locked breast, the subject of Two Men, etc. and the superstructure I reared upon it had almost no resemblance to, or nothing in common (*but* the subject!) with yours" (HGW, 82). We also know

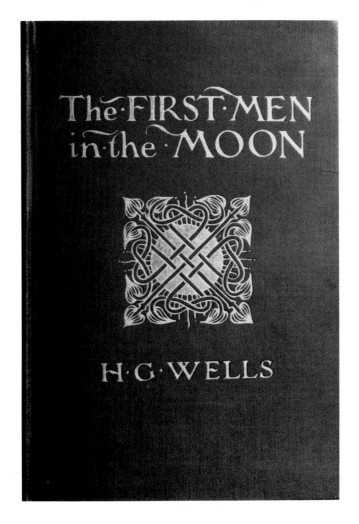

Figure 56. *The First Men in the Moon* by H. G. Wells, 1901
Contains the inscription, "To Henry James from H. G.
Wells."

how carefully James read *Twelve Stories and a Dream* (1903) in 1904, each of the tales collected therein being to him "as a substantial coloured sweet or bon-bon . . . which I just allowed to *melt* lollypop-wise, upon my imaginative tongue" (HGW, 94–95). The comments on the science stories end because they themselves end and Wells has abandoned the genre.

In *The Time Machine* we see certain details that may have influenced James. In conversation with the medical man, the hero of Wells's novel says that the machine can go either into the past or into the future. The hero chooses the future and so "flung myself into futurity."[5] When he loses the time machine in the world of the Morlocks, there "came the possibility of losing my own age, of being helpless in the strange new world. The mere thought of it was an actual sensation" (SSF, 29). Surely Ralph's anxiety about his own "liberation" could have had its original model in the above quotation, for he is to be "saved from all the horror of the growing fear of *not* being saved . . . of being *in* the past to stay, heart-breakingly to stay and never know his own original precious Present again" (SP, 294). Wells's hero is afraid of being lost in the future; James's hero is afraid of being lost in the past.

We know that James read "A Story of the Days to Come" because he mentions the blue food that is served in that tale in a letter to Wells (HGW, 62). When he writes to Wells about *The First Men in the Moon,* as noted above, he wants to collaborate with Wells, but it is certain details of *The Time Machine* that may have influenced the later-written notes of *The Sense of the Past.* In those notes, written in January 1900, one may see James's reflection of *The Time Machine* in parts. *The Sense of the Past* is James's science fiction novel, even though there is nothing about it that has the quality of science fiction, which even today is often devoted not to the future in time but to the far-off in space, to the life lived on planets of other stars. These stories are the direct descendants of Wells's fantasies. James's hero has "the backward vision," that of the past, and Aurora Coyne, Ralph's fiancée, who will accept him only if he will give up the past and engage in a true adventure, quotes from Ralph's essay on history: "There are particular places where things have happened . . . places . . . subject to the continuity of life mostly, that seem to put us into communication" (SP, 34).

Where the future comes into Ralph's life is where the figure in the portrait of 1820 wants to live and experience his future, which is Ralph's present. Ralph's time machine is the opposite of Wells's time machine: it is the stationary door knocker of the house he inherits: "an engine huge, heavy, ancient, brazen, polished, essentially defiant of any trifling, but now resoundingly applied" (SP, 62). It acts as his time machine, which lets him enter the past, as Wells's time machine had been the engine to penetrate the future. James uses in his novel the very words of the title of the first book of Wells's science novels he had read, *Tales of Space and Time,* only he reverses their order, because time was more important to him than space. Looking out of the window of his house in London, Ralph was "separated from the splashed Square and its blurred and distant life much more by time than by space" (SP, 65). "As the house was his house, so the time, and it sank into him, was his time" (SP, 66).

There is also a motif seemingly imported from *The Time Machine* which functions as it does in that novel. There the matches the hero finds in his pocket help him to escape from the Morlocks because they are afraid of fire, and the discovery determines a safe return to his own home in the present time. In *The Sense of the Past,* Ralph lights the matches he finds in his waistcoat pocket, and when he "raised aloft the glittering torch" made from the candles touched off with the matches "he was filled with the sense of a quite new relation to the house," for "it registered in a single brief insistance the fact that he was master." Just as the Time Traveler gains mastery over the Morlocks through his use of fire, so does Ralph over his house (SP, 84). It is through the lighted candle that Ralph can see that the figure in the picture has turned, the great discovery of the book, and that "what he had taken for a reflection of his light was only another candle" (SP, 87). It is by the lighted candle that the exchange of roles and personalities can take place, and the figure from the picture goes into his future while Ralph goes into his past. For Ralph the "spell" of communication with the past is "made to work by the imposition of hands . . . on an old object or an old surface" (SP, 34).

In 1891 "The Pupil" represented James's answer to Stevenson's way of writing an adventure story in his "boys' books," *Kidnapped* and *Treasure Island.* Ten years later James began another adventure story, basing it on yet making it as different as possible from the science fiction of H. G. Wells, the fiction he repeatedly wrote that he was rewriting. The invention now is taking off not from treasure hunts and juvenile literature but from the science literature that was going to become the adolescent romance of the twentieth century, the science fiction begun by Wells and flourishing in the works of Ray Bradbury and a hundred others today. Though the new science fiction was fixated in the subject matter and the vision of the future, and on inventions by Wells garnered from his training in the sciences, James based his adventure story on the only knowledge we actually have, that of the past. *The Sense of the Past* shows that James's adventure was a voyage into the past in space and time, and it is interesting that just when he was writing his preliminary chapters in January of 1900, the book he had received in November of 1899, *Tales of Space and Time,* offered him all kinds of solutions for handling science fictional thoughts. (A few months before, he had received Wells's novel *When the Sleeper Wakes,* but he had not yet, apparently, read it thoroughly—it is not very readable.) As for the other book, James wrote to Wells, "these new tales I have already absorbed and . . . assimilated." James adds certain details from the stories that show he has, in truth, done so, especially details from the tale "A Story of the Days to Come" (HGW, 62).

A far as Wells's later novels go, they are not concerned with science fiction, but James continued to be interested in them. *The Passionate Friends* elicited from James another avowal of his tendency to rewrite the work of others:

> To read a novel at all I perform afresh, to my sense, the act of writing it, that is of rehandling the subject accordingly to my own lights and over-scoring the author's form and pressure with my own vision and understanding of *the* way—this, of course I mean, when I *see* a subject in what he has done and feel its appeal to me as one: which I feel I very often don't. This produces reflections and reserves—it's the very measure of my attention and my interest; but there's nobody who makes these particular reactions less *matter* for me than you do. . . ." (HGW, 173)

He goes on to specify what is wrong with the book. He thinks that Wells's way is not the way "to give the truth about the woman of our hour." He thinks the woman is simply Stratton himself, the hero of the novel.

When it comes to *Ann Veronica* (1909), she is the new woman who is taking a higher scholastic degree but who lives at home. When her father refuses to let her go to a fancy dress party, she leaves home and wanders through the city. An older man, Mr. Ramage, who lives near and works as a barrister in London, tries to seduce her before he lends her forty pounds. She fights him off. She falls in love with somebody who heads a laboratory and is a student of Russell's, and when she realizes she is pregnant she marries him. When a woman really loves, she does not mind leading the traditional role with her husband; this is the general idea of the book.

At this time James was writing his short story "Mora Montravers," published in August–September 1909 in the *English Review*. Both are about "the new woman." (Sarah Grand had coined the phrase.) Mora and Ann Veronica both leave home because of their aunts. Actually, Mora marries so that she can leave some money to her friend, Mr. Puddick, the artist, but then she goes her own way, and we see her making friends with Sir B.B., a patron of the arts. She uses her femininity to get ahead in her field. Her charm works, and her disregard of marriage ties makes her revolutionary in her habits. Her step-uncle, Sidney Traffle, appreciates her character and her sense of life, since he has been hemmed in all his life and since he, too, had wanted to be an artist though he lacked the essential life force.

Henry James went on in his critique of *Ann Veronica* to say that "her projected Ego—the best thing in the book . . . rather wants clearness and *nuances* but the *men* are prodigious, all, and the total result lives and kicks and throbs and flushes and glares—I mean hangs there in the very air we breathe" (HGW, 123). James is measuring the woman against his Kate Cookham, the new woman whose psychology he presents in "The Bench of Desolation." Kate is, in spite of the fact that the central consciousness is that of Herbert Dodd, the main character in the book. But Kate is all there in her motivation, her working out of her plan, her feelings, and her thoughts.

James had finished all his tales. He had left only the woman in *The Sense of the Past,* and he had not done much with Aurora Coyne, who is simply the daughter of a billionaire—though she acts very much like Hilda Wangel (in *The Masterbuilder,* by Ibsen) who more or less invented the "new woman" of literature and spread her gospel around. Then there is Rosanna Gaw, of *The Ivory Tower,* who knows what she wants but who is too rich to be the new woman, for she does not have to make her way. James redoes *Ann Veronica* in his *Finer Grain* stories, yet *Ann Veronica* herself is not really a new woman. She calculates, even though she goes to jail for the suffrage movement. Still, when she falls in love, she gives her lover all she has. Kate Cookham, on the other hand, is a strong new woman who loves and gets her man even against all odds. By saying she loves him, Kate, by refusing to be refused, gets him back and gives him back what she had extorted from him. She is both a bad and a good woman combined. However, in spite of James's enthusiasm for Wells's books and his repeated desire to redo them his way, the fictions by Wells that really influenced him were the science fiction tales of the early years. It is in *The Sense of the Past,* James's kind of condensation of those tales, that we see a whole new frame of reference in which a typically Jamesian consciousness is placed.

# Notes

## Chapter 1

The Sleeping Beauty material is revised in part from my "Henry James and the Sleeping Beauty: A Victorian Fantasy on a Fairy-Tale Theme," *Topic,* Fall 1983, pp. 10–23.

1. Henry James, *The Art of the Novel* (New York: Scribner's, 1934), p. 254.

2. *Howells and James: A Double Billing,* ed. Leon Edel and Lyall H. Powers (New York: The New York Public Library, 1958), p. 50.

3. Henry James, *The Golden Bowl* (New York: Scribner's, 1905), II, p. 106.

4. *The Complete Tales of Henry James* (Philadelphia: J.B. Lippincott, 1964), XII, p. 358. Future references indicated by XII and page number.

5. Henry James *Watch and Ward* (Boston: Houghton, Osgood, 1878), p. 36. Future references indicated by WW and page number.

6. *The Complete Tales of Henry James* ed. Leon Edel (Philadelphia: J.B. Lippincott, 1962), I, 55. Future references indicated by I and page number. References to volume II indicated by II and page number.

7. *Perrault's Fairy Tales,* translated by A.E. Johnson (New York: Dover, 1969), p. 62. Future references indicated by P and page number.

8. James may have meant Lockley Hall to remind the reader of Tennyson's poem, "Locksley Hall," whose theme is based on the changes in England wrought by time. The poem appeared in *Poems of Alfred Tennyson* (London: E. Moxon and Co., 1857), p. 267. The copy belonging to Henry James is now in the Houghton Library, Harvard University, Cambridge and bears the following inscription: "From my Father (1858), H.J."

9. Tennyson's complete poem, *The Day Dream,* was printed in James's copy of Moxon's illustrated edition of Tennyson's poems cited above. The five main parts, "The Sleeping Palace," "The Sleeping Beauty," "The Arrival," "The Revival," and "The Departure," included the awakening of Sleeping Beauty and her marriage to the prince, with illustrations by J.E. Millais (see fig. 6).

10. Henry James, *Essays in London and Elsewhere* (New York: Harper, 1893), pp. 270–71. For material on the painters of the Sleeping Woman, see my "The Sleeping Woman: A Victorian Fantasy," *The Pre-Raphaelite Review* vol. 2, no. 1, November 1978, pp. 12–26.

11.  Martin Harrison and Bill Waters, *Burne-Jones* (London: Barrie & Jenkins, 1973), p. 103.

12.  Harrison and Waters, *Burne-Jones,* p. 151.

13.  Jerome Buckley, *The Victorian Temper* (Cambridge: Harvard University Press, 1952), p. 164.

14.  *The Complete Tales of Henry James* (Philadelphia: J. B. Lippincott, 1964), XI, p. 341. Future references indicated by XI and page number.

15.  Bruno Bettelheim, *The Uses of Enchantment* (New York: Knopf, 1976), pp. 225–26. Future references indicated by B and page number.

16.  Henry James, *Roderick Hudson* (Boston: Osgood, 1876), p. 185.

17.  Henry James, *Roderick Hudson,* p. 211.

18.  Juliet McMaster, "'Bluebeard at Breakfast,'" *Dickens Studies Annual,* vol. 8, 1980. Future references indicated by BB and page number.

19.  *The Works of Alphonse Daudet* (Boston: Little, Brown & Co., 1899), II, p. 259.

20.  Henry James, *The Sense of the Past* (New York: Scribner's, 1917), pp. 208–9. Future references indicated by SP and page number.

21.  *The Complete Tales of Henry James,* ed. Leon Edel (Philadelphia: J.B. Lippincott, 1962), III, p. 351. Future references indicated by III and page number.

22.  *Howells and James: A Double Billing,* p. 50.

23.  *The Complete Tales of Henry James,* ed. Leon Edel (Philadelphia: J.B. Lippincott, 1963), VI, p. 221. Future references indicated by VI and page number.

24.  *The Child's Own Book and Treasury of Fairy Stories* (New York: Allen, 1869), p. 72. Future references indicated by COB and page number.

25.  Henry James, *The Sacred Fount* (London: Methuen, 1901), p. 129. Future references indicated by SF and page number.

26.  *The Complete Tales of Henry James,* ed. Leon Edel (Philadelphia: J.B. Lippincott, 1963), VII, p. 90. Future references indicated by VII and page number.

27.  *The Complete Tales of Henry James,* ed. Leon Edel (Philadelphia: J. B. Lippincott, 1963), VIII, p. 468. Future references indicated by VIII and page number.

28.  *Howells and James: A Double Billing,* p. 50.

29.  *The Whole Family, a Novel by Twelve Authors* (New York: Harper, 1908), p. 145. Future references indicated by WF and page number.

30.  Henry James, *The Autobiography of Henry James,* ed. F. W. Dupee (New York: Criterion, 1956), p. 75. Future references indicated by AU and page number.

31.  *The Complete Tales of Henry James,* ed. Leon Edel (Philadelphia: J. B. Lippincott, 1964), X, p. 330. Future references indicated by X and page number.

32.  Charles Dickens, *Our Mutual Friend* (1864–1865) (New York: New American Library, reprinted 1964, 1980), p. 450. Future references indicated by MF and page number. Professor Juliet McMaster, University of Alberta, Edmonton, Canada, drew my attention to the Red Riding Hood references in *Our Mutual Friend.*

33. *The Works of Alphonse Daudet,* limited edition, XII (Boston: Little, Brown, 1899), p. 150. Future references indicated by AD and page number.

34. Henry James, *The Painter's Eye* (London: Rupert Hart-Davis, 1956), p.72.

35. *Contes de Perrault,* ed. G. Rougier (Paris: Garnier, 1967), pp. 114–15, and Perrault, *Contes* (Paris: Hetzel, 1862), p. 2.

36. *The Wallace Collection Catalogue* (London: His Majesty's Office, 1928), p. 243.

37. Hugh Walpole, *The Apple Trees* (Waltham Saint Lawrence: The Golden Cockerell Press, 1932), p. 58.

38. Leon Edel, *Henry James: The Treacherous Years: 1895–1901* (Philadelphia: J.B. Lippincott, 1969), p. 264.

39. Sigmund Freud, *Collected Papers* (London: Hogarth, 1948), III, p. 502.

40. Sigmund Freud, *Collected Papers,* IV, p. 236.

41. *The Notebooks of Henry James,* ed. F.O. Matthiessen and Kenneth B. Murdock (New York: Oxford University Press, 1947), p. 128. Future references indicated by N and page number.

42. Hugh Walpole, *The Apple Trees,* p, 53.

43. Robert Darnton, *The Great Cat Massacre* (New York: Basic Books, 1984), passim. This book was brought to my attention by Professor Anne Janowitz, Brandeis University.

44. Henry James, *The Ambassadors* (London: Methuen, 1903), p. 434. Future references indicated by AM and page number.

45. *The Novels and Tales of Henry James* (New York: Scribner's, 1909), XX, p. 270. Future references indicated by NYE, volume number, and page number.

46. I quote from Isaiah 39; the passage is the same as in II Kings 20, except for trivial differences.

47. Isaiah 39: 2 and 6.

48. Henry James, *Literary Reviews and Essays,* ed. Albert Mordell (New York: Twayne, 1957), p. 320.

49. *Henry James Letters,* ed. Leon Edel, IV (Cambridge: Harvard University Press, 1984), p. 131.

50. Donal O'Gorman argues for the Devil's existence in "The Turn of the Screw" where he appears incarnate in the two evil demons, Peter Quint and Miss Jessel. See Donal O'Gorman, "Henry James's Reading of 'The Turn of the Screw': Parts II and III," *The Henry James Review,* vol. 1, no. 3, Spring 1980, pp. 240–53.

## Chapter 2

1. "Holman Hunt's Scapegoat . . . so charged with the awful . . . I should have feared to face it all alone in a room." Henry James, *The Autobiography of Henry James,* ed. F.W. Dupee (New York: Criterion, 1956), p. 178.

2. Among the books on the East published before 1888 which James had in his library, we find in addition Théophile Gautier's *Constantinople,* 1865, and his *L'Orient,* 1877; Bryce's *Transcanasia and Ararat,* 1878; Alfred St. Johnson's *Camping among Cannibals,* 1883; Lyall's *Asiatic Studies,* 1884; and Edmund Gosse's *Firdausi in Exile,* 1886. See Leon Edel and

Adeline R. Tintner, *The Library of Henry James* (Ann Arbor: UMI Research Press, 1987), passim.

3.  Henry James, *"La Tentation de Saint Antoine*. Par Gustave Flaubert" (Paris: Charpentier; New York: F. W. Christern, 1874, *The Nation,* June 4, 1874. Reprinted in *Literary Reviews and Essays* by Henry James, ed. Albert Mordell (New York: Twayne, 1957), pp. 145–49.

4.  Letter from Henry James to Herbert Gilchrist, September 7, 1913. Author's collection.

5.  "Gobineau's 'Nouvelles Asiatiques.'" *The Nation,* December 7, 1876, pp. 344–45. James adds: "We may ask . . . whether now . . . it would not be worth some publisher's trouble to reprint Morier's charming tale?" (p. 344). In addition, James had in his Lamb House library a copy of Sir James Morier, *The Adventures of Hajji Baba of Ispahan* (London: Richard Bentley, 1851). Author's collection.

6.  Henry James, *The Painter's Eye* (London: Rupert Hart-Davis, 1956), p. 113.

7.  Henry James, *Watch and Ward* (New York: Grove Press, 1959), p. 49. Future references indicated by WW and page number.

8.  Henry James, *Roderick Hudson* (Boston: Osgood, 1876), p. 162.

9.  Henry James, *Europeans* (New York: New American Library, reprinted 1964), p. 25. Future references indicated by E and page number. There is no copy of Galland's translation in James's library list, but once he had moved to London at the end of 1876 he had the use of more than one club library.

10.  Henry James, *What Maisie Knew,* 1897, (Harmondsworth, Middlesex: Penguin, reprinted 1977), p. 127. Future references indicated by M and page number.

11.  Henry James, *Partial Portraits* (1888; reprint edition ed. Leon Edel, Ann Arbor: University of Michigan Press, 1970), pp. 231–34.

12.  Alphonse Daudet, *The Nabab,* translated by Prof. W. P. Trent (New York: Collier, 1902), p. 4.

13.  *Henry James Letters,* ed. Leon Edel (Cambridge: Harvard University Press, 1975), II, pp. 420–21.

14.  F. Marion Crawford, *Mr. Isaacs* (New York: Grosset & Dunlop, 1882), p. 12. Future references indicated by Is and page number.

15.  Letter from Henry James to Herbert Gilchrist, cited above.

16.  See my "Henry James and Byron: A Victorian Romantic Relationship," *The Byron Journal,* no. 9, 1981, pp. 52–64. Also my *The Book World of Henry James* (Ann Arbor: UMI Research Press, 1987), pp. 95–102.

17.  *The Complete Tales of Henry James,* ed. Leon Edel (Philadelphia: J. B. Lippincott, 1963), V, p. 150. Future references indicated by V and page number.

18.  *Poems by Alfred Lord Tennyson, D.C.L.* (London: E. Moxon and Co., 1857), p. 13.

19.  Philippe Jullian, *The Orientalists* (Oxford: Phaedon, 1977), p. 88.

20.  *An Arabian Tale from an Unpublished Manuscript* [Vathek] (London: J. Johnson, 1786), p. 200.

21.  *The Complete Tales of Henry James,* ed. Leon Edel (Philadelphia: J.B. Lippincott, 1963), VI, p. 123.

22. *The Complete Tales of Henry James,* VI, p. 125.

23. The twenty-three volumes by Pierre Loti in James's library have ten titles signed by James. The sixteen volumes dealing with the East begin with *Aziyadé* (1885), which is signed, as are nine other volumes of the Eastern novels. The last volume in the collection is *Un Pèlerin D'Angkor,* 1912. In addition to those by Loti, there were in James's library a number of volumes on the East published after 1886. Among them were Morton Fullerton's *In Cairo,* 1891; Sir G.S. Robertson's *The Story of a Minor Siege,* 1899, and *The Kafirs of the Hindu Kush;* E. Fitzgerald's *The Rubayat of Omar Khayam,* 1900; Viscount Wolseley's *The Story of a Soldier's Life,* 1903; The Ranee of Sarawak's *My Life in Sarawak,* 1913; George E. Woodbury's *North Africa and the Sahara Desert,* 1914. (See Edel and Tintner, *The Library of Henry James.*)

24. Pierre Loti, *Impressions,* with an introduction by Henry James (Westminster: Constable, 1898), p. 17. James wrote three essays on Loti: in 1888, 1897, and 1898.

25. Pierre Loti, *Into Morocco* (New York: Welch, Fracker, 1889) p. 314.

26. Loti, *Into Morocco,* p. 315.

27. Henry James, *The Golden Bowl* (New York: Scribner's, 1905), I, p. 219.

28. Loti, *Impressions,* introduction, p. 17.

29. Pierre Loti, *Propos d'exil* (Paris: Calmann Levy, 1887), pp. 115, 162.

30. Pierre Loti, *The Last Days of Pekin,* translated by Myrta L. Jones (Boston: Little, Brown, 1902), p. 79.

31. Loti, *The Last Days of Pekin,* p. 113.

32. Loti, *Impressions,* introduction, p. 17.

33. Henry James, *The Golden Bowl* (Harmondsworth, Middlesex: Penguin, 1978, reprinted 1905), p. 29. Future references indicated by G and page number.

34. James, *The Painter's Eye,* p. 150.

35. James, *The Painter's Eye,* p. 179.

36. Regina Soria, *Elihu Vedder* (Rutherford, New Jersey: Fairleigh Dickinson University Press, 1970), p. 38.

37. Soria, *Elihu Vedder,* p. 246. *The Questioner of the Sphinx* was given to the Boston Museum by Mrs. Martin Brimmer (Soria, *Elihu Vedder,* p. 283).

38. Henry James, *Parisian Sketches,* ed. Leon Edel and Ilse Dusoir Lind (London: Hart-Davis, 1958), pp. 151–52.

39. Jullian, *The Orientalists,* p. 102.

## Chapter 3

1. "Williams Morris's *The Life and Death of Jason: A Poem*" (unsigned review), *North American Review,* CV, October, 1867, pp. 688–92.

2. Bruce Redford, "Keeping Story out of History: Henry James's Biographical *tour de force,*" *American Literature,* vol. 57, no. 2, May 1985, pp. 215–25.

3. Henry James, *William Wetmore Story and His Friends* (Edinburgh: William Blackwood, 1903), I, p. 219. Future references indicated by ST, I, and page number.

4. Leon Edel, to whom I appealed for her identification, replied that "this is one of those exasperating and insoluble letters." He kindly checked the letters of this period in his files and found nothing after this letter until one of December 26 to Edmund Gosse which ends the December letters. Although Constance Fenimore Woolson was in London at the time, there is no evidence that she was the "venerable" enchantress, especially since she agreed with James to destroy his letters to her.

5. Henry James, *Essays in London and Elsewhere* (New York: Harper, 1893), p. 114. Future references indicated by EL and page number.

6. Leon Edel, *Henry James: The Conquest of London* (Philadelphia: J.B. Lippincott, 1962), p. 380.

7. *The Complete Tales of Henry James,* ed. Leon Edel (Philadelphia: J.B. Lippincott, 1962), VI, p. 151. Future references indicated by VI and page number.

8. Letter from Henry James to Isabella Stewart Gardner, May 2, 1884. Courtesy of The Isabella Stewart Gardner Museum, Boston, Massachusetts.

9. See my *The Book World of Henry James* (Ann Arbor: UMI Research Press, 1987), pp. 103–18.

10. Letter from Henry James to Isabella Stewart Gardner, April 16, 1882. Courtesy of The Isabella Stewart Gardner Museum.

11. Royal A. Gettmann, "Henry James's Revision of *The American,*" *American Literature,* vol 16, 1945, pp. 291–92.

12. *The Complete Plays of Henry James,* ed. Leon Edel (Philadelphia: J.B. Lippincott, 1949), pp. 232, 249.

13. Oscar Cargill, *The Novels of Henry James* (New York: Macmillan, 1961), p. 53.

14. Henry James, *The American* (Boston: Osgood, 1877), p. 136.

15. *The Novels and Tales of Henry James* (New York: Scribner's, 1907), II, p. 162.

16. Dora and Erwin Panofsky, *Pandora's Box* (New York: Harper, 1956), passim. Future references indicated by PA and page number.

17. *The Collected Tales of Henry James,* ed. Leon Edel (Philadelphia: J.B. Lippincott, 1963), V, p. 391. Future references indicated by V and page number.

18. Henry James, *Hawthorne* (New York: Harper, 1880), p. 127.

19. *The Complete Tales of Henry James,* ed. Leon Edel (Philadelphia: J.B. Lippincott, 1961), I, 143. Future references indicated by I and page number.

20. Adeline R. Tintner, *The Museum World of Henry James* (Ann Arbor: UMI Research Press, 1986), p. 22.

21. *The Complete Tales of Henry James,* ed. Leon Edel (Philadelphia: J.B. Lippincott, 1964), XI, p. 396. Future references indicated by XI and page number.

22. *The Notebooks of Henry James,* ed. F.O. Matthiessen and Kenneth B. Murdock (New York: Oxford University Press, 1947), p. 66.

23.  *The Complete Tales of Henry James,* ed. Leon Edel (Philadelphia: Lippincott, 1963), VII, p. 19. Future references indicated by VII and page number.

24.  *The Complete Greek Drama,* ed. Whitney J. Oates and Eugene O'Neill, Jr. (New York: Random House, 1938), II, p. 682. Future references indicated by GD and page number.

25.  Leon Edel, *Henry James: The Middle Years* (Philadelphia: J.B. Lippincott, 1962), p. 110.

26.  See my "The Sleeping Woman: A Victorian Fantasy," *The Pre-Raphaelite Review,* vol. 2, no. 1, November 1978, pp. 12–27.

This material first appeared in my "Euripides Echoed in James's Fiction," *A.B. Bookman's Weekly,* August 24, 1981, pp. 1011–16.

27.  Gilbert Murray, *A History of Ancient Greek Literature* (London: Heinemann, 1897), pp. 272–73.

28.  *The Library of Henry James,* ed. Leon Edel and Adeline R. Tintner (Ann Arbor: UMI Research Press, 1987). James owned a copy of *Specimens of a Translation of Theocritus* (London: Chiswick, n.d.). Author's collection.

29.  *The Notebooks of Henry James,* ed. F.O. Matthiessen and Kenneth B. Murdock (New York: Oxford, 1947), pp. 225–26.

30.  Communication, Joseph Wohlberg, Professor of Latin and Greek, retired, City University of New York, and source for general information about the intense interest in *The Bacchae* at the turn of the century in England.

31.  Henry James, *Notes and Reviews,* 1921, (Freeport, New York: Dunster House, reprinted 1968), p. 110.

32.  Henry James, *Notes on Novelists* (New York: Scribner's, 1914), p. 451.

33.  *The Complete Tales of Henry James,* ed. Leon Edel (Philadelphia: J.B. Lippincott, 1962), IV, pp. 362–64.

34.  Gilbert Murray, *A History of Ancient Greek Literature* (London: Heinemann, 1897), p. 259.

Some of this material appeared in my "James's Mock Epic: 'The Velvet Glove,' Edith Wharton and Other Late Tales," *Modern Fiction Studies,* vol. 17, no. 4, Winter 1971–72, pp. 483–501.

35.  *The Complete Tales of Henry James,* ed. Leon Edel (Philadelphia: J.B. Lippincott, 1964), XII, p. 233. Future references indicated by XII and page number.

36.  Henry James, *A Small Boy and Others* (New York: Scribner's, 1913), p. 28. Future references indicated by SB and page number.

37.  Henry James, *The Autobiography of Henry James,* ed. F.W. Dupee (New York: Criterion, 1956), p. 571.

38.  Letter from James to Gosse, ms. Leeds. Courtesy of University of Leeds.

39.  *The Complete Tales of Henry James,* ed. Leon Edel (Philadelphia: J.B. Lippincott, 1963), V, p. 305.

40.  *Henry James, Selected Letters,* ed. Leon Edel (Cambridge: Harvard University Press, 1987), p. 196.

41.  *The Notebooks of Henry James,* p. 57.

42. Letter from Henry James to "My Dear Athenian," 1899. Author's collection.

43. See my "James's Mock-Epic: 'The Velvet Glove,' Edith Wharton and Other Late Tales" for the attribution of the princess to Edith Wharton.

44. Henry James, *Essays on Literature, etc.* (New York: Library of America, 1984), p. 202.

45. James, *Autobiography,* p. 243.

46. *The Complete Tales of Henry James,* ed. Leon Edel (Philadelphia: J. B. Lippincott, 1964), IX, p. 296.

47. Adeline R. Tintner, *The Museum World of Henry James* (Ann Arbor: UMI Research Press, 1986), pp. 112–21.

48. Tintner, *The Museum World of Henry James,* pp. 192–94.

## Chapter 4

The material for this chapter first appeared in my "Iconic Analogy in 'The Lesson of the Master': Henry James's Legend of Saint George and the Dragon," *The Journal of Narrative Technique,* vol. 5, no. 2, May 1975, pp. 116–27.

1. Charles R. Smith, "The Lesson of the Master," *Studies in Short Fiction,* vol. 6, 1969, pp. 654–58), reviews the conditions in which the story was written and outlines the types of interpretation. Smith's paper gives the evidence from *The Notebooks* and letters of James and includes an annotated bibliography of the story's critical history. See also Ross Posnock, *Henry James and the Problem of Robert Browning* (Athens, Georgia: University of George Press, 1985); George Monteiro, review of Posnock's book in *Nineteenth Century Literature,* 1987, pp. 515–18.

2. Edward Burne-Jones, whom James admired as "the most distinguished artistic figure among Englishmen today" and whom he began to see regularly around 1886, had done a set of seven panels of the Saint George story, many studies for which were in his studio at the time James frequented it and at which time, according to Mrs. Burne-Jones, her husband was completing a new Saint George in oil (*Memorials of Edward Burne-Jones*). James had admired the painter as early as the 1877 Grosvenor Gallery exhibition in which Burne-Jones showed eight important works, among which was a Saint George. James reviewed and praised the Burne-Jones entries.

3. Henry James, *The Complete Tales of Henry James,* ed. Leon Edel (Philadelphia: J.B. Lippincott, 1964), IX, p. 60. Dencombe as a novelist was read a second time by Doctor Hugh.

4. Henry James, *The Complete Tales of Henry James,* ed. Leon Edel (Philadelphia: J.B. Lippincott, 1963), VII, p. 231. Future references indicated by VII and page number.

5. Henry James, *The Novels and Tales of Henry James* (New York: Scribner's, 1909), XV, p. 27. Future references indicated by NY and page number.

6. Henry James, *The Complete Tales of Henry James,* ed. Leon Edel (Philadelphia: J.B. Lippincott, 1964), IX, p. 69.

7. Henry James, *The Art of the Novel* (New York: Scribner's, 1934), p. 228.

8. James, *The Art of the Novel,* p. 229.

9. Jacobus de Voragine, *The Golden Legend* (New York: Arno Press, 1969), p. 236.

10. De Voragine, *The Golden Legend,* p. 237.

11.  De Voragine, *The Golden Legend,* p. 235.

12.  De Voragine, *The Golden Legend,* p. 235.

13.  James, *The Art of the Novel,* p. 226.

14.  Henry James *The Autobiography of Henry James,* ed. F.W. Dupee (New York: Criterion, 1956), p. 45. Future references indicated by AU and page number.

15.  Leon Edel, *Henry James: The Conquest of London* (Philadelphia: J.B. Lippincott, 1962), p. 314.

16.  Baroness Jemima Tautphoeus, *The Initials* (Philadelphia: Peterson, n.d.), p. 47. Future references indicated by I and page number.

17.  *The Complete Tales of Henry James,* ed. Leon Edel (Philadelphia: J.B. Lippincott, 1963), V, p. 357. Future references indicated by V and page number.

The material in this section first appeared in my "Henry James and Miss Braddon: 'Georgina's Reasons' and the Victorian Sensation Novel," *Essays in Literature,* vol. 10, no. 1, Spring 1983, pp. 119–25.

18.  S. Gorley Putt, *Henry James: A Reader's Guide* (Ithaca, New York: Cornell University Press, 1966), pp. 270–71.

19.  Letter of Henry James to Thomas Sargeant Perry, March 6, 1884. Quoted in Virginia Harlow, *Thomas Sargeant Perry* (Durham, North Carolina; Duke University Press, 1950), p. 316.

20.  *The Notebooks of Henry James,* ed. F. O. Matthiessen and Kenneth B. Murdock (New York: Oxford University Press, 1947), p. 60.

21.  *Notes and Reviews by Henry James,* preface by Pierre de Chaignon La Rose (New York: Books for Libraries Press, 1968), pp. 112–13.

22.  Mrs. M. O. W. Oliphant, "Sensation Novels," *Blackwood's Magazine,* May 1862, p. 584.

23.  Robert Lee Wolff, *Sensational Victorian: The Life & Fiction of Mary Elizabeth Braddon* (New York: Garland, 1979), p. 11.

24.  Wolff, *Sensational Victorian,* p. 10.

25.  *The Complete Tales of Henry James,* ed. Leon Edel (Philadelphia: J.B. Lippincott, 1962), VI, p. 63. Future references indicated by VI and page number.

26.  Mary Elizabeth Braddon, *Lady Audley's Secret* (New York: Dover, 1974), p. 195. Future references indicated by L and page number.

27.  *Oxford English Dictionary,* entry under "psychopath."

28.  In 1865 in a series of cases labeled as "moral insanity" and "moral imbecility" J. C. Pritchard was the first to describe systematically "so-called moral disorders." Kraepelin later termed the traits "excitability, impulsivity, lying, criminality, not constitutional in the sense of being inherited. . . . The traits in question were acquired early and were thoroughly ingrained in the personality." The "psychopathic personality . . . manifests itself in abnormally aggressive or seriously irresponsible conduct." Leland E. Hinsie and Robert Jean Campbell, *Psychiatric Dictionary* (New York: Oxford University Press, 1970), 4th edition, pp. 617–19.

29.  William James, *The Varieties of Religious Experience* (New York: Longmans, Green, 1907), p. 7.

30.  Miss F.P. Cobbe, *Daily News,* April 13, 1896, cited in the *Oxford English Dictionary.*

31.  Russell L. Cecil, ed., *A Textbook of Medicine by American Authors* (Philadelphia: Saunders, 1937), p. 1544.

32.  In order to appreciate what a good observer James was of this personality defect, we can check off Georgina's personal traits against the list of the following characteristics given by H. M. Cleckley in *The Mask of Sanity* (St. Louis: Mosby, 1976), pp. 337–38. "1. Superficial charm and good intelligence. 2. Absence of delusions and other signs of irrational thinking. 3. Absence of nervousness or psychoneurotic manifestations. 4. Unreliability. 5.Untruthfulness and insincerity. 6. Lack of remorse and of shame. 7. Inadequately motivated antisocial behavior. 8. Poor judgment and failure to learn by experience. 9. Pathologic egocentricity and incapacity for love. 10. General poverty in major affective reactions. 11. Specific loss of insight. 12. Unresponsiveness in general interpersonal relations. 13. Fantastic and uninviting behavior with drink and sometimes without. 14. Suicide rarely carried out. 15. Sex life impersonal, trivial and poorly integrated. 16. Failure to follow any life plan. The maladjustment is a chronic one, and the psychopath tends to project the blame for his actions onto others. He tends to act out his conflicts so that the environment suffers rather than the patient. He is a rebellious individualist and a non-conformist."

33.  *Henry James and Robert Louis Stevenson,* ed. Janet Adam Smith (London: Rupert Hart-Davis, 1948), p. 108.

34.  Mary Elizabeth Braddon, *The Doctor's Wife* (London: Maxwell, 1864), p. 14. Future references indicated by DW and page number.

A short version of this material first appeared in Leon Edel and Adeline Tintner, "The Private Life of Peter Quin[t]: Origins of 'The Turn of the Screw,'" *The Henry James Review,* vol. 7, no. 1, Fall 1985, pp. 2–4).

35.  *The Complete Tales of Henry James* (Philadelphia: J.B. Lippincott, 1964), X, p. 18. Future references indicated by X and page number.

36.  E.A. Sheppard in *Henry James and "The Turn of the Screw"* (Oxford: Oxford University Press, 1974), p. 114, sees Harley Street, at that time a fashionable London location not yet associated with physicians' offices, as coming from the street, la Rue Harlay-au-Marais of the pension where Henriette Deluzy of "L'Affaire Praslin" took refuge. She was the governess banished from the Duke de Praslin's home (after the murder of the duchess, a scandal of 1847), and Sheppard sees her as providing a possible model for James's governess.

37.  Sheppard locates the name Quint in *Henry James and "The Turn of the Screw,"* p. 129. She finds it as "the name of a New England mesmerist-healer and seer—Wilson Quint" in one of the "unpublished" American cases printed by F. W. H. Myers which she claims James "must" have seen in volume VIII of *The Society for Psychical Research Proceedings.* Sheppard believes that the real-life Quint was George Bernard Shaw and that Flora comes from Clement Shorter's *Charlotte Brontë and Her Circle* (1896), where he mentions the Reverend Patrick Brontë's *The Maid of Killarney; or, Albion and Flora.* Sheppard thinks that Miles's name might have been suggested by a Reverend Oddy Miles who was a resident at Haworth, by Charlotte's friend, Mary Taylor's novel, *Miss Miles, or a Tale of Yorkshire Life Sixty Years Ago* (p. 48), or by both.

38.  There are only two articles devoted to John La Farge's masthead drawing. The first, by S. P. Rosenbaum, "A Note on John La Farge's Illustration for Henry James's *The Turn of the Screw* (Henry James, *The Turn of the Screw,* ed. Robert Kimbrough, New York: W.W. Norton, 1966,

pp. 254–59), calls attention to the presence of *"another* darker hand" which he believes "presumes the ambiguity of the ghosts." The second article, my "An Illustrator's Literary Interpretation," *A.B. Bookman's Weekly,* March 26, 1979, reproduces the picture in order to show that both hands must anatomically belong to the governess, thus demonstrating her malevolent subconsciousness working along with her benevolent consciousness, and corroborating the Kenton-Wilson interpretation of the governor's hysteria.

39.  *Temptation. Frank Leslie's New York Journal of Romance, General Literature, Science and Art,* January–June 1855, p. 136. Future references indicated by TE and page number. Although the National Union Catalogue does not list any known author for *Temptation,* the *New York Journal* had announced in the June number of 1855 that *Temptation* would be followed by "A New Tale, 'MASKS AND FACES' by the same author." A novel by that name shows in the National Union Catalogue as the work of Tom Taylor. It was published in 1856, New York, by S. French, who, by that time, had bought Frank Leslie's *New York Journal.* Certain characteristics of this new novel indicate that the author was the same one who wrote *Temptation.* He introduces each chapter by a quotation from one of the English poets, chiefly Spenser, Milton, and Shakespeare, in addition to occasional selections from what the author calls simply "Old Play." *Masks and Faces* again features an heir born from a secret marriage who has difficulties in acquiring his fortune, but it is inferior to *Temptation,* a true thriller, filled with interlocking picaresque plots, arson, presumed insanity (or "mad" actions), virtuous characters overcoming evil characters, and the full panoply of the "sensation" genre, adroitly manipulated.

40.  The pages on which madness or insanity is mentioned in "The Turn of the Screw" are 48, 53, 81, 82, 83, 114. They are: "'without directly impugning my sanity'" (X, 48); "a disguised excitement that might well . . . have turned to something like madness" (X, 53); "'They're talking of *them*—they're talking horrors! I go on, I know, as if I were crazy; and it's a wonder I'm not. What I've seen would have made *you* so; but it has only made me more lucid, made me get hold of still other things'" (X, 81–82). And again we read, "'By writing to him that his house is poisoned and his little nephew and niece mad?' 'But if they *are,* Miss?' 'And if I myself, you mean?'" (X, 83); "'She was there, and I was neither cruel nor mad'" (X, 114). Then the word is introduced gratuitously as follows: "'Their more than earthly beauty, their absolutely unnatural goodness. It's a game.' I went on, 'it's a policy and a fraud.' On the part of little darlings—? 'As yet mere lovely babies? Yes, mad as that seems!'" (X, 82).

We expect the sensation tale to mention madness often and it does. When Martha escapes from her grandfather, Peter Quin, Mr. Griffiths refuses to let her into the lawyer Foster's office, and since he is a villain we discount his calling her "'some madwoman'" (TE, 135) and later some villain says "'Mad, she must be mad!'" (TE, 326) or "'Mad! He must be mad!'" The villains usually claim everyone is "mad," and Sir Richard himself says "'This is madness'" (TE, 327). He, by the way, is "haunted" by a figure, although it is never implied to be a ghost. Sir Richard Trevanian says his son, Edward, was "'half a madman'" (TE, 73). When Martha tells the moneylender Stork to burn the IOU he says, "'Mad—she must be mad!'" Martha tests Fanny by pretending to be poor, but Fanny greets her with love. "'Is the woman mad or drunk?'" (TE, 119). A Mr. Peapod "pitied the madness of the man" [Walter Trevanian] (TE, 107). He challenges him to a duel, and Walter dies (TE, 108).

The material from this section first appeared in my "Henry James's Use of 'Jane Eyre' in 'The Turn of the Screw.'" *Brontë Society Transactions,* 1976, part 86 of the Society's Publications, vol. 17, no. 1, pp. 42–45.

41.  William S. Peterson, "Henry James on 'Jane Eyre,'" *Times Literary Supplement,* vol. 30, July 7, 1971, pp. 919–20.

42.  James, *The Art of the Novel*, p. 155.

43.  Henry James, *Harper's Weekly* (London, dated January 15) February 6, 1897, p. 135.

44.  Henry James, *The Lesson of Balzac* (New York: Houghton Mifflin, 1905), p. 64.

45.  *The Letters of Henry James*, ed. Percy Lubbock (New York: Scribner's, 1920), I, p. 300.

46.  E.C. Gaskell, *The Life of Charlotte Brontë* (Edinburgh: John Grant, 1924), p. 285.

47.  Gaskell, *The Life of Charlotte Brontë*, p. 286.

48.  Charlotte Brontë, *Jane Eyre* (Edinburgh: Grant, 1924), I, p. 295.

49.  Brontë, *Jane Eyre*, I, p. 297.

50.  *The Letters of Henry James*, I, p. 301.

51.  Brontë, *Jane Eyre*, I, p. 296.

52.  James, *The Lesson of Balzac*, p. 82.

53.  *The Great Modern American Stories*, ed. William Dean Howells (New York: Boni and Liveright, 1920) p. vii.

54.  *Henry James Letters*, ed. Leon Edel (Cambridge: Harvard University Press, 1984), IV, p. 372. Future references indicated by HJL, IV, and page number.

55.  *The Complete Tales of Henry James*, ed. Leon Edel (Philadelphia: J. B. Lippincott, 1964), XII, p. 181. Future references indicated by XII and page number.

56.  Charles Dickens, *Oliver Twist*, ed. Peter Fairclough, introduction by Angus Wilson, with George Cruikshank's original illustrations. (Harmondsworth, Middlesex: Penguin, 1966, reprinted 1982), p. 423–24. Future references indicated by OT and page number.

57.  Henry James, *Notes on Novelists* (New York: Scribner's, 1914), p. 452. Future references indicated by NN and page number.

58.  Henry James, *Partial Portraits* (1888; reprint edition ed. Leon Edel, Ann Arbor: University of Michigan Press, 1970), p. 98.

59.  Leon Edel, *Henry James: The Treacherous Years* (Philadelphia: J. B. Lippincott, 1969), p. 247.

60.  *The Art of the Novel*, ed. Richard P. Blackmur (New York: Scribner's, 1934), p. 237.

61.  Mrs. Oliphant, *A Widow's Tale and Other Stories*, introduction by J. M. Barrie (Edinburgh: Blackwood, 1898), p. vi. Future references indicated by WT and page number.

62.  *The Nation*, September 30, 1875, p. 216, and May 30, 1878, p. 357.

63.  *The Complete Tales of Henry James*, ed. Leon Edel (Philadelphia: J. B. Lippincott, 1964), XI, p. 229. Future references indicated by XI and page number.

64.  Mrs. Oliphant, *Autobiography and Letters*, ed. Miss Coghill (Edinburgh: Blackwood, 1899), p. 4. Future references indicated by AL and page number.

65.  Mrs. Oliphant, *Kirsteen*, ed. J. M. Barrie (Edinburgh: Blackwood, 1898, originally published in 1890), p. 59.

66. Henry James, *The Portrait of a Lady* (revised version) (Harmondsworth, Middlesex: Penguin, 1977), p. 566. Future references indicated by R and page number. 1881 version indicated by PL and page number.

67. G. J. Whyte-Melville, *Digby Grand: An Autobiography* (Leipzig: Tauchnitz, 1862), p. 125. Future references indicated by D and page number.

68. Frederick Locker-Lampson, *My Confidences* (New York: Scribner's, 1896), p. 380. Future references indicated by C and page number.

69. Henry James, *Letters to A. C. Benson and Auguste Monod,* ed. E. F. Benson (London: Elkin Mathews and Marrot, 1930), p. 7. Future references indicated by B and page number.

70. Hugh Macmillan, *The Life-work of George Frederick Watts, R.A.* (London: Dent, 1903), p. 175.

71. James, *The Painter's Eye,* p. 142.

72. Mary S. Watts, *George Frederick Watts* (London: Hodder, 1912), II, p. 264.

73. Arthur Christopher Benson, *From a College Window* (New York: Putman's, 1907), p. 225.

74. Percy Lubbock, *Shades of Eton* (London: Jonathan Cape, 1929), p. 118.

75. Lubbock, *Shades of Eton,* p. 44. Howard Sturgis, an American, was also an Etonian, but his habits and tastes were eccentric.

## Chapter 5

1. Henry James, *The Autobiography of Henry James,* ed. F.W. Dupee (New York: Criterion, 1956), p. 46. Future references indicated by AU and page number.

2. Maria S. Cummins, *The Lamplighter* (Boston: Jewett, 1854), p. 38. Future references indicated by L and page number.

3. *The Complete Tales of Henry James,* ed. Leon Edel (Philadelphia: J. B. Lippincott, 1964), X, p. 122. Future references indicated by X and page number.

4. Edward Everett Hale, "My Double; and How He Undid Me," in *The Great Modern American Stories: An Anthology,* ed. W. D. Howells (New York: Boni and Liveright, 1920), p. 4. Future references indicated by GM and page number.

5. This is a real sect, a religious denomination named after a Scot, Robert Sandeman, which practiced a form of socialist pacifism.

6. Austin Warren, *The Elder Henry James* (New York: Macmillan, 1934), pp. 32–38.

7. *The Complete Tales of Henry James,* ed. Leon Edel (Philadelphia: J. B. Lippincott, 1964), VIII, p. 192. Future references indicated by VIII and page number.

8. "Two Unpublished Letters from Henry James," *Hound and Horn,* April–June, 1934, p. 416. The editorial note quotes from Joseph Pennell's *Adventures of an Illustrator,* 1925.

9. *The Complete Tales of Henry James,* ed. Leon Edel (Philadelphia: J. B. Lippincott, 1964), IX, pp. 75–76.

10. Leon Edel, editor's chronology in *Literary Criticism: French Writers, Other European Writers; The Prefaces to the New York Edition* (New York: The Library of American, 1984), p. 1344.

11. Virginia Harlow, *Thomas Sergeant Perry: A Biography* (Durham, North Carolina: Duke University Press, 1950), p. 245.

12. Harlow, *Thomas Sergeant Perry,* pp. 249–50.

13. Harlow, *Thomas Sergeant Perry,* p. 255.

14. Robert Lee Wolff, *Sensational Victorian: The Life and Fiction of Mary Elizabeth Braddon* (New York: Garland, 1979), p. 11.

15. Adeline R. Tintner, "Henry James and Miss Braddon: 'Georgina's Reasons' and the Victorian Sensation Novel," *Essays in Literature,* vol. 10, no. 1, Spring 1983, pp. 119–24. See chapter 4 above, "James and Miss Braddon."

16. *Literary Criticism,* p. 1255.

17. *Literary Criticism,* p. 1254.

18. *The Notebooks of Henry James,* ed. F. O. Matthiessen and Kenneth B. Murdock (New York: Oxford University Press, 1947), p. 11. Future references indicated by N and page number.

The following material first appeared in my "A Literary Youth and a Little Woman: Henry James Reviews Louisa May Alcott," in *Critical Essays on Louisa May Alcott,* ed. Madeleine B. Stern (Boston: Hall, 1984), pp. 265–69.

19. *Louisa May Alcott, Her Life, Letters, and Journals,* ed. Ednah D. Cheney (Boston: Little, Brown, 1911), p. 165.

20. Madeleine B. Stern, *Louisa May Alcott* (Norman, Oklahoma: University of Oklahoma Press, 1950), p. 133.

21. James, *The Autobiography,* p. 495.

22. Henry James, *Partial Portraits* (1888; reprint edition ed. Leon Edel, Ann Arbor: University of Michigan Press, 1970), p. 27.

23. Leon Edel, *Henry James: The Conquest of London* (Philadelphia: J. B. Lippincott, 1962), p. 31.

24. Alcott, *Her Life, Letters, and Journals,* p. 201.

The following material first appeared in my "James's 'The Beldonald Holbein' and Rollins's 'A Burne-Jones Head': A Surprising Parallel," *Colby Library Quarterly,* vol. 14 (1978), pp. 183–90.

25. Clara Sherwood Rollins, *A Burne-Jones Head and Other Sketches* (New York: Lovell, Coryell, 1894), p. 25. Future references indicated by B and page number.

26. *The Complete Tales of Henry James,* ed. Leon Edel (Philadelphia: J. B. Lippincott, 1964), XI, p. 291. Future references indicated by XI and page number. For the relation of "the Beldonald Holbein" to a real Holbein, see my *The Museum World of Henry James* (Ann Arbor: UMI Research Press, 1986), pp. 202–5.

27. James's story was unfortunately illustrated by Lucius Hitchcock who gave an approximation of how a contemporary woman could resemble a Holbein and still be considered attractive as a woman—which was counter to James's point (see fig. 46). Mrs. Rollins's story, since it was about a woman beautiful in conventional terms, was illustrated in her book with an actual Burne-Jones figure (see fig. 45).

28. Adeline R. Tintner, "John Singer Sargent in the Fiction of Henry James," *Apollo* (July 1975), pp. 120–30. See my *The Museum World of Henry James* (Ann Arbor: UMI Research Press, 1986), chapter 6.

29. *The Complete Works of Oscar Wilde: Intentions* (New York: William H. Wise, 1927) V. *Intentions* (1891) included *The Decay of Lying*, first published in January 1889 in *The Nineteenth Century*.

30. *The Letters of Henry James*, ed. Percy Lubbock (New York: Scribner's, 1920), I, pp. 396–97.

31. Henry James, *Essays on Literature: American Writers, English Writers* (New York: Library of America, 1984), p. 174. Future references indicated by LAE and page number.

32. F. O. Matthiessen, *Sarah Orne Jewett*, 1929, p. 21. Future references indicated by MA and page number.

33. J. I. M. Stewart, *Mark Lambert's Supper* (London: Gollancz, 1954), p. 92.

34. *The Letters of Henry James*, I, p. 285.

35. *The Complete Notebooks of Henry James*, ed. Leon Edel and Lyall H. Powers (New York: Oxford University Press, 1987), p. 197.

36. Edgar Fawcett, *A Romance of Old New York* (Philadelphia: J. B. Lippincott, 1897), p. 42. Future references indicated by R and page number.

37. *The Letters of Virginia Woolf*, ed. Nigel Nicolson and Joanne Trautmann (New York: Harcourt Brace Jovanovich, 1976), p. 548.

38. Edgar Fawcett, *New York* (New York: F. Tennyson Neely, 1898), p. 283.

39. Leon Edel, *Henry James: The Treacherous Years: 1895–1901* (Philadelphia: J. B. Lippincott, 1969), p. 303.

40. *Henry James Letters*, ed. Leon Edel (Cambridge: Harvard University Press, 1980), III, p. 193.

41. *Henry James Letters*, ed. Leon Edel (Cambridge: Harvard University Press, 1975), II, p. 421.

42. F. Marion Crawford, *The Three Fates* (London: Macmillan, 1892), p. 216. Future references indicated by 3F and page number.

43. Henry James, *The Ivory Tower* (London: Collins, 1917), p. 138. Future references indicated by IT and page number.

**Chapter 6**

1. Adeline R. Tintner, "Henry James: The Probable Original for Eustace Cleever in 'A Conference of the Powers,'" *The Kipling Journal*, in press.

2. Leon Edel, *Henry James: The Treacherous Years: 1895–1901* (Philadelphia: J. B. Lippincott, 1969), p. 52. Future references indicated by TY and page number.

3. Adeline R. Tintner, *The Book World of Henry James* (Ann Arbor: UMI Research Press, 1987), pp. 131–41.

4. Henry James, *Literary Criticism: French Writers, Other European Writers; The Prefaces to the New York Edition* (New York: The American Library, 1984), p. 1261. Future references indicated by EW and page number.

5.  Rudyard Kipling, *The Phantom 'Rickshaw and Other Stories* (New York: Scribner's, 1897), p. 9. Future references indicated by PR and page number.

6.  *Henry James and H. G. Wells,* ed. Leon Edel and Gordon N. Ray (London: Rupert Hart-Davis, 1959), p. 82.

7.  *The Complete Tales of Henry James,* ed. Leon Edel (Philadelphia: J. B. Lippincott, 1963), VIII, p. 137. Future references indicated by VIII and page number.

8.  Henry James, *Essays on Literature: American Writers, English Writers* (New York: Library of America, 1984), p. 1130.

9.  Rudyard Kipling, *Wee Willie Winkie* (Boston: Edinburgh Society, 1909), p. 17.

10.  Rudyard Kipling, *Mine Own People* (New York: Lovell, Coryell, 1891), xxi. Future references indicated by MO and page number.

11.  *The Notebooks of Henry James,* ed. F. O. Matthiessen and Kenneth B. Murdock (New York: Oxford University Press, 1947), p. 118. Future references indicated by N and page number.

12.  See my "Henry James as Eustace Cleever," in press.

13.  *The Complete Tales of Henry James,* ed. Leon Edel (Philadelphia: J. B. Lippincott, 1964), IX, p. 14. Future references indicated by IX and page number.

14.  *Henry James Letters,* ed. Leon Edel (Cambridge: Harvard University Press, 1980), III, p. 421. Future references indicated by EL III and page number.

15.  *Henry James Letters,* ed. Leon Edel (Cambridge: Harvard University Press, 1984), IV, p. 70.

16.  Leon Edel, *Henry James: The Master* (Philadelphia: J. B. Lippincott, 1972), p. 133.

17.  *The Complete Tales of Henry James,* ed. Leon Edel (Philadelphia: J. B. Lippincott, 1964), XI, p. 365. Future references indicated by XI and page number.

18.  Rudyard Kipling, *The Jungle Books* (New York: New American Library, 1951, 1981), reprint pp. 12–13. Future references indicated by JB and page number.

**Chapter 7**

1.  *Henry James Letters,* ed. Leon Edel (Cambridge: Harvard University Press, 1980), III, p. 98. Future references indicated by EL, III and page number.

2.  *The Notebooks of Henry James,* ed. F. O. Matthiessen and Kenneth B. Murdock (New York: Oxford University Press, 1947), p. 102. Future references indicated by N and page number.

3.  J. B. Priestley, *The Edwardians* (New York: Harper & Row, 1970), p. 23. Future references indicated by ED and page number.

4.  *The Complete Tales of Henry James* (Philadelphia: J. B. Lippincott, 1963), VIII, p. 234. Future references indicated by VIII and page number.

5.  Henry James, *Italian Hours,* 1909 (New York: Grove, reprint 1979), p. 42

6.  *Henry James Letters,* ed. Leon Edel (Cambridge: Harvard University Press, 1984), IV, p. 55. Future references indicated by EL, IV and page number.

7.  Leon Edel, *Henry James: The Treacherous Years: 1895–1901* (Philadelphia: J. B. Lippincott, 1969), pp. 179–80.

8.  *The Complete Tales of Henry James,* ed. Leon Edel (Philadelphia: J. B. Lippincott, 1964), X, p. 11. Future references indicated by X and page number.

9.  *The Complete Tales of Henry James,* ed. Leon Edel (Philadelphia: J. B. Lippincott, 1964), XII, p. 152. Future references indicated by XII and page number.

10. Henry James to Isabel Stewart Gardner, March 6, 1899. Courtesy Isabella Stewart Gardner Museum.

11. Henry James, *The Ambassadors* (London: Methuen, 1903), p. 295. Future references indicated by AM and page number.

12. Jean-Denis Bredin, *The Affair: The Case of Alfred Dreyfus* (New York: Braziller, 1986), p. 246.

13. Bredin, *The Affair,* p. 248.

14. Bredin, *The Affair,* p. 143.

15. Guy Chapman, *The Dreyfus Case* (New York: Reynal, 1955), p. 263.

16. Millicent Bell, *Edith Wharton and Henry James* (New York: Braziller, 1965), p. 178. For the relation between Edith Wharton and the heroines of *The Finer Grain* (1910) stories see my "The Metamorphoses of Edith Wharton in *The Finer Grain* by Henry James," *Twentieth Century Literature,* vol. 21, December 1975, pp. 355–79.

## Chapter 8

1.  *Henry James and H. G. Wells,* ed. Leon Edel and Gordon N. Ray (London: Rupert Hart-Davis), 1959), p. 81. Future references indicated by HGW and page number.

2.  Leon Edel, *Henry James: The Treacherous Years: 1895–1901* (Philadelphia: J. B. Lippincott, 1969), p. 329.

3.  Henry James, *The Sense of the Past* (New York: Scribner's, 1917), p. 104. Future references indicated by SP and page number.

4.  H. G. Wells, *28 Science Fiction Stories* (New York: Dover, 1952), pp. 730–820, passim.

5.  *Seven Science Fiction Novels of H. G. Wells* (New York: Dover, 1934), p. 17. Future references indicated by SSF and page number.

# Index

"The Turn of the Screw," 172–75
"Cinderella." *See under* Fairy tales
City Art Gallery (Manchester), 115
Clemenceau, Georges, 265
Coghill, Mrs. Harry, 192
*Collier's:* "The Turn of the Screw" in, 166
Collins, Wilkie, 160
Colvin, Sir Sidney, 225
Consciousness, human: James's concern with, 2–3
Cotes, Mrs.: James to, on Devil and art, 75–78
Cowper, John: "The Diverting History of John Gilpin," James's use of, in "The Siege of London," 3; poem, in *The Child's Own Book,* 3, 5
Crawford, Frank Marion (1854–1909): and I. Gardner, 236; James and, 236; James on, in *A Small Boy and Others,* 236
*Works:*
—*Mr. Isaacs* (1882): influence in "The Impressions of a Cousin," 85–86, 236; influence of *Arabian Nights* in, 86; Oriental influence in, xvi, 80, 86
—*The Three Fates* (1892): cabinet, influence in *The Ivory Tower,* 236–38; James's use of, xx; old and young men, 236–38
Cruikshank, George: illustration for *Oliver Twist,* 185, *187*
Cumming, Sir William Gordon: scandal, James to Stevenson on, 253
Cummins, Maria S., *The Lamplighter,* 156; influence in "The Turn of the Screw," 205; influence on James, xvii, 206, 211; James on, 203, 206; language in, 204; light in, 205; names, use in *Watch and Ward,* 211; orphan and surrogate parents, 204–5; plot, 203–4; popularity of, 203–4; "sets" of children in, 204
Curious woman theme, 24: Bettelheim on, 29; Dickens's use of, 24; in "A Day of Days," 24; in *The Sense of the Past,* 26; Thackeray's use of, 24

Darnton, Robert: *The Great Cat Massacre,* 70; on peasants, and fairy tales, 70
Daudet, Alphonse, 70; fairy tales, characters and roles in, 58–59; James and, 58; James's essays on, 48–49, 58, 85–86, 255; James's translation of, 140
*Works:*
—"Bluebeard," from Perrault, 58
—*Memories of a Man of Letters,* 255
—*Le Nabab* (1878), 85–86; use in "The Impressions of a Cousin," 86; Oriental in, 86
—*Port Tarascon,* James's translation of, 58
—*Le Petit Chose,* 25, 48

—*La Petite Paroisse* (1895), Little Red Riding Hood in, 58
—*Les Rois en exil* (1879), 255
—"The Romance of Little Red Riding Hood," xx, 25, 58; neurotic aspect, use in "Covering End," 58–60; seductress, 60, 67
—*Scenes and Fancies:* "The Eight Mrs. Bluebeards," 25; influence on James, 25–26
D'Aulnay, Madame, 3, 11
Decamps, Alexandre-Gabriel: influence on James, 80
Defoe, Daniel: "The Devil lies at Blye Bush," 78; *Political History of the Devil,* 78
Delacroix, Eugène, 82; influence of Orient on, 79; influence on James, 80; James's review of, 80, 87. *Works: The Death of Saradanapalus* (1826), 80, *82,* 87; Faust engravings, 78
Delaroche, Paul, 138
Devil: Defoe's use of, 78; James to Mrs. Cotes on, 75–78; James's relation to, 75; use in "Collaboration," 75; use in "Mrs. Medwin," 75–78; use in *The Wings of the Dove,* 75–78
Dickens, Charles: horror stories, Mrs. Oliphant on, 160; influence on James, xix, 181–83; James on, 181–82
*Works:*
—"Nurse's Stories," curious woman theme, 24
—*Oliver Twist:* Cruikshank illustrations, 185, *187;* influence in "Julia Bride," 181–83, 185; metaphor, 182–84; opening scene, 185; play, James to Navarro on, 181; slang in, 183–84
—*Our Mutual Friend* (1865): children's games in, 57; Cinderella in, 56; "Cock Robin," 55; influence in "Covering End," 54–57; "Jack and the Beanstalk," 55; James's review of, 54–55; Red Riding Hood motif, 54–55; reference to *Alice in Wonderland,* 56; reference to "The Three Little Bears," 56; use of fairy tales and nursery rhymes, 54–56
Dilke, Sir Charles: scandal, James to G. Norton on, 253
Disraeli, Benjamin: influence of Orient on, 79
Doran, Dr.: *Monarchs Retired from Business* (1857), 257
Doré, Gustave: illustration, for "Bluebeard," 26, *27;* illustration, for "Sleeping Beauty," *frontispiece,* 15; illustrations, for "Little Red Riding Hood," sexual aspects, 60–66; use in "Gabrielle de Bergerac," *frontispiece,* 9–11
Double: in E. E. Hale's "My Double; and How He Undid Me," 206–10; in "The Jolly Corner," 206; in "The Private Life," xvii, 206–13; in Wilde's *Dorian Grey,* 206; in "William Wilson," 206
Dreyfus case, xix-xx; anti-Semitism and, 262–64; Esterhazy and, 263; 265–67; facts, and